Formation for Life

Formation for Life

Just Peacemaking and
Twenty-First-Century Discipleship

Glen H. Stassen,
Rodney L. Petersen,
and
Timothy A. Norton

PICKWICK *Publications* · Eugene, Oregon

FORMATION FOR LIFE
Just Peacemaking and Twenty-First-Century Discipleship

Pickwick Publications
An Imprint of Wipf and Stock Publishers
199 W. 8th Ave., Suite 3
Eugene, OR 97401

www.wipfandstock.com

ISBN 13: 978-1-61097-986-3

Cataloguing-in-Publication data:

Formation for life : just peacemaking and twenty-first-century discipleship / edited by Glen H. Stassen, Rodney L. Petersen, and Timothy A. Norton, with a foreword by Richard J. Mouw.

xx + 298 pp. ; 23 cm. Includes bibliographical references and index.

ISBN 13: 978-1-61097-986-3

1. Peace—Religious aspects. 2. Christianity and justice. 3. I. Stassen, Glen Harold, 1936–. II. Petersen, Rodney L. III. Norton, Timothy A. IV. Mouw, Richard J.

BT736.4 S725 2013

Manufactured in the U.S.A.

Contents

Contributors

Martin Accad, DPhil (University of Oxford) is Associate Professor of Islamic studies, Fuller Theological Seminary, Pasadena, California, and Director of the Institute of Middle East Studies at the Arab Baptist Theological Seminary in Lebanon. Fluent in English, French, and Arabic, Accad has taught at seminaries in Egypt, Lebanon, and the United States. Accad has contributed chapters to various books, including *Rethinking Mission for the Middle East in Christian Presence and Witness among Muslims* (edited by Peter Penner, 2005) and "The Interpretation of John 20.17 in Muslim-Christian Dialogue (8th–14th cent.): The Ultimate Proof-Text" in *Christians at the Heart of Islamic Rule* (edited by David Thomas, 2003), as well as authoring journal and dictionary articles, such as the "Trinity" article in the *IVP Dictionary of Mission Theology: Evangelical Foundations* (2007). Accad is currently writing a book, through the Langham Writer's Grant, on moving beyond conflict in Christian-Muslim dialogue.

Warren S. Brown, PhD (University of Southern California) is director of the Travis Research Institute and Professor of Psychology, Fuller Theological Seminary, Pasadena, California. Brown has authored or coauthored over seventy-five scholarly articles in such peer-reviewed scientific journals as *Neuropsychologia, Psychophysiology, Biological Psychiatry, Developmental Neuropsychology, Cortex, Nature Review Neuroscience*, and *Science*; fifteen chapters in edited scholarly books; and over 150 presentations at scientific meetings. Brown has also written and lectured on the integration of neuroscience and Christian faith, and was principal editor and contributor to *Whatever Happened to the Soul? Scientific and Theological Portraits of Human Nature* (1998). He was also editor and contributor to *Understanding Wisdom: Sources, Science and Society* (2000), and wrote (with Nancey Murphy) *Did My Neurons Make Me Do It?: Philosophical and Neurobiological Perspectives on Moral Responsibility and Free Will*

(2007). His newest book, *Neuroscience, Psychology and Religion: Illusions, Delusions, and Realities of Human Nature* (with Malcolm Jeeves) was published in 2009.

Scott R. Garrels, PhD (Graduate School of Psychology, Fuller Theological Seminary) is Adjunct Professor in the School of Psychology at Fuller Theological Seminary, Pasadena, California, and a licensed clinical psychologist in private practice. He has written and lectured widely on the integration of René Girard's mimetic theory with contemporary empirical research on human imitation, including their implications for clinical theory and practice. He was awarded a Templeton Advanced Research Program grant from the Metanexus Institute (2006) and recently edited *Mimesis and Science: Empirical Research on Imitation and the Mimetic Theory of Culture and Religion* (2011).

Marc Gopin, PhD (Brandeis University), is the James H. Laue Professor of Religion, Diplomacy, and Conflict Resolution, and the Director of the Center on Religion, Diplomacy, and Conflict Resolution (CRDC) at George Mason University's Institute for Conflict Analysis and Resolution (ICAR). Gopin has lectured in universities and countries throughout the world on conflict resolution. He has engaged in back channel diplomacy with religious, political, and military figures on both sides of conflicts, especially in the Arab/Israeli conflict. Gopin is the author of *Between Eden and Armageddon: The Future of World Religions, Violence and Peacemaking* (2000), and *Holy War, Holy Peace: How Religion Can Bring Peace to the Middle East* (2002), a study on what was missing from the Oslo Process, and what will be necessary culturally for a successful Arab/Israeli peace process. He also wrote, *Healing the Heart of Conflict* (2004). Dr. Gopin was ordained as a rabbi in 1983. Gopin is now working in partnership with the Fetzer Foundation to create a web-based video series and book on enemies who become friends and close partners. Filming began in the summer of 2008. He is also the author of *To Make the Earth Whole: The Art of Citizen Diplomacy in an Age of Religious Militancy* (2009).

Jeffrey Gros, PhD (Fordham University) has been Distinguished Professor of Historical and Ecumenical Theology, University of Memphis. Gros has been involved in editing numerous books including: *Deepening Communion* (with William Rusch, 1998); *Introduction to Ecumenism* (with Ann Riggs, Eamon McManus, 1998); *The Church as Koinonia of Salvation; Its Structures and Ministries* (with Randall Lee, 2000); *Growing Concensus II* (with Lydia Veliko, 2005); *The Ecumenical Christian Dialogues and the*

Catechism of the Catholic Church (with Daniel Mulhall, 2006), *The Fragmentation of the Church and its Unity in Peacemaking* (with John Remple, 2001), *John Baptist de La Salle: The Spirituality of Christian Education* (with Jeffrey Calligan, 2004), *Evangelization and Religious Freedom: Ad Gentes, Dignitatis Humanae* (with Steven Bevans, SVD, 2008).

Raymond G. Helmick, SJ is professor of Conflict Resolution, Boston College, 1984. He has been Career Associate Director of the Center for Human Rights and Responsibilities, London, 1973–79, Institute Society Research, London, 1973–79; foundation, Co-director of the Center of Concern for Human Dignity, 1979–81; Senior Associate of the Conflict Analysis Center, Washington, 1982–; Senior Associate for the Center of Strategic and Internal Studies, Washington, 2000–2004; faculty Rotary Peace Center, Chulalongkorn University, Bangkok. He has worked with conflict in the following regions: Northern Ireland; Lebanon; the Arab-Israeli conflict; and elsewhere including Boston (USA). He is founder and Senior Associate Member of the Conflict Analysis Center. His publications include: *A Social Option: A Social Planning Approach to the Problems of Northern Ireland* (with Richard Hauser, 1975); *La Situation libanaise selon Raymond Eddé* (1990); *Forgiveness and Reconciliation: Religion, Social Policy and Conflict Transformation* (with Rodney L. Petersen, 2001); *Negotiating Outside the Law: Why Camp David Failed* (2004); *Living Catholic Faith in a Contentious Age* (2010).

Cheryl Bridges Johns, PhD (Southern Baptist Theological Seminary) is Professor of Discipleship and Christian Formation, Pentecostal Theological Seminary, Cleveland, Tennessee. Her published works include *Pentecostal Formation: A Pedagogy among the Oppressed* (1993) and *Finding Eternal Treasures* (1986). She is the past-president of the Society for Pentecostal Studies. She has been actively involved in numerous ecumenical initiatives including the Roman Catholic/Pentecostal Dialogue, Evangelicals and Catholics Together, Church of God-Mennonite Dialogue. She has represented her tradition with the World Council of Churches and Faith and Order for the National Council of Churches. Johns is on the board for Evangelicals for Human Rights, the Evangelical Partnership for the Common Good, and the National Religious Campaign against Torture. Her work has included several creation care initiatives, including "Scientists and Evangelicals Initiative on the Care of Creation." She is co-pastor of the New Covenant Church of God, a church she and her husband, Jackie, started in 1989.

Hajung Lee, PhDc (Boston University) is completing doctoral work in social ethics. Lee is an attorney and Co-director of the Center for Women in Ministry and Mission in Santa Clarita, California. Lee is interested in just peacemaking from a feminist perspective.

Philip LeMasters, PhD (Duke University) is Turner Distinguished Professor of Religion, Director of the Honors Program, and Dean, School of Social Sciences and Religion, Abilene, Texas. An internationally recognized scholar of Christian ethics, LeMasters has presented on the ethics of war and peace in Eastern Orthodox Christianity at conferences in Romania, Greece, Syria, and Northern Ireland. A widely published author, LeMasters' five books and many essays and reviews address a variety of topics in moral theology, including biomedical, political, and sexual ethics. His most recent book is *The Goodness of God's Creation* (2008). He has published an essay on the ethics of war and peace in the Orthodox Church in the March 2011 edition of *The Ecumenical Review*, a journal associated with the World Council of Churches. A member of Phi Beta Kappa, the American Academy of Religion, and the Society of Christian Ethics, LeMasters is also a member of the Board of Trustees of St. Vladimir's Orthodox Theological Seminary in Yonkers, New York. A priest of the Orthodox Church, he is also the pastor of a small congregation in Abilene.

David McMillan, PhD (International Baptist Theological Seminary) works with the International Baptist Theological Seminary (Prague) and is director of Clanrye Initiatives, involved in education and research with particular emphasis on theology, conflict, reconciliation, and peace-building. He has been pastor at Windsor Baptist Church, Belfast, Northern Ireland. He was director for seventeen years of ECONI (Evangelical Contribution on Northern Ireland), a catalyst for radical biblical discipleship, encouraging, and enabling Christians to think biblically about their life and witness in the world. In particular ECONI aimed to equip Christians to address the legacy of conflict in Northern Ireland and the reality of community division and to contribute to the long-term task of peacebuilding. McMillan has also held pastorates at other Baptist churches and been director at Newry and Mourne Co-operative.

Juan Martínez, PhD (Fuller Theological Seminary) is Assistant Dean for the Hispanic Church Studies Department and Associate Professor of Hispanic Studies and Pastoral Leadership in the School of Theology. Martínez joined Fuller from the Latin American Anabaptist Seminary in Guatemala

City, Guatemala, where he served as rector for nine years. A Mennonite Brethren pastor, Martínez also has experience in church planting and teaching in both religious and secular venues. He served as director of Hispanic Ministries for the Pacific District Conference of the Mennonite Brethren Church and of Instituto Bíblico del Pacífico, a Mennonite Brethren Bible Institute. Most recently Martínez has published the books *Los Evangélicos: Portraits of Latino Protestantism in the United States* (with Lindy Scott, 2009), *Walk with the People: Latino Ministry in the United States/Caminando entre el pueblo: Ministerio latino en los Estados Unidos* (2008), and *Vivir y servir en el exilio: Lecturas teológicas de la experiencia latina en los Estados Unidos* (with Jorge Maldonado, 2008). He is contributor to several books: *Hispanic American Religious Cultures* (2009), *Building Bridges, Doing Justice: Constructing a Latino/a Ecumenical Theology* (2009); *Evangelicals and Empire: Christian Alternatives to the Political Status Quo* (2008); and *Vivir y servir en el exilio: Lecturas teológicas de la experiencia latina en los Estados Unidos.* (2008). He was also a regional editor for the *Global Dictionary of Theology* (2008).

Richard J. Mouw, PhD (University of Chicago) is president of Fuller Theological Seminary, Pasadena, California since 1993. A philosopher, scholar, and author, Mouw joined the faculty at Fuller as professor of Christian philosophy and ethics in 1985 following seventeen years as Professor of Philosophy at Calvin College, Grand Rapids, Michigan. Mouw has a broad record of publication including editor of *Reformed Journal*, and current editorial board of *Books and Culture*. He is author of nineteen books, including *The God Who Commands*, *The Smell of Sawdust*, *He Shines in All That's Fair*, *Culture and Common Grace*, *Calvin in the Las Vegas Airport*, *Praying at Burger King*, an expanded and revised edition of *Uncommon Decency: Christian Civility in an Uncivil World*, and most recently, *Abraham Kuyper: A Short and Personal Introduction*, *The Challenges of Cultural Discipleship*, and *Talking with Mormons: An Invitation to Evangelicals*. Mouw is President of the Association of Theological Schools, and for six years has served as Co-chair of the official Reformed-Christian Dialogue, and is a leader for interfaith theological conversations, particularly with Mormon and Jewish groups.

Timothy A. Norton, MA (Southwestern Baptist Theological Seminary) is owner of Crux Communication, a communication, marketing and development consulting company that assists colleges, universities, and other non-profits with visioning, communicating, and funding their missions. He is also Co-executive Director of the Lord's Day Alliance of the U.S., having served the organization since 2000. An ordained Baptist minister, he has contributed to numerous faith-related publications and professional publications in the areas of philanthropy and marketing communications. He is founding director of the *Augustine Collective*, a network of independent, student-run Christian journals on college campuses. Together with Edward O'Flaherty, S.J. and Rodney Petersen, Norton edited *Sunday, Sabbath, and the Weekend: Managing Time in a Global Culture* (2010).

Rodney L. Petersen, PhD (Princeton Theological Seminary) is Executive Director of the Boston Theological Institute; Co-director of the Religion and Conflict Transformation Program, Boston University School of Theology; and, Co-executive Director of The Lord's Day Alliance of the U.S. In addition to this work with the BTI, he teaches in both the member schools and overseas in the areas of history and ethics, currently focusing on issues of religion and conflict. An ordained minister in the Presbyterian Church (USA), Petersen has served on several denominational committees and for seven years as the pastor of the Allston Congregational Church (U.C.C.). Prior work included teaching at Trinity Evangelical Divinity School (Deerfield, Illinois), Webster University (Geneva, Switzerland), and with the Fédération des Institutions établies à Genève (FIIG). He is author or editor and contributor of numerous publications, including *Preaching in the Last Days* (1993); *Christianity and Civil Society: Theological Education for Public Life* (1995); *Consumption, Population, and Sustainability: Perspectives from Science and Religion* (1999), with accompanying video, "Living in Nature;" The *Contentious Triangle: Church, State, and University. A Festschrift in Honor of Professor George H. Williams* (1999), *Earth at Risk* (2000), *Forgiveness and Reconciliation: Religion, Public Policy and Conflict Transformation* (2001), *Theological Literacy for the 21st Century* (2002); *Antioch Agenda: Essays in Honor of Orlando E. Costas* (2007); *Overcoming Violence: Religion, Conflict and Peacebuilding* (2010); *2010 Boston: The Changing Contours of World Mission and Christianity* (2012).

Tom Porter, JD (Boston University Law School) is Executive Director of Just Peace Center for Mediation and Conflict Transformation (UMC), the mission of which is "to engage conflict constructively in ways that strive for justice, reconciliation, resource preservation and restoration of community in and through The United Methodist Church and with the Church universal to the world in which we live." He is an ordained elder of the New England Conference of The United Methodist Church and served as conference chancellor for twenty-three years. He was a founding partner of the trial firm of Melick & Porter LLP in 1983 and has been a trial lawyer since 1974. Porter is a member of the Working Group on Restorative Justice of the Boston Theological Institute and has taught courses on the practice and theory of conflict transformation and peace building at Union Theological Seminary, Claremont School of Theology, and in numerous church settings. Co-director of the Boston University School of Theology Religion and Conflict Transformation program, he is author of *Conflict and Communion: Reconciliation and Restorative Justice at Christ's Table* (2006), and *The Spirit and Art of Conflict Transformation: Creating a Culture of Justpeace* (2010).

Kevin S. Reimer, PhD (Graduate School of Psychology, Fuller Theological Seminary) is Dean and Professor of Psychology at Fresno Pacific University. His research program considers moral identity through natural language processing. He has authored or co-authored more than sixty publications. Co-authored books include *The Reciprocating Self* (2005) and *A Peaceable Psychology* (2009). He recently authored *Living L'Arche* (2009) and co-edits *Theology and the Science of Moral Action* (2012). Reimer is co-principal investigator on a scientific research grant from the John Templeton Foundation entitled *Love, Compassion, and Care: Virtue Science and Exemplarity in Real Life and in the Laboratory.* He has received funding from the John Fetzer Institute, the Center for Theology and the Natural Sciences, and Institute for Research on Unlimited Love. He is ordained in the Presbyterian Church (USA).

April T. Scales lives in Waco Texas and attends Baylor University where she is pursuing a BA in Psychology. She enjoys writing and publishing poems and stories about her life experiences. She serves as a board member for Good Neighbor Settlement House-Waco, and a volunteer at Fuzzy Friends Rescue, an animal welfare organization.

T. Laine Scales, PhD (University of Kentucky) is Professor of Higher Education and Associate Dean of the Graduate School at Baylor University, Waco Texas. She served fifteen years as a faculty member in social work in three universities and has published over forty articles and chapters in the areas of teaching in social work, faith and social work practice, rural social work, and higher education. Her ten books include *Social Environments & Human Behavior: Contexts for Practice with Groups, Organizations, Communities, & Social Movements,* (co-authored, 2012) and *All That*

Fits a Woman, Training Southern Baptist Women for Charity and Mission, 1907–1926 (2000). She is former associate editor of *The Journal of Family & Community Ministries* and *Social Work and Christianity.*

Glen H. Stassen, PhD (Duke University) is Lewis B. Smedes Professor of Christian Ethics, Fuller Theological Seminary, Pasadena, California. He came to Fuller with thirty-four years of teaching experience at Duke University, Kentucky Southern College, Berea College, and Southern Baptist Theological Seminary. Stassen graduated from the University of Virginia with a degree in nuclear physics, and he studied systematic and historical theology, Christian ethics, and political philosophy during his graduate work at Union Theological Seminary in the City of New York and Duke University. He has done postgraduate study at Harvard University, the University of Heidelberg, Union Theological Seminary (New York), and the University of Notre Dame. Stassen's primary research and teaching interests are theological ethics, incarnational discipleship, peacemaking, social justice, and our need for healing in what he calls an "Age of Interaction." His book *Kingdom Ethics: Following Jesus in Contemporary Context* (2003) received *Christianity Today's* award for Best Book (2004) in Theology or Ethics. He has published several other books, including *A Thicker Jesus: Incarnational Discipleship in a Secular Age* (2012), *Living the Sermon on the Mount: A Practical Hope for Grade and Deliverance* (2006), *Just Peacemaking: The New Paradigm for Ethics of Peace and War* (co-edited, 2008), *Peace Action: Past, Present, and Future* (co-edited, 2007), *Authentic Faith: Bonhoeffer's Ethics in Context* (edited, 2007), *Living the Sermon on the Mount* (2006), *Authentic Transformation: A New Vision of Christ and Culture* (1996, with D. M. Yeager and John Howard Yoder), and *Just Peacemaking: Transforming Initiatives for Justice and Peace* (1992). Most recently, he co-edited John Howard Yoder's *War of the Lamb: The Ethics of Nonviolence and Peacemaking* (2009).

Hope Haslam Straughan, PhD (Barry University) is Associate Professor and Director of the Master of Social Work program at Wheelock College, Boston. Straughan's research and scholarship interests include spirituality within social work assessment and intervention, justice-based social work, and foster care and adoption. Her administrative roles at Wheelock are focused on helping the campus-wide community in their human rights and justice-based projects, research, and teaching. She serves as a volunteer foster care case reviewer for the Department of Children and Families and is on the board of FAMILY, Inc., and a leading member of the North American Association of Christians in Social Work (NACSW) Massachusetts chapter.

Straughan is co-author of "Spiritual Development," in *Christianity and Social Work: Readings in the Integration of Faith and Social Work Practices* (2011), and she contributed to *Wounded children, Healing Homes: How Traumatized Children Impact Adoptive and Foster Homes* (2010).

Najeeba Syeed-Miller, JD (Indiana University School of Law) is Assistant Professor of Interreligious Education at Claremont School of Theology, Claremont, California.

Syeed-Miller's involvements range widely, including conducting gang interventions, implementing diversity training in universities and public agencies, conflict resolution in public schools, interreligious dialogue among the Abrahamic traditions, and environmental conflict resolution. Her conflict resolution experience has made her a sought after trainer for those who work on conflicts in India, Latin America, Guam, Afghanistan, Israel, and Palestine. Her model of intervention is to build the capacity of those closest to the conflict. In particular her research and community activist efforts have focused on the role of women as agents of peacemaking. She has authored or co-authored numerous works including "Developing Appropriate Conflict Resolution Systems for Law Enforcement and Community Relations: The Pasadena Case Study" (*Ohio Journal on Dispute Resolution* 22:1 [2006]); *No Altars: A Survey of Islamic Family Law in America*, (2004); and, articles, "Cross Cultural Family Dispute Resolution" and "Mediating After 9/11, the Story of a South Asian Muslim Mediator" (*ACR Resolution Magazine*, September 2003).

Nimi Wariboko, PhD (Princeton Theological Seminary) is the Katherine B. Stuart Professor of Christian Ethics. He previously taught at New York University and at the Frank G. Zarb School of Business, Hofstra University (New York). His work focuses on economic ethics, metaethical theories, Pentecostal theology, and African studies. He was a strategy consultant to top investment banks when he worked on Wall Street. He is the author of eleven books and co-editor of three including *The Pentecostal Principle: Ethical Methodology in New Spirit* (2011); *Ethics and Time: Ethos of Temporal Orientation in Politics and Religion of the Niger Delta* (2010); *The Principle of Excellence: A Framework for Social Ethics* (2009), and *God and Money: A Theology of Money in Globalizing World* (2008). Wariboko has also published articles on economic history, corporate management, theology and science, and social theory. He is completing work on a forthcoming book, *The Spell of the Invisible: Pentecostal Spirituality in Nigeria*.

Foreword

RICHARD J. MOUW

WE DID NOT TALK about "spiritual formation" as such when I was young, but the Dutch Reformed tradition in which I was raised was very clear about what it meant to be formed for a life of conformity to God's will: we had to pay close attention to the Law of the Lord as set forth in Exodus 20. Reading the Ten Commandments every Sunday from the pulpit was a requirement. We were Calvinists and we knew what John Calvin taught about the "three uses of the Law": 1) the Decalogue reminded us of our sinful failure to live up to God's expectations of us; 2) it also gave us a framework for thinking about the general patterns of societal health; and 3) but—and in this as Dutch Reformed we differed, we knew, from the Lutherans and the Catholics—the Law was also a positive guide for our daily living.

It has been a long time since I have heard the Commandments read in a worship service, and I miss the recitation. I still think that attending church is, in an important sense, a re-gathering on Mount Sinai. Attending to the Lord's Day, the Sabbath, was a kind of covenant renewal. With ecumenical and inter-faith sensitivities today this is a reality worth recovering as appropriate to our different traditions.

If there was a defect in the way the Law was presented to us in my upbringing, though, it was that we seldom heard anything about the interrelationships among the various commandments. We were left with the impression that the Sinai Law was simply a report about ten distinct thoughts that loomed large in God's mind.

John Calvin actually warned against this way of seeing the Commandments. The Decalogue, he insisted, is not just a list of "dry and bare rudiments." It presents us with an integrated display, he said, of "all the duties of piety and love." Some of the Puritans took this a step further, arguing that, properly understood, each Commandment implies all of the others.

I like that emphasis, that is on seeing the integrated interrelationships among all of the Ten Commandments. I was delighted, then, when I discovered that the Lord's Day Alliance is paying much attention these days to the unity of the Decalogue. And I was immensely pleased when the Alliance proposed a co-sponsored conference at Fuller Seminary on the general implications of the "Thou shalt not kill" commandment, or the meaning of formation for a culture of life.

Recently in a faculty discussion focusing on our seminary's "community standards"—as set forth in a document dealing with issues such as plagiarism, sexual behavior, and the like—a colleague remarked that the real problem we face in Christian circles today is that we have lost a focus on *holy living*. Many heads nodded in approval when she said that.

The Sabbath commandment is explicit about holiness. We are to "remember the Sabbath day, for it is holy." If we want to understand the unity of the Decalogue, then, it is a good exercise to think about the "holiness" connection for each of the other commandments. Each of us is created in the image of God. This shapes not only our life of worship but the "holiness" of our relations with one another.

This fine book of essays, which emerged from cooperation between Fuller's Just Peacemaking Initiative and the Lord's Day Alliance, comprises an important exploration of holiness with respect to the Fourth and Sixth Commandments (in Jewish and Reformed numeration). God's mandate to ancient Israel regarding not-killing was a call to holy living—of a piece with all of the other divine calls to holiness.

God cares deeply about justice and peace. An active commitment to the practices of just peacemaking must be central to the life of Christian discipleship today. Worship on the Lord's Day, or the Sabbath, finds its proper complement in a life of justice and peace. The insightful essays in this book provide us with much needed contemporary instructions in holiness!

Introduction

GLEN H. STASSEN, RODNEY L. PETERSEN,
AND TIMOTHY A. NORTON

FORMATION FOR LIFE IS central to Christian discipleship as grounded in the resurrection. Formation for life is also at the heart of other religious traditions. But for followers of Jesus the reality of the resurrection challenges the sense of how one lives in the coordinates of space and time. From the earliest days of the church, gathering together on the Lord's Day, Sunday, became a way of challenging a culture of violence and death while pointing followers of Jesus toward a renewed life found in him. Among the other Abrahamic religions, Judaism finds its analogue in the Sabbath, which great tradition stands behind and challenges Christian practices of Sunday. Islam, while different, has a tradition of the Day of Assembly (*Jumu'ah*), on Friday, and also daily prayers.

In days of global political challenge, it is of value to remember that the promise given to Abraham, that his offspring would be a blessing to the nations (Gen 12: 2–3), is borne by each of these great traditions. For issues involved in the psychology of formation it is also important to remember the word of the Lord that came to Abram in a vision (Gen 15:1):

> Do not be afraid, Abram.
> I am your shield,
> Your very great reward.

The fourth commandment—"Remember the Sabbath day and keep it holy"—reminds us that each person is made in the image of God, and that how we think of the other is a measure of our regard for God. The sixth command, "You shall not murder" (Exod 20:13) challenges us to embrace a culture of life. Jesus illustrates his concern for life in many of the healing miracles (Matt 12:9–14), but the radical extent of this commandment is seen when he diagnoses how anger and disparagement lead to God's judgment because of the ways in which they kill the spirit.

Jesus commands the transforming initiative of quickly going to make peace with the other or with an adversary (Matt 5:21–26). "Blessed are the peacemakers" (Matt 5:9), we are counseled. We are called to include enemies in transforming initiatives that participate in God's gift to God's enemies of gentle rain and warm sunshine (Matt 5:43–48). Jesus wept over Jerusalem because they did not know the practices that make for peace, and warned that war would bring destruction (Luke 41:44).

The urgent question is: how can we do formation for life? The 10 practices of just peacemaking provide a lens for the formation of a culture of life rather than a culture of death. This is true for all peoples. The book *Interfaith Just Peacemaking* (2012), edited by Susan Thistlethwaite, draws this out for persons who find themselves in the Abrahamic religious traditions. Similar books might be written by others. The chapters in this book attend to the question of "formation for life" from a generally Christian perspective although chapters by Jewish and Muslim authors have been included for comparative purposes. Together we are interested in how we are formed to attend to the practices of just peacemaking and to the deep resonance throughout the Abrahamic traditions between the life of divine worship and that of ethical engagement (Isaiah 58).

Just peacemaking is a vision to which all are called. It is an ethos that must characterize persons in faith communities in the twenty-first century. These are the mutual concerns of the organizations that stand behind this volume, The Lord's Day Alliance of the U.S.A. (LDA) and the Just Peacemaking Initiative of Fuller Theological Seminary. It is a concern that was taken up at Boston University School of Theology in its conference on *Interfaith Just Peacemaking* (May 2012) and is increasingly of importance not only to the LDA and the schools mentioned here, to the ten schools of the Boston Theological Institute and additional schools represented in this volume, but of those interested in crafting a public theology for our times.

I

An Introduction to Part One

Just Peacemaking Practices and Formation for Life

Timothy A. Norton

THE PARADIGM OF JUST peacemaking is rapidly spreading, and even advocated in President Obama's Nobel Peace Award Address. But the question is: how do just peacemakers get formed? How does worship, or education, or community interaction form the kind of character that actually does what Jesus calls for—become actively engaged in being a peacemaker?

Jesus' words prior to his final departure, found in the Gospel of John 14:27, "Peace I leave with you; my peace I give to you; not as the world gives do I give to you. Let not your hearts be troubled, neither let them be afraid," quite simply forms the outline of the first section of this volume. For Jesus' words here remind us that the peace we seek is indeed the peace he has left with us, and in us, encouraging his followers that they should not be troubled by the circumstances they find themselves in, nor fearful of the unknown treatment that is in the future. Instead they should hear these words of Jesus' and actually do them (Matt 7:24).

The original impetus for this book came from the impact made by a conference sponsored by the Lord's Day Alliance of the U.S. and Fuller Theological Seminary's Just Peacemaking Initiative. We have added a few other authors to provide a rich, diverse, but certainly not exhaustive set of chapters built on the premise that spiritually formed persons are best equipped to be effective in doing the work of just peacemaking.

1

The writers of these essays come from a variety of backgrounds but each addresses the question of formation for just peacemaking. Christian ethicist Glen Stassen argues that effective formation for just peacemaking requires attention to four dimensions of interactive holistic character ethics, calling attention to emotions, perception of contexts, narratives and reasoning with moral guidelines. This opening chapter is followed by one by Scott R. Garrels, Kevin S. Reimer, and Warren S. Brown who sensitize us to issues of friendship, solidarity, commitment and virtue formation through mimetic compassion. Peacemaker and leading theorist of religious conflict, Marc Gopin, considers the elements of formation in his own life story as he learned to pursue a lifetime of peacebuilding. David McMillan writes of ways that a focus on just peacemaking has led not only to personal formation but also to ecclesial re-formation in his own Northern Ireland church. Developing the principles that guide the practices of just peacemaking in an Orthodox context is the focus of Philip LeMasters' chapter. Both Jeffrey Gros, FSC, and Raymond Helmick, S.J., offer insight on Ecumenical and Roman Catholic issues of formation, finding in the liturgy an antidote to violence. Finally, Cheryl Bridges Johns writes that only by yielding to a Spirit-directed life can we be formed to do the work of just peacemaking.

This first section of the book might be called "Venite," a Latin word meaning "come"—more specifically an invitation to prayer and worship as seen in Psalm 95 and 96 in verses like Psalm 95:6–7,

> [6] O come, let us worship and bow down,
> let us kneel before the LORD, our Maker!
> [7] For he is our God,
> and we are the people of his pasture,
> and the sheep of his hand.
> O that today you would hearken to his voice!

Calling herself only "Peace Pilgrim," Mildred Norman Ryder (1908–1981), walked 25,000 miles over the course of her last 28 years of life with the singular goal of highlighting the need for peace in the world. She is famously quoted as having said, "We who work for peace must not falter. We must continue to pray for peace and to act for peace in whatever way we can, we must continue to speak for peace and to live the way of peace; to inspire others, we must continue to think of peace and to know that peace is possible."

As you read, we invite you to "venite" as you consider how being a person formed by faith might best prepare you for the work of just peacemaking, as well as how your own faith tradition has something to offer in the larger context of being formed to do this work.

Holistic, Interactive Character Formation for Just Peacemaking

Glen H. Stassen

My argument is simple but important: Effective formation for just peacemaking—or any kind of moral formation—requires attention to four dimensions of interactive holistic character ethics:

1. *Emotions and loyalties*—as experienced in engagement with persons in different social contexts.

2. *Critical perception of the social context*—as it helps or hurts people.

3. *Basic convictions*—as embodied in narrative or historical drama.

4. *Reasoning* that relates moral guidelines to emotional responses.

I will seek to learn from important new psychological research on character formation. On the way, our understanding of the four dimensions will thicken and deepen. And more: we will learn how to do more effective formation from other chapters in the book on real-life examples—for example, the chapter by Scales, Straughan, and Scales on "Healing Hurt Kids," the chapter by McMillan on forming a congregation in the midst of "the troubles" in Northern Ireland, and the chapter by Marc Gopin on how he got formed as a just peacemaker.

Many Christian ethicists still repeat wisdom about how to form character that Aristotle taught two and a half millennia ago. But surely something has been learned since Aristotle. An understanding of character based on Aristotle's unmoving God focuses only on human striving toward ideals, and lacks the dynamism of God who brings God's kingdom interactively as grace, as gift.

Psychological research must offer significant learning that reaches beyond Aristotle's assumptions or Plato's ideals. My uniting theme is holistic, interactive, embodied character formation. I call ours the Age of Interaction. Psychology says humans are interactive, not closed to the influence of others and the world. Globalization says our nation and our lives are shaped by global interaction. Electronic interconnections are forming us. Quantum physics asserts that the physical world can be studied accurately only in terms of *relationships* between systems.[1] The new just peacemaking practices are interactions, not mere ideals. We are learning that selfhood is deeply interactive and holistic.

Warren Brown and Brad Strawn: The Physical Nature of Christian Life

Neurologist Warren Brown and Professor of Spiritual Development Brad Strawn report what neurological research has demonstrated: the Platonic dualistic view that we have a separate inner soul and an outer, material body does not fit actual evidence.[2] Nor does it cohere with a biblical understanding of holistic selfhood.[3] We are a complex integration of neurons, muscles, bones, and nerves, holistically interacting in our moral and spiritual relations. Moral formation does not happen to some hidden inner sanctum separated from the rest of our bodies, but is a holistic, integrated, interactive phenomenon. The dualistic belief that focuses almost exclusively on the soul as separated from the body is the ancient heresy of Gnosticism. Neurology confirms the holistic Hebraic understanding of selfhood and rejects Greek dualism.

This means that if we reduce character formation to "a matter of special spiritual knowledge to be acquired by individual persons via certain kinds of inner experiences," we are not only repeating the heresy of Gnosticism; we are also consigning ourselves to ineffectiveness. Character formation has to understand selves as holistic; it is about "reshaping the

1. Stassen, "Science: The Interactive Nucleus."

2. Brown and Strawn, *Physical Nature of Christian Life*. Page numbers that follow refer to the prepublication manuscript, and may change slightly in the final publication.

3. Murphy, *Bodies and Souls*; Green, *Body, Soul, and Human Life*; and the book that convinced me long ago: D. R. G. Owen, *Body and Soul: A Study on the Christian View of Man*.

whole embodied person—as in new habits, a different character, new virtues, and a greater capacity for hospitality, love, and care for others." In this more embodied view Paul's reference to "Christ in you" (Col 1:27 NIV) would be "a reshaping of our whole physical-mental-psychological selves into the image and likeness of Christ."[4]

Group Engagement/Group Reflection That Involves Emotions and Loyalties in Embodied Engagement with Persons in Different Social Contexts

Psychological research shows that moral formation takes place most effectively where there is embodied engagement, interaction and interdependence with other persons, with both trust and honesty. Brown and Strawn say that unfortunately most small groups in churches have a focus on comfortable, mutual affirmation, and study of the Bible as knowledge, rather than a covenant commitment to engage in longer-term confession and gentle confrontation plus embodied action. We need to be engaged in real mutual encounter, or in compassionate ministry and "the life of God's kingdom" so that we can learn to imitate one another bodily as well as emotionally. Brown and Strawn write:

> Intentional involvement in long-term small groups is often the place where a change process can best occur. . . . These groups may be therapy groups facilitated by a trained and licensed professional, or peer-led groups (such as Alcoholics Anonymous, Narcotics Anonymous, or Celebrate Recovery). Group situations that are transformative must present persons with opportunities for real, immediate, and authentic interpersonal interactions.[5]

Churches can organize themselves so that the worship service is followed immediately by small groups that discuss the implications of the worship service for their actual lives. Or they can form covenant groups, or *small groups with a mission*, that share together both in honest dialogue about the struggles in their lives and in a specific kind of service or mission that they focus on in the community near the church.

Brown and Strawn argue that much of our moral formation is learned and shaped by mimesis—imitation of others—especially persons to whom we have loyalties. Much of our learning by imitation occurs without our

---

4. Brown and Strawn, *Physical Nature of Christian Life*, 107–9.
5. Ibid., 78, 93, 117.

being aware of it. It is learned more effectively if we are engaged together in actual practices, in bodily actions that seek to provide some service to others. Hence membership in groups that are themselves engaged in practices for the good of others can be significantly formative. This is confirmed by sociologist Robert Wuthnow in his *Acts of Compassion: Caring for Others and Helping Ourselves*. Therefore I advocate the Church of the Savior model of *small groups with a mission*. Each group commits itself to a mission such as peacemaking, mentoring youth or school children after school, combating world hunger, housing the homeless, caring for families with a mentally challenged member, divorce recovery, etc. Members learn from each other, and are empowered by the strength and knowledge shared in the group, by contrast with the powerlessness of lonely individualism.

Critical Perception of the Social Context with Compassion for Persons

Older theorists like Piaget had said children lack much perception of social context until they develop more sophisticated cognitive abilities. But psychological research shows that babies only a few hours old start imitating and engaging with others. We are interactive from the start.

> Two- to three-day-old babies can discriminate smiles, frowns, and expressions of surprise, and can reliably recognize the smell of their own mother's breast milk. Newborns can differentiate their mother's voice from another woman's voice. Thus, fairly quickly, the dominant stimuli that come to have meaning for infants are the faces, voices, and physical presence of parents. . . .
>
> Infants are born predisposed to imitate other human beings. As early as the first hours of life, it has been shown that an infant will imitate facial gestures, like sticking out the tongue or opening the mouth—and the best part, smiling back. Given the openness of mental systems, the capacity to imitate allows an infant to learn about the nature of other persons. Infants engage in bidirectional learning effects, in which they both learn new behaviors by observing and copying the action of others and learn about the meaning of the action of others through their own imitative behavior. . . .[6]

Brown and Strawn point to Von Economo neurons that grow rapidly in small children, and that give us intuitive awareness of what is going

6. Brown and Strawn, *Physical Nature of Christian Life*, 2, 11, 52, 56.

on in other people's feelings. Mirror neutrons do likewise. The resulting ability to perceive the social context grows in adults, is nurtured in engagement in social groups, and helps form moral character. In rare cases, some people lack a key part of the brain's ability to interpret social context, so they lack the moral sense that others have. Sociologists, social ethicists, and political scientists study the complex perceptions of our social context more than psychologists do, but Brown and Strawn present highly interesting evidence for the importance of the dimension of perception of the social context, beginning from infancy and growing throughout life.

Basic Convictions as Narrative or Historical Drama That Aids Meaning and Reality Testing

Brown and Strawn argue that we need realistic stories as a framework for making sense of life. We make sense of our lives not merely by remembering abstract facts; we put them together in a narrative that gives us identity. Churches do likewise. "The church should tell and embody a core story about the kingdom of God that gives it a basis for understanding the nature of its communal life, as well as shedding light on a host of important cultural issues, such as wealth, power, politics, economics, war and international conflict, consumerism, individual rights and responsibilities, poverty and homelessness, sports and entertainment, marriage and family, neighborhoods, cities, and much more."[7]

They commend Stanley Hauerwas's argument for the importance of narrative that uses Richard Adams's book *Watership Down*. But significantly they do not mention the actual content of the story. Their theme is holistic embodiment; they say they want narrative that provides understanding of the actual world, with its wealth, power, politics, economics, individual rights and responsibilities, poverty and homelessness, etc. *Watership Down*, by contrast, is fiction about talking rabbits. Its interpretation of the culture is a dualistic either/or. Its narrative has only two kinds of rabbits: some represent Enlightenment liberalism: they despise tradition, and so they lack meaning. The others are authoritarian, reacting against the Enlightenment.

This bypasses the pluralism of American society, in which many people make sense of life through Constitutional minority rights, narratives of the civil rights struggle for human rights and human dignity for African Americans, and then for women, and the immigration struggle of Latinos and Muslims, and memories of the struggle for religious liberty by Baptists,

7. Ibid., 145; cf. 85.

Jews, and Catholics. We are in the midst of a struggle for American identity, including not only individualist liberalism and authoritarianism, but also the tradition of human rights and the common good that are under attack by an individualistic ideology of greed and selfishness. We need an American identity that supports fairness and justice so we have a way to encourage people to act with public responsibility. Brown and Strawn know that the kind of narrative we need for understanding the actual world makes room for including the pluralism of people in our actual world.

As John Paul Lederach writes, from a wealth of experience working to help people imagine a better, more peaceful future in situations of great conflict, "The moral imagination is built on a quality of interaction with reality that respects complexity and refuses to fall into forced containers of dualism and either-or categories."[8] I think Hauerwas agrees: his 2012 presidential address for the Society of Christian Ethics was an argument for the complexity and pluralism of the actual history that is our life. Hence in my *A Thicker Jesus*,[9] I argue for realistic embodied narrative that makes sense in our actual community with its pluralistic traditions and power structures. I call this kind of narrative "historical drama"—with the reality-testing of our actual history. Too often we tell romantic and dualistic stories about ourselves and our churches that focus on "spiritual" ideals or stereotype the culture as monolithically antagonistic and gloss over our actual histories in our actual communities. In our struggle for American self-understanding we need to include the common good, human dignity, and human rights in community, as Catholic encyclicals have been saying. In our struggle for the soul of the churches, we need a holistic theological ethic for all of life, not only life inside the churches. Christ is Lord through all of life, Sunday and all seven days of the week.

Brown and Strawn conclude their book by saying that the basic conviction that is crucial for the incarnational historical drama that makes sense of moral life in Christian faith is:

> the image of the embodied Christ, who forgave sins, healed bodies, and fostered interpersonal relationships characterized by kindness, justice, peace, and reconciliation. We understand Jesus' ministry as both the reconciliation of humans to God and a continuation of the prophets' call for justice for all people—all bodies! Jesus frequently engaged in scathing social commentary, making it clear that embodied and socially

8. Lederach, *Moral Imagination*, 36.
9. Stassen, *Thicker Jesus*.

embedded ministry in a physical world is at the heart of the Gospel. This ministry will not be realized by autonomous, individual Christians or by a one-dimensional and pale Christianity with no other call than to personal relationships with Jesus. The Kingdom of God will only come to ultimate fruition through the Body of Christ—the outcome of a truly embodied and embedded faith. It is this Body that continually forms human bodies into some measure of Christlikeness.[10]

Reasoning That Relates Moral Guidelines to Emotional Responses

By contrast with the kind of philosophical ethics that bases itself on allegedly universal ethical reasons, and Christian ethics that imitates such philosophical ethics, psychological research is showing that we are more powerfully influenced by our intuitive emotional perceptions.[11] Nevertheless, Brown and Strawn argue that reasoning with moral guidelines is important—if it connects with emotions and loyalties.

Some kinds of brain disorder damage this reasoning ability:

> A notable example is damage to the midline portion of the frontal lobe of the brain (between the eyes, just behind the forehead). Damage to this area can result in changes in the person's capacity to regulate his or her behavior with respect to either moral standards or normal social conventions, or to take into account the well-being of other people. These individuals are markedly capricious in their interpersonal and social behavior.[12]

What is missing in these persons signals the crucial importance of the dimension in our ethics of reasoning that relates moral guidelines to emotional responses.

---

10. Brown and Strawn, *Physical Nature of Christian Life*, 167–68.

11. Westen, *Political Brain*. This is a highly interesting and persuasive book for persons concerned about just peacemaking.

12. Brown and Strawn, *Physical Nature of Christian Life*, 33–34, 40.

Psychological Guidance for Forming Character (Holistically)

I turn now from neurological research to psychological research—again showing that character formation is more effective when it engages the four dimensions of holistic character ethics.

Marvin Berkowitz[13] reports on extensive research into school programs like the Child Development Project (www.devstu.org). Character formation takes place more effectively when students are engaged in a sense of empowerment for making decisions together and taking initiatives that develop a school-wide sense that the school community cares for each student, that the community includes rather than excludes others, that it stops bullying and teasing, develops older buddies for younger students, and develops and actually practices listening skills and conflict resolution skills. Students in these schools were led to take responsibility for helping set classroom norms and rules and planning schools' activities. Engaging pupils in initiatives to build a warmer community and in service projects is more effective than making public announcements.

F. Clark Power reports on the Just Community Project for schools, emphasizing the use of participatory democracy, and the goal of becoming a moral community "that shares an explicit commitment to a common life characterized by norms embodying high moral ideals. . . . We encouraged students to develop a sense of collective responsibility, which meant each member of the group shared responsibility for the group as a whole."[14] Psychologist William Damon writes similarly.[15] This confirms our dimension of group engagement with persons in diverse contexts that involves emotions and loyalties in embodied engagement with persons in different social contexts.

Furthermore, modeling is important. When significant others treat people in the child's presence with empathy, not violence and deceit, it impacts children's character formation. Schools must demand good character. This confirms Brown and Strawn's emphasis on mimesis.

Engaging the students themselves in community practices, with clear expectations, and in reflection sessions in which teachers lead them in integrating their experiences and actions with moral values, and with others' perspectives different from their own, impacts their character formation.[16]

13. Berkowitz, "Science of Character Education," 56–61.

14. Power, "Moral Self in Community," 50.

15. Damon, *Moral Child*, 147.

16. Berkowitz, "Science of Character Education," 61.

This supports our themes of group engagement/group reflection that involves emotions and loyalties to friends and mentors, perceptions of social context, and reasoning that relates moral guidelines to emotional responses.

As Berkowitz, Power, and the Child Development website indicate, "This elementary school reform program has been shown to promote pro-social behavior, reduce risky behaviors, stimulate academic motivation, create a positive school community, result in higher grades, and foster democratic values. Furthermore, it has identified the development of a caring school community as the critical mediating factor in the effectiveness of character education."[17]

It is especially important for our theme of *formation for just peacemaking* that such participative moral education decreases violence and increases conflict resolution and peacemaking practices. And conversely, teaching peacemaking practices to elementary school children increases moral education and subject learning. Berkowitz concludes: "Two of the most effective violence-prevention curricula, Second Step and Resolving Conflict Creatively, have been identified by the Character Education Partnership as character education initiatives. At the same time, the most effective character education program, the Child Development Project, is identified . . . as a model violence-prevention program and . . . as a model [substance abuse] prevention program."[18]

Berkowitz also writes: "At the college and university level, these same factors apply, plus it is greatly helpful to have consistent, well-supported, and justified whole-institution commitment to character education."[19] Berkowitz spent twenty years teaching at Marquette, a Jesuit University, as our sons studied at Boston College, also a Jesuit University, and Earlham, a Quaker College. Berkowitz himself has experienced what the research on schools supports: character formation is not only an individual project, but a community project. It is so much more effective when a school, a college, or a church actually practices it, articulates it, and encourages its members to practice it with each other in the community. Experiencing a community actually living the ethic connects with the dimension of perception of social context: members of the community perceive that it actually works and makes a difference when they experience it in action.

Striking evidence comes from a different context—working with delinquents who have done people damage or violence but do not feel remorse.

17. Ibid., 56–57.
18. Ibid., 58.
19. Ibid., 62.

Teaching them rational stages of moral reasoning would do little good; nor would "values clarification" about hypothetical situations have impact; their emotions, their feelings, their loyalties have to be engaged as they discuss the actual events. "From the extensive evidence available, it is clear that the values clarification approach does not live up to its ambitious claims."[20]

Psychologist William Damon writes that powerful effects have been obtained when delinquents discuss their own anger and moral apathy, and the effect on others of their actions, in small group discussions guided by a therapist who helps them face the emotional results of what they did. This has proven to be "one of the few successful means . . . for helping troubled youth develop this kind of interpersonal awareness and empathy."[21]

Here we see a focus on emotions and perceptions of how actions in the real world actually affect people. It is not hypothetical, but engagement in real experience. And it involves community that people can identify with—group discussion with fellow delinquents.

An analogous learning comes from psychologist Norman A. Sprinthall.[22] His Harvard team tried all the usual methods to teach psychology to high school students, with small group discussions, field trips, films, case studies, etc. But they detected no significant improvement in psychological growth. Then they shifted to training teenagers in several different states to do actual counseling of grade school and middle school children whose families had experienced a divorce. They were trained in group-discussion techniques as well as in problems that arise in families that experience divorce. "We found that adolescents were natural psychologists exploring questions of understanding causes of behavior. . . . The adolescents showed improvement in their level of ego maturity on Loevinger's index (of ego development) and on the Moral Judgment Inventory as well. The qualitative assessments of journals and other subjective observations all provided further validation." One key was actually engaging the teenagers in real experience rather than merely case studies, and the other was meeting with them during the process for group reflection on what they were learning. "In eleven studies in different states, different types of schools and colleges, socioeconomic levels, rural, urban, and suburban districts, with students from majority and minority backgrounds, we saw impressive growth." My own experience, though based on observation not psychological testing, echoes this: when engaging students in encounters with diverse others,

20. Damon, *Moral Child*, 140.

21. Ibid., 20–21.

22. Sprinthall, "Counseling and Social Role Taking," 86–97.

whether across racial differences or class differences or in teaching just peacemaking in Nicaragua, East Germany, or in Palestine and Israel, it is crucial to engage them in group reflection about perceptions of what they are learning. Both engagement and group reflection, with some probing leadership, are crucial.

Sprinthall's essay is part of a book with chapters by psychologists studying moral development in teaching school teachers, accountants, dentists, medical doctors, veterinarians, athletes, journalists, and others. The most impressive results were in the University of Minnesota nursing education program.[23]

There the moral teaching was integrated throughout the sequence of nursing courses, so that it regularly combined scientific knowledge with discussions of "ethics in the context of real practice." They combined moral reasoning levels (the dimension of reasoning that relates moral guidelines to emotional responses); along with a dimension of caring, empathy, sensitivity, courage, and perseverance (the loyalties in engagement); and also knowledgeable perception of the medical context (the dimension of perception of the social situation). Different faculty had responsibility for precisely defined parts of the sequence of courses, so students could experience mentors or models at the various stages. Group discussion was included in which students were encouraged to challenge each others' moral perspectives. "Engaging students in discussions with other students and faculty who clearly exhibit these attributes provides the students . . . who have less courage, ego-strength, toughness, and perseverance, with positive role models whom they may attempt to emulate" (as Brown and Strawn also suggest). An emphasis on caring was also essential. "Moral action could be taken in a manner that illustrates interpersonal warmth, empathy, compassion, and connectedness" with conflict-resolution techniques that are calm, caring, and respectful.

Similarly, the study found that "the moral reasoning ability of 244 pediatric residents was a predictor of their clinical performance. The authors concluded that high moral reasoning virtually excludes the possibility of poor clinical performance, and that the very highest level of clinical performance is rarely achieved by those at the lowest level of moral thought."[24] The book's chapter on integration of moral discussion with medical training got

23. Duckett and Ryden, "Education for Ethical Nursing Practice," 51–70.
24. Ibid., 64.

similar results, and also found that high moral reasoning scores had a highly significant correlation with having a religious orientation.[25]

Integrating moral education with experiential group engagement is important—especially experiential engagement with diverse others. In one study of college students, "The highest growth took place in majors that focus on understanding humans in all their diversity and/or majors that include a central integration of ethical considerations within the content of a professional course of study." Similarly, participation in voluntary off-campus learning experience that included engagement with other persons "showed a very strong growth on the DIT" measurement of moral reasoning, while students who did not have such experiences, or whose experiences were required rather than voluntary, did not show such growth. "This fits cognitive dissonance psychology, which says it is important that the dissonant experience be voluntary."[26]

Similar results come from psychological research on children's moral development in families. Based on extensive research, William Damon recommends that parents honestly share their moral and emotional responses to events in their own adult lives—"describing them clearly, and answering children's questions about them candidly. The purpose is to allow children to observe how respected adults manage moral feelings, thus providing children with models of emotional modulation." This fits the loyalties and emotions dimension of holistic character ethics, especially its variable of models, mentors, and friends, to be explained below. Parents are the first models and mentors, when children's emotional patterns are being formed. I testify that some of my father's comments on moral realities are still vivid in my memory. Damon says this may seem obvious, but his observation is that American parents too often shelter children from their adult emotional responses.[27]

Furthermore, parents can encourage children's natural loyalties to fairness and justice. "The outrage that a child feels when denied a fair share by a peer is as real as any moral emotion that will ever be felt. Children openly (and loudly) communicate such outrage to one another as well as to any supervising adults who may be at hand. . . . This web of feeling and communication presents the child with an irreplaceable opportunity to learn about the importance and meaning of justice."[28] The adult can ask

25. Self and Baldwin, "Moral Reasoning in Medicine," 155, 159.
26. McNeel, "College Teaching," 34–37.
27. Damon, *Moral Child*, 124.
28. Ibid., 29.

children what would be fair, and can suggest a solution like "you could play with it for five minutes, and then the other child could get a turn," thus affirming the sense of fairness and teaching a process of conflict resolution. "Through such engagements and the accompanying guidance of advising adults, children develop a rich understanding of fairness during the first decade of life."[29] I observe from my own parenting of our three sons that it is effective not simply to restate a rule, but to ask the child what the rule is, and leave space for an answer. This engages the child's moral perception and understanding rather than merely imposing an authoritarian rule. It is also effective to justify the rule in terms of effect on someone's feelings. This "supports the child's own natural empathic leanings."[30]

As we saw in research on college students engaging with diverse others, children's relations in school with peers promote a sense of fairness, justice, kindness, cooperation, reciprocity, mutuality and intimacy. "Mutuality means a high level of joint participation in discourse or other collaborative activities. Intimacy means a close affectionate bond leading to the shared disclosure of secrets and other confidences."[31] Trying to indoctrinate children in democratic values simply by lectures does not work. They need to experience the values working (perception of social context) among peers and in community (loyalties). "Such understanding can be fully acquired only through frequent participation in social engagements that are founded upon interactional procedures," that enact democratic values and conflict resolution.[32]

The ability of a leader to affect people's perception of the social context and thus to affect their actions is demonstrated in a chapter by David Moshman in the book, *Moral Development, Self, and Identity*.[33] Moshman presents a case study of the massacre of 767 men, women, and children in the small village of El Mozote, El Salvador. Captain Walter Oswaldo Salazar angrily addressed the men of the Atlacatl Battalion that had committed the massacre and were debating its rightness or wrongness: "What we did yesterday, and the day before, this is called war. This is what war is. War is hell. And, goddammit, if I order you to kill your mother, that is just what you're going to do. . . . Because what we did yesterday, what we've been doing on this operation—this is war, gentlemen. This is what war is."

29. Ibid., 45–46.
30. Ibid., 54.
31. Ibid., 76, 85.
32. Ibid., 118–19.
33. Moshman, "False Moral Identity."

The men who performed this and subsequent massacres were discussing their moral trepidations about their actions. But their captain persuaded them to see war as against communism, and to see communism as a worse moral evil than what they were doing. What they were doing was systematically raping the women before killing them, castrating the men before killing them, and killing babies by throwing them up in the air and spearing them with their bayonets as they came down. They massacred everyone in the village except the few who managed to escape. The people of the village were not fighting for communism; they were trying to stay out of the fight. They had done nothing to incite the massacre. But the captain gave the soldiers the perception that the threat from communism is worse; and that the effective way to defeat communism was to carry out such massacres and thus terrorize people away from joining with the revolutionaries.

When news of the massacres came to Washington in *The New York Times* and *The Washington Post*, members of the Reagan administration denied and obfuscated the truth because of their perceptions and loyalty to their policy of anti-communism by supporting military attacks, rather than defeating it by supporting human rights that would be better than communism. Thus the dimensions of perception of the social context (threat, authority, and truthfulness and openness) and loyalties (to the policy practices of the administration) led to immoral actions.

By contrast, consider the example of Rick Axtell, Chaplain and Professor of Christian Ethics at Centre College in Danville, Kentucky. During his student days, Rick volunteered to be a summer missionary in Bangladesh, which was then reputed to be the neediest nation in the world. He assisted Baptist missionary Carl Ryther, who had innovated a transformative agricultural program of growing rice, perch, rabbits, and vegetables all based on local resources rather than being dependent on the global economy. Carl was a mentor and model for Rick. He gave Rick moral *loyalty* plus a *perception of the social context*—what could be done effectively in the midst of Bangladesh's desperateness. Furthermore, they both shared *basic convictions* as followers of Jesus.

Rick came back with photos of his 6'5" slim frame with pure blond hair in the midst of a thousand dark-skinned, short Bengalis all staring at him. And he also came back with a vision and perception, and with new loyalties. He led the Southern Baptist youth in the church in Mississippi where he ministered to engage that church in an effective program feeding the hungry in their town, and thus changing their own perceptions and loyalties about the poor. He then got his Ph.D. in Christian ethics, writing a comparison of three strategies for combating hunger globally.

He has been organizing groups of students to engage in voluntary off-campus programs studying causes of poverty in Latin America. He is having huge impact on students of the elite college of Kentucky, and is much beloved by them. He has won three excellence in teaching awards from Bellarmine College and Centre College. He teaches just peacemaking to Centre's seniors—not only as a theory but also as experience. His teaching method includes group discussion and reflection on perceptions of the social context as well as on ethical values. This is how group engagement/ group reflection that involves emotions and loyalties in embodied engagement with persons in different social contexts can produce moral formation.

Lawrence Kohlberg and James Rest

In the 1950s and 1960s, Lawrence Kohlberg developed his six-stage theory of moral judgment. He offered people moral dilemmas and listened carefully to their reasoning for the solutions they advocated. He was focusing only on the dimension of reason with moral guidelines, and not on the other three dimensions.

Kohlberg acknowledged that his work implied "the reassertion of the Platonic faith in the power of the rational good. . . . Many psychologists (and moral philosophers) have objected to what they consider Kohlberg's excessive rationalism."[34] For example, Spiewak and Sherrod researched "how to motivate youth to engage in prosocial initiatives." Their finding was that Kohlberg's thinking-doing relationship is weaker than the relationship between emotions and doing, and between emotions and thinking. "Affective mechanisms are more effective motivators than their cognitive counterparts."[35]

Similarly, Lawrence Walker's research on moral exemplars concludes that "The danger of this overemphasis on moral rationality is that it separates people from their own personalities and risks destroying their motivation to be moral. . . . Thus, we hear increasingly frequent appeals to enrich the psychological study of moral development by integrating cognition with personality and character, thereby providing *more holistic understandings of moral functioning* and effective means to foster moral development."[36]

34. Bergman, "Identity as Motivation," 21.
35. Spiewak and Sherrod, "Shared Pathways," 76.
36. Walker, "Moral Exemplarity," 70–71 (emphasis added). Walker clarifies: "These

James Rest participated in Kohlberg's research at Harvard, and then with his own team of researchers at the University of Minnesota, developed a Defining Issues Test (DIT-P) that identified people's stage of reasoning more efficiently. This enabled him and his team to broaden the research base extensively, and to develop further confirmation and some disconfirmation in the 1980s and 1990s.[37]

Kohlberg himself acknowledged a problem in his claim that people would reason with moral judgments that fit one of six levels that he had identified, and not mix higher and lower levels: "In both Rest's data and in the longitudinal data (Kohlberg and Kramer 1969) . . . an excessive number of subjects skipped stages, or regressed. It was entirely reasonable, then, for Rest to question the simple stage model."[38] James Rest concluded: "These facts lead to the view that moral behavior is determined by several psychological processes acting together, and that [Kohlberg's levels of] moral judgment is only one of these."[39] Stephen Thoma writes that reviews of the interaction between moral cognition like the DIT and moral behavior find the correlation between Kohlbergian "moral judgment" and action to be only 10 percent to 15 percent. "There is a growing consensus in related areas that general interpretative systems such as moral judgments are insufficient predictors of specific behaviors in specific situations."[40]

Hence James Rest and colleagues developed and then revised a four-component model of moral behavior.[41] Rest's model, as modified subsequently, includes measures that roughly include the four dimensions that I am arguing for.[42] The Rest team's research found that their revised model predicted "over 60% of the variance in views on public policy issues (e.g., issues dealing with abortion, free speech, rights of the accused, women's roles, and the role of religion in public education."[43] This is a dramatically

---

criticisms of the rationalistic bias of contemporary moral psychology do not negate the essential role that moral reasoning plays; rather these concerns argue for a more full-bodied and balanced account of moral functioning that meaningfully includes moral personality and character."

37. Rest, "Longitudinal Study," 738–48; Rest and Narvaez, *Moral Development in the Professions*, 7. See also Rest, *Development in Judging Moral Issues*.

38. Kohlberg, foreword to Rest, *Development in Judging Moral Issues*, xiii.

39. Rest, "Background: Theory and Research," 21–22.

40. Thoma, "Moral Judgments and Moral Action," 201–2.

41. Thoma, Rest, and Davison, "Describing and Testing a Moderator," 659–60; Narvaez et al., "Individual Moral Judgment," 478–88.

42. This requires explanation that I do not have space for here.

43. Narvaez et al., "Individual Moral Judgment," 486–87.

high percentage for explaining variance in social science research, since people are so complex and vary in thousands of ways. It is striking confirmation of the power of a more holistic character ethics model.

Jonathan Haidt's Social Intuitionist Model

Psychologist Jonathan Haidt and others have now developed a Social Intuitionist Model that is achieving broad support among psychologists studying moral character.[44] Other researchers are coming to similar conclusions. They are concluding that the most powerful factor in moral judgments is our emotions and loyalties dimension, including as it relates to our perceptions dimension: "Moral intuitions (including moral emotions) come first and directly cause moral judgments. . . . Moral intuition is a kind of cognition, but it is not a kind of reasoning." Moral intuitions are immediate, quick, and come "by a process more akin to perception, in which one 'just sees without argument that they are and must be true' . . . rapidly, before any conscious processing has taken place. . . . Moral reasoning [by contrast] is an effortful process, engaged in after a moral judgment is made, in which a person searches for arguments that will support an already-made judgment."[45]

Haidt's Moral Foundations Theory says the five key moral perceptions are harm, suffering, and care; equality, fairness, and justice; ingroup/loyalty; hierarchy, authority, and obedience; and purity/sanctity of the human body and sacred spaces of meaning.[46] Haidt and associates tested this mapping of intuitive moral/emotional domains, with very large statistical bases of diverse kinds, for eleven world regions. Different religions and different regions emphasize different ones of these emotional and intuitive domains more than others. That causes persons raised in those social contexts to develop the emotions that their religious or regional cultures emphasize, and to allow the other emotions to shrivel, decrease, or remain relatively undeveloped.[47]

Usually, psychologists do not focus their research on distinctions among different kinds of basic religious convictions, so they do not

---

44. The model is most clearly laid out in Haidt, "Emotional Dog and Its Rational Tail," and Westen, *Political Brain*. Numerous articles by Haidt and associates and by Westen and associates develop various implications of the model.

45. Haidt, "Emotional Dog and Its Rational Tail," 814, 818.

46. Haidt and Joseph, "Moral Mind."

47. Graham et al., "Mapping the Moral Domain."

often confirm the importance of the basic convictions dimension. Here the very extensive research of Haidt and associates adds significant confirmation of the influence of religious or regional framing—basic convictions in embodied narratives. And the confirmation occurs in the dimension that their research shows is most influential—the intuitive, emotional, loyalties dimension. Their more recent research argues that moral identity based in a cosmic, existential, ideological, or theological narrative, such as the drama of the Compassionate Samaritan, does significantly influence moral character and action.[48]

It is interesting to notice that Jesus dealt with all five of these moral/emotional domains. Jesus explicitly prioritized care and fairness over purity and authority; and redefined the ingroup to include all to whom God gives sun and rain.[49] This fits well with the research behind the paradigm of just peacemaking, with its emphasis on economic justice and human rights as care for the common good and the vulnerable, over against possessive individualism. Just peacemaking also advocates love and community, and therefore international cooperation rather than nationalistic individualism—a broadening of the ingroup. Just peacemaking demonstrates that practices embodying these themes decrease war and increase peacemaking, in actual practice. Thus just peacemaking connects directly with the five basic emotions that Haidt and associates demonstrate are fundamental.

It is interesting to speculate that one reason evangelical churches and Christ-centered churches tend to grow more while many mainline churches are in decline may be their stronger connection with the emotional dimensions of the gospel as opposed to a more "academic and sophisticated" emphasis on the cognitive. In any case, many if not most Christians have strong emotional loyalty to Jesus; Jesus Christ is a person, our Lord and Savior, not merely a rational doctrine. If Haidt is right, and he surely is, moral formation of Christians needs to emphasize loyalty to Jesus Christ influencing and transforming Christians' other loyalties, with concrete attention to Jesus' actual teachings and actions.

Haidt observes: "The importance of affect-laden intuitions is a central theme of neuroscientific work on morality."[50] But he also clarifies that intuition is not only an emotion; it is a form of cognitive perception: "Affective evaluation occurs so quickly, automatically, and pervasively that

48. See also important support in Haidt, Graham, and Joseph, "Above and Below Left-Right."

49. For example, see Borg, *Conflict, Holiness & Politics.*

50. Haidt, "New Synthesis in Moral Psychology," 999.

it is generally thought to be an integral part of perception."[51] In several places, Haidt indicates that intuitive or affective evaluation is the result of perception plus emotional response, and that perception is in turn strongly affected by emotions.

Haidt also says we fool ourselves into thinking that our moral reasoning shapes the judgments that we reach, but since we lack awareness of our automatic intuitive processes, we do not realize how much we are influenced by our emotions and intuitions. "People have quick and automatic moral intuitions, and when called on to justify these intuitions they generate post hoc justifications out of a priori moral theories. They do not realize that they are doing this."[52] In conversation, Warren Brown has said he worries that this emphasis on the priority of emotions can fall back halfway into a view of selfhood as based in internal emotions disconnected from our bodies, our social contexts, and our embodied narrative frameworks. I agree with Brown and advocate a holistic and interactive understanding of selfhood that relates reasoning about moral guidelines to emotional responses. Elsewhere, Haidt acknowledges that interaction occurs in multiple directions, though the loyalties and passions are most influential, if often unseen. Haidt says that

> moral reasoning can be effective in influencing people before a conflict arises. Words and ideas do affect friends, allies, and even strangers by means of the reasoned-persuasion link. If one can get the other person to see the issue in a new way, perhaps by reframing a problem to trigger new intuitions, then one can influence others with one's words. Martin Luther King Jr.'s "I Have a Dream" speech was remarkably effective in this task, using metaphors and visual images more than propositional logic to get White Americans to see and thus feel that racial segregation was unjust and un-American.[53]

Haidt says elsewhere that metaphors and visual images can alter our perceptions and intuitions, and our emotions, and thus are often more effective than only dispassionate logic and facts. They actually engage all four of the dimensions of the holistic character model. "The social intuitionist model, therefore, is not an antirationalist model. It is a model

51. Haidt, "Emotional Dog and Its Rational Tail," 819.
52. Ibid., 822.
53. Ibid., 823.

about the complex and dynamic ways that intuition, reasoning, and social influences interact to produce moral judgment."[54]

The Holistic Character Ethics Model

Way back in 1969–72, independent from the psychological research that I have cited, I was trying to identify key elements in people's actual moral reasoning, and how those elements actually related to each other, so our Christian ethics could make a difference for moral formation of real people, rather than merely arguing about one hypothetical dimension that may or may not influence what they actually do. I observed a lot of bad ethics, a lot of racism and militarism that were doing enormous damage, and wanted to develop an ethical paradigm that could make a difference for people's actual, embodied ethics. I developed a *Holistic Character Ethics* model, based on analyzing contributions of philosophers Stephen Toulmin and H. D. Aiken, social theorists Talcott Parsons and Karl Deutsch, Christian ethicist Ralph Potter, the work on cognitive perception and misperception by Robert Jervis and John Steinbruner, and my own research in ethics and international relations as a research fellow at Harvard. I eventually published my holistic, four-dimensional model in *The Journal of Religious Ethics* in 1977, and, with David Gushee, subsequent versions elsewhere.[55] It developed the same four dimensions that I have been tracing in this essay. I am pleased to see it now confirmed by extensive psychological research. I also developed specific variables within each of the four dimensions that have proven highly useful for my students and for my own writing in Christian ethics, but that goes beyond our present purpose.

54. Ibid., 829.

55. Stassen, "Social Theory Model." Oddly, the *JRE* shuffled the pages without sending me the page proofs; after you read pp. 9–23, skip two pages to 26–27; then read pages 24–25, then 28–37. Other versions are Stassen, "Critical Variables," and Stassen and Gushee, "Holistic Character Ethics." As Karl Deutsch suggested, I also subjected the model to statistical testing in research published in the leading journal of international politics (Stassen, "Individual Preference versus Role-Constraint, Senatorial Response to Secretaries Acheson and Dulles"). This does not confirm all four dimensions, but does support a hypothesis about the formative power of the dimension of perception of the social context, as influenced by the dimension of passions and loyalties, for empirical action outcomes.

What We Learn for Formation for Just Peacemaking

1. Formation happens most effectively if people participate in embodied, voluntary engagement with other persons and new social contexts, such as a course on just peacemaking in Palestine and Israel, or service involvement with school kids who need mentoring or counseling when their parents divorce. *And if they meet in groups to share in analyzing what they are learning from their involvement.*

2. Formation happens if people join small groups with a mission, and with a covenant to work together honestly and sometimes confrontingly on real issues in their lives, including the emotional dimensions.

3. Formation happens if people play an active role in forming the ethics of their school, family, or church, and if that community becomes a community of discernment that shares together in discussing real, embodied issues in the world. It should include their loyalties and their perceptions of the social context.

4. Formation happens if all four dimensions of character are engaged interactively with other persons in community. Merely sharing rational information or detached "values clarification" or discussing universal principles and hypothetical cases is not effective.

5. Formation for just peacemaking happens if we frame our just peacemaking in the way of Jesus, very concretely, and in a way that makes emotional connection. Jesus wept over Jerusalem because they did not know the practices that make peace. He entered Jerusalem on a donkey, fulfilling the prophecy of Zechariah 9:9–10 that the Messiah of Peace would come on a donkey not a warhorse, and would abolish the war chariot and the war bow. Palm Sunday celebrations need to make this connection explicit and emotional. Jesus was deeply concerned that Jerusalem was building toward a rebellion against Rome, and the temple would be destroyed.

Sabbath Day and the Other Six Days

Psychologists usually do not include basic faith convictions in their research. The research we have seen is designed to assist character development in public schools and universities, where teaching does not usually have a particular faith basis. Nevertheless, studies of moral exemplars found that a more mature faith development was a crucial dimension for many moral exemplars.

Colby and Damon studied moral exemplars, as did Lawrence Walker. The moral exemplars were not distinguished in Kohlbergian principled moral reasoning. But they had:

- Considerable certainty about moral principles and values balanced by relentless truth-seeking and open-mindedness, precluding dogmatism,

- Active receptivity to progressive social influence and a continuing capacity to change,

- Positivity and optimism, humility (with moral courage), love for all people, *a capacity to forgive, and an underlying faith or spirituality*, and

- An exceptional uniting of self and morality, reflecting an identity that fused the personal and moral aspects of their lives. . . . They saw moral problems in everyday events and saw themselves as implicated in these problems and responsible to act."[56]

Similarly, M. I. Matsuba and L. J. Walker studied forty moral exemplars and found that "in contrast to the comparison group, the exemplar group was more mature in their identity, reflecting a stronger commitment to values and greater stability; they evidenced *more mature faith development, reflecting the process by which they make meaning in life*; and they used more advanced moral reasoning, confirming its critical role in moral functioning."[57]

Despite the usual practice of most psychologists to bypass faith considerations because they are seeking public advocacy in a society of religious pluralism, we have seen several psychological studies discovering that faith convictions were a significant ingredient in moral makeup. And when James Rest included a faith dimension in his model, along with a measure of ideological loyalty and perception of the situation, the predictive power of his model leapt from 10 percent to over 60 percent. This supports the importance of Sabbath-convictions from sources not used to noticing them.

But we have also seen the strong force of moral formation by engagement in experiences the other six days of the week. Schools, parents, colleges, engagement in civic organizations have a powerful effect on people's

56. Walker, "Moral Exemplarity," 65–79. Walker also reports on Colby and Damon, *Some Do Care*.

57. Walker, "Moral Exemplarity," 65–79.

moral development. Brown and Strawn persuade us to avoid an inner spiritualism divorced from holistic formation embodied in our social context. This means that formation for just peacemaking has a huge stake in the formation that takes place during the week. For real formation, we need tactical alliances with a public ethics of democratic values, the American tradition of human rights for all, *e pluribus unum*, the sanctity of human life and liberty and justice for all, in the culture that shapes schools, work places, political rhetoric, and community interactions. We have a huge stake in the tradition of human rights that began during the Puritan Revolution in England in the seventeenth century, was affirmed in the Preamble to the Constitution with its commitment to justice, liberty, and the general welfare (common good), in the Declaration of Independence with its commitment to the endowment by our Creator of the human rights of life (which includes the basic needs of life), liberty (religious liberty and civil liberties), and the pursuit of happiness (which must include dignity in community) for all. This tradition has been struggled for by Abraham Lincoln, Martin Luther King, and millions of Americans. It is now under threat by ideologies of selfishness, greed, uncaring, and militarism.

We are now in a battle for defending that tradition: defending that human rights are for the common good of all, in community practices, and require societal structures that defend the human rights of minorities and the marginalized, as over against ideologies of individualistic greed, possessive individualism, selfish interests, merely "my rights and let others fend for themselves." Such possessive individualism is the opposite of human rights for all in community, as exemplified by Martin Luther King, Jr. We can all be allies in that ongoing struggle for the tradition that in fact has helped America learn to incorporate varieties of ethnic groups and different religions with better dignity in community than we would have exemplified without it.

Jesuit ethicist Simon Harak has written profoundly that emotions and intuition-guided perceptions can be trained intentionally by engagement in experience. He describes his own experience on a "Walk for a Peaceful Future in the Middle East." He and two hundred others walked to support nonviolence by Israel and Palestine toward each other—and to support a solution in which each side would recognize the other as legitimate states in their own right. They walked across the "Green Line," the border between the two territories, in the face of the heavily armed Israeli military forbidding them to cross the line. Harak describes his sense of love and even eagerness for the confrontation, because of his own deep commitment to nonviolence:

> It seems to me that this eagerness, this willingness to encounter and undergo physical suffering, is the primary passion for the virtue of nonviolence. Like all passions, this passion must be trained—and this passion especially, lest it become a wrong passion, a passion for self-*destruction*. . . . [Gandhi] says, for example, "Suffering in one's own person is . . . the essence of nonviolence and is the chosen substitute for violence to others."
>
> More pointedly, this passion to accept suffering into the self is characteristic of Jesus who was crucified. . . . The Letter to the Hebrews tells us that Jesus "endured the cross, despising the shame" (12:2). And Christians are commanded to take up the cross as Jesus did and to suffer as he suffered.[58]

Bibliography

Bergman, Roger. "Identity as Motivation: Toward a Theory of the Moral Self." In *Moral Development, Self, and Identity*, edited by Daniel Lapsley and Darcia Narvaez, 21–46. Mahwah, NJ: Lawrence Erlbaum Associates, 2004.

Berkowitz, Marvin W. "The Science of Character Education." In *Bringing in a New Era*, edited by William Damon, 43–64. Stanford, CA: Hoover Institution Press, 2002.

Borg, Marcus. *Conflict, Holiness & Politics in the Teachings of Jesus*. Valley Forge, PA: Trinity, 1998.

Brown, Warren, and Brad Strawn. *The Physical Nature of Christian Life: Neuroscience, Psychology, and the Church*. New York: Cambridge University Press, 2012.

Colby, Anne, and William Damon. *Some Do Care: Contemporary Lives of Moral Commitment*. New York: Free, 1992.

Damon, William, editor. *Bringing in a New Era in Character Education*. Stanford, CA: Hoover Institution Press, 2002.

———. *The Moral Child: Nurturing Children's Natural Moral Growth*. New York: Free, 1988.

Duckett, Laura J., and Muriel B. Ryden. "Education for Ethical Nursing Practice." In *Moral Development in the Professions: Psychology and Applied Ethics*, edited by James Rest and Darcia Narvaez, 51–70. Hillsdale, NJ: Lawrence Erlbaum Associates, 1994.

Graham, Jesse, Brian A. Nosek, Jonathan Haidt, Ravi Iyer, Spassena Koleva, and Peter H. Ditto. "Mapping the Moral Domain." *Journal of Personality and Social Psychology* 101.2 (2011) 366–85.

Green, Joel B. *Body, Soul, and Human Life: The Nature of Humanity in the Bible*. Grand Rapids: Baker Academic, 2008.

---

58. Harak, *Virtuous Passions*, 130–31, as quoted in Stassen and Gushee, *Kingdom Ethics*, 46. See also Yoder, *Politics of Jesus*, chap. 7.

Haidt, Jonathan. "The Emotional Dog and Its Rational Tail: A Social Intuitionist Approach to Moral Judgment." *Psychological Review* 108.4 (2001) 814–34.

———. "The New Synthesis in Moral Psychology." *Science* 316 (18 May 2007) 998–1002.

Haidt, Jonathan, J. Graham, and C. Joseph. "Above and Below Left-Right: Ideological Narratives and Moral Foundations." *Psychological Inquiry* 20 (2009) 110–19.

Haidt, J., and C. Joseph. "The Moral Mind: How Five Sets of Innate Intuitions Guide the Development of Many Culture-Specific Virtues." In *The Innate Mind*, edited by P. Carruthers, S. Laurence, and S. Stich, 3:367–91. New York: Oxford University Press, 2007.

Harak, G. Simon. *Virtuous Passions: The Formation of Christian Character.* Mahwah, NJ: Paulist, 1993.

Kohlberg, Lawrence. Foreword to *Development in Judging Moral Issues*, by James R. Rest, xii. Minneapolis: University of Minnesota Press, 1979.

Lapsley, Daniel K., and Darcia Narvaez, editors. *Moral Development, Self, and Identity.* Mahwah, NJ: Lawrence Erlbaum Associates, 2004.

Lederach, John Paul. *The Moral Imagination: The Art and Soul of Building Peace.* New York: Oxford University Press, 2005.

McNeel, Steven P. "College Teaching and Student Moral Development." In Rest and Narvaez, *Moral Development in the Professions*, 27–50.

Moshman, David. "False Moral Identity: Self-Serving Denial in the Maintenance of Moral Self-Conceptions." In *Moral Development in the Professions: Psychology and Applied Ethics*, edited by James Rest and Darcia Narvaez, 83–110. Hillsdale, NJ: Lawrence Erlbaum Associates, 1994.

Murphy, Nancey. *Bodies and Souls or Spirited Bodies?* New York: Cambridge University Press, 2006.

Narvaez, Darcia, Irene Getz, James R. Rest, and Stephen J. Thoma. "Individual Moral Judgment and Cultural Ideologies." *Developmental Psychology* 35.2 (1999) 478–88.

Owen, D. R. G. *Body and Soul: A Study on the Christian View of Man.* Philadelphia: Westminster, 1956.

Power, F. Clark. "The Moral Self in Community." In *Moral Development, Self, and Identity*, edited by Daniel Lapsley and Darcia Narvaez, 47–64. Mahwah, NJ: Lawrence Erlbaum Associates, 2004.

Rest, James R. "Background: Theory and Research." In *Moral Development in the Professions*, edited by James Rest and Darcia Narvaez, 1–26. Hillsdale, NJ: Lawrence Erlbaum Associates, 1994.

———. *Development in Judging Moral Issues.* Minneapolis: University of Minnesota Press, 1979.

———. "Longitudinal Study of the Defining Issues Test of Moral Judgment: A Strategy for Analyzing Developmental Change." *Developmental Psychology* 11.6 (1975) 738–48.

Rest, James, and Darcia Narvaez, editors. *Moral Development in the Professions: Psychology and Applied Ethics.* Hillsdale, NJ: Lawrence Erlbaum Associates, 1994.

Self, Donnie, and De Witt Baldwin Jr. "Moral Reasoning in Medicine." In *Moral Development in the Professions*, edited by James Rest and Darcia Narvaez, 147–62. Hillsdale, NJ: Lawrence Erlbaum Associates, 1994.

Spiewak, Gabriel S., and Lonnie R. Sherrod. "The Shared Pathways of Religious/Spiritual Engagement and Positive Youth Development." In *Thriving and Spirituality among*

Youth: Research Perspectives and Future Possibilities, edited by Amy Eva Alberts Warren, Richard M. Lerner, and Erin Phelps, 167–82. New York: Wiley, 2012.

Sprinthall, Norman A. "Counseling and Social Role Taking: Promoting Moral and Ego Development." In *Moral Development in the Professions*, edited by James Rest and Darcia Narvaez, 85–100. Hillsdale, NJ: Lawrence Erlbaum Associates, 1994.

Stassen, Glen H. "Critical Variables in Christian Social Ethics." In *Issues in Christian Ethics: Festschrift for Henlee Barnette*, edited by Paul Simmons, 57–76. Nashville: Broadman, 1980.

———. "Individual Preference versus Role-Constraint in Policy-Making: Senatorial Response to Secretaries Acheson and Dulles." *World Politics* 25.1 (1972) 96–119. Reprinted in *The Analysis of Foreign Policy Outputs*, edited by William O. Chittick, 123–45. Columbus, OH: Merrill, 1975.

———. "Science: The Interactive Nucleus." In *Thicker Jesus: Incarnational Discipleship in a Secular Age*, chapter 6. Louisville: Westminster John Knox, 2012.

———. "A Social Theory Model for Religious Social Ethics." *Journal of Religious Ethics* 5.1 (1977) 9–37.

———. *A Thicker Jesus: Incarnational Discipleship in a Secular Age*. Louisville: Westminster John Knox, 2012.

Stassen, Glen H., and David P. Gushee. "Holistic Character Ethics." In *Kingdom Ethics: Following Jesus in Contemporary Context*, chapter 3. Downers Grove, IL: InterVarsity, 2003.

Thoma, Stephen. "Moral Judgments and Moral Action." In *Moral Development in the Professions*, edited by James Rest and Darcia Narvaez, 199–212. Hillsdale, NJ: Lawrence Erlbaum Associates, 1994.

Thoma, Stephen J., James R. Rest, and Mark L. Davison. "Describing and Testing a Moderator of the Moral Judgment and Action Relationship." *Journal of Personality and Social Psychology* 61.4 (1991) 659–69.

Walker, Lawrence J. "Moral Exemplarity." In *Bringing in a New Era in Character Education*, edited by William Damon, 65–84. Stanford, CA: Hoover Institution Press, 2002.

Westen, Drew. *The Political Brain: The Role of Emotion in Deciding the Fate of the Nation*. New York: Public Affairs, 2007.

Wuthnow, Robert. *Acts of Compassion: Caring for Others and Helping Ourselves*. Princeton: Princeton University Press, 1991.

Yoder, John Howard. *The Politics of Jesus*. 2nd ed. Grand Rapids: Eerdmans, 1994.

2

Redeeming Imitation

Virtue Formation
by Mimetic Compassion in Communities[1]

Scott R. Garrels, Kevin S. Reimer,
and Warren S. Brown

We live in a world of competition, where importance is given to success, a good salary, efficiency, distractions, and stimulations. Our world, however, needs to rediscover what is essential: Committed relationships, openness and the acceptance of weakness, a life of friendship and solidarity in and through the little things we can do. It is not a question of doing extraordinary things, but rather of doing ordinary things with love.

~JEAN VANIER

1. This chapter is a revised version of the article originally published as Brown, Garrels, and Reimer, "Mimesis and Compassion." It is reprinted here, as revised, with permission by the *Journal of Religion, Disability, & Health*.

Introduction

IMITATION IS CENTRAL TO Christian discipleship and its understanding of human formation. The apostle Paul urged his followers to "Imitate me, just as I also imitate Christ."[2] Imitating the kenotic, self-giving desires and actions of Jesus is considered essential to overcoming the fallible nature of our own desires, which, when left alone, invariably lead us into relentless cycles of selfishness, greed, deceit, and ultimately violence and death. In the Gospel of John, Jesus himself repeatedly tells his followers that he is not acting on his own accord, but is following the divine will of God the Father.[3] The *Imitatio Christi* is therefore central to the Christian church, not just in terms of Jesus' specific desires and actions, but, more centrally, as also remaining open to imitating a will beyond oneself in order to bring about the kingdom of God.

In contrast, the modern world tends not only to reject religious resources as essential models of wisdom to imitate in addressing our global and relational problems, but imitation in and of itself is considered anything but wise. In a culture that is proud of its hyper-individuality, the need to imitate is usually associated with being unoriginal, mindless, or demonstrating a general lack of maturity or intelligence. The popular saying "monkey see, monkey do" goes so far as to imply that the person who needs to imitate has not only failed to develop as a person, but hasn't even evolved as a species.

The irony of such devaluing generalizations concerning imitation is that they themselves are imitations—imitations of a cultural attitude that date back to the Enlightenment period when we began to view the human mind and person as self-contained and independently rational.[4] This Enlightenment view of the self as autonomous (exemplified by Descartes' credo, "I think, therefore I am") became so influential that the subject of imitation was substantially marginalized by the dominant psychological theories as they began to emerge in the twentieth century. This profound neglect can be seen by the absence of imitation in Freud's developmental theory of instinctual drives. In general, "until the 1970s the term 'imitation' did not even appear as a keyword in reference bases such as *Psychological Abstracts*."[5]

---

2. 1 Cor 11:1.

3. John 4:34; 5:30; 6:38; 8:22–29; 12:49–50; 14:30–31.

4. Gardner, *Myths of Freedom*, 53.

5. Nadel and Butterworth, *Imitation in Infancy*, 1.

However, in a dramatic turn of events, several recent and ground-breaking discoveries in the cognitive and developmental sciences now support the idea that imitation is unique to the human species. As it turns out, monkeys are very poor imitators. Not only that, but this rare human ability is active immediately at birth and may very well be what underlies our most prized forms of human intelligence, language, sociality, and culture. In short, the role of imitation is so pervasive and automatic that we barely notice its constant operation in our daily lives, leading to the illusory conclusion that our behaviors and motives are solely our own, uninfluenced by those of others.[6]

What is more, decades before advances in empirical research prompted a rise of interest in imitation, the French literary analyst and cultural theorist René Girard had already developed his own theory of imitation, or *mimetic theory*. Beginning in the early 1960s, Girard identified not only that imitation was essentially human, but that it was the founding social force that propelled humans to establish culture and religion through primitive forms of ritual sacrifice—a social mechanism that contained escalating in-group violence by deflecting it against an outside or surrogate victim. While contemporary research now emphasizes the essentially positive role of imitation in human formation, Girard's work further shows us, paradoxically, how the same imitative mechanisms are equally responsible for our most unique and problematic forms of human competition, rivalry, and violence.[7] The question therefore is not so much whether or not we imitate, but who our models are, and how they form who we become.

The goal of this chapter then is to discuss these renewed and paradoxical views of imitation as they pertain both to issues of human conflict and violence as well as personal transformation, just peacemaking, and Christian discipleship. We begin with an overview of Girard's description of the relationship between imitation, social vulnerability, violence, and the foundational nature of social scapegoating in human culture. We then argue that an orientation of service toward the socially marginalized and disabled of society connects us to our own shared existential vulnerabilities, thereby facilitating the process of personal formation away from mimetic rivalry, the romantic illusion of our own autonomy, and the need for scapegoating. In order to support this argument we focus on long-term caregivers in L'Arche communities—persons who give years of their lives at very low pay to live in

6. Bargh, "Most Powerful Manipulative Messages."

7. See Garrels, *Mimesis and Science*, for a recent integrative dialogue between scholars of Girard's mimetic theory and imitation researchers from the empirical sciences.

homes as assistants to persons with moderate to severe mental disabilities. Such persons seem to evidence little desire to compete for material possessions or increase their social status. While individuals such as L'Arche caregivers counter the dynamics of desire and rivalry of Girard's mimetic theory, we show how resources within the work of Girard can nonetheless help us understand these exemplars of compassion. Finally, drawing on the new science of human imitation, we provide reflections on how the transformations of persons into exemplars of compassion can be accounted for both from the perspective of the power of imitative interactions within communities, and from neuro-psycho-social perspectives on human formation. Such an analysis may help us understand both the role of imitation in generating human conflict and violence as well as fostering genuine compassion in communities and persons more fruitfully.

Mimetic Desire, Social Vulnerability, and Violence

In his book, *Deceit, Desire and the Novel*, Girard put forward his first major hypothesis that human desire is mimetic.[8] His initial research centered on the advent of the novel as a new literary genre in nineteenth- and early twentieth-century Europe, and included many of the principal authors, such as Cervantes, Flaubert, Stendhal, Dostoevsky, and Proust. From his comparative analysis, Girard observed that regardless of the author or period, human desire was almost always depicted as a "triangular" phenomenon involving a subject, a model, and the desired object. In contrast to Romantic or Enlightenment conceptions, Girard concluded that these great novelists intuitively understood that human desire was essentially imitated from, or mediated by, the desire of others.

Mimetic desire, therefore, refers to what Girard considers the nature of desire itself; that is, human desire is constitutively imitative rather than being an autonomous expression of the individual self. Whether we are aware of it or not, we are constantly looking to others to know what is desirable, how to act, what to acquire, and whom to become. Mimetic desire and behavioral imitation are inherently positive and necessary aspects of our uniquely human nature since they help us learn and adapt to all the complex rules of social, cultural, and familial life.

Girard notes, however, that mimetic desire can take on exaggerated forms directed ultimately toward acquiring what we *perceive to be* the ontological fullness or completeness of the other person. The desire to

8. Girard, *Deceit, Desire and the Novel*.

achieve such an illusory state of being is what Girard calls *metaphysical desire*. Webb[9] explains Girard's understanding of how these metaphysical longings are more commonly translated into expressions of desires for physical objects:

> Metaphysical desire as Girard describes it stems from the fear we each harbor that we are deficient in "being"—which means to us "power." Each of us comes into the world utterly helpless, surrounded by powerful, godlike others, and we long to possess the ontological plenitude we see in them . . . so we reach for the same objects in the illusory hope of gaining it too.[10]

In other words, what drives our desires is a basic longing for existential grounding, but we fundamentally misinterpret what generates this sense of vitality in others as the object(s) in their possession, which are potentially infinite. This is why we can "never get enough of what we don't really need," and why we often believe "the grass is greener on the other side," as well as feel a constant need to "keep up with the Jones."

As Girard's research points out, because we end up desiring what our 'neighbors' desire, our closest relationships are also those most susceptible to conflict. Because we desire to possess the same thing, even the best of relationships go from good to bad very quickly, especially when what we desire cannot be shared or when we desire to possess something exclusively for ourselves. Because only one person can possess an object exclusively for herself or himself, mutual appropriative mimesis can escalate into intense forms of rivalry and eventually violence. We become so caught up in the rivalry itself that we often forget what it was we were fighting over in the first place. Defeating one's rival becomes the primary desire, and not the object itself. This fascination/abhorrence vortex of emotional arousal is one of the most powerful of all human experiences, and one of the most difficult to stop or back away from once it has crossed a certain threshold of intensity. As individuals become more desperate in their attempts to defeat their rival, and therefore differentiate themselves from others, their behaviors eventually erupt into physical violence. This violence in turn is similarly imitated and increased reciprocally with each act. Ultimately, mimetic violence can become so intense that the only perceivable resolution is to kill one's rival. Indeed, there is no greater sense of differentiation and triumph than between one living and one dead.

9. Webb, "Eros and the Psychology," 1–14.
10. Ibid., 5.

The Disabled as Scapegoat

Within Girard's mimetic theory, the capacity of mimetic desire to invoke existential insecurities is not limited to conflict in one's sense of self and interpersonal relations. It can also threaten an entire social order. Much of Girard's anthropological research is an attempt to understand how humanity has survived its own violence.[11] Because violence is one of the most imitative of all human behaviors, once initiated it has the potential of spreading quickly to those within its proximity, upsetting existing bonds of community, and leading to cyclical acts of revenge and violent group contagion. In the absence of any instinctual elements of restraint, such as dominance patterns found in other animal societies, Girard reasoned that without some "natural" way to limit mimetic violence and bring it to an end, the likely result would have been the extinction of our species.

For Girard, the natural or "spontaneous" phenomenon that made social stability possible, and ultimately a cohesive human culture, was the mimetic displacement of violent tensions among members of the community onto an arbitrary or surrogate victim. While complex and wide-ranging, Girard's anthropology asserts that archaic culture and religion have their origin in the same type of event: a mimetic crisis of undifferentiation (all against all) that polarized into a collective murder (all against one). According to Girard, this event had the effect of creating an unprecedented sense of communal bonding that eliminated group tensions while at the same time establishing important social distinctions: that between a community and its antagonist. This, according to Girard, is the origin of human sacrifice. In the attempt to prevent such spontaneous episodes of uncontrollable violence, this scapegoat mechanism and its resolution was repeated and thus made available for imitation and cultural transmission on a ritual basis.

Even today, these two factors, mimetic desire and the scapegoat mechanism, work together in unconscious social life through attempts to provide our communities with a sense of control, resolution, and social differentiation (i.e., between good and bad, or sacred and profane). According to Girard,[12] the selection of victims by the community is less a function of the crimes they may or may not have committed, but rather of their membership in a social class that makes them particularly

11. Girard, *Violence and the Sacred.*
12. Girard, *Scapegoat.*

susceptible to persecution. Among these classes of victims are the physically and mentally disabled. Girard explains:

> Sickness, madness, genetic deformities, accidental injuries, and even disabilities in general tend to polarize persecutors. We need only look around or within to understand the universality. Even today people cannot control a momentary recoil from physical abnormality. . . . The "handicapped" are subject to discriminatory measures that make them victims, out of all proportion to the extent to which their presence disturbs the ease of social exchange.[13]

In a communal crisis characterized by loss of social differences, as is the case with mob violence, individuals that stand out based on physical qualities alone are often easy targets for victimization. This is true for the disabled not just because they might be weaker as a result of their physical disability, but also because the very nature of their physicality becomes associated with disorder. In the midst of mob mentality, blame for communal disorder is often irrationally transferred to those with physical disorders. Again, in Girard's own words, "If a disability, even as the result of an accident, is disturbing, it is because it gives the impression of a disturbing dynamism. It seems to threaten the very system."[14]

Compassionate Exemplars and L'Arche Communities

While it is not hard to see how Girard's claims concerning mimetic rivalry, violence, and social scapegoating are universal, there are nonetheless real world individuals and communities who appear to provide us with exemplary counter-examples. Such exemplars are worth examining in detail, since they provide us with powerful models worth imitating. It is here that we now turn to the exemplars of compassion found in L'Arche communities. In L'Arche homes (*L'Arche* is French for *The Ark*), people with developmental disabilities (also known as *core people* or *core members*) live in community with their caregivers (also known as *assistants*).

L'Arche was founded by Jean Vanier and Fr. Thomas Philippe in the early 1960s. The movement continues to spread across international boundaries, currently established in more than thirty countries worldwide. Community life is punctuated by deep spiritual commitments and experiences. L'Arche is a religious movement that embraces other traditions

13. Ibid., 18.
14. Ibid., 21.

while remaining committed to its Roman Catholic origins. L'Arche honors individuals as a sign of compassion and mutual respect.

In the United States, L'Arche communities typically exist on scarce financial resources. Besides room and board, assistants may live on several hundred dollars per month. Benefits (such as health insurance and retirement accounts) are scant or nonexistent. To serve as an assistant in a L'Arche community for an extended period of time offers no hope of financial gain, accumulation of possessions, or enhanced social status. To succeed long-term as a L'Arche caregiver one must give up certain mimetic desires and aspirations acquired from modern society.

The minimization of rivalry in these communities is striking, though deliberate. L'Arche communities are founded upon a Charter which cements compassion in everyday activity, anticipating conflict with social scaffolding for peaceful restitution of involved parties. Most importantly, mimetic inversion runs deep. In a sweeping paradox, L'Arche assistants insist the disabled are prophets and teachers who serve as models and exemplars in the community. By learning openness and the craft of compassion from these unlikely experts, assistants embrace the paradoxical notion of *downward mobility*—where the deepest human potential exists in simple relationships. To be downwardly mobile is to adopt an interpersonal posture lacking competition and exclusion. Compassion is animated in relationships between caregiver assistants who might be able to hide their brokenness through *askesis* (defined below) and those who cannot (e.g., disabled core members). Core members provide life instruction to assistants regarding how to live openly with disability and its existential implications. They must confront and resolve the inevitable shame which accompanies social stigmatization. From their experiences core members know profound isolation and suffering. Many have histories involving cruelty and abuse from institutional settings. Through a variety of circumstances they arrive in L'Arche where healing becomes a real possibility. For some the transition comes easily. Others require time to rehabilitate the trust necessary to function within community.

Novice and experienced L'Arche assistants were the focus of a large-scale study that involved extensive narrative interviews regarding self-identity.[15] In their responses, caregivers frequently aligned their narratives with examples from core members, recounting their own shame and "disability" in the form of traumatic experiences, harbored grievances, and fractured relationships. What became clear in these interviews is that rec-

---

15. Reimer et al., "Maturity Is Explicit"; Reimer et al., "From Novice to Expert."

ognition of one's own shame as mirrored in the experiences of those with disabilities contributes to reordered appraisals of others and themselves, coupled with the emergence of exemplary compassion manifest in long-term service to the disabled.

Thus, the narratives of many assistants make a significant demand on the reader to recognize and accept genuine compassionate mutuality in the core member-assistant dyad. Is this a legitimate example of the type of personal conversion in the face of rivalry and violence described by Girard or merely a sophisticated imitation of virtue to improve competitive advantage? Research on L'Arche caregivers reveals that both "apparent" and genuine virtue exists in these communities with most short-term or novice caregivers representing the "apparent" group. We believe that genuine compassion emerges in long-term caregivers through a significant personal transformation which comes about in sustained contact with, and care of, the core members, as these encounters reveal their own deeply felt social vulnerabilities. As Girard's own analysis shows, without the ability to sustain contact with our own limitations and vulnerabilities, we will forever strive to deny our core human dependency on one another.

The Novelistic Hero's *"Askesis"*

In *Deceit, Desire, and the Novel*, Girard concluded that the relational drama and conflict central to the great novels he was studying reflected a truth of the human condition: without a way to come to terms with our mimetic dependency on one another, our relationships will forever perpetuate the romantic lie of self-autonomy. Autonomy is a lie that can only be maintained through infinite forms of deceit, hypocrisy, greed, isolation, and even death.[16] This core dependency on others based on our innate mimetic tendencies is perhaps the most difficult aspect of our selves to acknowledge or admit to consciousness. By refusing to acknowledge the deepest fears of our own inadequacies and refusing to speak about such fears in our relationships, we defend against them with social strategies to demonstrate our potent abilities to others, thereby producing a variety of problematic relations.

One such strategy employed by the heroes of Girard's analysis is the practice of "*askesis* for the sake of desire." *Askesis* denotes asceticism, a practice of severe self-discipline in order to obtain spiritual and religious goals. According to Girard, *askesis* for the sake of desire occurs when one attempts

16. Girard, *Deceit, Desire and the Novel*, 155.

to hide her or his own mimetic tendencies and desires, in order to avoid appearing socially vulnerable and to stir desire in others toward oneself. The goal of *askesis* is to gain social favor and/or to possess desired objects, such as a potential lover, by turning oneself into a model for the metaphysical desire of others. While appearing virtuous to others, the novelistic hero's *askesis* is more accurately a form of hypocrisy, a feigning of superiority in order to fulfill one's own selfish desires. The characters perceive that if they can disguise their own needs well enough, especially in a way that displays indifference to such needs, they can then be seen as possessing enormous "strength of soul." This illusory image is used to draw admiration and ulti-mately to proclaim oneself as autonomous or superior to others.

Ironically, *askesis* for the sake of desire not only sets the hero apart but it creates an inordinate distance between him and others—a divide that cannot be crossed without leading to disillusionment. In other words, the ultimate goal of invulnerability becomes a barrier to genuine relation-ships since intimate contact will mean revealing the fundamental illusion of autonomy. The closer others are drawn to the novelistic hero based on his or her admirable "strength of soul," the more the hero has to push them away in order maintain the ascetic illusion. As such, the hero can never obtain the lover that his or her *askesis* seeks to attract. This leads the hero not only to greater forms of self-denial, but also more intense forms of deception and rivalry. Girard describes the hero's futile attempts at maintaining his or her illusion:

> Incapable of self-analysis and led on by his pride, he instinc-tively applies the precepts of underground mysticism which are always analogous to, but the inverse of, the principles of Christian mysticism: "*Do not ask and you will be given; do not search and you will find; do not knock and it will be opened.*" The further man strays from God, Dostoyevsky tells us, the deeper he plunges into the irrational, at first in the name of reason and finally in his own name.[17]

Thus, the hero attempts more severe and perverse forms of *askesis*, result-ing in a perpetual state of slavery to one's hidden desires. As a result, *ask-esis* for the sake of desire leads ultimately to the hero's tortured existence filled with dysfunctional relationships, intense conflict, and in some cases reciprocal violence. Without the ability to expose one's mimetic desires, thereby tolerating a certain amount of vulnerability, authentic relationality

17. Ibid., 156–57.

is never achieved. While appearing to be ascetic, "The most profound hypocrisy can be distinguished from virtue only by its poisoned fruit."[18]

The Novice L'Arche Caregiver Assistant

Although Girard's anthropology is unfamiliar to L'Arche, the manifestations of *"askesis* for the sake of desire" are widely recognized by these communities as an intentional target of novice caregiver socialization and development. Many assistants come to L'Arche motivated by metaphysical desire focused on models encountered in cultural or religious narratives or in their own experiences. In trying to emulate these models, they express a desire to engage in asceticism and self-discipline they imagine to be characteristic of L'Arche. To the degree this is true of their motives, their desire to be a part of L'Arche is primarily self-serving, covering a need to draw admiration toward themselves and proclaim autonomy, or superiority over others.

Consistent with other service organizations for the disabled, L'Arche communities experience high rates of turnover and burnout. Somewhere during the first year of service, caregiver assistants are typically forced to confront underlying elements of hypocrisy in their personal motivation for compassionate service. The confrontation is well known to the larger community, identified as opportunity for *discernment*—a period of coming to understand themselves in relationship to service to the mentally disabled. The first year of caregiver involvement is particularly difficult. During this period, novice assistants must come to terms with their own inadequate desires and weaknesses, and to grapple with the ethic of *downward mobility*. The ensuing crisis involves engagement with existential vulnerability and shame.

It would be a mistake to characterize the entirety of novice caregiver assistants on the basis of *askesis* for the sake of desire. However, when asked in the study about their personal goals, novice caregiver assistants responded with a range of motives, which reflect "virtuous" yet self-referential goals. Themes included *self-consistency* (e.g., ensure I am treated fairly, do my best, and do the right thing), *openness* (e.g., be open-minded, make contact with others, and consider future directions), *adventure* (e.g., seek new experiences, be financially independent, and seek new relationships), *empathy* (e.g., take care of people and be helpful in stressful situations), and *lifestyle* (e.g., live simply, waste few resources, and eat less). Thus, while goal themes suggest an authentic struggle and engagement

18. Ibid.

with existential vulnerabilities, the starting point for the struggle is typically self-referencing. By contrast, the personal goals of long-term L'Arche assistants differ considerably, with greater prioritization given to the other. The developmental process associated with the discernment experience unquestionably involves a weeding out of romantic attitudes and postures associated with metaphysical desire.

Outcomes are mixed regarding the number of assistants able to navigate the discernment process successfully. By some accounts, more than half of caregiver assistants who enter L'Arche are gone by the end of the first year. Of the remaining half, more than a third will leave through the process of discernment. Those caregivers able to resolve the crisis tend to become fixtures in the community, known through the study as *long-term or experienced L'Arche caregivers*. Remarkably, some of these individuals will remain in L'Arche for decades. Their narratives commonly reference a past history of upheaval associated with discernment and concomitant reordering of their mimetic desires. Downward mobility in L'Arche is the result of intentional socialization processes embedded within community. Coming to understand this transformation is the core topic of our discussion.

The Novelistic Conversion

In the novels that Girard analyzed, the heroes undergo a "conversion" experience toward the end of the story, which is often the result of a confrontation with their own mortality or based on some form of physical and social degradation. Once the heroes' condition deteriorates to an undeniable state of disability, often an end of life experience, they then are forced to see the futility of their efforts and renounce their pride. This confrontation is unavoidable since the heroes are unable to escape their physical bodies, and thus escape a dependent state of vulnerability. Yet this dying of the body produces a corollary awakening of the spirit.[19]

In essence, the hero is liberated from metaphysical desire and all desperate and exacerbating attempts at maintaining an illusion of superiority. In doing so she or he experiences true freedom. Girard argues that this freedom is the result of being released from the slavery of mimetic rivalry, which produces an inversion of all previous effects of *askesis* according to desire: "deception gives way to truth, anguish to remembrance, agitation to repose,

19. For Girard, the death of the hero is a metaphor for the author's own personal transformation—the death of the ego or pride—that allowed them to write their novelistic conclusion in the first place.

hatred to love, humiliation to humility, mediated desire to autonomy, deviated transcendency to vertical transcendency." Girard elaborates:

> This time it is not a false but a genuine conversion. The hero triumphs in defeat; he triumphs because he is at the end of his resources; for the first time he has to look his despair and his nothingness in the face. But this look which he has dreaded, which is the death of pride, is his salvation.[20]

Whereas metaphysical desire brought about certain forms of interpersonal relations, according to Girard, "true conversion engenders a new relationship to others and to oneself."[21] These new relationships are marked by the realization that self and other are the same and share the same fundamental desires, vulnerabilities, and hypocrisies. What the hero could previously only see in others he now sees in himself.

> Victory over self-centeredness allows us to probe deeply into the Self and at the same time yields a better knowledge of others. At a certain depth there is no difference between our own secret and the secret of others. Everything is revealed to the novelist when he penetrates the Self, a truer Self than that which each of us displays. . . . But this renunciation is very painful. The novelist can write his novel only if he recognizes that his mediator is a person like himself.[22]

Thus, the heroes realize how rivalry and pride have produced a form of blindness, whereas their renunciation produces a "breadth and depth of vision"[23] This vision allows them to look back on life and see it for what it was—vanity, loss, suffering, and sickness, all for the sake of pride. This conversion experience is also marked by a return to simplicity. The heroes take pleasure in things previously deemed unimportant. This simplicity may be perceived by others as banality since it is a departure from all the previous forms of social passions that were so constantly stirred as a result of mimetic rivalry. Girard concludes that "the novelistic denouement is a reconciliation between the individual and the world, between man and the sacred. The multiple universe of passion decomposes and returns to simplicity."[24]

20. Ibid., 294.
21. Ibid., 295.
22. Ibid., 298–99.
23. Ibid., 297.
24. Ibid., 308.

Transformation in L'Arche Caregivers

A similar form of conversion is potentially at work with long-term L'Arche assistants. Unlike novice caregivers, long-term caregiver assistants were found in the study to have *moral identities* characterized less by self-reference and more by commitment to the needs of others. Moral identity has received widespread attention in the work of Anne Colby and William Damon.[25] These authors spent time with nominated exemplars known for exceptional caring. Exemplars commonly reported experiences of transformation where social influences refashioned personal goals and values intrinsic to their self-understanding. The most powerful social influences came from close relationships (not distant models) in which exemplars were challenged to reach and grow. These relationships implicated a spectrum of mentor figures including friends, family members, and religious leaders. Key relationships galvanized exemplars to confront existential and moral issues associated with a given cause.

The community context of L'Arche exerts influence capable of shaping the moral identity of caregiver assistants. What is perhaps startling about this conclusion is that disabled core members, some with the cognitive capacities of a young child, offer powerful and lasting influence over caregivers. Core members influence others not as passive recipients of care, but as discrete moral agents. Through the life example furnished by core members, caregivers are confronted with their own limitations along with the possibility of existential restitution from shame. Caregiver self-understanding is altered in the encounter. When assistants have sustained close relationships with core members, they experience new appraisals of social situations that previously elicited shame.[26] A long-term caregiver assistant (seventeen years) offers a wrenching example:

> I was raped in high school. Even though my family moved around a lot and there was a lot of suffering and isolation, as a people person I was able to fit in and make friends quickly even

25. See Colby and Damon, *Some Do Care*. Colby and Damon's work greatly impacted the field of moral psychology. By focusing on exemplars known for remarkable caring, the book challenged the prevailing notion that morality is principally a function of Kohlberg's six-stage reasoning. Exemplars in the study were given Kohlberg's moral judgment interview, a moral reasoning metric. Despite their remarkable humanitarian achievements, exemplars scored no differently from the general population on Kohlberg's scale. Thus, moral identity captures aspects of maturity beyond the ability to reason through intractable dilemmas.

26. See Reimer, "Committed to Caring." Self-conscious emotions may also be implicated in moral reasoning. See Greene et al., "fMRI Investigation."

if I was dying inside. After the rape I gained 30 pounds, I probably became severely depressed, severely dissociated. This was an insane time. I never told anybody. My junior and senior year of high school I didn't have a single friend. There were some people I socialized with a little bit at school. I went from being someone who dated to someone who was overweight, invisible, severely depressed, and nobody noticed. If I let myself re-enter it, the pain was huge. What it gave me was that I experienced what it was like to be entirely on the outside looking in. And things looked really different that way. I think it brought me to a whole different level. It's interesting, I had a lot of feeling for people who were on the outside, I was the kind of kid who couldn't stand people being picked on. But I hadn't been completely that way. I just felt ugly and awful and icky. It was humiliating. I can still remember not having a date for my prom. Or not going to a single dance. But I think it gave me a whole experience of being a part of a world.

How did this relate to your work in L'Arche?

I look at the core members, I mean, what more rejected group is there? What group wears their pain in such a manner? Not that anybody should be ashamed, but let's face it, most people who are handicapped feel shame. And they wear it. To feel voiceless, to feel invisible, to feel unattractive. I used to think, I'll never get married. No man could ever love me. I've dwelt in the shadow lands. But I think it impacted receptivity in my heart. Much of that wasn't at a conscious level or awakening my own experience. That came later, over the years. I think I've been much more freed up at L'Arche, way less self-conscious. It's impacted my ability to be more forgiving. I think the community allows people to be free. I think it's a movement into more freedom, more joy. More peace, more tolerance for other people. I get less worried about things now. I feel like, I've always said God will provide, but now I'm living in it more.

This interview narrative suggests developmental transition away from debilitating shame. The contours of shame are unmistakable in the terribly painful recollection of rape and its aftermath. The caregiver recounts scenes of isolation punctuated by self-abasement. The experience of shame elicited what might be interpreted as an extreme form of *askesis* in her effort to camouflage her shame by feigned indifference to social interactions.

The move toward healing and other-oriented functioning was fostered by the example of disabled core members in a manner that liberates this woman from entrapment in shame. Revision of her *social scripts* or templates for social interaction is precipitated through changes to her expectations for relationships and understanding of herself in those relationships. From her L'Arche experience with core members, her pre-dispositions toward social situations evolved from self-deprecation to the appreciation and ratification of virtue in others. Instead of chronic self-consciousness she began to engage others freely, no longer bound to external judgments of self. Foundational to these changes is the caregiver's gradual move away from shame-related *askesis* and self-denial as the centerpiece of her self-understanding in favor of openness and freedom. By her own admission these changes are mostly "offline" or beneath conscious awareness. Her reflections suggest a gradual alteration of her self-understanding and moral identity. It seems likely that alterations to self-understanding that support such rich narrative reflections are consolidated only after transformation is well underway in offline experience and behavior.

How might such transformations in long-term L'Arche caregivers be understood from a Girardian perspective? In the novelistic conversion described by Girard the hero is forced to confront pride and brokenness through the inescapable condition of his/her physical disability and/or impending death. We argue that, in the case of L'Arche caregivers, this conversion, or death of the ego, is initially prompted not by the confrontation of one's disability, but by the physical disabilities of the other. The immersed experience with core members, and the resulting downward social mobility, forces the individual into self-evaluation and discernment. This process may very well be similar to that of the hero/author confronting his/her own frailty, pride, and hypocrisy. However, in the case of L'Arche caregivers, this frailty can once again be avoided if one so chooses. And in fact, this is what happens for many caregivers within a year's time—they choose to leave L'Arche. Those who stay, however, remain in the position of daily exposure to human weakness and vulnerability. In effect, they elect to stay in the position that the novelistic hero cannot escape—confrontation with severe disability. After some time, much like the heroes in the novels that Girard analyzes, attempts to avoid the suffering, disability, and shame and the mirroring of one's own vulnerability give way to a profound change in one's perspective. No longer are disabilities thought of as something primarily to be avoided and existing only in others. Instead, they are recognized as something fundamentally inherent in oneself as well. The novelist's recognition of the fundamental sameness between self and other described by Girard echoes the descriptions of long-term L'Arche caregivers.

Furthermore, we believe that, from a more anthropological perspective, L'Arche communities represent the inverse of the scapegoat mechanism described by Girard. As described earlier, Girard makes it clear that it is often the disabled who get singled out as scapegoats for the problems of mimetic desire and rivalry that occur between people. Instead of scapegoating, silencing, and marginalizing such persons through exaggerated and exclusionary acts filled with disdain and contempt, L'Arche places disabled persons at the center of the communities as prophets who reveal the truths of social vulnerability and self-other relatedness that most persons seek to hide at all cost.

Reflections on Imitation and Transformation in Communities

We have thus far focused on the developmental maturation of assistants in the care of core members as the key factor in the transformation of long-term caregivers. What other factors might be involved in L'Arche communities that foster the transformational process? We suggest here that a non-violent and caring form of *imitation and social contagion*, a *community narrative*, and *rituals* are key in fostering transformation as individuals attempt to face their own vulnerabilities and confront our human tendency toward competitiveness, conflict, and rivalry.

Imitation and Social Contagion

The power of Girard's mimetic theory is its being based on a universal and innate tendency of all human beings to imitate—a fact that has been recently substantiated by a wide range of important scientific discoveries, among which are the findings of neonatal imitation and mirror neurons. Infants are not only able to imitate adult facial and hand gestures immediately at birth,[27] but very early in development infants are able to read below-the-surface behavior of adults and imitate their underlying goals, desire, and intentions.[28] The role and power of imitation in the cognitive, affective, and behavioral development of infants and children has been extensively

27. Meltzoff and Moore, "Imitation of Facial and Manual Gestures"; Meltzoff and Moore, "Newborn Infants Imitate."
28. Meltzoff, "Understanding the Intentions of Others."

investigated from a wide range of developmental studies.[29] Whereas previous theories conceptualized imitation as a later development in early childhood—and rather rote and mindless activity at that—contemporary research stands this proposition on its head by showing how young infants register the acts of others and their own acts in corresponding terms right from the start. The recognition of self-other equivalences is seen as the primary means by which we relate to and understand other humans—a precondition for development, not the outcome of it.

In addition, the discovery of mirror neurons—first identified in monkeys[30] but also thought to exist in the human brain based on neuroimaging studies[31]—has been considered an important neurophysiological substratum for imitation in humans and in the operations of mimesis as described by Girard.[32] These brain cells are activated both when the subject performs a particular action and when the subject merely watches the same action being performed. In other words, when watching someone reach for an object, the same motor neurons are activated "as if" the observer were performing the action himself or herself. Observing other persons automatically and unconsciously puts us in their shoes and even prepares us to execute the same action. Understanding this primordial operation of the human mind has changed the way we think about fundamental aspects of human cognition, including the pervasive role of imitation in human life.

Particularly powerful is the imitation of one another that occurs in groups. Girard has referred to collective imitation as *contagion*—the exponential spreading of mimetic desire and rivalry throughout an entire community. However, this power of imitation can lead to the spread of other communal behaviors—particularly among small and highly interactive groups. The eighteenth-century theologian Friedrich Schleiermacher provides an analysis of care for the poor that illustrates the importance of imitation and contagion, but of a different kind.[33] Schleiermacher takes as a basic premise an ethic that would be familiar to L'Arche. He proposes that in a civil society, those who flourish within the cultural and economic environment ought to help those who are weakened by this same environment. The problem is that contemplation of one's undeserved privilege does

29. See Nadel and Butterworth, *Imitation in Infancy*, and Meltzoff and Prinz, *Imitative Mind*.

30. Rizzolatti et al., "Premotor Cortex"; Gallese et al., "Action Recognition."

31. Rizzolatti, Fogassi, and Gallese, "Neurophysiological Mechanisms," 663; Iacoboni et al., "Cortical Mechanisms of Human Imitation," 661–70.

32. Gallese, V., "Two Sides of Mimesis."

33. Schleiermacher, "Notes on Aristotle," as described in Welker, "We Live Deeper."

not elicit sentiments in most persons sufficient to give rise to meaningful benevolent actions. Thoughts and ideas about one's obligation are insufficient. Individual attempts at helping the poor typically do not yield strong enough rewards and satisfactions to sustain the action, partly because our individual benevolent acts are typically ineffective. By contrast, the multiplicity of compassionate acts that can occur as part of group action helps the underprivileged more significantly. What is more (and here is Schleiermacher's critical point), *action within groups strengthens the intensity of the benevolent motivations and sentiments of each individual within the group.*

Within groups of persons who engage in benevolent action together, there is reciprocal strengthening of compassion—a form of contagion based on reciprocal imitation. Both because the outcome is more significant and because of the power of reciprocal imitation, participating with a group in aiding the poor (or caring for core members) creates in participants even stronger motivations to be engaged in such acts in the future. Service in L'Arche communities provides long-term and intensive opportunities for imitation of caring between the small group of assistants in each community. A subtle but pervasive contagion of selfless caregiving is part of the ethos one enters when becoming a L'Arche assistant.

Community Narrative

In addition to the immediate effects of mimesis on the social group, Girard has also analyzed a great number of archaic myths, particularly myths of origin, in order to provide further support for his scapegoat hypothesis. Girard maintains that communal myths or narratives in archaic communities both concealed and revealed certain aspects of the culture's founding violence. According to Girard, scapegoating rituals only work if the victim is perceived as guilty. Mythological texts, therefore, never present an explicit theme of scapegoating or an accurate picture of the victim's identity; instead, myth camouflages scapegoating while representing patterns of meaning in stories of gods, ancient heroes, foundations of social order, rituals, etc.

While applying these insights to a wide range of religious and cultural texts, Girard realized that the Hebrew Bible and Christian Gospels represented a unique and revelatory movement away from such sacrificial narratives.[34] While these texts include all of the structural elements of archaic myth, including collective violence and sacrificial rituals, they

34. Girard, *Things Hidden.*

also feature religious leaders and communities who were openly troubled by these events and began to view their history from the standpoint of the social victims rather than the persecuting, or sacred social order. In contrast to surrounding communities whose gods demanded victims for their appeasement, the Judeo-Christian communities of the Bible began to revolve around a God who "demands mercy and not sacrifice."

Given that many (not all) assistants in L'Arche are Christian, and the movement has its roots in the Roman Catholic Church, biblical narratives no doubt are prevalent. Most religious or benevolent communities have a formative model (such as a founder of the organization, a previous exemplary member, or a historical figure) whose life and accomplishments provide the narrative within which the community attempts to live. Children grow up in families with narratives about parents, grandparents, uncles or aunts that provide models in their formation. For Christians, the ultimate model of the inclusive and non-violent will of God is found in the example of the life and death of Jesus, who placed himself in the role of the innocent victim in order to reveal once and for all the founding mechanism of human culture—violence directed toward surrogate victims. Additional models for L'Arche caregivers include exemplars of compassion, such as Saint Francis, Mother Teresa, Jean Vanier (founder of L'Arche), Henri Nouwen (a Dutch Priest and prolific writer who wrote a book on his year as L'Arche assistant), and others. We would suspect that such models provide the focus of the metaphysical desire such as it exists within L'Arche—particularly among novice caregivers. However, we have described a transformation that occurs in those who remain as assistants for many years of service. We believe that during this transformation, something about the narrative of core members becomes the most formative influence. This change from a focus on heroes of compassion to a focus on core members as models and sources of life narratives is clearly reflected in the interviews with long-term assistants.

Ritual

Girard's mimetic theory also points to the essential role of ritual as a means of cementing community cohesion by mimetically reenacting the collective victimization of a scapegoat. Without sacrificial rituals that serve to "cleanse" the community of its violent antagonisms in a planned and organized fashion, the community risks the outbreak of spontaneous violence directed at the very people it wishes to protect.

Not all rituals are violent, of course, nor do they need to be in order to generate collective bonding and prevent mimetic rivalry. A simple and profound ritual unites L'Arche. In the evening, those who live in the particular community—core members and assistants—sit in a circle and pass a candle from person to person. While holding the candle, each person has an opportunity to express themselves to the entire group—expression of a problem or concern, a word of thanksgiving, an apology, etc. This ritual has roots and meaning that are unique to L'Arche. While it serves to engender cohesion, it serves primarily to give all a voice and a significant place in the life of the entire community. It is likely that the equality expressed in this simple ritual plays a role in the compassionate, nonviolent and non-exclusionary life in L'Arche, as well as the transformation of assistants into persons who become capable of long-term caring for persons with mental and physical disabilities.

The mimetic repetition of such rituals works not only to enhance sentiments and motivations for compassionate action, but also engenders procedural learning and the developing of automaticity of caring behavior (i.e., habits). *Procedural learning* is the term given to things we learn to do, rather than the information that we know.[35] It is learning-by-doing (including what we learn by imitation). An important characteristic of procedural learning is that it remains unconscious. In most circumstances procedural knowledge is enacted in daily behavior without prior decision or conscious control over actions. The unconscious elicitation of behaviors linked to our procedural knowledge is referred to as *automaticity*.[36] Cognitive psychologists generally agree that a very small percentage of our daily behavior is the outcome of conscious decisions—some say as little as 5 percent. So, whatever is typical of our behavior and personality is mostly the outcome of the things we do automatically, without conscious forethought or conscious monitoring of the specifics of our behavior. Thus, through the continued experiences of reciprocal imitation of the caring expressed in the behavior of others, long-term L'Arche assistants become persons for whom providing care to core members is a form of unconscious automaticity. There is no need for thought or reason; over time, compassion is just something they do.

35. The concept of procedural knowledge is basic to the current understanding of human cognition. See, for example, the discussion of this topic in Anderson, *Cognitive Psychology and Its Implications*, 236–37.

36. Bargh and Chartrand, "Unbearable Automaticity of Being."

Bibliography

Anderson, J. R. *Cognitive Psychology and Its Implications*. New York: Worth, 2000.

Bargh, J. "The Most Powerful Manipulative Messages Are Hiding in Plain Sight." *Chronicle of Higher Education*, 29 January 1999, B6.

Bargh, J., and T. Chartrand. "The Unbearable Automaticity of Being." *American Psychologist* 54 (1999) 462–79.

Brown, W. S., S. R. Garrels, and K. R. Reimer. "Mimesis and Compassion in Care for People with Disabilities." *Journal of Religion, Disability, & Health* 15 (2011) 377–94.

Colby, Anne, and William Damon. *Some Do Care: Contemporary Lives of Moral Commitment*. New York: Free, 1992.

Gallese, V. "The Two Sides of Mimesis: Mimetic Theory, Embodied Simulation, and Social Identification." In *Mimesis and Science: Empirical Research on Imitation and the Mimetic Theory of Culture and Religion*, edited by S. Garrels, 87–108. East Lansing, MI: Michigan State University Press, 2011.

Gallese, Vittorio, L. Fadiga, L. Fogassi, and G. Rizzolatti. "Action Recognition in the Premotor Cortex." *Brain* 119 (1996) 593–609.

Gardner, Stephen. *Myths of Freedom: Equality, Modern Thought, and Philosophical Radicalism*. Westport, CT: Greenwood, 1998.

Garrels, S., editor. *Mimesis and Science: Empirical Research on Imitation and the Mimetic Theory of Culture and Religion*. East Lansing, MI: Michigan State University Press, 2011.

Girard, René. *Deceit, Desire and the Novel: Self and Other in Literary Structure*. Translated by Yvonne Freccero. Baltimore, MD: Johns Hopkins University Press, 1965.

———. *The Scapegoat*. Baltimore, MD: Johns Hopkins University Press, 1982.

———. *Things Hidden since the Foundation of the World*. Translated by Stephen Bann and Michael Meteer. Stanford, CA: Stanford University Press, 1987.

———. *Violence and the Sacred*. Baltimore, MD: Johns Hopkins University Press, 1977.

Greene, J., R. Sommerville, L. Nystrom, J. Darley, and J. Cohen. "An fMRI Investigation of Emotional Engagement in Moral Judgment." *Science* 293 (2001) 2105–8.

Iacoboni, M., R. Woods, M. Brass, H. Bekkering, J. Mazziotta, G. Rizzolatti. "Cortical Mechanisms of Human Imitation," *Science* 286 (24 December 1999) 2526–28.

Meltzoff, Andrew. "Understanding the Intentions of Others: Re-enactment of Intended Acts by 18-Month-Old Children," *Developmental Psychology* 31 (1995) 838–50.

Meltzoff, Andrew, and M. Keith Moore. "Imitation of Facial and Manual Gestures by Human Neonates," *Science* 198 (1977) 75–78.

———. "Newborn Infants Imitate Adult Facial Gestures." *Child Development* 54 (1983) 702–9.

Meltzoff, A., and W. Prinz. *The Imitative Mind: Development, Evolution, and Brain Bases*. Cambridge: Cambridge University Press, 1999.

Nadel, J., and G. Butterworth. *Imitation in Infancy*. Cambridge: Cambridge University Press, 1999.

Reimer, K. S. "Committed to Caring: Transformation in Adolescent Moral Identity." *Applied Developmental Science* 7 (2003) 129–37.

Reimer, K., C. Young, B. Birath, M. Spezio, G. Peterson, J. Van Slyke, and W. Brown. "From Novice to Expert: Moral Prototype Knowledge in Humanitarian Self-Understanding." *Journal of Positive Psychology* (under review).

————. "Maturity Is Explicit: Self-Importance of Moral Traits in Humanitarian Self-Understanding." *Journal of Positive Psychology* 7 (2012) 36–44.

Rizzolatti, G., L. Fadiga, L. Fogassi, and V. Gallese, V. "Premotor Cortex and the Recognition of Motor Actions." *Cognitive Brain Research* 3 (1996) 131–41.

Rizzolatti, G., L. Fogassi, and V. Gallese. "Neurophysiological Mechanisms Underlying the Understanding and Imitation of Action." *Nature Reviews Neuroscience* 2.9 (2001) 661–70.

Schleiermacher, F. "Notes on Aristotle: Nichomachean Ethics 8–9." *Theology Today* 56 (1999) 164–68.

Webb, E. "Eros and the Psychology of World Views." *Anthropoetics* 12.1 (2006) 1–14.

Welker, M. "We Live Deeper Than We Think: The Genius of Schleiermacher's Earliest Ethics." *Theology Today* 56 (1999) 169–79.

3

Pursuing Peace and Justice

Journey of a Lifetime

Marc Gopin

My Religious Youth: Love and Heartbreak

I GREW UP IN a very orthodox Jewish home in Boston, Massachusetts with people who had come from Europe, from northwest Ukraine, and Latvia/Lithuania. We were a big Jewish clan, and we were the part of the clan that was the most religious. I grew up praying three times a day and going to synagogue every morning, and three times on the Sabbath day and evening.

I have observed the Sabbath very strictly my entire life, no car driving, no cooking, no use of electricity. The Sabbath became a fundamental part of my ecological philosophy of leaving the earth alone for 24 hours in celebration of Creation, and in a deliberate limitation of my own power and impact, since all creative work is also destructive. I believed that despite the passionate work of social justice that I have come to do in my life that I must find ways to stop on Saturday, even though non-communication through electronics has become harder and harder the more my projects involve life and death issues concerning war and peace. To this day I balance the love of Sabbath and the urge to do the work of social justice and peace seven days a week, 24 hours a day.

As I grew up in Boston the distant and ancient city of Jerusalem was in every single one of our prayers, and these prayers go back thousands of years. I grew up in a totally Orthodox Jewish world. I didn't even know any non-Jews, except for the wonderful Irish Catholic cleaning lady who loved me; I didn't even associate with Jews who were not Orthodox. In that environment Jerusalem meant everything to me as a symbol of Jewish identity, as a symbol of Jewish care, and as the center of Jewish spirituality.

I started coming to Jerusalem when I was very young. When I was thirteen years old, instead of having a big Bar Mitzvah I asked that my family come to celebrate my becoming thirteen in Jerusalem. We were there three weeks, and the most important highlight of that was coming to the Western Wall.

I spent twenty years of my life just studying Torah as part of my education. I studied a lot of secular studies, but I spent twenty years intensively on Torah. It's hard for me to imagine just how much that was a part of my life. Every one of those texts, every one of those prayers, seven days a week, always had in them something about Jerusalem. For me, Jewish Jerusalem was a dream come true. And I'd say that until I was about twenty-two this was a rather positive dream. It was a sense of care of what was happening to Jewish people.

As I got into my early twenties, I was already in rabbinical school. Because of the combination of things that I learned from my teachers, from my master teacher Rabbi Joseph Soloveitchik, I had been brought up to believe that Judaism and the Jewish people were a symbol of *enlightenment* for the world, the pinnacle of spirituality but the pinnacle also of positive values: of compassion, of justice—*and* that we were teaching this to the world.

The Evolution of Hard Questions

Come my early twenties, and I started to sense that something's going badly, that people in some quarters of my community are more and more talking in racial terms, and in terms of who is superior and who is inferior. There are people who are carrying guns. This was in New York, and I realized that all the wars and the occupations that involved the Jewish people were having a corrosive effect on Jewish spirituality.

The height of it came in 1982, with the Lebanon War, and the massacre in Sabra and Shatila, in Beirut. That was hundreds and hundreds of Palestinians—civilians, families—who were murdered. This was a turning point for me, it was a very low point for my teacher, my master teacher Rabbi Soloveitchik, and I started to question many things. That's when I started coming to Israel on a fairly regular basis, and was starting to have a much more negative experience—but also a determination to reach out beyond the Jewish people. This is when I discovered the hard road of just peacemaking, because it is the combination of commitment to justice and peace that makes you ask hard questions of your own community, whatever community on the globe that may be.

Beginnings of a Journey toward the Enemies of My People: 1983–2000

I started experimenting with pursuit of peace, as we frame this in Judaism, and naturally I felt compelled to do this in Israel. I avoided organizations for the most part, and I went on my own with taxi drivers, with Arab taxi drivers, and then meeting people on the street. With every step that I took out of the very, very closed environment that I had grown up with, my spiritual sensibility, my emotions, everything was changing.

I found myself in between peoples. That started a journey of the next twenty years, of reaching further and further into what my family considered "the enemy," all the way to nine years ago in 2003, ending up in Damascus. I was the only rabbi ever, and the first conflict resolution professor, to give major talks, public talks, in that closed police state that would ultimately turn its massive arsenal on its own people starting in 2011. I appeared many times with the Grand Mufti of Syria on Syrian state television, on Al-Jazeera, public ceremonies of reconciliation, in this toughest of the Arab states that was the most bitter enemy of Israel.

Every step of the way, as I moved from a Jewish very, very closed, safe environment, to more and more into the realm of my so-called enemies, every step was painful, excruciatingly laced with guilt and doubt—but it was liberating at the same time.

Early Peacemaking Experiences and a Turning Point at Neve Shalom

My early peacemaking experiences were very halting. I remember walking the streets of Jerusalem, and more and more—a pattern in my life—I was going through emotional trauma. I found my own way to meet strangers on the streets, which is not always the best way to figure things out, because it depends on where you go and whether you're in danger. But to me, each time this was breaking a barrier.

I remember the first time I resented the fact that people in my family warned me not to speak to "those people," warned me about the dangers. And, I, at the same time, I was scared, because my elders in my family were telling me to be scared of these people. Every one of the instincts of my community was telling me that Arabs were dangerous. And yet there was something driving me on that's hard for me to figure out to this day.

I think that all the values I had been brought up with, that I thought were universal Jewish values such as social justice and peace, were being contested by the reality in Israel, that the reality there was saying something very different. So I pushed myself on, but inside I was terrified.

I remember one time going to a place called *Neve Shalom*, which was just beginning in the early 1980s. It was a place in Israel where Jews and Arabs were living together, and that's unheard of. It was an intentional community of Jews and Arabs. I went up, I just took a cab, and I went there on my own, and I walked up this dirt road—they didn't have the rights at the time to get a road! They weren't recognized as a community because they were not a Jewish community.

I went to the center of town and said who I was. Now the Jews there were busy, they worked. The Arabs there were not busy, and so they sent me over to talk. I ended up being given a tour by a wonderful young Arab man who was married, and he took me around the hilltops there. We were very friendly, and I noticed some very powerful things right away. First of all, he knew every single herb. He was picking up herbs from the ground, and I'd never seen that before, I had never seen anybody in Israel know every single piece of grass! I could tell that this was a person of the land, this was a person who knew the place. I was starting to understand the Arab attachment to the land, and how special that was, and how unique it was. And then I would come back to the other side, and Jews would disparage them as primitive, as violent, and yet I saw something deep and cultural. So the differences were starting to emerge.

Then I asked him a question. I said, "That's a lovely group of pine trees over there," and he just didn't say anything. I started to learn that in Arab culture—and in many cultures—when people don't say anything, it means that they don't agree with you. In my culture, they have to yell at you before you can get that they don't agree with you. And even if they yell at you, sometimes they actually *do* agree, but just want to have a good argument! So

I was learning new signals from a very different culture. And so I said, "Well, why, why are you uncomfortable with the pine trees?" He said, "I'll take you for a walk there, I'll show you a well." I said, "What do you mean, a well?" He says, "The well, from the village." I said, "What do you mean a village?" He said, "There was a village there." So I said, "It's a group of pine trees. I don't see a village." He said, "Yeah, there was a village there, they put the pine trees to cover up the village." "Why did they put the pine trees there?" "Because they drove the people out in 1948 and they wanted to cover up the evidence." He said, "All along here, all throughout this region, you'll see pine trees, and they're covering up villages that used to be there."

That was tough, because for the first time in my life, pine trees, which for me are a symbol of beauty, and are—I later found out—all over my ancestral home in Ukraine, now is a symbol of conquest, as opposed to olive trees, which were the stock and trade of Arab culture. So suddenly there's a war of trees as well as a war of holy places as well as a war of peoples.

I remember as a child in first grade, the biggest source of pride was that I got to give a little bit of money to plant a tree in Israel, from the Jewish National Fund. And I had a poster from the Jewish National Fund on my wall year after year, that I had planted a tree in Israel. And at twenty-five I discovered that I had planted that tree on top of a village. On top of a village where people used to live! And suddenly, I was part of the conquest.

I think what happened at that moment of my life was that this Arab man, whom I was making a strong connection to, was about five, ten years older than I, and so I respected him, I was interested in him. I had never read anything about the Arab or Palestinian narrative, and this was all new to me. I had only had a Jewish narrative my whole life. I had every year religiously, in the Passover season, seen the film with Paul Newman, *Exodus*. That was my narrative of Israel, but suddenly this was a new narrative and I knew in my heart that it was a true narrative that had been kept from me deliberately. I had already known that I was going into new territory, but this almost became for me a moment of new identity.

Listening and Confiding, Embrace of and Debate with Enemies

I challenged the Palestinian man in Neve Shalom, but I didn't challenge him aggressively because I have some pretty good skills with this work. Even as a child I was brought up in dealing well with conflict. But I asked him a question. I said, "Let me ask you a question. That's a *kibbutz* down there, yes?" We were up on a hill. And he said, "Yes, that's a *kibbutz*." So I asked him, "That *kibbutz* down there, if that was your land, would you fire from up here on that piece of land? If you had a gun, if you could?" He said, "If it was my land, yes I would."

I was shocked by his honesty, but what I was asking was about the nature of the conflict here, especially over high and low places. Everything in military conflicts is about who has the higher terrain. Everywhere in Israel and the West Bank that you can see that there is Jewish settlement, and Jewish enclaves, it's always higher than the Arab places, in order to have the line of fire. And I was sitting with him, and I was asking him what he would do if he could. I was thinking to myself that because he would fire, that's why people have guns.

Later on in the day, he invited me over to his house, and I actually ended up sleeping in his house. He didn't even have a floor (just a dirt floor), but he welcomed me in, and it was quite wonderful with his wife and himself. He invited friends over, because they had this American there who wanted to know the truth about the conflict, a Jew, and they wanted to talk to me. And so, before I know it, I'm in this small room, in a very poor house, with ten Arab men, and I was shaking like a leaf because my whole life I had been surrounded by religious Jews. And suddenly, I'm with ten Arab Palestinian men. And I knew inside my heart, what was going on in me, and I decided just to be honest about it.

I said, "You know, I'm scared," to the group. And they started laughing! They said to me, "Why are you afraid of us? You're the ones with the guns." So then I thought about it, and I said to my host, "Well, you remember how you said to me today—we were on the hilltop—that if that was your land, you would shoot. So, that's why I'm afraid. And that's why some people have guns here, and some people don't."

That was my earliest Arab-Jewish dialogue. It was my first experiment with that process of listening and communication, and it was quite beautiful and we had a very good relationship. But as for me on my life journey, I was moving further and further away from my origins, and yet not moving away at the same time. I was moving away from ethnocentric fears and prejudices that had gotten my people into deep trouble with millions of Palestinians, and hundreds of millions of Arabs. But I was moving toward a far deeper understanding of my ancestors' prophetic and rabbinic commitments to pursuing peace and pursuing justice as a calling, as a driven mission, that requires constant vigilance, patience, persistence and faith in what is right.

Passing Over to the Other Side During the Intifada: Encounters with Arafat

Many years passed, and I grew further and further into my role as a rabbi pursuing justice and peace. There was a moment in 2000, the Intifada had already begun, and I was crossing the border with two extraordinary peace-makers, Rabbi Froman and Sheikh Abu Salakh, and a series of others. At the Palestinian/Israeli border the Sufis I was with had absolutely no plans on how to cross over during a war. We came to the border unlike anybody else—without a car! The soldiers thought we were insane—they were right. We sat there, and there was no way to get from there to Ramallah, and we had an appointment—a real appointment—with the *rais*, with Arafat.

Suddenly a small van came, and the door opens. And—I swear to God—the windows were blackened, the windows were dark, and the man who is driving says, "Get in." We had no idea who this person was and where he came from. So one person with us says, "The angels are all around us, no problem getting in." And Rabbi Froman? His weapon of defense was reciting constantly from some mystical book. So we got in and somehow this man took us around the border, because the Israeli soldiers would not let us in, and he took us to a small alleyway where hundreds of Palestinians were going back and forth to work (across the border).

Thus we went on, this strange entourage, with Rabbi Froman's beard down to the floor and the Sheikh's white robes, and we went to Arafat that way. The truth is that we had a very, very powerful and deep discussion with Arafat, and at least on that day, we had a relationship with him. We also had an agreement—that unfortunately the Israelis and Americans did not agree to—on a spiritual approach to a ceasefire, and to peace building. I was there, I was witness to his explicit agreement, and his request that we ask the Israeli leadership to agree to it also. But that is as far as we got because then, as now, mainstream leaders and diplomats have a hard time understanding that religious and spiritual people matter, that involving them in peace is critical, and that if they don't do this they will find their institutions overwhelmed by religious rebellions, as we are seeing today.

The most important thing I have learned from spiritual and religious partners is that matters of the heart and spiritual matters go deeper into people's needs, into suffering, into poverty, into questions of dignity. This sometimes reaches even the most hardened warriors, especially if part of why they are fighting involves some religious identity motivations. None of us would ever believe that we had all the answers to the war between Palestinians and Israelis, nor that we had the only key necessary to Arafat's heart. But we were sure that the willful neglect of religion, of spirituality, of matters of the heart, had done deep damage to all efforts at negotiations, and that, then as now, a much deeper appeal to whole peoples is called for when you want to truly undermine the cycles of violence that make some relationships on this earth chronically violent.

First Encounter With My Syrian Peace Partner Hind Kabawat

As the Intifada dragged on, and so many innocent people died, I needed a break because a door had closed to my work in Palestine, we could no longer pass between enemies. But then somehow a door immediately opened in Syria. I remember the moment very vividly when I first met my Syrian peace partner. We were at a session together at the World Economic Forum, it was a very elite atmosphere of world leaders, and I was very excited to be there but also a little bit lost. I ended up sitting next to Hind at a session, and as the session chair called for questions Hind shot up her hand like a young school girl, saying she had a question. Her questions were all about human rights, and she announced, "I am from Syria and I want human rights to be observed all over the world *by all regimes.*" I was stunned by her courage and by her outspokenness to say this openly despite the traditional habit of Syrians to be utterly mute in 2003 about their own regime's behavior. I said to myself that I needed to meet this person.

Hind and I started chatting at that conference, and we hit if off very nicely, and we were talking about many issues that we had shared a common concern about in the region, in terms of the unjust behavior of states. I was very excited to meet someone like her, and then we seemed to just leave it like that. But then I happened to send her an email saying I was going to be "in the region" [code for Israel and Palestine] doing work. Out of the blue she sent me an email saying, "Why don't you come speak in Syria?" I was completely shocked by that invitation, and that's how that our work together began.

Shared Values and Common Passion for Peace

I went back and checked out Hind's website, and Hind's website completely shocked me. Hind was the first Syrian I'd ever met, and I grew up in a very conservative Jewish home in the United States. I was terrified of the Arab world. All of my work in the last twenty-five years has been about overcoming those fears and working with people in the Arab world towards just peace in the Middle East. But in all of those years I had never met anybody from Syria, nor did I really want to. It had been a forbidden territory, and so Hind was the first one. When I went to the website it was all about democracy and social justice, and also a very fun and exciting approach to the world. She went on about how beautiful Syria is—it was very patriotic Syrian—and at the same time about peace and justice values. I was stunned and I said to myself, "This is interesting!" And so in some ways we were dancing in this moment of, "Can we trust each other? Can we move in to a new space of actually working together in a way that was unprecedented?" And I didn't know where it was going to go.

Crossing the Border to an Enemy Country for my First Time

Crossing the border to Syria inaugurated a deep relationship with many people, and I developed a very profound sense of connection with the Syrian people that I have maintained to this day, feeling the pain of their every loss. From then until today, almost every day of my life since then, I have used the Syrian soap made in the villages of Syria, and it reminds me every day in the shower of a connection to simple people.

I was overwhelmed from the moment I crossed the border at midnight. I come from a very frightened kind of atmosphere and I was going farther into enemy territory than anybody Jewish had gone before. My heart was pounding so hard in my chest as I entered through their security check. Nobody from my world and my community had ever gone over to a radical Arab state as a religious representative, and I didn't know what to expect.

From the very second I got over there, however, I was treated like an honored guest and met at the border, which made me feel welcome and comfortable from the very beginning. That was just the beginning of four years of being treated like an honored guest, because the best elements of Syrian culture are all about welcoming people and making people feel like they are at the center of attention and the center of importance.

I also felt like I was coming home in the sense that from an ancient perspective my ancestors had come from north of Israel, from Assyria. Abraham had traveled that whole region, and I felt that I was returning to an ancient place of *Abraham*, also where my favorite prophet Jonah had gone, where the other prophets had traveled to, and where the ancestors had come from. It was an amazing feeling and that feeling has never stopped. I didn't even want to leave Damascus many times when I came. I would ask myself, "Why am I leaving?"

Goals of the Speech At the Assad Library in 2003

When I gave a major speech at the Assad Library, their national cultural center, I wanted to convey the possibilities of what non-violent resolution of conflicts is all about and how we could build something together, a new Middle East, and my basic theme was, "A New Middle East." I knew that Syria was a place where many people of vision had high hopes for the future, for democracy, but who were trapped by the wars, by the dynamic between the nations, and by their corrupt and brutal regime. I knew we had invited many forward-thinking people in Damascus, as well as the diplomatic elite. But at the same time I didn't want to get too specific in my speech because the Mukhabarat, the secret police, were watching every word I said to judge whether they would retaliate against my hosts for bringing me. I had to make, in other words, a good first impression because the stakes were very high.

I also knew that my own country, the United States, had made some big mistakes in the region, and so had all of the major powers, and how their alliances and interests kept the regional conflicts going. I wanted to be very honest about the mistakes that *everyone* had made, I wanted to be honest about the mistakes that Israel had made as well, as I knew I would be cross-examined on all these matters. I wanted to honor Syrian history and Syrian culture, and have them understand that my job and my hope is to see Syrian society flourish in a new Middle East. I even talked about walking around the streets of Damascus and how I immediately saw this ancient town that could be the center of the world's attention with millions of tourists, which I really believed as I walked around. This is how I was trying to create a bridge that would become the basis of our intercultural peace work in subsequent years.

Hind and I had many goals with our work in Damascus, some of them more on the surface and some of them much more subtle. On the surface we were interested in helping to promote civil society and inter-faith tolerance in Syria. This was a time when people were talking about a new era with a new president. So we were fitting in with those goals of building civil society, interfaith tolerance, and it was building on my own work and reputation in interfaith peacebuilding. Of all places in the Middle East, Syria actually had a secular government that was committed to interfaith tolerance in principal, and Syria had a very liberal Mufti who had reached out to many religious minorities and in support of women. I witnessed this work, and we did work closely with him from time to time.

More subtly, we wanted to demonstrate the possibility of a relationship between Arabs and Jews as people, because everybody knew that I was traveling the region and that I had worked for ten, twenty years in Israel. Since I had championed Palestinian rights for so long, and this was well known, I thought that we could create a good bridge in Syria on that basis. Indeed this is what happened with many people, and I succeeded in developing some Palestinian friendships that would have never been possible anywhere else. We set the early stage for at least the possibility of a connection in the region and a way to talk about things that were painful, with grievances but without hatred, and without intention of war.

My hope and my intention of coming was actually to have people provoke me with questions, with issues, and to get upset about the United States, about Israel, about the whole region. This would create debate and it would allow me to talk to them honestly about a Palestinian-Israeli just peace, a better role for the United States in the region, more justice for Syria, more fairness in the region so that Syria could become part of a global economy. All of these things I wanted them to be able to speak to me in an atmosphere of non-violence, *because that is the alternative to war. The alternative to war is relationship, difficult conversation, visioning together.* And that's exactly what we did.

We ended up having many press conferences since then over a period of eight years, and many programs. Another agenda was to get the society used to the idea of training in conflict resolution, the practice of working out problems without violence. We both really believe in diplomacy and conflict resolution in combination with progressive values, and we wanted to teach people that. Alas, we were just getting going with two years of great students in 2009 and 2010 when the Arab Spring and the Syrian Revolution hit hard, and slammed right into all the delicate relationships across ethnic and religious boundaries that we were cultivating.

I want to return for a moment to 2006 and describe an event that was also formative for me as a just peacemaker. Sometimes being a just peacemaker is not about choosing sides or going against your own group or your own country, it's just solidarity with everyone's needs, and this changes people. Solidarity with everyone gives intellectual nuance and emotional subtlety to the art of combining peace and justice, or conflict resolution and human rights. It takes courage to embrace one's own people and others at the same time, even when they are angry at or hate your own people.

There was a period of time in 2006 during the war between Hezbollah and Israel when Lebanon was being destroyed by bombs, people were terrified in Syria, and people were getting bombed in Israel. I was on the phone within an hour with a Rabbi in Israel who had Jewish people in his home who were refugees from northern Israel that was being bombed by Hezbollah, and with Hind in Damascus who had friends who were refugees from Lebanon, who also had run away from Israel's bombs. My heart broke as I wept, on the phone with friends, helpless to offer anything, anything except tears; sometimes that is all a peacemaker can offer.

The linkage through relationships we created between all these groups of suffering recipients of missiles was unprecedented, to have a triangle of conversations with people in the West Bank, and in Israel who were being bombed, and then in Damascus with Lebanese who had been bombed in Lebanon. To know all these people at once, that changes reality, because Hind could tell it to her friends and I could tell it to my friends, and we were starting to make linkages between enemy peoples that had never been made before. This makes war different, it makes it closer and humanizes it, and it makes it that much harder in the long run to continue to commit this human travesty. Such connections prevent war from being an abstraction, and it becomes a way that everybody is linked through relationships of care. That was our purpose, and that is what we accomplished in the midst of these terrible orgies of killing, orgies that some consider valorous but we do not. This is really the purpose of partners across enemy divides, because they create linkages where there were none.

Mutual Respect: The Essential Ingredient for Incremental Change[1]

One of the things that we have thought about a great deal is how exactly to move incrementally from situation A to situation B in terms of political and social constructs, how to move incrementally toward a situation where human needs are addressed and thus peace and justice are achieved. We have found that dignity is at the core of those needs, or that dignity encapsulates the essence of what justice calls for.

---

1 For more on "positive increments of change" as a new method of conflict resolution, see Gopin, *To Make the Earth Whole*.

In essence, dignity for all, or mutual respect, is the goal, love and care is the way, and peace is the result. Dignity relates to equal education, jobs and opportunities. Empowerment through education, but particularly a creative approach to job creation that builds economies but at the same time builds a middle class, these are all essential ingredients of a peaceful and just society.

Now how do you get there? How do we build economies across adversary lines in war-torn societies? It takes things that are actually emotional. It takes a focus on honor and respect in the positive sense, it takes a focus on the courage required for mutual apologies, for acknowledging our own responsibility for what has gone wrong. It takes the emotional capacity to mourn the past—but also build a future. It takes many things that are deeply cultural, deeply emotional, in order to set the stage for doing the rational thing about, for example, job creation for all young people, and equality of women. Finally, it takes a lot for the men of wounded civilizations to build enough courage and inner strength to allow women to become truly equal, and it takes women a great deal of courage to move men in this direction. Finally, the just peacemakers, the glue of healing processes, must possess an immense amount of love and emotional strength to accept and overcome all the surrounding pain, while also giving guidance and vision to the new future. When you build relationships based on respect and honor, on listening, on apology and forgiveness, you can then get to the rational plan for how *everybody* takes responsibility and changes.

It is hard for me to fathom, as I look at my life's journey, where I began and where I have arrived. I began life immersed in a community that housed ancient traditions and texts that embraced a God of justice, of peace, of compassion, but also a God of anger and stern judgment of a deeply imperfect humanity. I studied day and night the words of a God who insisted that I not only love peace and justice, but that I pursue them relentlessly, that I feel the poor in my bones as I look at them.

I was also in a community housing the memories of unimaginable suffering, two thousand years of prejudice based on completely idiotic theological excuses. The history of Abrahamic hatred and sadism would be comical if it were not so tragic. The people I grew up with laughed, ate and sang their lungs out despite the legacy, and in exultation at newly found freedom in the United States.

Such an ambivalent legacy I inherited. All those texts and traditions that embodied justice, the rule of law, and the commitment to a messianic world of peace and justice, embodied in the symbolic dream of Sabbath. It was so deep and beautiful as a dream.

Nothing prepared me, however, for the agony of making even the smallest part of the world, or the tiniest speck of human history, into an oasis of peace, justice and love. No one prepared me for how agonizing it would be as I came out of my ethno-religious cocoon in order to turn even a single enemy into a friend, let alone try to prevent wars and heal their devastating effects. I learned slowly how to work, through many of my own wounds, and giving up so much of my cherished and cloistered lifestyle. The ancient Talmud says, "Who is a war hero? He who turns an enemy into a friend." Well, I and my beloved partners, Jewish, Palestinian, Syrian, Iranian, Afghan, Christian, we have done this many times, and I am proud of what we have achieved, I am proud of every one of them, despite how far in the distance our goals appear to be right now. This is what the long view of history requires, this is the sacrifice that is required of the human being with such a short lifespan, to work for the distant future, the most important characteristic of the just peacemaker.

I finish this essay while sitting on a bus at the base of the Egyptian Pyramids. I sit here writing while I watch my students having a great time on camels and horses. I see my young Palestinian students, Christian students, Syrian students, Moroccan students, Afghan students, students from the State Department, Christians from across America. We all came here in solidarity with the youth of Egypt in 2012, hoping to express support for greater freedom and greater justice in this ancient land. It occurs to me that I am blessed in this journey toward justice and peace, blessed by the miracle of youth, blessed by a younger generation that is ready for the path of peace, justice, and courageous love of strangers.

Bibliography

Gopin, Marc. *To Make the Earth Whole.* Lanham, MD: Rowman and Littlefield, 2009.

4

Building Just Peacemaking Churches
Reflections from Experience in Northern Ireland

DAVID MCMILLAN

Introduction

THE ROLE OF RELIGION and churches in particular during the Northern Ireland conflict has been much debated. Commenting in the introduction to one of his books,[1] Sociologist Steve Bruce observed that it was once generally assumed that religion and nationalism had long been superseded by class and economic interests as significant factors in social construction and conflict. However, Bruce did much to kick-start a serious sociological engagement with the issues of religion, politics, and conflict in the Northern Ireland situation. His work paved the way for a succession of studies seeking to understand and untangle the significance and relationship between religion, politics and conflict.[2]

A thorough consideration and critique of the role of churches in the Northern Ireland conflict has been provided by Brewer et al. in *Religion, Civil Society, & Peace in Northern Ireland*. Reflecting on the role of

1. Bruce, *Paisley: Religion and Politics*, vii.

2. See, for example, Mitchell, *Religion, Identity and Politics*; Ganiel, "Framework for Understanding." Ronald Wells has made a number of significant contributions in this area, the most recent of which is *Hope and Reconciliation*.

churches in the conflict and subsequent peace process, they criticize the churches' contribution in the following terms:

> The problem was perceived to be violence itself rather than a sectarian social structure of which the churches were themselves an integral part, so negative peace became the solution rather than positive peace, conflict transformation the emphasis rather than social transformation.[3]

They do not conclude that the churches were irrelevant or primarily responsible for the conflict, nor that they were completely ineffectual, but that their vision of peacemaking was limited, flawed, and ultimately based on self-preservation. They work within an analytical structure that firstly distinguishes between active and passive peacemaking (the former assumes direct involvement, the latter a non-engaged expression of values and aspiration) and then between two aspects of active peacemaking which, following Galtung,[4] work for positive peace or negative peace. Positive peace assumes the need to resolve underlying social realities, addressing justice, equality, and fairness issues, as an essential part of peacemaking, while negative peace is limited to conflict resolution and ending violence. On the basis of Brewer's earlier work,[5] they further distinguish between two kinds of peace process—a social peace process and a political peace process. A social peace process is concerned with relationship building and reconciliation, while a political process is concerned with hammering out peace deals and political arrangements. While the categories are not hermetically sealed and often "bleed" into one another, they provide a useful topographical map of religious attitudes to and engagement with peacemaking. Brewer et al. argue that in Northern Ireland churches made a significant contribution to the social peace process, helped create the conditions for the political peace process (and contributed directly at times) but did so within the mindset and framework of negative peace, and thus have failed to provide leadership or make a significant contribution to the ongoing challenges facing Northern Ireland. It will be interesting to see how Brewer et al.'s analysis is received within the academic community and by the churches in Northern Ireland, but there can be little doubt that they have highlighted many critical issues that have to be addressed by churches in conflict situations.

---

3. Brewer, Higgins, and Teeney, *Religion, Civil Society, and Peace*, 207.
4. Galtung and International Peace Research Institute Oslo, *Peace by Peaceful Means*.
5. Brewer, *Peace Processes*.

They are not the first to appreciate the challenge facing churches in regard to long-term positive peacemaking. In 2007 David Stevens, former leader of the Corrymeela Community (a Christian community of reconciliation) wrote the following at the dawning of the new political arrangement that was to see archenemies begin to share power in Northern Ireland:[6]

> So yes this is an historic moment. But . . . reconciliation and a shared future have not arrived. The central challenge in Northern Ireland is to change the historic pattern of community relating—of distrust, fear, exclusion and violence—and to create a shared future of equity, diversity and inter-dependence.[7]

The challenge Stevens so clearly articulated in 2007 remains as great today as it was then and, as Brewer et al. have shown, the churches' capacity to meet this challenge remains problematic. The nature of that problem is twofold. On the one hand, many churches of all denominations have become more preoccupied with maintaining their own market share of members and adherents in a post-conflict context than addressing the issues of building a shared future. On the other hand, churches that understand the challenge find there is little leadership or energy within denominational structures to facilitate meaningful engagement in civic society. Brewer et al. suggest that much of the contribution to the social and political peace process from within the church sector came from "mavericks" or those working with only the tacit support of denominational structures and leadership.[8] Such "mavericks" and "maverick" churches within denominations still exist, but it is hard to identify any group of churches seriously committed to the task of active positive peacemaking—to use Brewer et al.'s terminology.

In Northern Ireland and perhaps in most Christian contexts, Christian formation is essentially introspective and devoid of the vision and tools to form individual Christians and Christian communities as active positive peacemakers. My purpose here is to explore the possibility of

---

6. The DUP and Sinn Fein had come to an arrangement that paved the way for them to work together in the government of Northern Ireland, an arrangement that to many had previously seemed unthinkable.

7. http://www.corrymeela.org/comment/40.aspx accessed 30–31-2012. Also available on the Corrymeela website at http://www.corrymeela.org/comment/29.aspx is the excellent "Briefing Paper on Northern Ireland" prepared by David Stevens in 2007, a valuable resource for those looking for an accessible and comprehensive introduction to the politics and religion of Northern Ireland.

8. Brewer, Higgins, and Teeney, *Religion, Civil Society, and Peace*; see, for example, 110–14.

appropriating the practices of Just Peacemaking as the basis for the formation of relationships within Christian community, creating an embedded
vision of incarnational discipleship and incarnational mission. Ultimately
the ambition is to enable Christian communities to see the responsibility
to engage in Just Peacemaking and be empowered to seize the opportunities to do so. To this end we will revisit the concept of Just Peacemaking
and its biblical roots, reflect on the basis of associating together in church
life, and consider if the practices of Just Peacemaking can become embedded in the life of Christian communities in the context of Christian
worship. Ultimately we will be addressing the question, "Is it possible in
the 21st Century to conceive of building Just Peacemaking Churches in a
manner not dissimilar to the tradition of Peace Churches that have made
a considerable contribution to the search for justice and reconciliation in
contexts of conflict?"

Context

My interest in this theme arises out of my personal context and journey.
Born into a Baptist family in Protestant East Belfast, I was nurtured in a
separatist conservative Baptist tradition. Our church community considered the responsibility to be separate from the world as part of the defining nature of what it meant to be truly saved, and we therefore had little
engagement with other Christian churches, social clubs, or political
parties. The conviction—though it transpired to be a myth—was that we
were apolitical and given to eternal matters rather than temporal. All was
fine until 1969 and the emergence of the Northern Ireland Civil Rights
Association (NICRA). NICRA grew out of a number of grassroots movements and protests, mainly within Catholic communities that had held
longstanding grievances over the poor condition of housing and the Protestant Unionist control of local councils and housing policy. While the
emergence of NICRA is not directly related to the Civil Rights movement
in the USA or any of the other developments in Europe, it was not unrelated. One of the leaders of NICRA, Michael Farrell, explains the background
to the rise of the civil rights movement in Northern Ireland and how it
became world news very quickly:

> In the late 1950s and early 1960s, especially with the advent of
> television, attitudes were changing. Horizons were widened.
> People were no longer prepared to accept things just because
> that was the way they had always been. But the housing—and

> jobs—situation was not getting any better or, at least, any
> fairer. . . . In Derry, a new Housing Action Committee took
> up the baton from the Springtown residents at the end of 1967
> and picketed, protested and blocked roads in the city through-
> out 1968 until they eventually called the second Civil Rights
> march on October 5th, 1968. It was the attack on that march
> by the RUC [Royal Ulster Constabulary] which brought the
> Civil Rights movement to world attention.[9]

The television images of the police mishandling the October marchers
were broadcast round the world and from that day for the next thirty
years Northern Ireland would be characterized on the world stage by violence. Anger at the brutality of the police against a peaceful march, and
the recognition that the issue was now before world attention, led to three
days of trouble and rioting in Londonderry. In the weeks that followed
there was a series of Civil Rights marches and, at the same time, counter
protests by Protestant loyalist groups protesting against and seeking to dis-
rupt the Civil Rights marches. One of the groups making up NICRA, the
People's Democracy, organized a march from Belfast to Londonderry for
1st January 1969. By the time the march was approaching the city of Derry
(Londonderry and Derry are one and the same) it was attacked by a large
group of loyalists including, it is believed, off-duty part-time police then
known as B Specials. The results of this were to be felt in further unrest in
the months ahead. By August 1969 British troops were being deployed on
the streets of Northern Ireland.

At this stage the true nature of the political convictions of my community came to the fore. We were united in our disgust, not at the police
handling of the marchers, but at the destabilization of the State by what
we saw as organized Catholic agitators who, as a consequence of their civil
disobedience, got their just deserts at the hands of the police. As the situation deteriorated it was not long until NICRA was being overshadowed,
if not overtaken, in 1970 by the re-emergence of the IRA and the revival
of the "armed struggle" against what was termed "the British occupation,"
characterized as being the source of injustice in Ireland. By this stage, not
least in response to the violence of the IRA, we were unashamedly reaf-
firming our essentially Protestant Unionist identity and our belief that the
defense of the State was our Christian responsibility. Many of us played
our part in maintaining the peace, and the State, by joining the part-time
Royal Ulster Constabulary Reserves. While longing for and praying for

9. Farrell, "Historical Reflections."

peace, the concept of being peacemakers in any other sense than supporting the State was completely foreign to our thinking and understanding.

In the early 1980s I took up my first pastorate in a small Baptist church in the town of Newry. Newry is located on the border between Northern Ireland and the Irish Republic and at that time had been a center of IRA activity. It was an overwhelmingly Catholic community and for us a totally alien environment in which to minister and bring up a family. However, it was clear that the vast majority of Catholic people held their Irish Nationalist aspirations with dignity and were utterly opposed to the use of force and violence. We experienced a degree of hospitality extended to us as outsiders from the Protestant community that would not have been reciprocated to Catholics in the section of Belfast from which we had come. In 1985 Margaret Thatcher signed the Anglo-Irish Agreement with the Irish Taoiseach, Garret FitzGerald, which led to massive opposition and uproar within the Protestant and Unionist community.[10] A significant element of that opposition was led by the Rev. Ian Paisley (leader of the Democratic Unionist Party and Moderator of the Free Presbyterian Church) who, as well as expressing political opposition, mobilized opposition on the basis of a dire threat to the cause of the gospel and the Ulster Protestant heritage if the Irish Republic were to have any say in the affairs of Northern Ireland, given that the Irish Republic was, in his opinion, completely dominated by the idolatrous and blasphemous Catholic Church. Neutrality or silence in the face of such blatant anti-Catholic religious and political rhetoric was not an option, and it was at this time that I and others began to find our voices and feel the necessity to articulate a different vision publicly, which gave rise to the establishment of the organization ECONI (Evangelical Contribution on Northern Ireland).[11]

Ours, it has to be acknowledged, was at first a limited vision that sought to rescue an Evangelical understanding of the gospel from entrapment in sectarian anti-Catholicism and political nationalism. It was not a vision of a just society but of more righteous Christian living in the context of violence, fear, and threat.[12] However, the response to the material

---

10. For a detailed chronology of events and reports on the Northern Ireland conflict see the extensive resources on the CAIN website at the University of Ulster: http://cain.ulst.ac.uk/.

11. The story of the emergence and development of ECONI is recounted in Mitchell, *Religion, Identity and Politics*, 260–98. Brewer et al. in Brewer, Higgins, and Teeney, *Religion, Civil Society, and Peace*, outline ECONI's contribution throughout their analysis of the churches and the Northern Ireland conflict.

12. ECONI, "For God." This initial publication by ECONI set out ten biblical

we published pushed us further into the world of peacemaking and reconciliation, ultimately bringing us into face-to-face contact with politicians of all parties and members of paramilitary organizations, both Republican and Loyalist. The journey over twenty years between 1969 and 1989 was a period of significant theological and practical reappraisal of our essential calling as Christians in the context of conflict. It was a learning process, a journey to become, at best, active peacemakers in pursuit of an essentially negative peace, (using the criteria of Brewer et al.), while recognizing there was something more to be achieved—positive peace. I suspect that the inherent nationalism and dormant sectarianism that underlay the avowed separatist theology of my background is not untypical of the situation for many Christians, whatever their context or theology. It often takes violence, unrest or threat to uncover our deepest convictions and to lay bare the paucity of Christian formation as peacemaking, incarnational disciples of Jesus.

Reflection on the Role of the Just Peacemaking Paradigm

The question of the church's peace witness has long been problematic. Miller and Gingerich's book *The Church's Peace Witness* two decades ago explored the challenge of finding ecumenical agreement on the church's peace witness among the various traditions and differing hermeneutical approaches to Scripture. Their conclusion was modest, stating that the intention was "to begin a conversation rather than state conclusions of a finished debate,"[13] but the model was essentially one of seeking to reconcile different paradigmatic readings of Scripture which, however valuable and well intentioned, and while it improved mutual understanding and relationships, clearly could not provide a common confession around which the traditions could unite.

In *Just Peacemaking: Transforming Initiatives for Justice and Peace,*[14] Stassen recounts the origins of the Just Peacemaking project. Faced with frustration at the predictable dichotomy between Just War theorists and Pacifists when discussing the likely invasion of Iraq Stassen writes:

> I came away frustrated that we lacked a third model . . . with something like the seven clear criteria of the just war theory . . .

principles by which Christian attitudes and behavior are to be guided in the context of the Northern Ireland situation.

13. Miller and Gingerich, *Church's Peace Witness*, 206.

14. Stassen, *Just Peacemaking: Transforming Initiatives*.

for guiding ourselves and the people in our debates and actions about peacemaking.[15]

A third model, or a third way, is necessary not only for the academy of ethicists but the church.

Stassen's work on the Sermon on the Mount identified the pattern of transforming initiatives in the text which, in conjunction with other New Testament material, provided a basis for the development of his eight concrete steps of peacemaking. This was in turn to become the "Seven Steps of Just Peacemaking" as the implications of the biblical material were refashioned as a "public ethic" drawing on the work of other ethicists and political scientists.[16] Since then, in collaboration with other academics and practitioners, Just Peacemaking theory has developed as ten practical steps for the avoidance of war.[17] The trajectory of Stassen's work runs from biblical studies—particularly on the Sermon on the Mount—to the identification of transformative initiatives, to eight concrete steps of peacemaking, to the public ethic of seven steps of Just Peacemaking and ultimately to the contemporary collaborative work of thirty interdenominational ethicists and political scientists on the ten practices of Just Peacemaking as the new paradigm for the ethics of peace and war. The direction of flow has been from a specific text and need for a 'third way' to unite pacifist and non-pacifist in the discipleship of peacemaking to the public space and the ten specific practices. However, while those who collaborated in *Just Peacemaking* advocate the challenge and opportunity for churches to engage in Just Peacemaking, one cannot help but feel that the significance of Just Peacemaking theory has largely gone unnoticed by the churches. Stassen expects it will take a new generation of church leaders, trained in present-day Christian ethics rather than merely repeating past paradigms. It is not that the contributors to Just Peacemaking have failed to address the churches. In the introduction to the latest edition they comment that

> Our focus on practices and on churches and groups that encourage and foster those practices means that we recommend to every individual and every church that they form groups to nurture such practices. . . . Churches should have a peacemaker group, a

---

15. Ibid., 17–18.

16. Ibid., 94.

17. Stassen, *Just Peacemaking: The New Paradigm*. This, the most recent edition of *Just Peacemaking*, is the work of some thirty scholars.

Peace and World Hunger committee, or a Peace and Justice leadership group that will lead the church in peacemaking action.[18]

However, such expectation perpetuates the paralysis within the churches in regard to moving from passive peace (expressing the hope for peace) to active peace (getting engaged in Just Peacemaking) in the social and political spheres. The establishment of peacemaking groups within churches and the proliferation of para-church peacemaking organizations reinforce the sense that while peacemaking is a "good thing" it is not core to the churches' calling. It is perceived as the domain of those exercised on this matter rather than the calling of all Christians as incarnational disciples of the Jesus of the Sermon on the Mount. The contributors to Just Peacemaking recognize that churches may have a unique role to play:

> Churches can serve a special role in nurturing a spirituality that sustains courage when Just Peacemaking is unpopular, hope when despair or cynicism is tempting, and a sense of grace and the possibility of forgiveness when Just Peacemaking fails.[19]

But, again, this suggests that the main role of churches is to be available and willing to support this 'good thing' of peacemaking, not that peacemaking and the practice of peacemaking is to be at the heart of their understanding of discipleship. Brewer et al. observed that much of the active peacemaking emerging from the churches in the Northern Ireland context was done by individuals or para-church groups. Indeed they referred to some of the most effective contributors to the peace process as "mavericks" precisely because churches and church leaders were hesitant, sometimes for good reason, to take the lead in peacemaking within the community. There remains, therefore, the challenge of how Just Peacemaking as a core expression of incarnational discipleship becomes more commonly part of the DNA of spiritual formation and discipleship within the life of churches in the twenty-first century.

Placing Just Peacemaking at the Heart of Christian Discipleship

Writing in 1992, Stassen made reference to the "turnings" taking place at that time. There was "The Turning"[20] in the fall of the Berlin Wall and

18. Ibid., 36–37.
19. Ibid., 34.
20. Stassen, *Just Peacemaking: Transforming Initiatives*, 14.

the end of the Cold War; the turning to a new century and, perhaps most significantly in terms of Christian thinking, the turning toward the Sermon on the Mount.[21] That turning toward the Sermon on the Mount and the practical call to become followers of Jesus has continued unabated since the early 1990s, epitomized by the appearance of *Kingdom Ethics*[22] (and many other significant texts in both academic and popular publications), which states unashamedly:

> Christian churches across the theological and confessional spectrum, and Christian ethics as an academic discipline that serves the churches, are often guilty of evading Jesus, the cornerstone and center of the Christian faith. Specifically, *the teachings and practices of Jesus*—especially the largest block of his teachings, the Sermon on the Mount—are routinely ignored or misinterpreted in the preaching and teaching ministry of the churches and in Christian scholarship in ethics. . . .We write to redress this problem.[23]

However, how to address the problem at the level of church practice is another challenge altogether. Duane Friesen makes the point that being able to articulate ethical norms is of itself insufficient if "we do not nurture moral communities that can form people of character,"[24] and there can be little doubt that his reflection on the corrosive nature of "self interest" applies as much to church life as to any other element of civil society. The challenge of inspiring and equipping churches in the task of discipleship formation that embraces the concepts of Just Peacemaking is not insignificant.

In his work *Tracks and Traces*,[25] Paul Fiddes sets out a methodology of reflecting on what has gone before and forging a vision for the future on the basis of some clearly articulated convictions. He provides a useful model for addressing the role of the church, with all of its tradition and baggage, in its contemporary setting. Adopting a similar methodology in regard to Stassen's contribution may enable us to be clearer about how our sense of identity is shaped in relation to Jesus and, therefore, clearer in our

21. Ibid., 33–36.

22. Stassen and Gushee, *Kingdom Ethics*.

23. Ibid., 11.

24. Friesen, "Encourage Grassroots Peacemaking Groups," 202.

25. Fiddes, *Tracks and Traces*. Fiddes speaks of "tracks made by Baptists in the past that have the potential still to offer guidance for the present day" and the "traces of theology" which "point to God and enable us to participate in God's life" (ibid., 1).

understanding of our vocation as disciples and witnesses. Ultimately, the important issue that has to be addressed in the life of contemporary local congregations is whether we associate on the basis of theological dogma and principles—however they have been formed—or on the basis of a commitment to the practice of following Jesus in the everyday journey of life together in community, within the wider community of society.

Fiddes is particularly interested in the concept of covenant and, at the outset of his thesis in *Tracks and Traces*, comments:

> In early Baptist life, a confession was often associated with the "covenant" by which the community renewed its pledge of faithfulness to its Lord, and committed itself to a common life and mutual caring.[26]

While Fiddes' subtitle makes clear that his primary interest is in "Baptist identity in Church and Theology," his approach speaks to a wider community and offers a potential means of thinking of how to integrate the biblical and ethical reflections on Just Peacemaking with the life of churches in discipleship formation. Reflecting on the contributions of Schleiermacher, Barth and McClendon, Fiddes draws the conclusion that experience in community, how the community talks about God, and the narrative life of the community, shape theology.[27] All too often theology is fossilized in confessions or statements of faith which, while serving to articulate a set of doctrinal beliefs or theological propositions, fail to provide the resources and impetus for the formation of churches as communities of Christian virtues and practice. That purpose is better served by the use of covenants that are

> about relationship and trust, about "walking together," which is in some mysterious way part of the journey of salvation . . . I suggest that a theological and practical distance should be kept between confessions and covenants; confessions should be regarded as the *context* for covenant making, but never the *required* basis for "walking together."[28]

Herein lies a possible route to integrate the practices of Just Peacemaking into the life of churches as an agent of formation leading to authentic incarnational discipleship and mission. Can we follow the trajectory observed earlier from biblical studies—particularly on the Sermon on the Mount—to the public ethic of the ten practices of Just Peacemaking

26. Ibid., 9.
27. Ibid., 12.
28. Ibid., 45–46.

and direct the flow into the life of local churches through renewal of the concept of church covenant under the rule of Christ?

Renewing Covenant in the Local Church

While living in Newry during the mid 1980s and struggling to know how to address the upheaval and fear associated with the protests against the Anglo-Irish Agreement, we were reviewing the old minute books of Newry Baptist Church. The church was founded in 1889 above a shoe-maker's shop in the centre of the town. We were less than four years away from celebrating the centenary of the church and keen to gain an understanding of the life of the community over the 100 years. It transpired that the original minute book was still intact, even though many years of church activity were unaccounted for in the intervening period. It was fascinating to discover that at its foundation the members of the church signed a covenant and not a statement of faith, a covenant that spoke clearly in terms of a relational commitment in the light of Christian belief. For example, they had used 1 Peter 1:1–3 as their stated understanding of Christian calling and then proceeded:

> Therefore we desire as a community of believers by lifestyle and in teaching to proclaim the truth as it is in Jesus, to proclaim the riches of his grace, and by loving sympathy and encouragement, to help one another in the Christian life.[29]

For the founders of our small Baptist church the covenanting together in relationship was inseparable from doctrinal belief, which itself was not expressed in theological propositions but in simple Bible quotations. It was an epiphany, a moment of recognition of the bankruptcy of so much of our experience of church life with its confessions, creeds and doctrinal statements, yet better known for fractious, aggressive articulation of its fears than for following, relationally, in the ways of Jesus.

Adopting or renewing the role of covenant may be one of the ways of diverting the trajectory of Just Peacemaking into the life of churches to enable a renewed process of formation in incarnational discipleship. At a Baptist conference I took the opportunity to introduce around eighty delegates over the course of two seminars to Just Peacemaking theory and in particular to the eight concrete steps and seven practices of Just Peace-making as outlined in Stassen's 1992 work. Having set the biblical basis

---

29. "Newry Baptist Church Covenant."

from which Stassen had been working, we rephrased the eight concrete steps and the seven practices in terms of a mutual covenant intended as a commitment to the conduct of relationships in the life of local churches. The proposals were a very rough reworking of the Just Peacemaking material and read along the following lines:

As disciples of Jesus and in obedience to his commands in our relationships with each other we commit to:

- acknowledge our common alienation and shared dependence on God's grace
- go, talk, welcome one another, and seek to be reconciled when tension or conflict arises
- take transforming initiatives rather than resist vengefully
- invest our time and resources in delivering justice among us and beyond us
- love our enemies and affirm their valid interests
- pray for our enemies, and persevere in prayer
- avoid judging others; instead repent and forgive
- commit together to do peacemaking as disciples of Jesus or, alternatively based on the seven practices

We covenant to:

1. affirm each others' common interests and concerns
2. take independent initiatives to resolve tension or conflict when it arises
3. talk with our brother or sister when relationships are under threat
4. seek justice and the interests of others in any dispute
5. acknowledge the vicious cycles of enmity that can develop. and instead commit ourselves to participate in peacemaking
6. avoid judgemental speech and make amends when we offend
7. work with the whole community for transparency and truthfulness

The discussions that ensued were in some measure predictable, expressing anxiety about abandoning doctrinal statements, but also intriguing in the acknowledgement that there was something fundamentally and profoundly different about committing to practices rather than theological principles. Some participants expressed a sense of nervousness about making such specific commitments, e.g., how could they be maintained, what happens when we fall short? At the same time there was acknowledgement that following the flow of Stassen's reading of the Sermon on the Mount on the basis of transforming initiatives, the implications of discipleship were stark, challenging and potentially transformational. The intention of the seminar was then to press those attending to consider whether church life based around this kind of covenant would better equip or enable Christians to imagine the possibility of making a contribution to Just Peacemaking within civil society. The seminars were an opportunity to explore ideas, gauge reaction, identify fears and possibilities. I left convinced that there is great potential in developing this process.

As if to reinforce the need for some such initiative I had been invited to share in a private ecumenical gathering of Christian leaders from across the denominations in Northern Ireland to "explore how Christians can channel our vocation, faith and vision into transforming the social, cultural, religious and political realities and estrangements which still restrict healthy development of our community."[30] While it was agreed that the conversations were private, there is no secret in recognizing the struggle, some would say "failure," of the churches to make any significant contribution to the discussion and creation of a shared future for the people of post-conflict Northern Ireland. Despite the element of support for those engaged in peacemaking, despite the consistent condemnation of violence during the conflict, and despite official statements that acknowledge the need to work for a shared future, there is not sufficient capacity within the churches to engage with the challenge of addressing the past and shaping the future. Indeed, just as politics in Northern Ireland has, as David Stevens feared, settled into a manageable sectarianism, so too have the churches been content to maintain segregated education, and to embrace quasi-political/sectarian organizations. As Brewer et al. commented, they have hoped that politics will continue as normal rather than addressed the need for fundamental social change. We need a new way of thinking about being church, relating both within and beyond our local congregations, denominational structures and sectarian identities. The radical call to place relational covenant before doctrinal confession is as necessary as it is absent.

---

30. Private correspondence from the organizers of the meeting.

Formation and Re-Formation

Part of the challenge in putting the concept of Just Peacemaking at the heart of twenty-first-century Christian self-understanding is that Christian communities are already formed through a variety of narratives, traditions and practices. There is no blank page onto which Just Peacemaking can be written in clear, bold letters. Indeed there is clearly much within existing traditions that reflect meaningful patterns and practices of discipleship, and some traditions have valued the role of relational covenants over many generations. However, whether it is on the small stage of Northern Ireland or in the much bigger arena of the United States, the state of inter-church relationships and the relationship between churches and civil society indicate that there is much to be done in coming to grips with a form of discipleship that models and follows the practice and teaching of Jesus. Indeed there is a considerable challenge in gaining a hearing for Just Peacemaking amidst the cacophony of voices vying for the attention of the Christian community and Christian market. However, over the past two decades considerable energy has been expended in promoting Just Peacemaking theory in the academy and the political arena, to good effect. The same strategic thinking and energy directed towards the churches may yet see a re-formation within the various traditions in which the concept of incarnational discipleship informed by Just Peacemaking theory and practices becomes embedded as part of the ongoing formation of Christian disciples in the twenty-first century. Relocating the values and practices of peacemaking from the periphery of church life to the centre is a goal for which it is worth striving. As the Kreiders write:

> putting peace on our churches' agenda can . . . transform our churches' "domestic life"—our way of relating to each other and making decisions. Furthermore, it can deeply affect our churches' outward life—our approaches to worship, work, wealth, war and witness.[31]

With its proven capacity to unite those from Just War and Pacifist traditions, Just Peacemaking theory has the potential to inspire rather than threaten, enrich rather than deplete, and unite rather than divide.

Joel James Shuman, in his contribution to Hauerwas's *Festschrift*, observes that "gathered Christian worship—church—is the most important place that Christian formation takes place; in the Christian gathering

---

31. Kreider and Kreider, *Becoming a Peace Church*, 12.

for worship the Christian body is crafted."[32] Shuman is clear that gathered Christian worship is not the only means by which formation occurs and that worship is not primarily intended for moral formation. Nevertheless worship in community has the potential to shape the worshippers' character and behavior. I say "potential" because it hardly needs stating that participation in worship does not guarantee any particular effect in the life of the individual. To use Shuman's phrase, "Worshippers retain moral agency"[33] and may or may not allow worship to be a formative influence on attitude and practice. However, Shuman's discussion on the relationship between discipleship, craft, and the role of worship in the crafting of disciples helpfully directs our attention to the role and significance of corporate Christian worship in discipleship formation or re-formation.[34] Astley follows a similar theme, claiming that "Christian doctrine and the formation of Christian attitudes must take place together. . . . Christian worship is the paradigm situation for that joint activity."[35] In a similar vein, Timothy O'Connell reflects on the embodied nature of worship and the importance of gesture and ritual. The very existence of a worshipping community, the power of gesture and ritual within the community, and the language of the community, have the capacity to "energize, support and guide the values out of which we daily live."[36]

As the Kreiders reflect on the challenge of churches becoming "Peace Churches," they too emphasize the significance of worship in the formation of peacemakers. "Worship is . . . an engine of peacemaking,"[37] as the Lordship of Jesus is declared, our unity in Christ affirmed, God's purposes for the world are retold, intercession for peace is made, and "God shapes our vision and mission" in the context of his reconciling grace. Undoubtedly the Kreiders' terminology and description of worship would be appropriated by most, if not all, Christian churches, which begs the question why peacemaking, within congregations and as an expression of incarnational discipleship and witness, seems so often to be foreign to church life? The answer would appear to lie in the rift between principles and practices,

32. Shuman, "Discipleship as Craft," 325.

33. Ibid., 330.

34. Clayton Schmit comments on Don Saliers's three levels of worship—participation in the rites of worship, in the body of Christ, and in the life of God—by using a phrase from Miroslav Volf, who speaks of worship that is authentic as occurring within "the rhythm of adoration and action" (Schmidt, "Worship as a Locus," 30).

35. Astley, "Role of Worship," 250.

36. O'Connell, *Making Disciples*, 138.

37. Kreider and Kreider, *Becoming a Peace Church*, 23.

between worship that is abstracted and worship that is embodied. I well remember the fervent and heartfelt prayers prayed in our church prayer meetings during the "troubles" in Northern Ireland. We were not indifferent to what was happening in our community, but there had been no crafting in a discipleship of peacemaking, no covenant made between us as to how we would relate to one another so that, unfortunately, at times our own relationships were as broken as those in our society. Our worship was sincere, our people good people. However, the security and strength of relationships to one another were based primarily on the thin ground of affirmation of doctrinal positions just as our bonds within the wider community were predicated upon our voting patterns, our various national identities and political loyalties.

What happens on Sundays, or whatever other days or occasions Christian communities gather for worship, is not incidental to discipleship formation but critical in the formation process of both identity and mission. Corporate Christian worship is the environment where we can learn what it means to be Christian, retell the story of Jesus that shapes our narrative, and enact the grace and practices of forgiveness and reconciliation in a communion that shapes the wider ministry of reconciliation of which Paul speaks in 2 Corinthians 5. It was for this reason that ECONI initiated "ECONI Sunday" in Northern Ireland. As a para-church organization ECONI did not attempt to speak for the churches or in any way attempt to set itself up as a church, but it did believe strongly in resourcing clergy and church congregations in the process of peacemaking discipleship. It could not be claimed that over the number of years ECONI Sundays were promoted they led to any great transformation in the churches of Northern Ireland. Indeed the number of churches participating was limited.[38] ECONI did, however, provide substantial resources of biblical material, sermon suggestions, prayers, hymns, and discussion materials to enable the language of peacemaking to be heard within the practices of reading, reflecting and praying in the context of worship.[39] The production of such material is not unique to ECONI's work. Other churches and Christian organizations involved in peacemaking, world development, civil rights,

---

38. Patrick Mitchel records that "over fifty-five churches took part in the first ECONI Sunday on 7 Nov. 1993 representing the involvement of 10,000 people" (Mitchel, *Evangelicalism and National Identity*, 263n17).

39. ECONI published a compendium of the material offered over the seven years of ECONI Sundays (ECONI, *Thinking Biblically Building Peace*). By the end of the seven years ECONI Sundays were organized, over four hundred churches had made use of the materials.

and other causes, have produced material for use in churches. It can seem a small contribution in the grand scheme of things but it can often have significant results. However, when church denominational bodies are willing to participate in the renewal of worship practices, much can be achieved. Timothy O'Connell's reflections on the post Vatican II re-introduction of the rite of the peace are interesting in the context of this discussion:

> by the simple expedient of a modest gesture of peace-wishing, . . . the bishops of Vatican II reconstructed the theology of church of a worldwide, multicultural, often uneducated, and sometimes unresponsive congregation in the astonishingly brief period of twenty years.[40]

Discipleship, like the "good thing" of peacemaking, is too often perceived to belong to the more peripheral element of church life—the Sunday school class, discipleship class, or Bible study group. Both discipleship and peacemaking need to be placed at the core of corporate worship, which itself should be predicated on covenant commitment to one another, reflecting Jesus' teaching and example. We need a liturgical addition that incorporates renewal of a covenant commitment to one another on a weekly basis and an intercessory structure that incorporates prayers for peace in the church and in the world. There needs to be a means to celebrate the gift of faithful covenant relationships, of admonishment when the relational covenant is broken, and a commitment to reconciliation when relationships are fractured. We need to discover that the greatest shame and failure is not doctrinal deviance but the absence of incarnational discipleship, that believing is a verb and following is believing, that the church is not ours to hold but Christ's to give, that God blesses the peacemakers and opposes the proud, that what we are and how we live say more about our worship than we ever say in a worship service.

Is it possible in the twenty-first century to conceive of building Just Peacemaking Churches in a manner not dissimilar to the tradition of Peace Churches? Most certainly. Just Peacemaking theory and practice have the potential to draw together the themes of formation, peacemaking and worship and empower the church to re-form its life and witness in the pattern of incarnational discipleship with a renewed incarnation mission in Just Peacemaking. The transformative initiatives pattern Stassen

---

40. O'Connell, *Making Disciples*, 129. O'Connell comments that there may be an element of exaggeration in his comments, but his point is well made. However, not everyone would see the re-introduction of the rite as positive nor accept that it is properly understood and practiced, as a survey of Catholic blogs would soon make clear!

identified in the Sermon on the Mount needs to be let loose in the church so that the 'grace-filled deliverance' in the transforming initiatives can do their work in forming disciples equipped for "positive participation in peacemaking initiatives"[41] to the glory of God and the good of the world.

> MAKING PEACE[42]
> God, as a people set apart for you,
> we confess that we have neglected
> to follow Jesus in the path of peace.
> That our words and acts have at times
> perpetuated fear and suspicion
> and fuelled our sectarian conflict.
> Help us to be peacemakers in our divided community.
> To guard our words when we speak.
> To overcome hostility with openness and love.
> To cultivate skills to resolve conflict.
> And to value the gift of peace when we find it in others.
> God, let the peace of your Son rule in our hearts.
> Amen

Bibliography

Astley, Jeff. "The Role of Worship in Christian Learning." In *Theological Perspectives on Christian Formation*, edited by Jeff Astley, Leslie J. Francis, and Colin Crowder, 245–51. Grand Rapids: Eerdmans, 1996.

Brewer, John D. *Peace Processes: A Sociological Approach*. Cambridge: Polity, 2010.

Brewer, John D., Gareth I. Higgins, and Francis Teeney. *Religion, Civil Society, and Peace in Northern Ireland*. Oxford: Oxford University Press, 2011.

Bruce, Steve. *Paisley: Religion and Politics in Northern Ireland*. Oxford: Oxford University Press, 2007.

ECONI. "For God and His Glory Alone." Belfast: ECONI, 1988.

ECONI. *Thinking Biblically Building Peace*. Belfast: ECONI, 2002.

Farrell, Michael. "Historical Reflections on the Civil Rights Movement." Paper delivered at the Desmond Greaves Summer School, Dublin, XX MONTH 2008. Accessed 30 January 2012. http://www.nicivilrights.org/articles/historical-reflections-on-the-civil-rights-movement/.

Fiddes, Paul S. *Tracks and Traces: Baptist Identity in Church and Theology*. Carlisle, UK: Paternoster, 2003.

Friesen, Duane K. "Encourage Grassroots Peacemaking Groups and Voluntary Associations." In *Just Peacemaking: The New Paradigm for the Ethics of Peace and War*, 2nd ed., edited by G. Stassen, 186–96. Cleveland: Pilgrim, 2008

41. Stassen, *Just Peacemaking: Transforming Initiatives*, 42.

42. Prayer taken from the ECONI Sunday resource: ECONI, *Thinking Biblically Building Peace*, 116.

Galtung, Johan, and International Peace Research Institute Oslo. *Peace by Peaceful Means: Peace and Conflict, Development and Civilization.* London: Sage, 1996.

Ganiel, G. "A Framework for Understanding Religion in Northern Irish Civil Society." In *Global Change, Civil Society and the Northern Ireland Peace Process: Implementing the Political Settlement*, edited by Christopher Farrington, 159–82. New Security Challenges Series. Basingstoke, UK: Palgrave Macmillan, 2008.

Kreider, Alan, and Eleanor Kreider. *Becoming a Peace Church.* New Ground: Christian Discipleship in the Radical Tradition. London: HHSC Christian, 2000.

Miller, Marlin E., and Barbara Nelson Gingerich, editors.. *The Church's Peace Witness.* Grand Rapids: Eerdmans, 1994.

Mitchel, Patrick. *Evangelicalism and National Identity in Ulster, 1921–1998.* Oxford: Oxford University Press, 2003.

Mitchell, Claire. *Religion, Identity and Politics in Northern Ireland: Boundaries of Belonging and Belief.* Aldershot, UK: Ashgate, 2006.

"Newry Baptist Church Covenant." Newry: Newry Baptist Church, 1987.

O'Connell, Timothy E. *Making Disciples: A Handbook of Christian Moral Formation.* New York: Crossroad, 1998.

Schmidt, Clayton J. "Worship as a Locus for Transformation." In *Worship That Changes Lives*, edited by Alexis D. Abernethy, 25–40. Grand Rapids: Baker Academic, 2008.

Shuman, Joel James. "Discipleship as Craft." In *Unsettling Arguments: A Festschrift on the Occasion of Stanley Hauerwas's 70th Birthday*, edited by Kelly S. Johnston, Charles R. Pinches, and Charles M. Collier, 315–31. Eugene, OR: Cascade, 2010.

Stassen, Glen H., editor. *Just Peacemaking: The New Paradigm for the Ethics of Peace and War.* 2nd ed. Cleveland: Pilgrim, 2008.

Stassen, Glen H. *Just Peacemaking: Transforming Initiatives for Justice and Peace.* Louisville: Westminster John Knox, 1992.

Stassen, Glen H., and David P. Gushee. *Kingdom Ethics: Following Jesus in Contemporary Context.* Downers Grove, IL: InterVarsity, 2003.

Stevens, David. "Briefing Paper on Northern Ireland". http://corrymeela.o28ni.org.uk/joomla16/phocadownload/Stevens/Miscellaneous/a%20briefing%20paper%20on%20northern%20ireland.pdf Last accessed 27 February 2013.

Stevens, David. "Two Cheers for Devolution". http://www.sicrieproject.org/view.php?preview_part_id=165947&part_id=165947&page=archive__two_cheers_for_devolution.html&random=512e7862a7691 Last accessed 27 February 2013.

Wells, Ronald. *Hope and Reconciliation in Northern Ireland: The Role of Faith-Based Organisations.* Dublin: Liffey, 2010.

5

Developing the Practices of Just Peacemaking

Reflections from the Experience of the Orthodox Church in North America[1]

Philip LeMasters

THE ORTHODOX CHURCH IN North America provides several resources for the formation of disciples who bear witness to the eschatological peace incarnate in Jesus Christ. Those who share in the Lord's victory over death become "partakers of the divine nature" (2 Pet 1:4) and are called to manifest the healing and fulfillment of the broken social orders characteristic of life in the fallen world. The Divine Liturgy celebrated every Sunday and major feast day contains many petitions for peace; indeed, the Eucharistic worship of the Church is a liturgical icon of the peace of God's reign. Though there are tremendous theological, liturgical, and spiritual resources to support Orthodox engagement in the practices of just peacemaking, Orthodox social ethics has only recently begun to give explicit attention to the practices of just peacemaking.[2]

---

1. This essay is a revised version of paper of the same title presented at the International Orthodox Consultation titled "Orthodox Contribution to a Theology of Just Peace," Saidnaya, Syria, 18–22 October 2010.

2. For the practices of just peacemaking, see Stassen, *Just Peacemaking: The New Paradigm*. For an account of the relationship between Orthodoxy and just peacemaking, see LeMasters, "Dynamic Praxis of Peace."

Unfortunately, the actual praxis of peacemaking is obscure in the Orthodox community. With the social location of a religious minority associated with immigrants,[3] the Church in the Western Hemisphere is not yet jurisdictionally united. The three largest jurisdictions in the United States (the Greek Orthodox Archdiocese of America, the Orthodox Church in America, and the Antiochian Orthodox Archdiocese of North America) have at times been embroiled in strife—both internal and in relation to one another—at various points during recent decades.[4] The Church has not been a beacon of reconciliation and peacemaking in its internal relations. These circumstances present challenges for acting in a coordinated, effective manner to promote peacemaking in contemporary culture. Unfortunately, serious engagement with the dynamics of forming parishioners in the life-affirming way of Christ often falls to a relatively small number of activists and academicians.[5] This state of affairs is ironic in a church that begins each Sunday liturgy with a petition "for the peace of the whole world . . . and the union of all men." The just peacemaking practice of cooperative conflict resolution would surely strengthen the Church and its witness to the peace of Christ.

Various statements from the different Orthodox jurisdictions, as well as from the Standing Conference of the Canonical Orthodox Bishops in the Americas (SCOBA), offer guidance on the praxis of peace. At least implicitly, they affirm many of the practices of just peacemaking, including nonviolent direct action, cooperative conflict resolution, and fostering just and sustainable economic development. SCOBA has endorsed several organizations that embody peacemaking dimensions of the Orthodox social witness: International Orthodox Christian Charities (IOCC); the Orthodox Peace Fellowship of North America (OPFNA); the Orthodox Christian Prison Ministry (OCPM); the Orthodox Fellowship of the Transfiguration, which promotes the ecological witness of the Church; Project Mexico, which supports an orphanage and builds homes for the poor; the Fellowship of Orthodox Christians United to Serve (FOCUS), a domestic ministry to the needy; and Zoe for Life, a ministry that assists pregnant women and facilitates adoption. Taken together, these collective efforts of the Orthodox Church to share with the poor, reconcile enemies,

3. See Krindacht, "Orthodox Church Today," for the results of a recent survey of American Orthodox Christians.

4. See Michalopulos and Ham, *American Orthodox Church*.

5. Bos and Forest, *"For the Peace from Above,"* is an important anthology of texts related to peacemaking in Orthodox Christianity.

and care for the helpless are disciplines that form those who participate in them as embodied witnesses of the peace of Christ.

Despite such statements, organizations, and practices, the Orthodox witness for peace is often ineffectual. For example, statements by Orthodox hierarchs and an appeal by the Orthodox Peace Fellowship of North America against the NATO bombing of Yugoslavia on Pascha (Easter) in 1999 were not successful in changing American policy and drew little public attention. The same is true of the American response to statements against the invasion of Iraq in 2003 by Orthodox hierarchs around the world, as well as to the appeal issued by OPFNA. Similar pleas against the legality and prevalence of abortion, or concerning ongoing conflicts in the Middle East, have not achieved any changes in public policy or discourse on the issues at stake.

What steps could American Orthodoxy take in order to develop the ability to engage the larger society toward the end of just peacemaking? The establishment of a single, united Orthodox jurisdiction would both be a witness to peace in itself and make it possible for the entire Church to speak with one voice. The statements and ministries of the Church would then likely receive more attention in the larger culture, which would increase the likelihood of effective engagement. The work of the Assembly of Bishops toward this end is a welcome development.[6]

The formation of clergy and laity as just peacemakers is essential for the Church to bear witness to the eschatological harmony of the kingdom in the midst of a broken world. For such formation to occur, the Orthodox community must begin to recognize peacemaking as a fundamental vocation for all Christians. The Orthodox Peace Fellowship of North America and the Institute for Peace Studies in Eastern Christianity at Boston College provide provocative initial models for highlighting the centrality of peace in the life of the Church. There are areas of notable charitable and social service work in the Church, such as IOCC and FOCUS. Since these ministries address needs that are often the product of long-term political and economic problems, they provide a basis for engaging governmental and societal agencies in cooperative long-range peacemaking efforts in areas of common concern. Whenever Orthodox believers participate in social ministries that aid the poor and needy, they engage in a praxis that may form them as more faithful disciples of the Prince of Peace.

6 See the website of the Assembly of Canonical Orthodox Bishops of North and Central America, http://assemblyofbishops.org.

The Orthodox Peace Fellowship of North America promotes the praxis of peace through conferences, publications, and other educational efforts directed at both clergy and laity. Articles in the OPF journal *In Communion* address different dimensions of peacemaking in the family, the parish, American society, and around the world. Contributors include well-known clergy, monks, nuns, and scholars. Unfortunately, the membership of the organization and the circulation of the journal are not large. Though OPFNA is an important witness for Orthodox peacemaking, its visibility and influence in the Church, and especially in the larger culture, are limited.[7]

The website of the newly formed Institute for Peace Studies in Eastern Christianity states that its mission is "to conduct research, educate, and offer consultancy to educators, policymakers, and religious leaders in exploring and implementing methods of peacemaking emerging from the traditions of Eastern Christianity." The Institute co-sponsored an initial international Orthodox consultation on peace ethics in Bucharest in 2009 and in Saidnaya, Syria, in 2010. Its director, Marian Gh. Simion, has written two seminal papers on peacemaking: "Prolegomena to a Peace Studies Model for Eastern Christianity" and "Seven Factors of Ambivalence in Defining a Just War Theory in Eastern Christianity." This new Institute promises to strengthen the peacemaking witness of American Orthodoxy in a variety of ways, but it is too early to gauge its effectiveness.[8]

In every Divine Liturgy, the Church prays for the peace of the whole world, the unity of all people, and God's blessing upon those who are in danger and in need. The peace for which the Church prays concerns real-life situations of nations and regions threatened by famine, genocide, and various forms of political oppression. The Church also prays in the Anaphora of St. Basil the Great for the armed forces and civil authorities, asking God to "grant them a secure and lasting peace . . . that we in their tranquility may lead a calm and peaceful life in all reverence and godliness." While mourning the broken reality of warfare, Orthodoxy accepts the existence of armed states and prays for a peaceful life for all. Just peacemaking practices such as reducing offensive weapons, working with emerging cooperative forces in the international system, supporting nonviolent direct action, and cooperative conflict resolution serve to decrease instances of warfare. Orthodox social ethics strongly endorses such steps to make peace and avoid the tragedy of war, whenever possible.

---

7. See the website of the Orthodox Peace Fellowship, www.incommunion.org.
8. See the website of the Institute for Peace Studies in Eastern Christianity.

The 2003 invasion of Iraq prompted explicit discourse in American Orthodoxy on peacemaking in the midst of armed conflict.[9] Statements by Orthodox hierarchs focused primarily on the tragic nature of war and the physical and spiritual threats to all involved. For example, in October, 2002, His Eminence Metropolitan Philip, Primate of the Antiochian Archdiocese of North America, criticized the prospect of an American invasion of Iraq for fear that "Such an attack will destabilize the entire region, cause untold harm to countless children and other civilians as well as bring political and social unrest to an already troubled area of the world." He presciently warned that "overthrowing ... the Iraqi government could cause the breakup of the country into warring factions for many years to come," and urged the "President and Congress to seek the difficult and tiresome road of peace rather than the bloody and dark road of war.[10]

Once the war began, the statements by American hierarchs were pastoral in tone and did not make specific arguments about public policy. For example, the bishops of SCOBA in their "Appeal for Prayer" were "compelled by our spiritual obligation as peacemakers, to express the anguish in our hearts that, once again, due to the presence of sin and evil in the world, nations and people of faith have been unable to avoid a dreadful confrontation." They called for prayers for peace and for all those at risk in the war, including "the security and well-being of our military personnel . . . our President and all civil authorities, for their discernment and divine guidance during this difficult time." The bishops noted that "[t]his tragic war, combined with the threat to security at home, has created enormous fear and anxiety throughout the world," which "[o]nly the Prince of Peace . . . can allay."[11]

A pastoral letter from the Holy Synod of Bishops of the Orthodox Church in America strikes a similar tone. Written in the first days of the war, it notes that the world "is hardened and cold, unable to recognize the peace given to us by Our Lord, Jesus Christ, and unwilling to pursue His divine peace in its conflicts and disputes. Our Lord Himself recognized that . . . conflict and war would continue to manifest themselves in the world." In this context, the Synod called for prayer and fasting for the quick

9. Much of the following discussion of the American Orthodox response to the 2003 invasion of Iraq is taken from LeMasters, "Ethics of Peace." It was originally presented at the International Orthodox Consultation on Peace, Bucharest, Romania, 2009.

10. Metropolitan PHILIP, "On Iraq"; Metropolitan PHILIP, "Iraq War Peace Appeals by Hierarchs."

11. "SCOBA Hierarchs Issue Appeal for Prayer."

resolution of "the present crisis . . . with as little bloodshed as possible," asking the Lord to turn "that which is evil" into what "is not only good, but godly." The bishops call for prayer for "our own sons and daughters in military service, our chaplains, and especially those who have no one else to pray for them," for the Lord's protection and aid in their "battle against temptations which would render them hopeless and heartless. May God fill them with every desire to do good and to show compassion in the midst of their spiritually challenging ordeal." The statement also calls for prayer for national and world leaders "that they will be moved to bring about an end to the conflict in a speedy manner, focusing their attention on producing a just and lasting peace."[12]

A lively exchange occurred in response to the OPFNA statement against the invasion of Iraq, as demonstrated by a condemnatory article in *The Washington Post* by Orthodox layman Frank Schaeffer, who objected to the implication that his son, who served in the armed forces, was a murderer.[13] Schaeffer later retracted his statement and stated that the invasion of Iraq was not justified.

Father Patrick Reardon also criticized the statement in the journal *Touchstone* for a simplistic and misleading interpretation of Orthodoxy's stance on the morality of war, as well as for giving the impression that the Church is "committed to a pacifist ethic [that] could not be a central feature of American political and social life."[14] Had the OPFNA statement appealed explicitly to the practices of just peacemaking, it would have been less subject to such misinterpretations. Pacifism may well have a bad name for many Americans, but there is far greater acceptance of pragmatic steps that provide realistic alternatives to armed conflict.

Father Alexander Webster, a priest of the Orthodox Church in America, is another important voice in this debate. He has argued in support of an ethic of morally justified war in Orthodoxy. In *The Virtue of War,* and an essay in *St. Vladimir's Theological Quarterly,* he maintains that a justifiable war is a "lesser good" than peace. Writing in the context of post-9/11 America, he denies that fighting or supporting such a war is a "lesser evil," arguing that Christians should never do evil, whether greater or lesser. If a war is justified for the protection of the innocent and vindication of justice, and fought in a just manner, he concludes that it is a morally good

12. Webster, *Virtue of War,* 114, finds this statement "to eschew military action as *ipso facto* unworthy of Orthodox Christians." I do not think that this conclusion is warranted by the text of the statement.

13. See "OPF Iraq Appeal"; Schaeffer, "Stripped of Spiritual Comfort."

14. Reardon, "Not So Quiet."

endeavor.[15] Several Orthodox authors responded to Fr. Webster's position in the November, 2003, edition of St. *Vladimir's Theological Quarterly*. Most were not convinced by the argument that war is a lesser good than peace on a scale of virtue, and instead stressed its tragic nature and connection to death, destruction, and damage to the soul.[16]

These debates about the morality of the Iraq invasion, and of war in general, had no visible impact upon American public policy or opinion. They did not attract much attention even within the Church, for the dominant cultural ethos shapes the social and political vision of many clergy and parishioners more decisively than do the pronouncements of bishops, let alone the always obscure writings of scholars. The relative obscurity of the discussion on the Iraq war stands as a clear example of the need for more robust peacemaking witness in the Church. If the Orthodox Church spoke and acted with explicit reference to just peacemaking practices, and other churches increasingly did likewise, the larger culture would likely be more receptive to its appeals.

True peace displays right relationships between nations, peoples, and other social groups. In this context, how should Orthodox Christians understand just peacemaking? The Church's praxis of peace appeals implicitly to both restorative and distributive views of justice through the work of Orthodox charitable groups, such as FOCUS, which "serves the hungry, thirsty, stranger, naked, sick and imprisoned by providing Food, Occupation, Clothing, Understanding, and Shelter."[17] Likewise, the vision statement of IOCC indicates that the organization "seeks to respond, without discrimination, to those who are suffering and in need, to enable them to continue to improve their own lives and communities and to have means to live with dignity, respect, and hope."[18] The goal of Orthodox Christian Prison Ministry is "to bring the love of Christ to those who are in prison by providing encouragement, material support, transition and reintegration services, Christian education, spiritual guidance and the sacramental life of the Church to prisoners and their families."[19]

15. Webster, "Justifiable War," 53.

16. See, for example, Breck, "Lesser Good or Lesser Evil?," 109, and LeMasters, "May Christians Kill?"

17. See the website of the Fellowship of Orthodox Christians United to Serve, http://www.focusnorthamerica.org/index.php?option=com_content&view=article&id=19&Itemid=90

18. See the website of International Orthodox Christian Charities, www.iocc.org.

19. See the website of Orthodox Christian Prison Ministries, *www.ocpm-scoba.org.*

American Orthodox ministries and charities rarely use the language of justice in describing their work. Instead, they present themselves as charitable ministries, as organizations that manifest the merciful love of Christ to those who lack the necessities of life. St. Basil the Great preached that those who could give to the poor, but did not, were guilty of injustice and should restore excess goods to their rightful owners. "The bread you are holding back is for the hungry, the clothes you keep put away are for the naked, the shoes that are rotting away with disuse are for those who have none, the silver you keep buried in the earth is for the needy. You are thus guilty of injustice toward as many as you might have aided, and did not."[20] Likewise, St. John Chrysostom proclaimed that "not giving to the poor of what one has is to commit robbery against them and to attempt against their very life, for we must remember that what we withhold is not ours, but theirs."[21]

Seen in this light, charitable ministries to the needy are also works of both restorative and distributive justice, for those who have more than they need owe the surplus to their rightful owners, the poor. Likewise, such restoration is based on a view of distributive justice; namely, that goods should be distributed according to the principle of need. The peace for which the Orthodox pray every Sunday in the Divine Liturgy implies that everyone should have what is necessary for a decent human life: "For our deliverance from all tribulation, wrath, and necessity, let us pray to the Lord." Orthodox peacemakers should work to help all human beings live with the dignity appropriate to those created in God's image and likeness. This commitment coheres with the just peacemaking practices of just and sustainable economic development and human rights.

Whether the language of human rights fits coherently within an Orthodox vision of peacemaking is, however, open to debate. Many American Orthodox statements endorse human rights in a manner consistent with the Universal Declaration of Human Rights. On the thirtieth anniversary of the Declaration, SCOBA "urged all Orthodox Christians to pray 'for those whose human rights are being denied and/or violated,' specifically for their religious beliefs or in their pursuit of 'justice, shelter, health care and education.'"[22] The "Statement on Human Rights" by the 24th Biennial Clergy-Laity Congress of the Greek Orthodox Archdiocese affirmed "a right of divine love" that God has granted humanity such

20. Basil, "I Will Tear Down My Barns," 70.

21. John Chrysostom, "Homily on Lazarus 6," as cited in Gonzalez, *Faith and Wealth*, 206.

22. Webster, *Price of Prophecy*, 146.

that there are "divinely inherent human rights" to freedom of "thought and expression" and equal opportunity in society. The next Clergy-Laity Congress, meeting in 1980, cited "the United Nations Declaration of Human Rights," strongly affirmed "an inalienable right" to the free practice of religion, and urged governments to act consistently for "the preservation of human rights."[23] In 1990, the "clergy-laity congress added to the list of human rights another one especially relevant in the last decade: 'freedom from terrorism.'"[24] Since the Turkish invasion of Cyprus, several congresses have called for respect for "the human and civil rights of both Greek and Turkish Cypriots" and "effective international guarantees with security and justice for all . . . inhabitants.[25]

All-American Councils of the Orthodox Church in America have passed many resolutions "on issues of freedom and human rights," including opposition to abortion, euthanasia, and capital punishment, and support for the rights of native peoples in Alaska to their traditional "lands, resources, and properties" and means of subsistence.[26] The council of 1986 condemned "expedient 'considerations of political ideology and political strategy' and explicitly cited human-rights abuses by governments on both the 'right' and the 'left' of the political spectrum."[27]

Conventions of the Antiochian Archdiocese have passed several resolutions "concerning freedom and human rights" in countries around the world, including "scores of resolutions on Lebanon, Palestine, and the plight of Arabs elsewhere." The 1979 convention affirmed "an ambitious litany of material 'rights' . . . possessed by children, including the right to 'experience affection, love and understanding both in home and in society, . . . to adequate nutrition and medical care, . . . to opportunity for play and recreation, . . . to a name and nationality, . . . to be brought up in a spirit of peace, freedom, and love."[28]

Other Orthodox statements have also appealed to the language of human rights in defense of life in the womb. For example, Jim Forest of OPFNA has highlighted the statement of the late scholar Jaroslav Pelikan that abortion is "the great human rights issue of our time."[29] Forest himself

---

23. Ibid., 156.
24. Ibid., 147.
25. Ibid., 149.
26. Ibid., 158–59.
27. Ibid., 160.
28. Ibid., 171.
29 See Forest and Forest, "Great Human Rights Issue."

prefers to say that "abortion tops the list" of human rights issues, "for once you allow yourself to kill the unborn, no one can claim a right to life."[30] The North American Orthodox-Catholic Theological Consultation has connected opposition to abortion to a broader defense of human rights, for "the 'right to life' implies a right to a decent life and to full human development, not merely to a marginal existence. We affirm that the furthering of this goal for the unborn, the mentally retarded, the aging, and the underprivileged is our duty on a global as well as a domestic scale."[31]

A similar affirmation of human rights is found in "The Manhattan Declaration," a statement signed by a variety of Catholic and Evangelical leaders, as well as by His Beatitude Metropolitan Jonah of the Orthodox Church in America, His Grace Bishop Basil of the Antiochian Orthodox Archdiocese, and Father Chad Hatfield, Chancellor of St. Vladimir's Orthodox Theological Seminary, and several other Orthodox clergy. The declaration affirms "the profound, inherent, and equal dignity of every human being as a creature fashioned in the very image of God, possessing inherent rights of equal dignity and life." It also affirms "religious liberty, which is grounded in the character of God, the example of Christ, and the inherent freedom and dignity of human beings created in the divine image."[32]

Caution about Orthodox use of the language of human rights has been expressed by American scholars such as Vigen Guroian and H. Tristram Engelhardt, Jr., on the grounds that it is a secular concept that reflects a greater commitment to the allegedly autonomous reason of the Enlightenment than to a theologically sound perspective on the place of humanity before God.[33] Father Emmanuel Clapsis of Holy Cross Greek Orthodox School of Theology writes that "The Orthodox critique[s] of human rights tradition focus on their reduction, especially in affluent western countries, to a basis that fortifies the self, leads to self-centeredness, and legitimizes

---

30. Forest, email.

31. North American Orthodox-Catholic Theological Consultation, "Agreed Statement." See also the Consultation's "Statement by the Orthodox and Roman Catholic."

32. See the full text of "The Manhattan Declaration" and a list of signers at www.manhattandeclaration.org/the-declaration/read.aspx. See also Jatras and Farley, "Orthodox Church Supreme Court Brief."

33. See, for example, Guroian, *Rallying the Really Human Things*, 228–31, and Engelhardt, *Foundations of Christian Bioethics*, 84–85. It is interesting to note that recent statements by SCOBA on topics such as environmental stewardship, the plight of Christians in the Middle East, and the need to address spiritual and moral issues in society have not employed the language of human rights. See www.scoba.us/news/official-statements.html.

self-gratification."[34] Such an approach forgets that humans "have their being in relationship to God, to themselves and to [the] world . . . of personal and social interaction as [well as] a material cosmos."[35] Father Stanley Harakas states that while there is a place for rights language, Orthodox moral theology appeals more naturally to "relationships that are 'fitting and appropriate" . . . [and] express a common vision of the Kingdom of God and find implementation as each person grows in the image and likeness of God, toward *theosis*."[36] Harakas writes that "Modern social and political theory in the West assumes the primacy of the individual over society. In this context, the exercise of freedom is an individually based right to do whatever one wants to do."[37] In contrast, Orthodoxy teaches that "Genuine freedom is teleological and consequently only corporately flexible." We find the fullness of our freedom in the divine image and likeness through "a quest of human fulfillment [in God] which cannot take place unrelated to others or without communion with others."[38]

Harakas claims that "Our creation in the image of God, the Trinity, places us experientially in a relationship of mutuality and inter-personal relationship. This . . . is certainly much more than the minimal claims of duties and right. But it includes duties and rights."[39] Though "rights are not at the center of Orthodox Christian ethical concern, they are not to be ignored" as they reflect "our inviolate dignity as creatures of God created with the destiny of achieving perfection." He lists the rights to life, self-determination, property, and education as being fundamental. In contrast to constant assaults upon human dignity in contemporary society, Harakas teaches that "the Church will do well to highlight such rights."[40]

Most Orthodox in America surely affirm that societies should recognize basic human rights in light of the dignity of the human being created in the image and likeness of God. Matters become more complicated, of course, when those rights are defined in detail and applied practically in culture and politics. Activists on all sides of controversial issues in the United States—such as abortion, marriage between persons of the same sex, gun control, and public funding of health care—appeal to rights

34. Clapsis, "Human Dignity in a Global World," 6.

35. Ibid., 7.

36. Harakas, *Living the Faith*, 187.

37. Ibid., 103.

38. Ibid., 104.

39. Harakas, *Toward Transfigured Life*, 192.

40. Ibid., 198–99.

language in what often seem to be interminable debates. In such a context, it is easy for the Orthodox witness on the dignity of the person to become subsumed by dominant political agendas that obscure and truncate the Church's distinctive vision of the human being before God. For example, Engelhardt states that the Orthodox "position regarding abortion can only be adequately understood outside of a language of rights, even one of a right to life. The language of the tradition regarding abortion, as well as other biomedical matters, is preeminently that of commands, proscriptions, injunctions and invitations to holiness, which direct to a life aimed at the pursuit of the kingdom of heaven. Even to talk of a right to life may obscure the integral character of the Christian life by suggesting that there are ultimate reference points for the moral law outside of the pursuit of the kingdom through Jesus Christ."[41]

No doubt, rights language falls short of the fullness of an Orthodox view of the dignity and destiny of the human being before God. On the one hand, appeals to human rights may serve as a point of contact with the larger culture toward the end of facilitating cooperation in practical efforts to protect human beings from abuse. To the extent that there is even a broken, opaque understanding of the glory of the human person in the language of human rights, there are present important dimensions of truth. Peacemakers should be grateful, for example, when secularists want to respect human freedom or protect the innocent from harm. On the other hand, the distinctiveness and fullness of an Orthodox view of the place of humanity before God will often be obscured by the use of language and concepts strongly associated with a dominant culture so imbued with individualism, pragmatism, and rationalism.

The Orthodox Church in North America must embody "a dynamic commitment to the praxis of peace" in order to be able to form just peacemakers who bear witness to the life-affirming way of Jesus Christ.[42] This witness must become more than mere words contained in the resolutions of conventions or the writings of scholars; instead, it must be an experiential reality manifest in the life of the Church, in the daily lives of Orthodox believers, and in efforts to engage cultural trends and challenges that present opportunities to embody the fullness of Orthodox teaching on the human being as one whose personhood finds fulfillment in eschatological peace of the Holy Trinity. Such fulfillment is not individualistic or reserved only for the distant future, but calls for "the peace from above and the salvation of

41. Engelhardt, *Foundations of Christian Bioethics*, 279.
42. Inter-Orthodox Preparatory Consultation, *Called to Be "Craftsmen."*

our souls" for all people in the world as we know it, as well as for the blessing of the entire creation. In order to speak with integrity about what this vision means for contemporary challenges to human dignity, the Orthodox Church in North America must live out the praxis of peace and become a living icon of salvation. If the Church fails to become such an epiphany, its statements will lack the power to form disciples who manifest the blessed peace of the kingdom of God that the Church celebrates in every Divine Liturgy. But if the members, ministries, and organizations of the Church enact the practices of just peacemaking, their actions will embody and make present the peace for which the Orthodox pray.

Bibliography

Assembly of Canonical Orthodox Bishops of North and Central America website. http://assemblyofbishops.org.

Basil the Great, Saint. "I Will Tear Down My Barns." In *On Social Justice*. Translated by C. Paul Schroeder. Popular Patristics Series 38. Crestwood, NY: St. Vladimir's Seminary Press, 2009.

Bos, Hildo, and Jim Forest, editors. *"For the Peace from Above": An Orthodox Resource Book on War, Peace and Nationalism*. Bialystok, Poland: SYNDESMOS, 1999.

Breck, John. "'Justifiable War': Lesser Good or Lesser Evil?" *St. Vladimir's Theological Quarterly* 47.1 (2003) 97–109.

Clapsis, Father Emmanuel. "Human Dignity in a Global World." 2 March 2011. Website of the Greek Orthodox Archdiocese of America. http://www.goarch.org/ourfaith/dignity.

Engelhardt, H. Tristram, Jr. *The Foundations of Christian Bioethics*. Lisse, The Netherlands: Swets & Zeitlinger, 2000.

Fellowship of Orthodox Christians United to Serve (FOCUS) website. www.focusnorthamerica.org.

"FOCUS Announces Local Feeding Ministries." *The Word* 54.7 (September 2010) 27.

Forest, Jim. Email to the author, 22 September 2010.

Forest, Jim, and Nancy Forest. "The Great Human Rights Issue of Our Time." www.incommunion.org/2004/12/12/the-great-human-rights-issue-of-our-time.

Gonzalez, Justo. *Faith and Wealth*. San Francisco: Harper & Row, 1990.

Guroian, Vigen. *Rallying the Really Human Things: The Moral Imagination in Politics, Literature, and Everyday Life*. Wilmington, DE: ISI, 2005.

Harakas, Father Stanley. *Living the Faith: The Praxis of Eastern Orthodox Ethics*. Minneapolis: Light and Life, 1992.

————. *Toward Transfigured Life*. Minneapolis: Light and Life, 1983.

Institute for Peace Studies in Eastern Christianity (IPSEC) website. http://www.orthodoxpeace.org/.

International Orthodox Christian Charities (IOCC) website. www.iocc.org.

Inter-Orthodox Preparatory Consultation towards the International Ecumenical Peace Convocation. *Called to Be "Craftsmen of Peace and Justice."* Leros, Greece: World Council of Churches, 2009. http://www.

overcomingviolence.org/fileadmin/dov/files/iepc/expert_consultations/090921_
InterOrthodoxPrepConsLerosFinalStatement.pdf.

Jatras, James George, and Paul Farley. "Orthodox Church Supreme Court Brief on Roe
v. Wade." http://orthodoxinfo.com/praxis/abortion.aspx

Krindatch, Alexei D. "The Orthodox Church Today: A National Study of Parishioners
and the Realities of Orthodox Parish Life in the USA." Berkeley, CA: Patriarch
Athenagoras Orthodox Institute, n.d. http://www.orthodoxinstitute.org/files/
OrthChurchFullReport.pdf.

LeMasters, Philip. "A Dynamic Praxis of Peace: Orthodox Social Ethics and Just
Peacemaking." *Revista Teologica* 4 (2010) 69–82. http://www.revistateologica.ro/
articol.php?r=24&a=3666.

———. "The Ethics of Peace: Orthodox Perspectives in the Americas and Western
Europe on the Invasion of Iraq." In *Just Peace: Orthodox Perspectives*, edited by
A. Semegnish, A. Chehadeh, and M. Simion, 98–116. Geneva: World Council of
Churches, 2012.

———. "May Christians Kill?" In *The Goodness of God's Creation: How to Live as an
Orthodox Christian*, 69–88. Salisbury, MA: Regina Orthodox, 2008.

"The Manhattan Declaration." www.manhattandeclaration.org/the-declaration/read.
aspx.

Metropolitan Philip "Iraq War Peace Appeals by Hierarchs." www.incommunion.org.

———. "On Iraq." www.incommunion.org.

Michalopulos, George C., and Herb Ham. *The American Orthodox Church: A History of
Its Beginnings*. Salisbury, MA: Regina Orthodox, 2003.

North American Orthodox-Catholic Theological Consultation. "An Agreed Statement
on Respect for Life." 24 May 1974. www.scoba.us/resources/orthodox-catholic/
respectforlife.html.

———. "A Statement by the Orthodox and Roman Catholic Bilateral Consultation
on Persecution of the Greek Orthodox Community in Turkey." 25 January 1978.
www.scoba.us/resources/orthodox-catholic/turkeypersecution.html.

"OPF Iraq Appeal: A Letter to President Bush." http://www.incommunion.
org/2004/10/19/iraq-appeal.

Orthodox Christian Prison Ministries (OCPM) website. *www.ocpm-scoba.org.*

Orthodox Peace Fellowship website. www.incommunion.org.

Reardon, Patrick Henry. "Not So Quiet on the Eastern Front." *Touchstone*, November
2003. http://www.touchstonemag.com/archives.

Schaeffer, Frank. "Stripped of Spiritual Comfort." *Washington Post*, 6 April 2003, B07.
http://www.stpaulsirvine.org/html.war%20on%20iraq.htm.

"SCOBA Hierarchs Issue Appeal for Prayer." www.incommunion.org.

Standing Conference of the Canonical Orthodox Bishops in the Americas (SCOBA).
www.scoba.us/news/official-statements.html.

Stassen, Glen H., editor. *Just Peacemaking: The New Paradigm for the Ethics of Peace and
War.* 2nd ed. Cleveland: Pilgrim, 2008.

Webster, Alexander. "Justifiable War as a 'Lesser Good' in Eastern Orthodox Moral
Tradition." *St. Vladimir's Theological Quarterly* 47.1 (2003) 3–57.

———. *The Price of Prophecy: Orthodox Churches on Peace, Freedom, and Security.*
Grand Rapids: Eerdmans, 1993.

———. *The Virtue of War.* Salisbury, MA: Regina Orthodox, 2004.

6

Christian Formation for Just Peacemaking as We Practice the Sabbath

Jeffrey Gros, FSC

When I taught high school religion, I would begin my course on Christian social responsibility with a film on the horrors of the Nazi Holocaust, to form my students in an understanding of the conflict, not only at the heart of the twentieth-century history in a particular culture and nation, but more especially the conflict at the heart of the human person, the inherent sinfulness of all of us—perpetrators and the silently complicit alike. If we are to form for a life of peacemaking, it is essential to focus on the very nature of the human person and our capacity for violence and redemption; on the core of the gospel as a graced call to responsibility and human community; and on the eschatological hope and imperative of building bridges and signs of the kingdom, on the journey to that future which only the Holy Spirit can give.

In this essay I will focus three themes for our discussion: 1) the Christian vocation, 2) the nature of the church as a community of dialogue, and 3) the strategic approach to prophetic witness. I have been at this Fuller Conference on Just Peacemaking in a listening mode, and very much enriched by all of us as we reflect on God's call to the human family, and to our Christian responsibility within the world. As I will note later, I have been very much enriched by the Just Peacemaking work of Glen Stassen[1] and the research of Howard Loewen.[2]

---

1. Stassen, "Baptists as Peacemakers." See also Stassen, *Just Peacemaking: Transforming Initiatives.*

2. Loewen, "Analysis of the Use of Scripture."

I. The Christian Vocational Call to Peacemaking

In the postmodern world, where we have moved beyond the Constantinian vision of a society that claimed to embody and enforce Christian values; all of our churches are, in effect, free churches, functionally voluntary, intentional associations in which members are drawn to the gospel by the free grace of God in Jesus Christ, without legal or cultural coercion.[3] This, of course, does not mean that we have no responsibilities as Christians to advocate for values we consider grounded in the common good for civil society, and for laws that reflect our particular vision of peace, justice and respect for creation. It means we do not expect society to impose our values for religious reasons.

However, we have come to expect that political and legal elements in society will use religious rhetoric instrumentally to further cultural ends that may, indeed, not represent the consensus of religious persons. Nor will they represent the biblical truths about society that some will read in God's revelation in Jesus Christ, whether derived from Scripture or from an interpretation of natural law. We may have come to separate religion from social controls, but religion is never separated from society and its policy debates. As Christians, it is important to continue to approach political rhetoric and even religious political rhetoric with a healthy hermeneutics of suspicion.

In fact, we have to form our people to see their vocation to discipleship in Christ in personal and ecclesiological terms.[4] Convictions about their faith and about Christians' obligations in society can no longer presume on a cultural Christianity or the supports of secular power. This was a hard-won conviction in my church, when the confession of Religious Freedom was promulgated in 1965; and it remains a challenge to be received in the life, faith, education and social witness of our Catholic people in places like Latin America.[5] There is still a tendency of some leadership in my church, and others, to slip back into an attitude of "aggrieved entitlement" to influence and respect, which was not the experience of Jesus, nor will it be for the church's often solitary witness in a pluralistic society.

The commitment to human dignity and religious freedom is a conviction that has yet to be received in some sectors of the U.S. community, as the current debates about Islam in our pluralistic society, or the ecclesial

3. Kauffman, *"Follow Me."*
4. Hahnenberg, *Awakening Vocation.*
5. Bevans and Gros, *Evangelization and Religious Freedom.*

and rhetorical legitimating of certain partisan political positions, continue to demonstrate. No party or policy can be identified with the Christian gospel. Yet, at the same time, the Christian vocation to peacemaking calls for engagement in the messy process of politics and policy judgment.

The vocation to Christian discipleship, and its call to peacemaking, is a voluntary conviction to which each must be formed to respond, personally with decision, content, and conversion. However, this does not mean we must all become Anabaptists. Indeed, a strong sacramental sense of church, the solidarity of the human family, and God's gracious call preceding any response on our part, is important for building a community of reconciliation and witness to God's will for the peace of the world. This sacramental and ecclesiological conviction is an essential counterpoint to the personal responsibility which is entailed in church membership.

Again, my church is beginning a sacramental renewal that should entail refocusing on an adult, conscious and faith-filled participation in the role of the community as sign, witness and sacrament of unity and peace for a world, torn by conflict. The "core ecclesiology of the Second Vatican Council made peacemaking essential to the church's identity. This is illustrated in the Council's profession that the church is 'the sacrament of union with God and of the unity of humankind' and in its commitment that 'the promotion of unity' is one of the primary ways in which the church serves the world."[6]

The process of Christian Initiation for Adults becomes a formation paradigm for training all to a sacramental worldview that contrasts to the culture of conflict, exploitation and inequality, which is the sinful human experience. To become Christian/Catholic is to become responsible for the peace of the human community and to a sacramental vision that sees all creation as diaphanous to the glory of God.

As the draft for the World Council of Churches 2011 Conference puts it:

> At its most fundamental level, the Church is a sacrament. That sacramental character is centred in its being a sacrament of the Trinity: the Creator's sending the Word and the Spirit into the World, and God's reconciling the world through Christ and the action of the Holy Spirit. This fundamental fact is represented and re-presented in the liturgy, especially the celebration of the Eucharist. The liturgy is an act of memory of what God has already done for us in Christ's Incarnation, life, death and

---

6. Christiansen, "Ethics of Peacemaking"; see also Christiansen, "Wider Horizon."

resurrection. It is also the window on the eschatological hope of the bringing together of all things in Christ that has been promised to us. This ritual act—where sin is confessed and forgiven, where God's Word is once again heard, where praise of God recalls God's great works, where the needs and the suffering of the present are commended to God, and where the Great Thanksgiving is enacted and shared in the banquet of Christ's presence in our midst—this ritual action draws us back into the Trinitarian life itself, that Life which is the beginning and end of true peace. In the Divine Liturgy as celebrated by the Orthodox churches, peace is named ("the peace from on high", "peace for the whole world") and extended to one another again and again. The sharing or passing of the peace is a common ritual feature in many of the Churches. And the injunction to go forth from the Eucharist in the peace of God is a mandate to carry God's peace into the world. So the Eucharistic benediction of the Syrian Orthodox Church says: "Go in peace, our brethren and our beloved ones, as we commend you to the grace and mercy of the Holy and glorious Trinity, with the provisions and blessings which you have received from the altar of the Lord." This carrying forth of God's peace into the world is what Orthodox theologians have called "the liturgy after the liturgy" and Roman Catholic theologians "the liturgy of the world." Such expressions remind us that the liturgy and the world are not separate entities. They are both enfolded in God's design for creation.

The liturgy, then, is the source and font of peace. . . .

That the Church is a sacrament of God's peace is the source of its being able to be a prophetic sign and instrument of God's peace in the world.[7]

Formation for a vocation to a critical gospel witness to the way the world ought to be, in its eschatological call to human solidarity in peace and justice, and responsibility for creation and society; cannot, in my view, be reduced to a merely voluntary, congregational ecclesiology.

[J]ustification is the work of the triune God. The Father sent his Son into the world to save sinners. The foundation and presupposition of justification is the incarnation, death, and resurrection of Christ. Justification thus means that Christ himself is our righteousness, in which we share through the Holy Spirit in accord with the will of the Father. Together we [Lutherans, Methodists and Catholics] confess: By grace alone, in faith in

7. International Ecumenical Peace Convocation, *Initial Statement*, 135 para. 52–55..

> Christ's saving work and not because of any merit on our part, we are accepted by God and receive the Holy Spirit, who renews our hearts while equipping and calling us to good works.[8]

It is grace that enables our voluntary good works; grace that gives the incarnational solidarity of the church as sacrament and prophetic sign of that peaceful community to which the world itself is called in the fullness of the kingdom; and God's grace that calls us to the penultimate, imperfect peace we build on earth by our nonviolent action amid the conflicts of human sinfulness. For the Christian, the justification we talk about as a gift is intimately related to the justice for which we hunger and thirst in the fourth Beatitude (Matt 5:6).[9]

There are scholars who attribute the vitality of twentieth-century Christianity to the voluntary principle within, especially, American ecclesiology.[10] While I can agree on the great contribution of Christian voluntaryism documented by Noll for example, I have lived among Southern Evangelicals long enough to understand that the international solidarity of the church catholic, with its interdependent accountability, is an important counterpoint to a cultural captivity that congregational and voluntary ecclesiologies can enable. Reconciliation among Christians is a calling and a sign of the reconciliation among peoples and with creation, that is our gospel calling.

The vocation to a global vision of the unity of the church and its call to peacemaking may be offensive to many who feel that the compromise of such solidarity is too high a price to pay for the purity of witness seen as the gospel command. These voices would oppose intentional, often pacifist, community to catholic universality and ecumenical unity. I have appreciated John Howard Yoder's challenge to his own community to see its witness as a prophetic, public call to the whole human family, and not the elite, ethnic preserve of the silent in the land. John D. Rempel argues for "a non-separatist but non-conformed" church, following Menno Simons and especially Pilgrim Marpeck. Certainly the strategies of the Just Peacemaking movement have charted ways of overcoming this sectarian tendency with integrity.[11]

---

8 *Declaration on the Doctrine of Justification.*

9. Stassen and Gushee, *Kingdom Ethics*, 43.

10. Noll, *History of Christianity*; Noll, *American Evangelical Christianity*; Noll, *New Shape of World Christianity*.

11. See Christiansen, "The Ethics of Peacemaking," 395.

We need to form Christians to see the vocation to nonviolent peace-making as the responsibility of all, at all times, even if some among us have a special vocation to carry that witness in a special way, whether it be particular ecclesial traditions, religious orders, issue-oriented coalitions, or movements that challenge all of us to the centrality of peacemaking. I am not called to live in a Catholic Worker house, but I try to serve on the food line once or twice a year so as not to lose the vision of my more radical confreres. The debates in my church at the highest levels during the 1980s as to whether, in this age, we needed to move away from Augustine's just war perspective, were productive for those who followed them. Pope John Paul and his then advisor, Joseph Ratzinger, moved away from this proposal, as the world was faced with the humanitarian, peacekeeping imperatives of Somalia and the Balkans.[12] However, part of this discussion has led Catholic leadership to move away from support of the death penalty in contemporary society. Certainly, the ecumenical initiatives of Stassen and others to provide concrete practices that transcend our theological differences are of fundamental importance, while the more theological debates continue.

In the age of terrorism, nuclear capability and global technological interdependence, peacemaking demands more sophisticated models than just war or pacifism, especially when nations with a significant number of Christians can legitimate wars of unilateral intervention, which clearly violate all of the prescriptions traditionally held by Christian peace teaching on the just war. However, this demand for more sophisticated visions of just peacemaking are not causes for paralysis and despair, but rather spurs to creativity in our Christian hope and discernment of what the fidelity calls for as we discern God's will for the church in new signs for our times.

Yes, formation needs to focus on:

- the vocation of the individual Christian as personally called to peacemaking;

- the vocation of the church to visible unity and visible witness to the mission of peacebuilding in service to the kingdom, and public prophetic witness to justice and sensitivity to creation; which are integral to the biblical understanding of peace, and

- the vocation of specialized movements and individual communities within the church to providing the strategies, and to holding

12. Schreiter, *Peacebuilding*; Philpott and Powers, *Strategies of Peace*.

us accountable to the reconciling ministry and mission to which we are all called.

II. Dialogue as a Privileged Tool in the Formation for Peace

The church is dialogical by nature—as the community that witnesses to God's dialogue with the human family in divine revelation; the community that brings its own members into dialogue about their heritage and calling and their responsibilities to one another, society and creation; and the community that dialogues about how best to proclaim the gospel, including the gospel of reconciliation, peace and solidarity. Concretely, our task is to build into the life of our churches experiences of dialogue, peacebuilding and analysis of and response to the conflicts we experience in our world, and experiences of prayer for and with our perceived enemies.

a) For my students, I always begin by putting them into dialogue with their own tradition and its resources before inviting them into ecumenical dialogue with the longer and wider reality of the church. Religious illiteracy is a major problem for all U.S. Christians.[13] For example, as president of the Society for Pentecostal Studies I am generating dialogue on the African American Pentecostal tradition centered on the Church of God in Christ (COGIC) and its Memphis heritage.[14]

We have to remind even our COGIC students of their peacebuilding heritage, and help them to witness to others around them. Founding Bishop C. H. Mason was jailed for, among other things, his pacifism during the First World War. He continued that witness during the Second, while encouraging his members to buy War Bonds, because of the justness of the cause against so great an evil as Nazism![15] At our March convention 2011, we had a COGIC speaker, Dr. David A. Hall, witness to the challenges of their Pentecostal eschatological millenarian rapture confession, and its deleterious effects on peace in the Middle East, when utilized to support certain military and political options in Palestinian and Israeli relations. Dialogue with the best of our peacekeeping histories and our sad failures,

13. Pew Forum on Religion and Public Life, *U.S. Religious Knowledge Survey.* See also Prothero, *Religious Literacy*; Smith, *Soul Searching*; and Petersen, *Theological Literacy.*

14. See the website of the Society for Pentecostal Studies, "Annual Meeting" page. See also Gros, "Ecumenical Challenge."

15. Clemmons, *Bishop C. H. Mason*; Hall, *Essays to the Next Generation*, 151–67.

equip us to build a more effective future, and understand one another's resources for building a just peace witness for our society.

b) I find pilgrimage among the biblical spiritual disciplines that nourish my own formation and enrich my understanding of the faith and its fruitfulness in the lives of our forbearers. In Memphis, the Lorraine Motel Civil Rights museum,[16] Mason Temple where Dr. Martin Luther King, Jr. gave his last *Mountain Top* address recalling the prophetic heritage of Christianity,[17] Bishop Mason's jail cell/shrine in Lexington, MS, and the historic churches of all traditions that supported the 1968 sanitation strikers; are all places that nourish the nonviolent legacy enshrined there. Bringing visiting colleagues through these pilgrim sites is a means of enriching the dialogue of peace and justice for us together.

c) In the summer of 2010, with Reformed colleagues from Grand Rapids, we made the journey to the now famous 300-year-old Oberammergau Passion Play.[18] Recounting its evolution from a traditional, anti-Semitic rendering of the medieval drama; to a depiction that emphasizes the Jewishness of Jesus and his disciples, the guilt of the whole human family for the tragic death that becomes our redemption, and dramatizing a clear internal division among the Jewish leadership; all demonstrate how the violence of the *Shoah* has pressed this small German community to reassess the violence that has been generated over the centuries by particular erroneous interpretations of the Christian narrative.[19] Study of this process itself is a significant contribution to understanding the culture of violence and its reform.

On our journey to Bavaria, places like Dresden, Prague and Cracow were among our stops. Reflection on the destruction and rebuilding of Dresden, its anti-Jewish iconography,[20] and the *Krstallnacht* which was initiated there; reflection on the modern Communist era churches of Poland including Nowa Houta with its chapel to Maximilian Kolbe and its stunning Way of the Cross set amid the devastation of Nazi and Communist eras,[21] the Cracow ghetto—and nearby Auschwitz; and reflection

16. See National Civil Rights Museum website, home page.

17. King, "Rev Martin Luther King Jr."

18. Weis and Dalsenberger, *Oberammergau Passion Play 2010*.

19. Shapiro, *Oberammergau*.

20. Frauenkirche Dresden, "Leben in der Frauenkirche." As one will note, below Paul you have a bent over Moses signifying the supersession of the gospel over the Law, and below the apostle Philip you have Aaron, representing the replacement of the displaced ritualism of Temple sacrifice with Protestant preaching.

21. Catholic Radio & Television Network, "Nowa Huta."

on the tragic Christian Thirty Years' War and murder of Jan Hus, so vividly commemorated in Prague, were part of the formation for the final experience at Oberammergau.

While the play itself is a fiction, like Mel Gibson's the *Passion of the Christ* or *The Da Vinci Code,* it demonstrated yet again how our view of the gospel evolves in the Christian imagination, and can be fuel for violence when the story is used to stigmatize and exclude the other; or as a resource for reconciliation, outreach, and proclamation of the love, which is the core message of our Lord's death and resurrection.

d) I work a bit with the Mennonite Benedictine dialogue called Bridgefolk.[22] I would love some day to provide a dialogue/retreat for this group in urban D.C. on the National Mall.[23] The retreat would allow for an open-air dialogue with the great monuments: Viet Nam,[24] Korean,[25] and World War II[26] monuments, possibly with films recalling the history of these violent wars. The Viet Nam and Korean are veterans' memorials, not celebrations of the wars, and carry quite a different character, representing quite a different America, than the World War II memorial. The stark wall that is the Viet Nam shrine, and the poignant aluminum soldiers, evoke the tragedy of the Korean conflict; while the traditional majesty of victory characterizes the memory of the Second World War. Of course, it would be ideal to include a contemplative day among the memorials at Hiroshima in Japan.[27]

I would like to provide focused questions to stimulate reflection and journal writing that would ask the sculpture ensembles about the mood of the country as it: a) legitimated the wars, b) remembered the experience, and c) healed the post-war wounds in the American society-psyche, the global human community, and the economic, political and ecological heritage of the globe. More reflection questions might ask how we can heal the memories, avoid the pitfalls, and hold out to our people a more peace-building future. Such a retreat could include a brief AM introduction,

22. See the Bridgefolk website for more information about this movement.

23. To imagine the setting for such a retreat, watch the YouTube video "Washington DC Memorials."

24. See, for example, the reflection in Garcia-Rivera, *Wounded Innocence,* 100–109.

25. See the Vimeo documentary "Vietnam Veteran's [*sic*] Memorial Wall and Korean War Memorial."

26. See the video "World War II Memorial" for images of the memorials.

27. Stassen suggests a week of listening prayer to enhance discernment of what God's coming kingdom entails and demands (Stassen and Gushee, *Kingdom Ethics,* 459).

possibly with some readings,[28] a day of silent wandering and contemplation, and a PM discussion; noting whether Mennonite and Catholic pieties brought different, conflicting or complementary interpretations, prayer perspectives, and hopes to the contemplative day.

I do not know that such a retreat would help us discern what God was doing in our past and calling us to in our future, but it would give us the opportunity to dialogue with the history that is our burden, and the challenge which is our gospel hope. It could enliven our imaginations to help us transcend, without avoiding, our heritage, and ponder how artists and society have attempted to contribute to our healing.

Experiences of dialogue with one's own tradition, with one's own history, and with the wider histories of the human family, can enable the growth toward that zeal for peace, healing, and reconciliation that are at the heart of the Christian calling.

Direct experiences of conflict, conflict resolution, and service in the world are essential elements in the formation for peace that Christians so desperately need. At our Memphis Theological Seminary we do a lot with Catholic Worker immersions;[29] Mexican-US border experiences;[30] Merton, King and Gethsemane explorations; an annual Gandhi-King Conference;[31] Northern Ireland journeys; and the like. Boston Theology Institute's work with Colombia and other such exposure to conflict situations, and those building peace in these contexts, are often life-changing experiences.

Formal dialogues, like those among the Peace Churches and the rest of our traditions, like those of Reformed, Catholic, and Lutheran bodies with the Mennonites—including the recent public apology from the Lutheran World Federation for its anti-Anabaptist confession and persecution;[32] working together on practices of nonviolent living and devotion;[33] and like the Benedictine–Mennonite US *Bridgefolks* dialogues,[34] or the Puidoux conferences between the historic peace churches and the classical Protestant and Catholic churches,[35] provide opportunities for experiencing the other, for learning techniques for peace formation from expert colleagues,

28. Like, for example, Geyer, "Acknowledge Responsibility."
29. Gathje and Kimbrough, *Sharing the Bread of Life.*
30. See BorderLinks website.
31. See 2012 Gandhi-King Youth and Community Conference website.
32. Lutheran World Federation Eleventh Assembly, "Lutherans Take Historic Step."
33. Bridgefolk, "Bridgefolk Conference Explores Footwashing."
34. See Bridgefolk website.
35. Peachey, "Puidoux Conferences."

and for working out formal strategies for peacemaking, and Christian formation in the skills of reconciliation.

The World Council of Churches *Decade to Overcome Violence* has produced some important discussion,[36] and has held an International Ecumenical Peace Convocation in Jamaica May 2011.[37] The results of these encounters have the potential for bringing grassroots groups together in prayer, support, study, and action.

III. The Prophetic Is in the Strategic

a) At the Franciscan School where I had the good fortune to teach in 2010, I gave the homily on the feast of the medieval Dominican Saint, Catherine of Siena. She is a great favorite of mine. She has a fascinating story: she was an urban mystic, who lived in her family home in prayer and service in the community rather than in a convent, which would have been cloistered from the world, in her fourteenth-century Italy. She lived in difficult times for the church, with the popes living away in Avignon, now part of France. She characterized the church and its leadership as afflicted with leprosy, so dire was her analysis of the corruption.[38]

However, she was also a shrewd and pious lady. While there is much to tell about her story, she is known for her diplomatic skills in convincing the pope to return from Avignon to Rome, to begin the task of cleaning up the mess of the era, and restoring piety, order, and discipline to the church. In this she was successful. As one of my Franciscan historian colleagues noted: "What Catherine wanted, Catherine got!" The points of my homily were: 1) the importance of a deep spirituality for those active in the world, 2) the compatibility of a political, diplomatic, activist ministry with the contemplative life, and 3) most especially, a strategic approach to prophecy.

For Catherine, her concern was not to demonstrate the weakness of the papal court, the lax discipline of the church, or the irresponsibility of papal leadership. She knew all of this and could easily demonstrate it, if called upon to do so. She could have preached against corruption. What she wanted, however, was change and change that would affect the good, and reform in the best way she knew how: restoring focused leadership and credible discipline through the institutional instruments available at the

36. International Ecumenical Peace Convocation, *Initial Statement*. See also Enns, "Glory to God and Peace on Earth."

37. See International Ecumenical Peace Convocation website.

38. Luongo, *Saintly Politics*.

time: a papacy located in Rome and carrying out its task in ensuring the proclamation of the gospel and the reform of Christian life in the church.

If we are to be prophets of the church's peace witness, we are called to develop formation and action strategies that are realistic and that work, and not content ourselves with being "right," righteous and perceived as prophetic. Some of the best prophetic voices are those that go unheard, but get bridges built, violence diminished, and communities mobilized to live nonviolent lifestyles in service of human reconciliation. This is why the ten strategies of Just Peacemaking hold such appeal.

We need to be as wise as serpents and as prudent as doves in our service to the gospel call to peacemaking and to forming our church communities in steps that will influence society toward a more nonviolent approach in international and personal relationships. Sometimes, it is careful research, and even journalistic excellence, that will make for a clearer and more effective witness.

b) Sometimes social movements become romanticized and develop a rhetoric that oversteps the bounds of the possible, displaying a temptation to Pelagian kingdom-building. It is important to energize the newly converted by a vision of a just and peaceful world that provides an imaginative concreteness to our Christian hope for society. However, this enthusiasm for a penultimate utopia needs always to be subordinated to the graced character of the future which will be given by God's in-breaking alone, and not built by our good works.

Such a zealous, but modest expectation, in service of Christian hope and charity, is a necessary, realistic, and strategic spirituality that continues to serve our vocation as peacebuilders, in the face of all the reversals that will inevitably be our experience in Christ's service. Some expressions of liberation theology are overly optimistic and undercut the spiritual commitment to the future kingdom that can only be expected in God's transcendence of time and human works. We continue to work as if everything depended on us, and pray knowing that everything depends on God.

c) The Latin American consciousness-raising methodology, grounded in Aquinas' understanding of prudence, can serve us well in our peacemaking formation: observe, judge, and act.

- Observation sometimes means scientific social and political analysis, or investigative journalistic probing, but always a careful realistic discernment of the demands of the times and resources for response.

- Judging always means drawing on the sources of Scripture and the Christian heritage for making decisions in service of the church's peace mission. Specific reexamining the texts in the Abrahamic traditions that have often been used to legitimate violence, injustice, and exploitation of God's creation, are important initiatives for us in providing the biblical judgments that will make peacemaking action possible in our traditions.

- Action means laying out a strategic plan for taking steps that will effectively lead to a goal that will bring more peace in, with steps as realistic and practical as possible. In this the practical just peacemaking practices give form to the vision and analysis.

The gospel of peacebuilding requires nothing less than the best formative skills we can bring to it. Christian prayer requires nothing less than an incarnational view of the concrete realities of what God is calling for: in relationships among people, communities, nations and the created universe. I am particularly appreciative of the Just-Peacemaking processes and the "Ten Practices for Abolishing War," that stand behind the annual Lord's Day gatherings and emphasis upon the integration of Sabbath with the other commands of the Ten Commandments.

1) These ten practices; emphasizing initiative, justice, and community, are clear, specific and practical, so they can be used with small parish groups, Pax Christi chapters, or full courses; like those of my colleague in ethics, Pete Gathje, in his syllabi from labor relations to global solidarity.

2) These practices transcend the significant, but long-term, traditional, theological confessional differences over pacifism or just war; on behalf of the concrete action of the churches together in the real world, here and now.

This is especially important for our Memphis Seminary students, who work in the militarized Bible Belt culture, whether it be the rural white south or the urban African American community. While we recognize the socially liberal character of the African American community and their churches, we also recall that the bulk of our armed services are drawn from the minority cultures of our country, and therefore are inclined to be less critical of U.S. military policies than we might expect. More can be said about the peacemaking, cultural impact of the voluntary draft in our country, but that question can be left for another discussion!

To illustrate the importance of this second point, let me recall the contribution, and limitation, of one of the great initiatives of John Howard Yoder. It was his conviction, from early in his career, that the pacifist witness of the Mennonites was not a social ethical particularity of one Christian community; but a confessional, church-dividing issue as central as any other element for the church's faith and order, as essential for unity as any article of the Nicene Creed.[39] Richard Mouw and I shared the conviction that this affirmation belonged at the table of church unity discussions in faith and order, whatever the convictions of our own churches on the matter.

We have been successful in including the historic Peace Churches' conviction in the discussion of the Apostolic Faith, with this pacifist confession taken as seriously as the sacramental, Christological, or authority issues that divide Christians. However, as the Notre Dame consultation in the 1990s demonstrated, that discussion is a long-term project of reconciliation, in which Mennonites will not yet recognize those of us who admit the possibility of any use of violence resistance, as gospel peacemakers.[40]

While important reconciling theological dialogue continues, it is imperative as the just-peacemaking process invites us, for Christians and—indeed—all persons of good will, to find concrete strategies for changing our hearts, our communities and our world here and now.

Indeed, it was wise for the Mennonite-Vatican dialogue[41] to focus on healing of memories and common peace witness rather than church-dividing ecclesiological questions; and for *Bridgefolk* to focus on peacemaking strategies, liturgy, and sacraments, rather than to tackle the major theological divisions of these traditions. We have a hurting world to serve and reconcile here and now, as we continue the calling to reconcile Christian churches.

3) My third note of appreciation to the just-peacemaking process is its commitment to organize and translate the rich research necessary to deal with the technical military, political, economic, legal, and theological issues that are changing in our world each day, into categories and conclusions that are available to those of us outside this arcane ethical world, in such a way that they can inform our prayer, pastoral and pedagogical life.

It is much like the contributions of the theologians who dialogue with quantum physics and molecular biology that feed my teaching of Christian evolution or the sacraments, or ethical specialist who help unravel the conundrums of Christian responsibility in the health care, immigration and economic reform debates for us. These professional ethicists provide prudential options on the complex decisions for ballet box and pulpit in the field of global and local peacemaking and economic justice. These are

39. Yoder, *Royal Priesthood*; Yoder, "Anabaptist/Reformed Dialogue"; Mouw, "Abandoning the Typology."

40. Rempel and Gros, *Fragmentation of the Church*.

41. Joint Commission between the Roman Catholic Church and the World Methodist Council, website.

rich resources on which we depend for nourishing our faith and action in an ever more complex world.

For all of these contributions to our formation and that of our people we can only be most grateful.

Finally, we reflect on how we provide for a day of the Lord, aside from the distractions of the week and the proximate imperatives of our culture. We take this occasion for a renewed reassessment of our vocation as Christian peacemakers, our formation to become a church of dialogue, and our prophetic calling to develop realistic strategies for building a just peace. These are all gifts of grace and not merely good works of our own doing. Our formation needs to provide resources for reinvigorating our vocation; for strengthening our zeal for and skills in dialogue, and for being attentive to wise and realistic strategies for changing the situation in the world in which we live.

We walk in a path that has been trod before us, toward a goal which we are given in Christian hope:

> Therefore, since we are surrounded by such a great cloud of witnesses, let us throw off everything that hinders and the sin that so easily entangles, and let us run with perseverance the race marked out for us. Let us fix our eyes on Jesus, the author and perfecter of our faith, who for the joy set before him endured the cross, scorning its shame, and sat down at the right hand of the throne of God. Consider him who endured such opposition from sinful men, so that you will not grow weary and lose heart. (Heb 12: 1–3)

As one of these witnesses so eloquently challenges us:

> We shall have a choice today: nonviolent coexistence or violent co-annihilation. We must pass indecision to action. Now let us begin. Now let us rededicate ourselves to the long and bitter— but beautiful—struggle for a new world. The choice is ours and, though we might prefer otherwise, we must chose in this crucial moment of history.[42]

42. Martin Luther King Jr., quoted in Steele et al., "Use Cooperative Conflict Resolution," 86.

Bibliography

Bevans, Steven, SVD, and Jeffrey Gros, FSC. *Evangelization and Religious Freedom: "Ad Gentes," "Dignitatis Humanae."* New York: Paulist, 2008.

BorderLinks website. http://www.borderlinks.org/.

Bridgefolk website. http://www.bridgefolk.net/.

———. "Bridgefolk Conference Explores Footwashing." http://www.bridgefolk. net/2010/08/10/conference-press-release/.

Catholic Radio & Television Network. "Nowa Huta—A Sea of Red—Trailer." Uploaded 2 October 2008. http://www.youtube.com/watch?v=nYZcSwBd_oM.

Christiansen, Drew, SJ. "The Ethics of Peacemaking: The Genesis of *Called Together to Be Peacemakers*, Report of the International Mennonite-Catholic Dialogue (2004)." *Journal of Ecumenical Studies* 45.31 (2010) 385–416.

———. "The Wider Horizon: Peacemaking, the Use of Force and the Communion of Charisms." In *Just Policing, Not War: An Alternative Response to World Violence*, edited by Gerald W. Schlabach, 192–214. Collegeville, MN: Liturgical, 2007.

Clemmons, J. I. *Bishop C. H. Mason and the Roots of COGIC*. New York: Pneuma Life, 1997.

Declaration on the Doctrine of Justification. 1997. Centro Pro Unione website. Lutheran World Federation/Roman Catholic Church; http://www.prounione.urbe.it/dia-int/l-rc/doc/e_l-rc_just.html#15.

Enns, Fernando. "'Glory to God and Peace on Earth'—The Decade to Overcome Violence, 2001–2010." *Ecumenical Trends* 39.6 (2010) 6–11.

Frauenkirche Dresden. Web page entitled "Leben in der Frauenkirche." http://www. frauenkirche-dresden.de/.

Garcia-Rivera, Alejandro. *A Wounded Innocence*. Collegeville, MN: Liturgical, 2003.

Gathje, Peter R., and Calvin Kimbrough. *Sharing the Bread of Life: Hospitality and Resistance at the Open Door Community*. Atlanta: Open Door Community, 2006.

Geyer, Alan. "Acknowledge Responsibility for Conflict and Injustice and Seek Repentance and Forgiveness." In *Just Peacemaking: Ten Practices for Abolishing War*, edited by G. Stassen, 87–101.. Cleveland: Pilgrim, 1998.

Gros, Jeffrey. "Ecumenical Challenge in the African American Pentecostal Community." *Ecumenical Trends* 38.11 (2009) 1–5.

Hahnenberg, Edward. *Awakening Vocation: A Theology of Christian Call*. Collegeville, MN: Liturgical, 2010.

Hall, David. *Essays to the Next Generation: An Interpretation of Church of God in Christ Faith and Practice*. Memphis: Church of God in Christ, 2004.

International Ecumenical Peace Convocation. *Initial Statement towards an Ecumenical Declaration on Just Peace: Glory to God and Peace on Earth*. Geneva: World Council of Churches, 2011. http://www.overcomingviolence.org/fileadmin/dov/files/iepc/peace_declarations/drafting_group/Initial_Statement_JustPeaceDeclaration_full.pdf.

International Ecumenical Peace Convocation website. http://www.overcomingviolence. org/en/peace-convocation.html.

Joint Commission between the Roman Catholic Church and the World Methodist Council website. http://www.prounione.urbe.it/dia-int/m-rc/e_mr-c-info.html.

Just Peacemaking Initiative. www.justpeacemaking.org.

Kauffman, Ivan. *"Follow Me": A History of Christian Intentionality.* Eugene, OR: Cascade, 2009.

King, Martin Luther, Jr. "Rev Martin Luther King Jr I've Been to the Mountain Top Pt 1." Uploaded 7 April 2008. http://www.youtube.com/watch?v=C2EnnclLMX4.

Loewen, Howard John. "An Analysis of the Use of Scripture in the Churches' Documents on Peace." In *The Church's Peace Witness*, edited by Marlin E. Miller and Barbara Nelson Gingerich, 15–69. Grand Rapids: Eerdmans, 1994.

Luongo, Thomas. *The Saintly Politics of Catherine of Siena.* Ithaca, NY: Cornell University Press, 2006.

Lutheran World Federation Eleventh Assembly. "Lutherans Take Historic Step in Asking for Forgiveness from Mennonites." 22 July 2010. http://www.lwf assembly. org/experience/lwi-assembly-news/news-detail/article/461/8/neste/4/.

Mouw, Richard. "Abandoning the Typology: A Reformed Assist." *Theological Students Fellowship Bulletin* 8.5 (May–June 1985) 7–10.

National Civil Rights Museum website. Home page. http://www.civilrightsmuseum.org/.

Noll, Mark A. *American Evangelical Christianity.* Oxford: Blackwell, 2000.

———. *A History of Christianity in the United States and Canada.* Grand Rapids: Eerdmans, 1992.

———. *The New Shape of World Christianity: How American Experience Reflects Global Faith.* Downers Grove, IL: InterVarsity, 2009.

Peachey, Paul. "Puidoux Conferences." In *Global Anabaptist Mennonite Encyclopedia Online.* 1989. http://www.gameo.org/encyclopedia/contents/P856.html.

Petersen, Rodney. *Theological Literacy for the Twenty-First Century.* Grand Rapids: Eerdmans, 2002.

Pew Forum on Religion and Public Life. *U.S. Religious Knowledge Survey.* Washington, DC: Pew Research Center, 2010. http://www.pewforum.org/U-S-Religious-Knowledge-Survey.aspx.

Philpott, Daniel, and Gerard F. Powers, editors. *Strategies of Peace: Transforming Conflict in a Violent World.* New York: Oxford University Press, 2010.

Prothero, Stephen. *Religious Literacy: What Every American Needs to Know—and Doesn't.* New York: HarperOne, 2008.

Rempel, John, and Jeff Gros, editors. *The Fragmentation of the Church and Its Unity in Peace Making.* Grand Rapids: Eerdmans, 2001.

Schreiter, Robert J. *Peacebuilding: Catholic Theology, Ethics, and Praxis.* Maryknoll, NY: Orbis, 2010.

Shapiro, James. *Oberammergau: The Troubling Story of the World's Most Famous Passion Play.* New York: Vintage, 2001.

Smith, Christian, et al. *Soul Searching: The Religious and Spiritual Lives of American Teenagers.* Oxford: Oxford University Press, 2005.

Society for Pentecostal Studies. "Annual Meeting." http://www.sps-usa.org/#/meetings.

Stassen, Glen H. "Baptists as Peacemakers." In *The Fragmentation of the Church and Its Unity in Peace Making*, edited by John Rempel and Jeff Gros, 103–18. Grand Rapids: Eerdmans, 2001.

———, editor. *Just Peacemaking: Ten Practices for Abolishing War.* Cleveland: Pilgrim, 1998.

———. *Just Peacemaking: Transforming Initiatives for Justice and Peace.* Louisville: Westminster John Knox, 1992.

————. Homepage. http://documents.fuller.edu/sot/faculty/stassen/cp_content/homepage/homepage.htm.

Stassen, Glen H., and David P. Gushee. *Kingdom Ethics: Following Jesus in Contemporary Context.* Downers Grove, IL: InterVarsity, 2003.

Steele, David, Steven Brion-Meisels, Gary Gunderson, and Edward LeRoy Long Jr. "Use Cooperative Conflict Resolution." In *Just Peacemaking: Ten Practices for Abolishing War,* edited by G. Stassen, 63–83. Cleveland: Pilgrim, 1998.

2012 Gandhi-King Youth and Community Conference website. http://www.gandhikingconference.org/.

"Vietnam Veteran's [*sic*] Memorial Wall and Korean War Memorial." Uploaded in 2011. http://vimeo.com/groups/480/videos/12101021.

"Washington DC Memorials." Uploaded 5 March 2009. http://www.youtube.com/watch?v=wt5A3GDzF1s&NR=1&feature=fvwp.

Weis, Othmar, and Joseph Dalsenberger. *Oberammergau Passion Play 2010: Text Book.* Edited by Christian Stuckl and Otto Huber. Oberammergau: Gemeinde Oberammergau, 2010. http://www.passionplay-oberammergau.com/.

"World War II Memorial—Washington DC: An Inspiring Tour DVD." Uploaded 2 February 2009. http://www.youtube.com/watch?v=XnaKsO_vvmM.

Yoder, John H. "Anabaptist/Reformed Dialogue: Reformed vs. Anabaptist Social Strategies; An Inadequate Typology." *Theological Students Fellowship Bulletin* 8.5 (May–June 1985) 2–7.

————. *The Royal Priesthood: Essays Ecclesiological and Ecumenical.* Grand Rapids: Eerdmans, 1994.

7

An Antidote to Violence

Liturgy Grounded in the Resurrection

Raymond G. Helmick, SJ

For a Catholic to attend church on a Sunday, or for those many who do so more often or even every day, the experience differs from that of Protestant Christians in a marked way. Catholics put great stock in sacramental signs, and understand their relation to Christ through them. For Catholic people gathering to worship, much as for the early Christians who gathered around St. Paul, celebration of the Eucharist is the most natural way to express their faith whenever they meet: Mass with very nearly everything.

Characteristically, the Reformers of the sixteenth century suspected the medieval and Renaissance church of having infused the celebration of the Mass with superstition. They reacted sharply against many of the externals of traditional Eucharistic worship: vestments, incense, ritual gesture, the cult of the consecrated species apart from the action of the Mass. They opposed the understanding of the sacrament all but exclusively in terms of sacrifice and wished to interpret it primarily as the table sharing to which the tragedies of life could be brought for reconciliation, even shearing the language of sacrifice out of the ritual. The manner in which Christ was present in the sacrament became a matter of controversy, as it had often been before in Christian history.

Catholic reaction to these strictures was defensive, emphasizing even more those elements to which Protestants objected. While for the leading

Reformers themselves—a Luther, a Calvin, a Melancthon, and much later a Wesley—the sacrament was precious heritage, their followers tended to be wary and the sacramental celebration became progressively rarer, a thing to be done among a small part of the congregation at a service, often with no sermon, apart from the major one, sometimes for only a small number of participants.

A disjunction in the minds of Christians of two things that belonged together, which for Luther were the two basic marks of the church, Word and Sacrament, followed, and remain the separate marks of Protestant and Catholic Christians in their worship to this day. Catholics "go to Mass." They have become quite used to services, sometimes shabbily performed, at which there is at times no preaching or where the preaching is drastically inadequate. *Ex opere operato*, from the very fact that the Mass has been offered, it is sufficient, and those who attended have done what they need to do, fulfilled their Sunday duty. The inattentive part of that is a matter of older habits, and much has been done in recent decades to overcome it. But Catholics have come for sacramental communion with Christ and feel keenly that that has been accomplished when they go to Mass.

The reforms to the Second Vatican Council aimed to broaden this concept of Communion into a sense of communion *in* Christ, with one another. That called for such changes as the use of vernacular language and the celebrating priest facing the people so that they can more fully participate in the action. As an added result, in more recent decades, biblical consciousness has grown greatly among the more committed or aware Catholics. They have experienced a new-found hunger for the word. They look for real biblical preaching and a truly reverent and moving presentation of the ritual at a Mass, a genuine renaissance of Scriptural awareness. If they get it, they are enormously pleased. But it is a bonus. With it or without it, they've been to Mass.

For Protestant consciousness, the Word is primary. While the sacramentality of Catholic worship dictates that music, sung or instrumental, should be basically processional in character, accompanying actions or proceeding to them, hymns for Protestants are a basic vehicle of prayer. They are sung in all their verses. Spoken prayers and readings must be presented meaningfully and with care. The sermon, it is expected, should truly reach into the hearts of the congregation. If it does not, people are going to replace the Pastor. And yet a convergence has come about. Protestants, especially those of the traditional "mainstream" churches, have in more recent times become much more sacramentally aware. The Table of the Lord is far more frequently celebrated and in some denominations even becomes a normal part of the Sunday service, its form more and more resembling what happens in Catholic churches. If it is so, and is presented with reverence and care, the congregation is very much pleased. But for them this is a bonus. The Word was the most important part of the worship experience, understood to be communion with Christ.

The Fathers of the Second Vatican Council, responding to a movement that had been gathering strength in the Catholic Church throughout the 20th century, gave high priority to reform of the liturgy, even insisting that their Constitution on the Sacred Liturgy, *Sacrosanctum Concilium*, should be the first completed of their major documents, promulgated by Pope Paul VI on December 4, 1963. It defines its aim clearly, including this deliberately sought ecumenical convergence even in its introduction:

> to impart an ever increasing vigor to the Christian life of the faithful; to adapt more suitably to the needs of our own times those institutions which are subject to change; to foster whatever can promote union among all who believe in Christ; to strengthen whatever can help to call the whole of mankind into the household of the Church.[1]

Christian life, then, not merely ritual, should find its expression in the liturgy. This is how "the work of our redemption is accomplished," The eucharist "is the outstanding means whereby the faithful may express in their lives, and manifest to others, the mystery of Christ and the real nature of the true Church."[2] It was to be conducted in a way that contributed to union with other Christians. To those ends, the Council desired "that, where necessary, the rites be revised carefully in the light of sound tradition, and that they be given new vigor to meet the circumstances and needs of modern times."[3]

Implementation of these ideals, clearly enunciated in the Constitution, took the Catholic people, both clergy and lay, into *terra incognita*. New ways had to be discovered, sometimes clumsily, but there were clues in ancient practices of the church.

That the actual arrangement of the worship space should change, with the altar drawn out from the wall and the priest put in facial contact with the gathered people was not actually legislated, but quickly became an obvious conclusion. Even as they voted for the reform, the bishops

1. Constitution on the Sacred Liturgy, para. 1.
2. Ibid., para. 2.
3. Ibid., para. 4.

hardly imagined that the translation of the whole transaction into the people's language would follow. People had commonly done something else, such as reciting their rosaries or, in earlier times, reading a "book of the hours" during the Latin Mass, but the "active participation" of the whole community called for in the Constitution[4] soon required the vernacular. Bishops' conferences were authorized to prepare the translations, and norms laid down that the language should, with all elegance, be the real language of social intercourse and always wholly intelligible. The translators into various languages took their ecumenical responsibilities into account, and gave attention to finding language common to the usage of other Christians.

A sense of mystery had long been cultivated by keeping the rites distant from the lay faithful, a property of the clergy alone. Thus the most sacred parts of the action had long been conducted inaudibly, sometimes with the people singing something else while the constitutive prayers of the Mass were recited by the priest silently and alone. In an earlier epoch, a rood screen, often preventing even the sight of the action from the body of the church, had stood before the sanctuary, and even when that was removed a railed enclosure, at which people would kneel for communion, had marked the separation of the sacred space from their intrusion. Now all was to be heard clearly, with new participatory responses added for the people and the space was reordered to provide a sense of openness. Effort was made to restore the ancient sense of bringing actual food and drink to the altar, from which some could be set aside for liturgical use while the rest was for distribution to those in need. The collection of money to maintain the needs and works of the community was associated with it. Reintroduction of the ancient ceremony of offering a gesture of peace to one another, long disused, expressed the relatedness of members to the whole community in an especially moving way. Gradually, Catholics ceased to see themselves in solitary relation to Christ and came to understand the whole community, communion in Christ, as supporting one another in faith.

All of this correlation of worship to life was consonant with the presentation of Eucharist in the New Testament texts. St. Paul describes the procedure of his Corinthian congregation, who, when they met, regularly shared a meal in the course of which the works of Christ would be recalled, letters of the Apostles read and discussed, and the institution narrative was told over bread and wine. Yet he tells them (1 Cor 11:17–34) this is not the supper of the Lord that they eat, because they do not share with one

4. Ibid., para. 27.

another. "Each one goes ahead with his own meal, and one is hungry and another is drunk. What! Do you not have houses to eat and drink in? Or do you despise the church of God and humiliate those who have nothing? What shall I say to you? Shall I commend you in this? No, I will not."

Sharing of the Eucharist, then, is to express truly the fabric of the rest of life, which will be constituted by sharing, care for one another and for all on the model of Christ. "For as often as you eat this bread and drink this cup, you proclaim the Lord's death until he comes."

"Whoever, therefore, eats the bread or drinks the cup of the Lord in an unworthy manner will be guilty of profaning the body and blood of the Lord. . . . For anyone who eats and drinks without discerning the body eats and drinks judgment upon himself. . . . So then, my brethren, when you come together to eat, wait for one another . . ." The manner of our conduct toward the other, which should be Christ-like, is consequently intrinsic to the sacrament.

This is consistent with the Eucharistic texts in the Gospel narratives: multiplication of the loaves so that those who have come to hear may not hunger on their way; the sharing of food with the needy, especially those who are spiritually needy; the disciples at Emmaus who recognize the risen Christ in the breaking of the bread. A refrain familiar from the prophets runs through Christ's repeated instruction: "I desired mercy and not sacrifice," and in the judgment scene (Matt 25) he tells us that what we do for the least of the brethren we do for him. The Eucharist as sacrament, then, enters in at every point in our lives.

"Discerning the body," of course, is the neuralgic point between Catholic and Protestant in understanding the Eucharist, Catholics taking a real corporeal presence reading of it. Protestant theology, in all its complex diversity on the topic, is careful not to make the presence of Christ an unreality but is uncomfortable with the literal physicality of the Catholic position. Christian positions, East and West, have varied greatly over the church's history, with the Eastern church generally emphasizing the work of the Holy Spirit and the spirituality of Christ's presence in the sacrament. The entire subject belongs in the realm of the most basic summons to faith that appears as a constant throughout the Hebrew Scripture: "The Lord says, 'Have no fear, be not alarmed; take courage; have faith; because I am with you.'"[5] This "I am with you" is the fundamental promise of God, the summons to put our faith in him, resumed just as constantly in the

---

5. These many passages are the topic of an extensive study of the author's own: Helmick, *Fear Not*.

gospel writing of the New Testament, where Jesus himself, the Word made flesh, is the ultimate fulfillment of that promise. His presence, promised unfailingly to the church, in the Holy Spirit, is seen in this sacrament of his body and blood, as also in his word, manifested to us in multiple ways, in the communion of our gathering—body of Christ—and in every person who comes to us, as the "least of the brethren," in need. This is the central fact of our lives to be testified and brought to fulfillment in our worship, on Sundays and whenever we turn to God.

From the beginnings of the Catholic liturgical reform there were dissidents, devotees of the old ways who saw any change in the distant and awe-inspiring mystery presentation of the presence of Christ in Eucharist as betrayal. Much more widely, for others the new-cast liturgy, illuminating so much of the reality of Christian life, was welcomed as a new window, opening up a liberating revelation of the full meaning of the sacrament and of the following of Christ. Practice of liturgy, with this new active participation, came to be linked with activism for justice and the pursuit of peace in the violent Cold War world of the time. Some saw all this, of course, simply as a change of spectacle, were reluctant to change their habits of piety, heard the new hymns as trivial and resented the disappearance of signs of devotion and symbols that were precious to them. But other lay people were energized to bring their Christian faith out from the sanctuary into the forum of life. There were extravagances, of course, bizarre happenings that further alienated those who found all this merely strange.

The reforms of Vatican II are fifty years old now, and one thing that has happened is a falling off of Catholic practice. Sunday attendance, once the norm taken for granted by Catholics, is down to low percentages—just over 16 percent in the traditionally Catholic Archdiocese of Boston—and it has become clear, a matter constantly under review in successive studies by the Pew Foundation, that while Catholics still remain the largest single religious denomination in America, the second largest is ex-Catholics. The Catholic Church right now is in a crisis of confidence with its own people, with extremes that put their faith either in the maintenance of a tight-ship discipline under hierarchical control or in a near-anarchy, distrustful of any authority, and of course a bewildered middle disappointedly wondering what has happened. Alienation is rife.

Different and contradictory reasons are given for this. For many traditionalists, bothered by the vanishing of familiar landmarks, the reforms themselves are to blame. Others would blame regression to older forms of a hierarchy fixated on power and the reinstatement of control, things that the Council had striven mightily to reform. The Catholic Church has gone through many shocks, most recently the sex-abuse scandal which burst on public consciousness in the earliest years of the twenty-first century, things arguably related to the assertion and protection of overweening clerical power, but the decline in faith and practice is older than the sex crisis.

What is notable for our study, though, is that the urge to pull back and circle the wagons has penetrated now to the realm of liturgy. New translations, imposed by power figures in the hierarchy who have taken the authority entirely out of the hands of regional conferences of bishops, have broken with any recognition that the language in which we address God should be the language we really use. An artificial language which seeks to mirror Latin prototypes down to the minutiae of syntax and even punctuation has rendered the texts artificial and practically opaque, and preference for literal cognates of Latin terms, even where they are themselves poor renderings of Greek originals, has often distorted even the doctrinal content of the prayers. Choices have been made that seem calculated only to reinforce clericalism in the church. After all the disillusionment that has gone before, we have to expect that this will reduce Catholic practice even more.

The current crisis in Catholicism is reminiscent of two comparable previous times of crisis that have left a legacy of disunion and alienation among Christians: the East-West division of the eleventh century and the Reformation period of the sixteenth. In each of those, the reaction of the hierarchical church was defensive and self-righteous. An equally defensive response now, we can be sure, will lead as much to division as before, but this time, rather than the formation of new church bodies, it is likely that people will simply walk away.

It was the insight of Pope John XXIII at the end of the 1950s, when the Catholic Church seemed too institutionalized and even sclerotic, that a Council of the Church, a grand consultation on the deepest meanings of Christian faith by its responsible leaders, was the way to revive it. Much was accomplished, but much of that has since been stifled. Many hope that this way of addressing it, a new Council, relying on the Holy Spirit whose presence has been promised to the church, will be chosen again.

In the meantime, what can we expect of Catholic worship as the seedbed for active lives of Christian faith? The best news is of a growing demand among Catholics for strong biblically based preaching. A contest is on with those who believe nothing else is worth talking about in church except the tired "social issues" which, important as they are, can hardly carry real weight on their own if they cannot show themselves as part of a consistent life of Christian service for the good of others attentive to the serious issues of our time.

Many Catholics of strong conviction are in fact finding, as they choose the most helpful places for their Sunday worship, that they are bonded, in Christ, to address such issues as the plight of the poor in our own country and abroad, the still powerful strains of racial discrimination in our society, the militarism of American life, with its appeals to a nationalistic messianism, the threats of global warming and disastrous climate change and the reluctance of our economic and political establishment to acknowledge them or act against them.

Those who share these concerns and make these a part of their worship are a minority, their voices easily drowned out by those who are so tied to the dominant political powers that they become captives of wedge issues that sully their Christian commitment. Catholics traditionally need their bishops on their side if they are to bring their convictions into the public forum. It is in the context of worship that they can build the strength and the formation, both in individual practice and shared community practice, to effect such change, including for just peacemaking.

Bibliography

Helmick, Raymond G., SJ. *Fear Not: Biblical Appeals to Faith*. Newton, MA: IPSEC and Boston Theological Institute, 2012.

Roman Catholic Church. *Constitution on the Sacred Liturgy:* Sacrosanctum Concilium. http://www.vatican.va/archive/hist_councils/ii_vatican_council/documents/vat-ii_const_19631204_sacrosanctum-concilium_en.html.

8

Yielding to the Spirit

Following Jesus in Just Peacemaking

CHERYL BRIDGES JOHNS

THE AGE WE LIVE in, like the ages past, is a time of war. The United States, in particular, seems to have a morbid fascination with this pastime. The making of war has become our country's largest industry, with an annual budget of somewhere between 800 million and 1.03 trillion for the fiscal year of 2010. As the United States continues to budget for empire building we spend over 43 percent of the world's share of military expenditure.[1]

In light of these statistics, it is becoming increasingly clear that as never before, Christians must discern the times and live faithful to the gospel's call for just peacemaking. Yet, it is hard not to be ravished with wonder at the shock and awe of empire building. Its glories attract us with enticing promises of security. And, it seems that many are willing to pay a high price for this security. Polls indicate that many Evangelical Christians see nothing wrong with torture and are willing to turn a blind eye to the new war policies in which mass assassinations are being carried out by special forces.

The heroic figure of Jack Bauer, who tortures people in order to save the United States from the impending threats of terrorists, serves as an icon for a generation. In its day "24" was one of the most popular television programs among young Christians. Many of my theology students planned their schedules so as not to miss an episode.

---

1. Stockholm International Peace Research Institute (SIPRI), *SIPRI Yearbook 2010*.

With such unprecedented build up of mechanisms of war, the loss of Geneva Conventions, outsourcing of secret torture chambers, Fuller's inauguration of the Initiative on Just Peacemaking is especially timely. Unless Christians make concerted efforts to counter the current obsession with war, we will continue to be swept into the glories and thrills of empire building and find that along the way, somewhere between "24" and the nightly news, we have ceased to be authentically "Christian."

The Failure of Reductionist Discipleship

Historically, Christian peacemakers have turned to the New Testament, and, in particular, the life and teachings of Jesus, as their source of ethical reflection. And, rightfully so; it is in Christ that we find our identity. The way of Jesus, the crucified way, demands that we swear allegiance to the kingdom characterized by justice, peace, love. It is to this "peaceable kingdom" that we are called.

I am afraid, however, that modern discipleship, with its reductionist tendencies fails to address the epiphanies of darkness that are present in a post-Holocaust world. In light of great suffering, war and injustice, many Christians are unable to provide a fully developed approach to just peacemaking. Instead, they seem to offer simplistic answers to complex and deep issues.

One reason for this failure is the neo-Gnostic lens of the Enlightenment in which people are viewed as primarily "thinking things."[2] The Christian worldview movement is a good example of reductionistic, neo-Gnostic thinking. This movement is represented among Evangelicals in the phrase "what would Jesus do?" and is probably best represented in George Barna's recent book, *To Think Like Jesus: Make the Right Decision Every Time.*

Biblical worldview ideology represents the height of Enlightenment thinking and modernity's emphasis upon rationalism. People are primarily "thinking beings" who operate out of information and principles. In fact, in the biblical worldview camp Jesus was primarily led by his power of reason and his ability to draw from his biblical foundation that was "clear, reliable and accessible."[3] Jesus was the ultimate Thinking Being. His Bible was a list of clear principles.

There is something missing in this model of discipleship, namely the huge divide between knowing the truth of God and becoming like God.

2. Smith, *Desiring the Kingdom.*
3. Barna, *To Think Like Jesus,* 6.

Larry Rasmussen, in his work on "Green Discipleship," takes note of this missing link and asks some probing questions: "Have we inadvertently been reductionist about following Jesus? Should our discipleship be more Christocentric than Jesus' discipleship?" Rasmussen goes on to point out that Jesus is utterly God-centered and Spirit-led. And he asks another question:

> Is there a discipleship of the Spirit? Discipleship is always associated with following Jesus. But is this a proper reading if what Jesus himself does he does "in the power of the Spirit," and, if he says he must depart so that the Spirit might dwell among us, guide us, and produce in us the fruits of the Spirit. . . . Or, if Jesus dares to say that his followers will, in the power of the Spirit, do even greater things than he? Are we sufficiently Trinitarian in our discipleship?[4]

According to Rasmussen, the lack of a robust Trinitarian framework for discipleship is that the God-centered Christology of an alternative servant community has been eclipsed by a "Christ centered theology of a universalizing empire."[5] Furthermore, "this absorption of virtually all of God in Jesus of imperial Christianity is the greatest possible remove from the theocentric Jesus and his yeastly, salty, seedy community way."[6]

If we marry a view of the human being as primarily a "thinking thing" with the transcendent *logos* Christology of Western Christianity, then it follows that ethical reflection becomes primarily a matter of rational discourse. It becomes a matter of simply asking, "what would Jesus do?" Or, a matter of reflecting upon the principles of peacemaking found in the Bible and following them. However, this type of rational discourse could not bear the weight of the holocausts of the twentieth century; it will not be able to face the coming challenges of the twenty-first. We are in need of a more powerful way forward.

We are in need of new ways for ethical reflection, ways that speak to us as full-orbed humans living in a world of terror. Even Pope Benedict, the great champion of *logos* Christianity, has called the reliability of reason into question. It is human reason, he points out, that created the atomic bomb, and the power of sin can make the irrational appear rational and can justify evil. Benedict calls this "the pathologies of reason."[7] It should be noted, however, that while acknowledging that reason needs purifica-

---

4. Rasmussen, "Green Discipleship."

5. Rasmussen, *Moral Fragments and Moral Community*, 142.

6. Ibid.

7. Habermas and Ratzinger, *Dialectics of Secularization*, 77.

tion, Benedict does not seek to move away from the *logos* foundation of Hellenized Christianity. As a consequence, he continues to plead for the Western World to turn to a *logos* Christ. He fails to realize how his very image of Christ has contributed to the demise of a robust Christianity in a postmodern world.

The question that begs for response is "how do we overcome the 'pathologies of reason' that have taken over our world? How is reason to be purified so that we can truly live justly and walk in peace?" I believe that Rasmussen's observation that we need a "discipleship of the Spirit" is a move in the right direction. Pathologies of reason are not easily overcome and epiphanies of darkness do not easily give way to the revelation of light. The truth of the gospel of peace is not easily embraced. Clearly, we are in need of a power beyond ourselves, one that takes us beyond the domesticated forms of contemporary Christian discipleship.

The Way of the Spirit

Jesus announced his ministry with the words "The Spirit of the Lord is upon me" (Luke 4:18). Before that event Luke portrays Jesus being "full of the Spirit" and "led by the Spirit" into the wilderness (4:1). Mark's Gospel uses forceful imagery stating that the Spirit "drove" him into the wilderness (1:12). From the beginning through the middle and to the end, Jesus' ministry was accomplished in the company of the Father and in the power of the Spirit. While Jesus was grounded in the divine life, he divested himself of his glory, submitting to the driving force of the Holy Spirit, "becoming obedient to the point of death" (Phil 2:8).

The divine life that Jesus empties himself of is, in turn, offered to his followers. In becoming nothing, Jesus allowed his disciples to gain access to the divine inaccessibility. Jesus told his disciples "I will not leave you orphaned; I am coming to you. In a little while I am coming to you. . . . On that day you will know that I am in my Father, and you in me, and I in you" (1 John 14:18–20).

It is by the Holy Spirit that we have access into this life of God, and it is only by the Spirit that we are able to faithfully follow the commands of the kingdom of God. Thus, a discipleship of the Spirit is necessary for us. Just as Jesus yielded to the Spirit, we too are to divest ourselves of claims to autonomy, power or glory and be "driven by the Spirit," "led by the Spirit," and "filled with the Spirit." Thinking like Jesus thereby comes as a result of our union with the divine life and our experience of the Holy Spirit transforming us, so that the good we know to do is the good we become.

One of the greatest obstacles to a discipleship of the Spirit is the ontological claim of the human being as the rational subject over the world. In this Enlightenment claim the world exists as the object. It can be acted upon, owned, manipulated, managed and conquered. As a result of centuries of this belief about humankind and the world, all of life has become objectified and commodified. Violence against other people and against the natural world is a natural outcome of commodification.

A Dialogue with Praxis[8]

During the late twentieth century the word *praxis* became popularized among those seeking liberation and justice for the oppressed. *Praxis* is an ancient concept that is grounded in Aristotle's vision of knowledge. Aristotle saw praxis as a way of knowing which was basically related to one's reflective engagement in a social situation. It was one of three ways of knowing, the other two being *theoria and poesis. Theoria* was the highest form of knowledge which utilized only the intellect. *Praxis* merged though with doing in the sense of interaction with society. *Poesis* merged thought with making, for example, the artisan's shaping of material objects.

G. W. F. Hegel re-introduced the term *praxis* in modern times. Hegel took the term and adapted it to the Enlightenment's emphasis on critical reason. He placed theory and practice together in a manner even more dialectical than Aristotle. Hegel saw *praxis* in relation to *Geist*, the all-powerful and encompassing Spirit which guided the universe toward the actualization of itself.

Karl Marx was influenced by Hegel's concept of *praxis*. He, however. put humankind in the place of *Geist*, calling for humans to influence and shape their own history. Thus *praxis* became totally an endeavor within nature, void of any transcendent authority. Human critical reflection and action would be sufficient for the ongoing of social reality.

For the most part, modern Christian activists operate out of the assumption that people are active subjects in the historical process. This belief enables empowerment and provides a sense of active human responsibility in history. However, at best, God is often relegated to a subjective presence in the historical process.

---

8. This section is based upon Johns, *Pentecostal Formation.*

Furthermore, despite all efforts to join theory and practice into a singular moment, there remains in *praxis* a fundamental dualism between matter and reason. Because of this dualism *praxis* assumes an unbridgeable distance between the knower and the known. The entire system elevates theory (in the form of reasoning skills) above all other forms of knowledge. The objectification of the other is an unavoidable aspect of this knowledge and the power of transformation is of necessity grounded in the "spirit" of the individual.

Praxis is, therefore, an insufficient means of knowing God and achieving human transformation in the way of just peacemaking. Human-reflection-action, while important, is distorted and may become self-serving, thereby hindering true knowledge of God. Without an authority beyond the self that transcends and even negates reflection-action, we are left, in spite of our worthy intentions for the transformation of society, with sinful *praxis*.

The Hebrew concept of *yada* offers more hope for the type of knowing that will lead us toward just peacemaking. It offers a knowledge that arises from active engagement and lived experience. Furthermore, *yada* is grounded in covenant, a relationship initiated and maintained by God. Knowledge, therefore, is measured not by the information one possesses but by how one is living in response to God. As Rudolph Bultmann explains:

> This knowledge has an element of acknowledgment. But it also has an element of emotion, or better, of movement of will, so that ignorance means guilt as well as error. . . . To know Him or His name is to confess or to acknowledge Him, to give Him honor and to obey His will.[9]

Bultmann points out that the New Testament, while employing Greek terms, continues the Hebraic understanding of "to know." Knowing the Lord is still viewed as being in relationship with God and in submission to his will. Thus, the Christian view of knowledge is in keeping with the Old Testament, and to know God requires obedient and grateful acknowledgment of God's deeds and demands. Therefore, "Christian knowledge is not a fixed possession but develops in the life of the believer as lasting obedience and reflection."[10] Christians are not merely called to "think like Jesus," they are called to follow the pattern of Jesus' intimate, experiential and obedient knowledge of the triune God.

9. Bultmann, "ginōsko," 698.
10. Ibid., 707.

Pentecost Knowledge

Before his departure Jesus spoke to his disciples about how they could, like him, live with intimate, obedient knowledge of God. The Paraclete Sayings in the Gospel of John point toward a new vision of knowledge, namely one that would come about with the coming of the Holy Spirit. By the Paraclete Jesus' disciples would not be left orphaned, but would receive "the Spirit of truth, whom the world cannot receive" (John 14:17). This Spirit of truth will prove the world wrong about sin and righteousness (16:8); guide into all truth and declare the things that are to come (16:12, 13); glorify Christ, taking what is Christ's and declaring it to the disciples (16:15).

As the Paraclete sayings make clear, it is the Spirit who knows all things and searches all things, who holds the key to the fund of knowledge. This knowledge arrives not through human critical reflection. Rather, it comes as a gift to the world. This gift stands in stark contrast to Western civilization's trickle down model of knowledge.

The Feast of Pentecost is the celebration of the receiving of this gift of the Paraclete and the gift of knowledge that arrives upon the winds of the Spirit. It is a feast that offers us a way forward beyond the reductionist "what would Jesus do?" model of Christian discipleship. This feast calls into question the modern project that places the human subject reigning supreme over the world. It does not offer a *logos* metaphysics in which there is a Christology removed from the earthy, salty, and Spirit-filled community.

The Feast of Pentecost offers a radical re-ordering of epistemology. It brings to humanity the possibility of *yada*, a knowing that is based upon intimate encounter with God. If offers to humanity a knowing of the Spirit, the same Spirit who searches all things and knows all things. Such knowing goes far beyond the limitations of reason and it exceeds the critical reflection of *praxis*.

What is not often realized is that Pentecost offers to humanity not only a new order of knowing, but an ontological re-ordering as well. Pentecost brings into the world a mockery of the human subject as grounded within itself. It offers an escape from the idea that the human subject has ultimate power over the world. Pentecost teaches us to relinquish the desire for control.

These desires for control do not leave us easily. One of the most important symbols of Pentecost, fire, speaks of the de-centering that is necessary in order for humanity to truly know the world. Pentecost brings about the re-configuring of the fire at Horeb. Rickie Moore points out that the events at Horeb and those at Pentecost are events that "claim" the participants. He notes that "to be thus claimed is at the same time to be disclaimed, to be seized, taken captive and dispossessed of everything previously claimed. . . . It is an experience so radically confessional that we, like Isaiah, can say nothing less than 'I saw God!'"[11]

Such events bring about what, in postmodern terms, is known as "the death of the subject." This death involves the purging of "all essentialized or ontological identities before the God who speaks us into existence."[12] Entering into the fires of Pentecost means entering into the fires of death. Such a death involves a de-centering of human affections, knowledge and will.

Pentecost brings into the world a mockery of the human subject as grounded within itself. It offers an escape from repressive human discourse and its accompanying arrogance. It points to an ultimate deconstructive power that offers death as the only way forward toward freedom. While modernity has taught us to objectify the world in order to know it and to master it, Pentecost teaches us to relinquish this desire for control. Under the canopy of Pentecost the self is eclipsed and transformed into an integrated, new world. Knowledge arises out of this new configuration of self and world.[13]

Moreover, the fund of knowledge is reversed from human standards. The Spirit who holds the fund of knowledge reveals the world to those who receive its gifting. Thus, knowledge is a gift of love. And, its distribution is given out among those who, in the standards of the world are unfit—the lowly. Thus, the uneducated can know the deep mysteries of God and the illiterate can read the world with a new critical lens.

Following Jesus thus becomes a way of "radical participatory ontology." The human subject is freed to actively participate in the Spirit's work in the world. As in the life of Jesus, there is synergy of Spirit-human vocation. And, as in the life of Jesus there is the ability to be led by the Spirit.

Love's Knowledge

The knowledge brought about by the fires of Pentecost may be characterized as "love's knowledge." It is a knowledge that does not arise from one's mastery and power over the world. Rather, as a knowledge that comes

11. Moore, "Deuteronomy and the Fire of God."

12. McClure, *Otherwise Preaching*, 7. See also Johns, "Epiphanies of Fire."

13. It is my understanding that glossolalia is a sign of the deconstruction of the self. It is the great equalizer—giving the uneducated and the elite the same language. With tongues, no one gets to "name their own world" or "speak their own language."

from a re-configured passion for God, it overflows with love. Martha Nussbaum suggest that "knowledge might be something other than intellectual grasping—might be an emotional response, or . . . even a complex form of life."[14] Borrowing from Nussbaum, Craig Dykstra observes that the lack of love's knowledge results in "liturgies eviscerated by the clouded eyes and perfunctory gestures of presiders who communicate all too clearly through their bodies that they do not know or do not believe what they are doing."[15] Furthermore, "Complacency before injustice. Fear of taking initiative until success is all but assured. These are all signs and symptoms of the loss of love's knowledge."[16]

The loss of love's knowledge is evident in our world. Knowledge is more defined as power, in particular power over the world. Pentecost re-configures knowledge, bringing it into the life of God. In this re-configuration love becomes the primary characteristic of knowledge. It is relational, dynamic and discerning. Persons filled with this knowledge love as God loves.

Love's knowledge becomes the primary characteristic for just peacemaking. The ten just peacemaking practices are, at the heart, practices of love's knowledge. Non-violent direct action can only be brought about when there is a relinquishment of self and power. It is a paradox to say that human violence is negated in the fires of Pentecost. Its deconstructive power negates human will to power and negates human violence.[17] The initiative to use cooperative conflict resolution comes about through the power of love's knowledge. Acknowledging responsibility for conflict and injustice comes about through the deconstructive power of the Spirit who knows all things and searches the human heart.

Just peacemaking initiatives that are Spirit-led and Spirit-empowered bring into the arena of human conflict the dimension of the Holy. This dimension transcends human knowing and human power. It brings about a fusion of the human with the divine. In this fusion there is greater efficacy than with mere human initiative.

The epiphanies of darkness that surround human existence do not give way easily. "Thinking like Jesus" or "following the principles of Jesus" are not enough in the face of this great darkness. We need a power greater than our own power. We need a love greater than our own ability to love. We need

14. Nussbaum, *Love's Knowledge*, 283.

15. Dykstra, "Love's Knowledge."

16. Ibid.

17. For an insightful analysis of the meaning of Pentecost for the peace movement see Valliere, *Holy War and Pentecostal Peace*.

the power of Pentecost. Until we are ravished with wonder with this great power, Christians will continue to be seduced with the glories of empire.

Bibliography

Barna, George. *To Think Like Jesus: Make the Right Decision Every Time.* Brentwood, TN: Integrity, 2003.

Bultmann, Rudolf. "ginōsko." In *Theological Dictionary of the New Testament*, edited by Gerhard Kittel and Gerhard Friedrich, translated by Geoffrey W. Bromiley, 1:689–714. Grand Rapids: Eerdmans, 1964.

Dykstra, Craig. "Love's Knowledge: Theological Education in the Future of the Church and Culture." Address to the joint plenary of the Association of Theological Schools and the American Theological Library Association, Denver, Colorado, June 22, 1996.

Habermas, Jürgen, and Joseph Ratzinger. *The Dialectics of Secularization.* Freiburg im Breisgau: Herder, 2005.

Johns, Cheryl Bridges. "Epiphanies of Fire: Para-Modernist Preaching in a Postmodern World." Paper presented at the annual meeting of the North American Academy of Homiletics, 1996.

———. *Pentecostal Formation: A Pedagogy among the Oppressed.* Eugene, OR: Wipf & Stock, 2010.

McClure, John. *Otherwise Preaching: A Postmodern Ethic for Homiletics.* St. Louis: Chalice, 2001.

Moore, Rickie. "Deuteronomy and the Fire of God." *Journal of Pentecostal Theology* 7 (1995) 11–13.

Nussbaum, Martha. *Love's Knowledge: Essays on Philosophy and Literature.* New York: Oxford University Press, 1990.

Rasmussen, Larry. "Green Discipleship." *Reflections: A Magazine of Theological and Ethical Inquiry* (Yale Divinity School) (Spring 2007) 68–72.

———. *Moral Fragments and Moral Community.* Minneapolis: Fortress, 1993.

Smith, James K. A. *Desiring the Kingdom: Worship, Worldview, and Cultural Formation.* Grand Rapids: Baker Academic, 2009.

Stockholm International Peace Research Institute (SIPRI). *SIPRI Yearbook 2010.* Stockholm: Stockholm International Peace Research Institute, 2010. http://www.sipri.org/yearbook/2010/.

Valliere, Paul. *Holy War and Pentecostal Peace.* New York: Seabury, 1984.

II

An Introduction to Part Two
Just Peacemaking as the New Paradigm for the Ethics of Peace and War

GLEN H. STASSEN

Here are the ten practices of just peacemaking, to which the following chapters on formation for just peacemaking refer. We list them here so you can refer to them as you read.

Initiatives

1. Support nonviolent direct action. (Jesus' way of transforming initiatives: Matt 5:38ff.).

2. Take independent initiatives to reduce threat perception (also Matt 5:38ff.).

3. Use cooperative conflict resolution (Matt 5:21ff—Go make peace with adversary).

4. Acknowledge responsibility for conflict and injustice; and seek repentance and forgiveness (Matt 7:1–5).

Justice (Matt 6:19–33)

5. Advance human rights, religious liberty, and democracy.

6. Foster just and sustainable economic development.

Include Enemies in the Community of Neighbors (Matt 5:43)

7. Work with emerging cooperative forces in the international system.

8. Strengthen the United Nations and international efforts for cooperation and human rights.

9. Reduce offensive weapons and weapons trade. (Matt 26:52).

10. Encourage grassroots peacemaking groups and voluntary associations (Jesus' disciples and groups).

This section exemplifies the ten Just Peacemaking practices as they illuminate specific cases of conflict and peacemaking in specific settings. The International Ecumenical Peace Convocation of the World Council of Churches' sponsored Decade to Overcome Violence, Jamaica 2011, issued *An Ecumenical Call to Just Peace*. These chapters serve to make specific what was called for at that convocation. Lawyer and church leader Thomas Porter introduces us to methodologies for addressing conflict, in ourselves as well as in engagement with others, particularly appropriate for churches as well as wider relationships. Inter-religious educator and activist Najeeba Syeed-Miller illustrates the work of Muslim women in the Islamic public square, a growing force for justice and peace. Through the lens of personal experience and as professional sociologists, Hope Straughan, Laine and April Scales draw us to practices of just peacemaking in the family. Nimi Wariboko looks at the world of finance and relationships generated by money through the eyes of a Wall Street banker, consultant to the Nigerian state, and a trained social ethicist. Martin Accad, Professor of Islamic Studies in the Middle East and North America, takes us to the heart of global challenges facing Islam and the West. Guatemalan Juan Francisco Martínez exposes us to the hard questions around the phenomenon of "disposable people" in the twenty-first century. Korean ethicist Hajung Lee carries us to the Korean peninsula, highlighting President Kim Dae-jung's "Sunshine Policy" and its relation to just peacemaking practices in an effort to find a peaceful solution to the long-divided Korea. Finally, bringing us back to the International Ecumenical Peace Convocation, Rodney Petersen provides what, in effect, is a summary reflection on the two parts of this book, issues of formation and practice.

Here is a brief explanation of the ten practices of just peacemaking as they arose from meditation on the way of Jesus, especially as revealed in the Sermon on the Mount. They arose from deep, personally formational meditation on Jesus' teachings as they relate to practices many are enacting in hopes of reducing the number of wars in our world. We hope they can be personally formational for you.

Dietrich Bonhoeffer begins his *Discipleship* (a.k.a. *Cost of Discipleship*) "It is not ultimately important to us what this or that church leader wants. Rather, we want to know what Jesus wants."[1] So he interprets the Sermon on the Mount—Jesus' teachings on the way of discipleship—the largest block of Jesus' teachings in the New Testament and the most often cited in the early church—thickly and richly, as concrete and specific commands. In Greek, they are commands. They are not optional; they are God's will, revealed in Jesus Christ as Lord. And they are grace—grace as Jesus' entering into our presence and offering us participation in community with him as he brings God's breakthroughs into our lives and our society. God in Christ is calling us into community of participation in God's deliverance, God's shalom. Bonhoeffer says:

> It is . . . the exact opposite of all legalism. Again, it is nothing other than being bound to Jesus Christ alone. This means completely breaking through anything preprogrammed, idealistic, or legalistic. No further content is possible because Jesus is the only content. There is no other content besides Jesus. He himself is it.
>
> So the call to discipleship is a commitment solely to the person of Jesus Christ: a breaking through of all legalisms by the grace of him who calls. It is a gracious call, a gracious commandment.[2]

And Bonhoeffer distinguishes the Sermon on the Mount from the cheap grace that reduces it to a thin principle and whitewashes it so it does not call us to repentance and a change in our action.[3]

In the two drafts of *History and the Good* in his *Ethics*, Bonhoeffer points to a further development in his hermeneutic for interpreting the Sermon on the Mount: The Sermon on the Mount is not high and absolute Platonic ideals applied to history from above, but points to what God is actively doing in history and in the responsibility we have to others in the world as it is.[4] So these are not "ideals" or "principles," but *practices* actually happening in our history.

1. Bonhoeffer, *Discipleship*, 37.

2. Ibid., 58–59.

3. Ibid., 43–56.

4. Bonhoeffer, *Ethics*, 219–88. Twice Bonhoeffer says he intends to write a chapter titled "Politics and the Sermon on the Mount," which would develop this more

Jesus identified with the prophetic tradition, which focuses not on mere ideals, but on actual history, realistically. He identified most especially with the tradition of the prophet Isaiah. He went about Galilee proclaiming, "so that what had been spoken through the prophet Isaiah might be fulfilled, . . . 'Repent, for the kingdom of God has come near'" (Matt 4:13–17). Reading the Gospels in English, we see Jesus quoting Isaiah often, but scholars who know Aramaic detect more than we can notice—Jesus citing dozens of verses from the Aramaic version of the prophet Isaiah by memory. Jesus was steeped in Isaiah—we might even say formed in part by meditating on Isaiah.

Jesus heard John the Baptist proclaiming God's word as in the prophet Isaiah, and Jesus said "yes!" He presented himself for baptism by John. Both Jesus and John taught in the tradition of Isaiah. And Isaiah repeatedly proclaimed that peace is God's will—as Jesus proclaimed all the more clearly. This means Jesus was commanding peacemaking as Isaiah had—*because it is God's will.* Peacemaking is God's will—in Isaiah's time, in Jesus' time, and now—which is still Jesus' time, the time in which Jesus Christ is Lord over our life.

Jesus proclaimed peacemaking also because it was desperately needed in his historical context. Anger was building in Israel against colonial domination by Rome, as anger is building among some Palestinians now against colonial domination by Israel. Repeated rebellions against Roman domination led by false Messiahs always ended with the Israelis massacred by the Roman troops. Jesus wept over Jerusalem because they did not know the practices that make for peace. He warned that Israel's lack of peacemaking would lead its enemies to "crush you to the ground, you and your children within you, and they will not leave within you one stone upon another" (Luke 19:41–44). Six times in the Gospels (including the Gospel of Thomas), Jesus warned that the temple would be destroyed. His prophecy came tragically true in 70 CE: Israel engaged in massive rebellion against Rome, and the "wars and rumors of war" that Jesus had warned against took place. Jerusalem was destroyed by the Romans, and Jews were exiled from Israel, as the prophets and Jesus had warned.

Jesus intended his commands to practice peacemaking for the real world of Israel's relations with Rome and relations with each other, just as Isaiah meant his prophecies for the real world of idolatrous reliance on horses and chariots, foolish military adventurism, and practices of

---

incarnational and grace-based understanding of the Sermon (*Ethics*, 244 and 298n191; the editors conclude similarly in 236n68).

injustice, which led to Babylonian exile. It is not right to relegate Jesus' teaching on peacemaking practices only to one small corner of life, or to a realm of Platonic ideals, and avoid Christ's lordship in practices of peacemaking in the real world. When we talk about formation for just peacemaking, we mean peacemaking in all realms of life, individual, church, and those policies of nations whose wars kill almost a million people each year and cause enormous grief and deprivation for many more millions.

So let us notice briefly some of the teachings of Jesus' Sermon on the Mount in terms of their meaning in Jesus' own historical context, and then seek analogous meanings in our historical context—as they point to *the ten practices of just peacemaking.*

In Matthew 5:21–26, Jesus commanded his followers to deal with their anger by going and making peace with their "brothers" (other disciples) and their "adversaries" (including the Romans). As N. T. Wright has written, Jesus' followers obeyed this teaching, became the peace party in Israel, and did not participate in the war against Rome. Instead, they practiced loving their enemies. This proved a more effective strategy of evangelism than trying to knife Roman soldiers. Rome eventually became mostly Christian. Jesus' command pointed to the grace of deliverance from vicious cycles of hostility. Going to make peace with an adversary against whom we have anger is participation in the grace of God's coming to us in Christ to make peace when there is anger between God and us. When people obey his command and practice conflict resolution with their adversaries rather than setting out to make war, it is the breakthrough of the reign of God—participation in Christ and in the Holy Spirit.

What practice of peacemaking in our time functions analogously to Jesus' command to go and make peace with our adversary? I suggest it is *the just peacemaking practice of cooperative conflict resolution.* When former president Jimmy Carter went to adversary North Korea and practiced conflict resolution over their beginning nuclear enrichment program, he achieved a halt in their nuclear program and international inspection of their nuclear facilities. When, however, the George W. Bush administration cut off the oil shipments that were key to the negotiated solution, threatened war against the "axis of evil" of Iraq, Iran, and North Korea, and refused to practice conflict resolution by negotiating with North Korea, it led to North Korea's developing nuclear bombs. The same may be true of Iran. It proved less realistic than Jesus' strategy of going and practicing conflict resolution.

In Matthew 5:38–43, Jesus diagnosed the vicious cycle of revengeful retaliation, and commanded the peacemaking practice of nonviolent independent initiatives—going the second mile, turning the cheek of equal dignity, giving the shirt, and lending to the beggar. The analogy in our time is the practice of *independent initiatives* that enabled president Bush senior and prime minister Gorbachev to reduce nuclear weapons by 50 percent in a short time. Another analogy in our time is the practice of *nonviolent direct action* practiced by Mohatma Gandhi in India, Martin Luther King and the civil rights movement, the Iranians who toppled the Shah, the Tunisians and Egyptians in the Arab Spring, and many others. These practices have proven to be a way of deliverance, indeed a way of grace.

In Matthew 7:1–5, Jesus diagnosed the vicious cycle of relating to others judgmentally, condemningly. We have seen that vicious cycle in U.S. policies of "war against terrorism," war against Afghanistan, war against Iraq, and torture of defenseless prisoners, in some groups' ideological and hateful promotion of Islamophobia, and in Congress's polarization and partisan blocking of jobs stimulus programs. Jesus commanded us to take the log out of our own eyes—that is, to take initiatives of our own repentance. The analogy in just peacemaking practice is to *acknowledge responsibility for conflict and injustice and seek repentance and forgiveness.*

Isaiah identified four kinds of injustice—greed that deprives the poor, domination that oppresses the powerless, exclusion that shuts out Gentiles and others, and violence. And he prophesied that by contrast, "the effect of *tsedaqah*—delivering justice—will be peace" (Isa 32:17–18). Isaiah strongly emphasized practices and policies of justice throughout his prophecies, and their causal relation with peace.

Isaiah 32:1 and 6f. and many other passages show that the meaning of the Hebrew *tsedaqah* is much better conveyed by *delivering justice* than the usual translation of *righteousness*, because in our culture righteousness is thought of as in individual possession rather than a practice and policy that delivers the hungry and the poor from the injustice that they experience. The meaning of *tsedaqah* is *delivering justice or restorative justice*, paralleling the meaning of *mishpat, fairness justice*. I will translate them that way in what follows. Both especially concern meeting the needs of the hungry and the poor, and confronting the power of the domineering.

Isaiah 32:1 says: "See, a king will reign in *delivering justice*, and princes will rule with *fairness justice*." Isaiah 32:6–7 says: "For fools speak folly, and their minds plot iniquity: . . . to leave the craving of the hungry unsatisfied, and to deprive the thirsty of drink. The villainies of villains are evil; they devise wicked devices to ruin the poor with lying words, even when the plea of the need is right."

Furthermore, Isaiah 32:16–18 shows not only the parallel meaning of *mishpat*—fairness justice—and *tsedaqah*—delivering justice—but also the intimate causal relation between justice and peace:

> Then justice will dwell in the wilderness,
> and delivering justice abide in the fruitful field.
> The effect of delivering justice will be peace,
> and the result of delivering justice, quietness and trust forever.
> My people will abide in a peaceful habitation,
> in secure dwellings, and in quiet resting places.

Again Isaiah 33:5 and 15 connect *mishpat* and *tsedaqah* as parallel, assert their confrontation of oppression and greed, and connect them with peace: "The Lord is exalted, he dwells on high; he filled Zion with fairness justice and delivering justice. . . . Those [can live] who walk righteously and speak uprightly; who despise the gain of oppression, who wave away a bribe instead of accepting it, who stop their ears from hearing of bloodshed."

Jesus taught extensively on justice, confronting the authorities for the same four kinds of injustice that Isaiah focused on—greedily depriving the poor, jealously dominating who would be healed, self-righteously excluding outcasts, and angrily advocating violence. In Matthew 6:19–34, he commanded that we not hoard our money for ourselves, but invest in God's reign and God's justice.

The just peacemaking analogies advocate the delivering justice *practices of democracy, human rights, and religious liberty; and just and sustainable economic development.* The spread of human rights has led to the spread of democracy, and during the entire twentieth century, not one democracy with human rights made war on another democracy with human rights. Political scientists call this "the iron law of international relations"—democracies with human rights do not make war on each other.

Furthermore, Ted Gurr won the national award from the American Political Science Association for his *Why Men Rebel*, which demonstrates that economic deprivation relative to expectations is a major cause of civil war, rebellion, and, by extension, terrorism. By relative deprivation, Gurr does not mean absolute poverty, but deprivation that seriously disappoints expectations. This is what most terrorists have experienced. Just peacemaking advocates *just and sustainable economic justice.*

Jesus diagnosed the vicious cycle of loving only our friends and hating our enemies. He commanded we love our enemies and pray for them, as God shines warm sun and rains life-giving rain on God's enemies as well as friends (Matt 5:43–47). Isaiah 49:5 also proclaimed "I will give you as a light to the nations, that my salvation may reach to the end of the earth." And: "Do not let the foreigner . . . say, 'The Lord will surely separate me from his people'. . . . The foreigners who join themselves to the Lord, . . . these I will bring to my holy mountain, and make them joyful in my house of prayer; . . . for my house shall be called a house of prayer for *all peoples.*"

The analogous practice in war-prevention is to *engage all nations, including enemies, in international community—in the United Nations, in regional organizations, in trade, in human travel and internet communication, etc.* Empirical evidence in the book *Just Peacemaking: the New Paradigm for the Ethics of Peace and War* indicates that the more nations engage in international community, the less often they make war or have war made against them. So two just peacemaking practices are "Work with emerging cooperative forces in the international system," and "Strengthen the United Nations and international efforts for cooperation and human rights."

Furthermore, in line with the prophets' warnings against idolatrous, exaggerated, foolish trust in war horses and war chariots instead of the Lord (Isa 31:1–5), Jesus intentionally rode into Jerusalem on a donkey, not a war horse, fulfilling Zechariah 9:9–10:

> Rejoice greatly, O daughter Zion!
> Shout aloud, O daughter Jerusalem!
> Lo your king comes to you,
> Triumphant and victorious is he,
> Humble and riding on a donkey,
> On a colt, the foal of a donkey,
> He will cut off the chariot from Ephraim,
> And the war horse from Jerusalem,
> And the battle bow shall he cut off,
> And he shall command peace to the nations.

On the Lord's Day that is Palm Sunday, every church should make clear to its people that the meaning of Palm Sunday is Jesus' fulfillment of Zechariah's prophecy of the coming of the King of Peace. We should read that prophecy and display it so people get the message.

In Matthew 26:52, Jesus also taught:

> Put your sword back into its place:
>> For all
>>> who take up the sword
>>> by the sword
>> will perish.

The analogous practice that just peacemaking advocates is to *reduce offensive weapons and the weapons trade*. Empirical evidence indicates that nations are realizing war does not pay, since the weapons possessed by an opponent have become so destructive that they can do enormous damage in response to an attack. Hence nations are initiating war less often. The exception sometimes occurs when a government believes it has such preponderant offensive power that the other side cannot retaliate effectively. Serbia during Milosevic's rule believed that, and the United States during George W. Bush's presidency believed that, and each declared three wars—which worked out very badly for everyone. Thus reducing offensive weapons reduces the temptation to make war.

Finally, Jesus worked on developing a group of disciples, and traveled from village to village, beginning groups of followers in various villages. Isaiah and other prophets likewise had a group of disciples. The analogous practice in our time is to *join grassroots peacemaking groups* both in churches and in the society. Alone, we feel uninformed and powerless. Together, we are better informed, and can become connected by internet to other peacemaker groups acting simultaneously to make changes for peace. A joke in Egypt during the Arab Spring has former Egyptian leader Nasser saying he was deposed by poison, Sadat saying he was deposed by gunshot, and Mubarak saying he was deposed by Facebook.

These ten just peacemaking practices are also supported by many other biblical teachings beyond the Sermon on the Mount. They are supported by widespread Christian teachings of grace, the common good, human rights, love, and justice. Grace is not simply about refraining from doing something, such as violence, but even more about God's taking initiative toward us and calling us to take initiatives of love, reconciliation, justice, compassion, and peace. Just peacemaking is not an ethics simply of refraining from doing violence, but of taking initiatives that are effective in delivering us from violence.

Milton Leitenberg of the University of Maryland's School for International and Security Studies has estimated that war and state-sponsored genocide in the first 45 years of the twentieth century killed as many as 190 million people, both directly and indirectly. That comes to an average of 4.2 million deaths per year. His analysis found that wars killed fewer than one-fifth of that total in the last 55 years of the twentieth century—750,000 per year.[5] The second half of the twentieth century is when

5. Milton Leitenberg, "Deaths in Wars and Conflicts in the 20th Century," Cornell University Peace Studies Program Occasional Paper #29, 3d edition (August 2003, 2005,

the ten practices of just peacemaking were developed and began to be practiced. They get results. They reduce the number of wars dramatically, They call for our support. They call for us to prod governments to practice them, and to practice their analogous initiatives in our congregations and in our relationships. They are for Sabbath relationships, and for relationships in the world the other six days of the week.

This has been intentionally a *brief summary* of the ten practices of just peacemaking that are in fact preventing many wars. Fuller accounts can be found in the books *Just Peacemaking* and *Interfaith Just Peacemaking*, as well as in discussions of contemporary issues on the www.JustPeacemaking.org website. We are urging people not simply to advocate just peacemaking as a general concept, but to know and advocate the *ten specific practices* that are achieving the actual peacemaking results so they can urge friends to support them. They are easy to remember: four transforming initiatives—nonviolent action, independent initiatives, conflict resolution, and acknowledging responsibility; two justice practices—human rights and sustainable economic justice; four community practices—international networks, United Nations, reduce weapons, and join groups.

We do not quite claim these ten practices have authority equal to the ten commandments, but we do claim they are present-day implications of Jesus' teachings on peacemaking, and they are proving effective in preventing actual wars. It is important to remember and to advocate the ten practices of just peacemaking, and it is crucially important to form people who do.

Other books have written about just peacemaking practices, but none has focused on formation of people and congregations that practice just peacemaking. Our focus here is how to form actual just peacemakers. We think this is enormously important, and is empowering. We can all work on formation. It is enormously important. We hope you will agree, and get to work.

Bibliography

Bonhoeffer, Dietrich. *Discipleship*. DBWE, vol. 4. Minneapolis: Fortress, 2001.

———. *Ethics*, DBWE, vol. 6. Minneapolis: Fortress, 2001.

Horgan, John. "Does Peace Have a Chance?" *Slate*, 4 August 2009. http://www.slate.com/id/2224275/.

World Council of Churches. *An Ecumenical Call to Just Peace*. Geneva: World Council of Churches, n.d. http://www.overcomingviolence.org/fileadmin/dov/files/iepc/resources/ECJustPeace_English.pdf.

2006). This includes civil wars and wars against people within states, in both periods.

9

Learning to Engage Conflict Well

Mediation Strategies

THOMAS PORTER

FOR THE PAST TWELVE years, I have had the good fortune of working for the JustPeace Center for Mediation and Conflict Transformation of the United Methodist Church, developing a faith-based understanding of what it means to be a justpeace practitioner and a justpeace church—a church that practices the ministry of reconciliation. Since 2004, I have also been part of the Religion and Conflict Transformation program at Boston University School of Theology, where we take seriously the need for the spiritual formation of religious leaders as ministers of reconciliation, deeply informed by theology, theory and practice. In this work, I have personally experienced my life as a lawyer, mediator, minister, teacher and citizen coming together in a remarkable way—the JustPeace Way. I want to tell some of what I have learned. It will especially articulate the just peacemaking practices of cooperative conflict resolution, and to some extent the practices of justice and of acknowledgment, forgiveness, and repentance.

Early on in this work, the board of JustPeace suggested that we put on a wallet card the major themes of this practice—this way of life. I admitted that our work was not rocket science, but I could not imagine how we could do justice to these themes on a card. They insisted and the following was the result, with the four ways of preparing oneself and coaching others on one side, and the six ways of engaging others on the back of the card.

Prepare Yourself for Conflict Transformation
Create a well, not a wall.

Create in yourself an openness to conflict as a natural and necessary part of God's creation, an opportunity for growth and revelation.

Allow the well to fill.

Open your heart and mind to God's love, drawing you toward reconciliation and being a reconciler.

Be well prepared.

Be prepared to listen for understanding, speak the truth in love, use your imagination, and practice forgiveness.

Be well. Be a well.

Be a mediating presence in the midst of conflict.

Engage Others in Conflict Transformation
Create a common well together.

Design a circle process for a good conversation to get to a better place together.

Share the well.

Together open yourselves to God through ritual and to each other through a relational covenant

Appreciate the life-giving waters.

Elicit stories of peak experiences, grace-filled moments, and dreams of a preferred future.

Go beneath the surface.

Move from positions to interests and needs, generating options to reach consensus.

Drink deeply the healing waters.

Move from retribution to restoration: healing the harm, affirming accountability, and creating a new relationship.

Be well together.

Celebrate each step toward communal healing.
Be prayerful, persistent and patient.

These themes were more fully developed, first, in a pamphlet entitled *Engaging Conflict Well*,[1] and then in a book, *The Spirit and Art of Conflict Transformation: Creating a Culture of JustPeace*.[2] As you will see the emphasis is on the local church, the local community whether in Des Moines or in Johannesburg, as a locus and focus for building justpeace and doing the work of reconciliation. This emphasis is shared by the writers in the Introduction to *Just Peacemaking*, "Political science and sociology are now discovering how crucial are grassroots groups, nongovernmental organization, churches, meeting houses, mosques, and synagogues, and civil society to build the foundation for secure and peaceful societies . . ."[3] We ask ourselves this question: What if every church in the world became a neighborhood reconciliation center? These ten themes, we believe, are essential to the formation of such a people. As religious leaders we need to prepare ourselves for this work of conflict transformation, peacebuilding, and reconciliation and we will be called on to coach others as they prepare for this work. Let's begin with the first four practices.

Preparing Ourselves and Coaching Others

Nothing is ever linear in this work. However, we do not get very far if our *attitude* towards conflict says that it is always destructive and that we should avoid it, allowing it to fester to the point where we explode with destructive responses of our own. Our attitude to conflict is important to our practice and determines whether it becomes destructive or constructive. Often a constructive response will first heighten conflict before dialogue and mediation can begin. Ultimately, our attitude to conflict is a matter of faith. Dealing with conflict is where the rubber of faith meets the road of life. Do we believe the scripture which says, "Be strong and courageous; do not be frightened or dismayed, for the Lord your God is with you wherever you go" (Josh 1:9)? Injustice is not addressed without conflict. Growth and revelation do not occur without conflict. We can engage conflict in constructive ways or destructive ways. The point here is that we can engage it and not just avoid it. Yes, it takes courage. Yes, it involves risk. But God is with us.

1. This booklet was published in 2001 by the JustPeace Center for Mediation and Conflict Transformation.

2. This article summarizes the major themes of this book with excerpts, with the permission of the publisher.

3. Stassen, *Just Peacemaking: The New Paradigm*, 29–30.

Our *theology* matters! It matters to our practice. Peacebuilding is at the heart of the gospel. Paul often calls God the "God of peace" (Rom 15:21; 16:20; 1 Cor 14.33; 2 Cor 13:11; Phil 4:9; 1 Thess 5:23). At Jesus' birth the angels proclaimed peace on earth (Luke 2:14). Each of the first six of Jesus' beatitudes prepares for and builds to the seventh beatitude: "Blessed are the peacemakers, for they will be called children of God" (Matt 5:9). In Acts, Luke sums up the ministry of Jesus as "preaching peace" (Acts 10:36). The Bible teaches us what is now being confirmed, for example, by neuroscience. We are made for relationships. We are interconnected and interdependent. We are who we are because of our relationships. We are created for relationship with God and neighbor. The Great Commandment is not only the sum of the law and the prophets; it is the central truth and reality of life. Key to our practice is an understanding that we are called to love God, neighbor and self in all we do. We are called to a journey of reconciliation (2 Cor 5:18–20). In short, we need to rediscover, to be grounded in and guided by reconciliation and peacebuilding as the essential themes of the Bible and of the life, ministry, death, and resurrection of Jesus, who was Emmanuel, God with us.

Skills matter! We can have a faithful attitude and theology, but we also need the skills to make our actions constructive. The skills that we emphasize are listening for understanding, speaking the truth in love, using our imagination and practicing forgiveness. For us, the skills are spiritual disciplines that are critical to the spiritual life, the relational life. They involve a lifetime of practice. These skills come together in a conversation that is transformative and healing. These skills are always formed, informed and guided by a love that is compassionate, kind, humble, meek, patient, forgiving, and grateful (see Col 3:12–15).

Listening for understanding is an art and practice of caring—a gift to the other. Being listened to provides the opening we need to tell our stories, to express feelings and ideas we would otherwise be afraid to voice or unable to voice. Listening creates the possibility of learning and being changed, enriching our lives. If we do not listen, our creativity, flexibility, and ability to grow and learn are diminished; our universe is diminished. Listening involves creating the space for listening, asking questions that open up the other's story and letting the other know that she or he has been heard.

Speaking the truth in love is an art of communicating our story in a way that opens up a conversation. God speaks and there is light (Gen 1:3). In my study of the Truth and Reconciliation Commission in South Africa, I saw the power of stories and the importance of providing a space where these stories can be told. Nothing is more powerful in changing our views and opinions than hearing the personal story of another. How we tell our stories matters. Later we will talk about the importance of Holy Communion in the formation of the peacebuilder, but here we can affirm what Jesus taught us at the Last Supper: to name the truth, "one of you is going to betray me," and then to give bread, not a stone or punishment. Naming to give bread, to heal, changes the way we speak the truth.

Using our imagination releases our creativity, opens our minds and hearts to the leading of the Holy Spirit, which involves being carried by the Spirit to places and ideas we never dreamed possible. Much of our destructive conflict is due to the failure of our imagination. Violence is the ultimate sign of a failure of the imagination. Using our imagination involves improvisation, reframing, brainstorming, being flexible, and being open to the moment, to the other, and to the deep resources of the Spirit.

Being forgiving is an essential practice for breaking out of the cycles of violence and retribution in this world. As Bishop Tutu says, there is "No Future without Forgiveness."[4] Forgiveness is a journey that includes mourning as well as a rehumanizing of the one who harms us; a choice, a decision we make; primarily a gift we give to ourselves; and a gift we give the other. Forgiveness is not reconciliation, but it is critical to reconciliation. L. Gregory Jones describes forgiveness as a craft that can be learned. We will have plenty of opportunities to practice.

So our attitude, our theology and our skills matter. We also need to be formed by the character and *virtues* of the peacebuilder, and we need to understand the *role* that we can and should play. Both are important to our own well being and the well being of those with whom we engage in peacebuilding. What follows is a summary of some of the virtues and practices that we have found helpful to those who facilitate peacebuilding.

Let Go of Striving for Status or Control

- Give up the desire to control the outcome.
- Let the conversation flow without feeling you need to control it.
- Give all the credit for any success to the participants.

---

4. Tutu, *No Future without Forgiveness*, the title of the book.

Develop a Relationship of Respect and Trust with Each Party

- Help others see their interdependence and interconnection with each other.
- Spend as much time as needed with each party to develop a relationship of respect and trust, motivated by curiosity and genuine caring.
- Prayerfully open up space in one's self for the Spirit and each of the parties.
- Maintain confidences.
- Be impartial, fair, principled and committed to the legitimate needs of all.
- Trust your own instincts.

Bring a Sense of Gratitude and Abundance to the Process

- See each party as a child of God with unique gifts and resources.
- See yourself as a discoverer of the gifts and resources of the parties.
- Empower the parties to find their own voice, tell their own stories and find their own healing solution.
- Express gratitude to the parties for their courage and their wisdom in coming together and for their faith in being able to resolve their differences.
- Open the imagination and abundant resources of the parties, helping them expand the pie.
- Bring a playful spirit, a lightness of being, to the process.
- Exercise before a process to relieve some of the tension in your own body.
- Be forever hopeful and optimistic that the parties can come to a better place together.
- Help the parties be patient, while you are persistent.

Express Humility As Wonder and Awe

- Recognize God is in control; the parties have the wisdom to resolve their own problems.

- Recognize one's own limits, even failures without feeling defeated or lacking self-worth.

- Do not bring a spirit of judgment to the parties.

- Recognize the limits of one's vision.

- See complexity as a friend, avoiding dualities.

- Be open to suggestions and criticism.

Be in Solidarity With All Creation

- Seek wellbeing and right relations for all the parties.

- Believe the parties can find common ground as well as higher ground.

- Help create a new sense of relationship and community among the parties.

These virtues are related to our understanding of our role. In our work, we suggest that we abandon the need and the burden to see ourselves as fixers or miracle workers. The motivation is a caring one, although it can carry with it a sense of superiority and the imposition of our will. The reality is that people can and must solve their own problems in order to own and be committed to the solution. We cannot bring about healing or reconciliation by ourselves. We can only create the environment in which it can occur or the context for the Spirit to work. Our understanding of our role as a peacebuilder has evolved into being a mediating presence, a person who is present between and among the parties, who brings people together in good conversation to solve their own problems and get to a better place together. This role will be fleshed out in the six ways in which we engage others. I hope that as you experience this role description, you feel your body relaxing, a burden being removed from your shoulders, and a sense of excitement about playing the role of the mediating presence, not the fixer.

We will never be fully prepared for this work. It is not about perfection. It is about being human. All this preparation is not an end in itself, but in this relational world we are preparing ourselves to be engaged with others in a way that heals relationship and creates a new sense of community.

How do we engage people with whom we are in conflict? How do we facilitate the engagement of others who are in conflict? We need to understand and design good process, a process that provides space where we can have a good conversation to get to a better place together.

In her book *Turning to One Another: Simple Conversations to Restore Hope to the Future*, Margaret Wheatley talks about how we can change the world through "simple, truthful conversation where we each have a chance to speak, we each feel heard, and we each listen well." She goes on to say, "This is how great changes begin, when people begin talking to each other about their experiences, hopes, and fears."[5]

In JustPeace, we use the term "facilitated conversation" to describe what we are doing. We use this term instead of "mediation" as much of our work in the church involves values and deals with harm. People do not like to enter into a process thinking where they are mediating their values, but they can and will talk about them. People also do not want to mediate their harm, but they will talk about their harm, where there is a process for addressing their harm. Describing an engagement as a facilitated conversation is broad enough to describe mediation, or negotiation, or dialogue, or a consensus building process or simply a healing conversation. Such facilitated conversations draw on lessons learned from the theory and practice of all these fields, but we always describe what we are doing as a facilitated conversation, regardless of the issue or the process.

In a relational world, the process we use to deal with a conflict is as important, or more important, than any solution. "You can't get to a good place in a bad way."[6] The way decisions are made is critical to the ownership and success of the decision. Generally people can live with a decision they may not actually prefer if they have had a voice in that decision or resolution. Everyone needs to feel valued, and to be treated fairly. Bad process can be a source of conflict, yielding resentment, feelings of being treated unfairly, and a sense of powerlessness.

When I began to move from the two adversarial tables of the courtroom to the one table of collaborative conversation, I searched for a process that would be most consistent with the theology and practices of the faith. What does a faith-based conflict transformation process look like? I was trying to understand how to create the space and the time where people can

- find sacred space, a relatively safe space;

5. Wheatley, *Turning to One Another*, 3.

6. A Native American insight quoted in Boyes-Watson, "Healing the Wounds of Street Violence," 18.

- recognize their interdependence and connection;
- find a sense of equality and respect;
- have voice—even the quiet ones;
- experience deep listening and respectful speaking;
- feel responsible and accountable for the outcome;
- solve their problems and find healing.

The answer came from many sources, all about the same time. I learned about circles from Chief Justice Yazzi of the Navaho Nation. He and I were both board members of the *Journal of Law and Religion*. As Chief Justice, he followed the laws and practices of the American judicial system. However, he realized that the adversarial retributive system was not healing the people of his nation, especially the youth. He then returned to the ancient process of his own people, peacebuilding Circles, and gave people the opportunity to choose which process they wanted. I also heard about circles from my study of restorative justice with Howard Zehr at Eastern Mennonite University. There I was introduced to the work of Judge Barry Stuart, who started using First Nation circle processes in his courtroom in the Yukon. In a meeting with one of the general secretaries of our church, he reported that he had just experienced the most powerful conversation he had ever experienced, using something called "the circle process" that Meg Wheatley was using with all her work. Finally, I came to know Kay Pranis, who was the restorative justice planner for the Minnesota Department of Corrections. She became my teacher, and her books *Peacemaking Circles: From Crime to Community* with Barry Stuart and Mark Wedge, and *The Little Book of Circle Processes: A New/Old Approach to Peacemaking* were transformative for me. Kay taught me that circles combine the ancient traditions, for example, of Native Americans, "with contemporary concepts of democracy and inclusivity in a complex, multicultural society."[7] In short, I found the circle process a great gift to the church and the world. As one participant said, "The circle process has helped bring us back to a better and more faithful way of being church."

Sitting in circle expresses in a physical and symbolic way the interconnectedness, interdependence, and unity of all life as found in God with deep appreciation for diversity and the unique wisdom and contribution of each person. Everyone in the circle is the alpha and omega of the circle, with equal responsibility and accountability for the work of the circle. The

7 Pranis, *Little Book of Circle Processes*, 3.

circle emphasizes collective and communal wisdom and discernment. We are all on the same side of the table. The circle symbolizes and establishes the community we want to be.

One of the more obvious connections of circle process and the rhythms of church life is that in circle process, opening and closing rituals frame the whole time and space together as sacred. The circle is a sacred space. In fact, circle process calls the church back from doing business like the Chamber of Commerce, to doing "worshipful work," and seeing its task to discern in and through community the will of God. Circle process has helped me understand again the power of ritual to transform lives and create community. At the center of the circle is a continuous reminder of the presence of God, for example a candle. Ritual helps create a space safe enough, physically and emotionally, for the telling of our stories and the speaking and hearing of truth.

Circle process involves the participants in defining how individuals should be treated in the conversation and life of the circle. These guidelines are best expressed, in the theology and tradition of the church, by the word "covenant," a mutual agreement that binds people together, honors the other party, and requires mutual accountability and responsibility. We found the creating and living out of such a relational covenant the most important act that can be taken to prevent destructive conflict.

The use of a talking piece in the circle is the most helpful ritual I know to encourage deep listening and respectful speaking. The talking piece enables everyone to have a voice, including the quiet ones, often the wisest, and enables the talkers to listen. When you hold the talking piece, you get to talk and everyone else gets to listen. The talking piece goes from left to right around the circle, giving everyone the opportunity to speak without interruption. A person can pass for any reason; including feeling too emotional to talk or feeling what they wanted to say has already been said. The talking piece is something respected by the community. In Native American circles, a feather is often the talking piece. The Bible is the talking piece I most often use, but only when the group finds it appropriate. The talking piece is used wisely and not mechanically, with the facilitator moving as needed between passing it and holding it with open conversation, one at a time, in the circle. The talking piece removes much of the burden of facilitation from the facilitator. The steward on occasion will speak without the talking piece, but only rarely in my experience. For me, the circle process is easier to practice than other forms of facilitation, in large part because of the use of the talking piece.

Circle process is grounded in the value of consensus. Coming to consensus for Quakers is a way of communal discernment of the will of God. I understand consensus as a process of seeking the common mind without resort to a formal vote, engaging in genuine dialogue that is respectful, mutually supportive, and empowering while seeking to discern God's will. Consensus, which is not the same as unanimity, is declared when one of the following occurs: all are in agreement about an outcome; or most are in agreement and the few for whom it is not their first preference, nonetheless accept that they have been fairly heard and can live with the outcome. Another way to put this is to say that a consensus is reached when no one feels a need to oppose it. This process involves everyone seeking alternatives that address everyone's concerns and interests, something greater (higher ground) than anyone's preconceived ideas (newness). Once a consensus is reached, there is communal ownership, and more effective and sustainable agreements.

The concept of the "guardian" or "keeper of the circle," terms used in Native American circles, liberates leaders or facilitators from the burden of thinking they alone must fix or solve the problems being dealt with in the circle, or heal the relationships that are broken. Critical to the concept is the recognition that everyone in the circle is responsible for the good work of the circle. The concept is congruent with an understanding of servant leadership. Instead of "guardian" or "keeper" of the circle, we have used the term "steward" for such servant leadership, a term that is more familiar in the church. Stewardship involves the caring for what is entrusted to you. A circle steward is one who helps create and monitor the sacred space and time for dialogue where the community can solve its own problems and experience healing together. The steward does this work by:

- setting a tone of respect and hope that honors and supports every participant;

- framing the circle as sacred by beginning and ending with ritual;

- obtaining agreement on the relational covenant;

- raising powerful questions and issues to address before passing the talking piece;

- encouraging the telling and hearing of stories;

- helping everyone practice listening for understanding, speaking the truth in love, using their imagination to reach higher ground, and being forgiving;

- at the end of passing the talking piece, or at other times as needed, summarizing the contributions of the circle;

- allowing participants in the circle to resolve their own conflicts, find healing, justice, and right relations, and even reconcile with one another;

- assisting the participants to put any agreements in writing.

Often there are two stewards, not just one. Two heads are often better than one. Different styles and experiences come together to provide greater knowledge, skills, and insights. A balance in terms of diversity can assist parties in feeling more comfortable, especially in conflicts involving race, ethnicity, or gender. Co-stewards can take turns and divide up the work. One may focus more on issues and facts while the other focuses on feelings or emotions, or one can lead and direct the process while the other monitors and ensures that important elements are not overlooked.

Preparation for the circle—the work done before the circle comes together—is critical to success, especially for a circle dealing with conflict. Preparation is essential to understanding the issues, the people involved, and the structures within which the conflict developed. The preparation time is also the time when you create credibility and trust with all the parties. Finally, it is the time when the circle is designed, so that agreement is reached on the primary focus of the circle, who will be present, what will be included in the relational covenant, and when and where the circle will meet. Sometimes we bring like-minded people together in affinity circles, before bringing the sides together in a joint circle. These circles allow people to vent, focus on the underlying issues and concerns, and develop together their hopes for a constructive outcome. Affinity circles also educate participants in the circle process. Participants in these circles can assist in choosing who should be in the joint circle.

A circle works best with eight to twelve people, but we have facilitated much larger circles. We have also facilitated a thousand people divided into circles, reporting their work to the whole. In the context of a United Methodist grievance procedure in a complaint against a pastor for stealing money, the circle might include members of the church who have been harmed; the district superintendent and a member of the board of ordained ministry, who represent the covenant of ministry that has been breached; the minister and the minister's spouse and a best friend of each; and an ex-offender. In a dispute between two churches, we had five representatives of each church in the circle surrounded by another four hundred people, who understood that their only role was to listen. In this circle, we provided complete transparency.

Ideally each circle includes those affected by the conflict, those who might block any decision if they were not in the circle, as well as those who can bring wisdom to the process. Everyone needs to know who will be in the circle so there are no surprises. The persons who are going to be part of the circle need to understand the circle process, the role of the facilitator or steward of the circle, the use of ritual, the talking piece, and the consensus nature of the decision-making process. The participants decide what they would like to use as a talking piece. Together they work out a relational covenant as to how they all want to be treated in the process, which includes confidentiality when that is required.

For JustPeace, the circle is the space for three movements within the conversation of the circle, the movements of Appreciative Inquiry, Interest-Based Negotiation or Mediation, and Restorative Justice. Although we like to start with Appreciative Inquiry and then move to Interest-Based Mediation and Restorative Justice, we sequence the process in a way that meets the needs of the group and the flow of the conversation. The work of conflict transformation is improvisational.

The first movement, in most situations, is to share and build on the positive and best in all the parties—peak experiences, grace-filled moments, and dreams of a preferred future. This movement is informed by the field of Appreciative Inquiry (hereinafter, AI). The word *appreciate* means "valuing; the act of recognizing the best in people or the world around us; affirming past and present strengths, successes, and potentials; to perceive those things that give life (health, vitality, excellence) to living systems." Inquiry is "the act of exploration and discovery . . . to ask questions."[8]

AI is a philosophy of positive change and a methodology for discovering and building on the positive core of any human system. "At the heart of AI is the understanding that human systems move in the direction of what they continuously study, analyze, and discuss. AI is therefore a call to study 'root causes of success,' rather than 'root causes of failure.' "

Carl Jung at the end of his career stated that "he had never seen people grow *from* a problem. Instead, he suggested, they grow *toward* some more compelling life force."[9] Appreciative Inquiry begins with the assumption that all human systems have something to value in the present or in their past. Together parties to these systems search for what is

8. Whitney, Liebler, and Cooperrider, "Appreciative Inquiry," 27.
9. Ibid., 27, 49.

valued. This search involves appreciative questions aimed at *discovering* this "positive core."

Think about how this approach might help us as we work to create positive change in the church. This approach is different from our usual problem-solving approach, looking at the problems, at the negative, and trying to figure out how to solve the problems—for example, declining numbers, declining giving, increasing conflicts, losing the youth. With this focus, we often find ourselves even more stuck in the problems. The problem is often a small part of the overall picture, but it overwhelms our ability to see other aspects of the person or institution or situation. AI recognizes, for example, that every church, no matter how troubled, has had good moments. People would not be in the church if things were all bad. Start from the positive, from people's best moments, their peak experiences, and their grace-filled moments, instead of from the negative or the problems. Focusing on strengths is more effective than focusing on problems. And it is more constructive to build on what is known and appreciated in the system than trying to imagine an abstract ideal of a better self or a better community. In the context of a conflict, sharing stories of peak experiences and dreams of a preferred future may serve to resolve the presenting problem. But when the original problem or problems persist, the group needs to address them. Having shared the positive, people can now more readily address the negative. Sometimes the conflict is so emotional that we must start with the problem and then later move to the positive core or grace-filled stories.

A *"problem" is an* issue such as a dispute over worship styles with one group taking the position that they want contemporary music and the other taking the position that they want traditional music in worship. For interest-based mediation, a focus on problems involves moving from positions to interests and needs, generating options, evaluating options and reaching consensus on an agreement. The methodology of interest-based negotiation or mediation was developed in a book entitled *Getting to Yes: Negotiating Agreement Without Giving In*, by Roger Fisher and William Ury. Most people enter into discussions around conflicts talking primarily in terms of their positions or demands: "I want the minister to stay." "I want the minister to leave." Criticizing people or their positions or trying to get parties to compromise and "back off" from their demands generally causes them to cling more stubbornly to them. Focusing on positions leads to impasse, sometimes compromise, but rarely to creative solutions that meet everyone's needs and interests. Positions are statements or demands framed as solutions. They express a solution to deep needs and interests. Interests and needs motivate people to take positions. Positions often obscure what parties really want. The good news is that a position usually represents just one possible solution to the needs and interests of the parties. Knowing this, instead of focusing on positions, we can help the parties verbalize underlying interests and needs and find common solutions to these interests and needs. The other good news is that, although needs and interests may conflict, shared and compatible ones can be discovered. Different interests can create opportunities as well.

An example often used is the story of two children arguing over an orange. The position of each child was that they wanted the orange. If one child gets the orange, then the other child loses. The loser does not think this is a wise agreement and the relationship has not been improved. If someone plays Solomon and splits the orange in two, a compromise has been reached, but no one is fully satisfied and, as you shall see, there is a lost opportunity. At the heart of the alternative to positional negotiation is getting beneath the positions to find out why each child wants the orange. Asking the question, we discover one child wants the orange for the juice and the other wants the peel in order to make a pie. Knowing this, both parties can get all they want—their interests can be met by what is described as a win/win agreement and the relationship is sustained. In this process the parties discover there are many compatible and shared interests and needs. We all have, for example, basic human needs, including security, economic well-being, a sense of belonging, recognition, some control over one's life. Once you recognize and agree on meeting the shared interests, the conflicting ones are more manageable. Parties usually have several interests. The more interests that are surfaced, the more options you can generate for meeting at least some of the interests. Some interests are more important than others. This process allows for setting priorities as to which are most important. Relatively minor ones might be part of a compromise when the major ones are met.

Once the interests and needs are known, the most creative part of the process begins—generating options to meet these interests and needs. Newsprint, which can be posted on the wall, and an easel are the two essential props in most facilitations. As you go through the process of storytelling and then working to understand needs and interests, you will list these interests and needs on the newsprint without preference or priority. Before moving to try to meet these interests or needs, ask if there is anything that was not yet listed, any other issues to be considered. Give people time to think; this is the time to state all concerns. You do not want to work out an agreement and then discover significant issues have not been discussed.

Once everyone has agreed on the list of concerns to be addressed, you can begin the process of seeking options for meeting the interests and needs of all the parties. You may, as I often find, have several sheets filled with interests and needs. The parties look at this list and wonder where to start. You can lead a process of organizing the interests and needs, finding that they generally group into a few issues that become manageable. You then list the issues on newsprint in the order you would like to address them. Now start to work on one issue at a time. We usually start with the easiest one to resolve. Here you brainstorm as many ideas as possible, without critical evaluation. Encourage everyone to turn off their censors and let the ideas flow. This is where it gets exciting! Ideas are generated or discovered that no one had thought of when they entered the room. You never know who will express the best idea. Welcome every idea and list them all without comment. Once the group has exhausted its ideas, move to evaluating the pros and cons of the options to determine which ones best meet the interests and needs of the parties. The best part of this process is when people begin to improve the preferred or favorite ideas, making them even better. Proceed to the next issue and follow the same process. The end result is an agreement in writing.

The final movement is necessary in most conflicted situations—the addressing of the harm experienced by the parties. This movement is informed by the field of Restorative Justice.[10] In the book of Amos, God says:

> "I hate, I despise your festivals,
> and I take no delight in your solemn assemblies. . . .
> Take away from me the noise of your songs;
> I will not listen to the melody of your harps.
> But let justice roll down like waters,
> and righteousness like an ever-flowing stream."
> (Amos 5:21, 23–24)

Justice is more important to God than worship. The worth of worship is contingent upon being just and righteous in one's relationships, fulfilling the demands of relationships. In his book *The Prophets*, the Jewish theologian Abraham Heschel asks, "Why should religion, the essence of which is worship of God, put such stress on justice . . . ?" Heschel approaches this question by looking at the partnership of God and humanity in the creation of

10. An outstanding articulation of restorative justice with extensive grounding in biblical exegesis is Marshall, *Beyond Retribution*.

history. God needs humans to help in accomplishing God's "grand design."[11] The Bible moves from unlimited retribution in the law of Lamech in Genesis 4:24 ("seventy-sevenfold"), to an eye for an eye, to unlimited forgiveness ("seventy-seven times" in Matthew 18:22). We see the justice God seeks is ultimately not retributive. What is the justice God desires?

The concept of restorative justice became much clearer to me when I studied the Truth and Reconciliation Commission in South Africa (hereinafter the TRC). Critics of the TRC asked, "Where is justice?" "Where are the adversarial retributive trials such as were experienced at Nuremberg after World War II in Germany?" I listened to Bishop Tutu agree that retributive justice was not the justice the Truth and Reconciliation Commission was seeking. There was another form of justice, restorative justice, which was consistent with the desire to seek truth and reconciliation. Retributive justice defines crime or wrongdoing as violation of the law. The question is whether the defendant broke the law, and, if so, how is he/she going to be punished. The focus is on the offender, not on the people who have been harmed. The law assists us in understanding when someone is harmed. However, the harm is harm to a person. Jesus says, "The sabbath was made for humankind, and not humankind for the sabbath" (Mark 2:27). The law was made for men and women, not men and women for the law. Restorative justice poses a different essential question: who has been harmed and how have they been harmed? While retributive justice regards the state as the victim rather than the person or person directly harmed by the wrongdoing, restorative justice sees the harm in terms of people, relationships, and community. My experience is the person harmed is often harmed twice, once by the wrongdoing and then by the trial process, including cross-examination, where the person is seen primarily as a witness for the state. Restorative justice says we must start with the person harmed and then ask what the harm was to the community as a whole. The aim of retributive justice is to establish blame, guilt, or liability. The aim of restorative justice is to identify the needs of the person harmed and to determine the obligations of the offender—and even the community—in addressing these harms.

Instead of a punishment system, restorative justice creates an accountability system. What does the offender need to do personally to address the needs of the person harmed, to make things right? We are talking about real accountability to the victim. In the retributive system, third parties determine the punishment. This is coerced accountability,

---

11. Heschel, *Prophets*, 198.

and, in my experience, the third-party punishment does not lead, in most cases, to acceptance of responsibility and to actions on the part of the offender personally to address the harms created. Punishment is often counterproductive to such accountability as it discourages empathy and encourages denial of responsibility. Punishment stigmatizes through shame, and shame is a primary cause of violence. Most people in prison see themselves as victims, and in many ways they are. In fact, their crimes often come out of their own victimhood; and the punishment system adds to this sense of victimhood. Restorative justice is able to see the offender in context, but, more importantly, gives the offender the chance to take personal responsibility for the actions that harmed another human being—to make things right. For some offenders, this accountability might involve the need for restraint.

Zacchaeus is a biblical example of such accountability. He agrees to give half of his possessions to the poor and to restore fourfold to anyone whom he defrauded. Jesus' response to Zacchaeus was to tell him, "Today salvation has come to this house" (Luke 19:9). Three words sum up restorative justice: *harm, accountability, engagement*. Restorative justice addresses victims' harms and needs, holds offenders accountable to make things right, and engages the victims, offenders, and communities in the process.

The ultimate goal of all our preparation and engagement for conflict transformation and peacebuilding is to find healing in our relationships, to flourish in community, to *be well together*. It involves more than just addressing a single conflict. It is about creating a different way of living together, a culture of justpeace. I have talked about the importance of getting people to a table where they can engage one another and work together to address the issues, the harm, and the problems that divide them. For me, that table is the Table of Holy Communion. This Table is the place, for me, where a search for a better way to deal with conflict ended. For me, this Table summarizes and empowers all that we have been discussing. This is a Table of relational healing, restorative justice and reconciliation. At this Table we are formed into peacebuilders, ministers of reconciliation.

The invitation is to those who seek to live in peace with one another. We are then sent out with the admonition to "go forth in peace." The essential power of this Table is that the One who reconciles and heals is the Host of this Table. I believe that the One in whom I have experienced God incarnate is present at all tables, but here at this Table, we recognize the Host and consciously open ourselves to this One. At the heart of the liturgy lies the good news of God's everlasting love and forgiveness in spite of our failures. At this Table we see ourselves as a forgiven people who are called to the spiritual practice of forgiveness. In fact, we are asked to work beyond forgiveness to reconciliation, as we hear the invitation to "offer one another signs of reconciliation and love." No one at this Table is unaware of the destructive conflicts in our world, in our communities, in the workplace, and in our homes. We bring all these conflicted worlds to the Table. The greatest issue of our day is how we are going to break out of the cycles of retribution and violence that are tearing our world and our relationships apart. At the Table of Holy Communion, each time we commune, we are reminded that the only way out of these cycles is through the path of forgiveness. At this Table we celebrate the defeat of the powers of retribution and violence through the word of forgiveness from the cross and through the resurrection. We are freed to give up the idolatry that violence is redemptive, that it will save us.

One of the toughest problems in the work of conflict transformation is how to get people who disagree to the table. At the Table of Holy Communion, we find ourselves all standing together, regardless of our differences. I have a growing conviction that on some issues we are not, at least in the near term, going to find common ground, but we can find at the Table higher ground, transcendent ground to which we are invited and where we can stand together. What better place to bring our conflicts, especially those that seem intractable? What would the body of Christ look like for the world if we began to celebrate this gift and this reality of higher ground, instead of being focused on our differences?

The most important lesson for me about the Table has come through studying what Jesus did at the Last Supper, the meal we are called to remember. This lesson has led to the conviction that the Table might become transforming and formative for us and for the world when we begin to recognize, with Jesus, that the Table is a place to name and engage our conflicts and practice reconciliation. After the disciples have taken their places and are eating, what are the first words Jesus said? According to the Gospel of Mark, he said, "Truly I tell you, one of you will betray me, one who is eating with me." He added, "It is one of the twelve, one who is dipping bread into the bowl with me" (Mark 14:17–20). Isn't this startling? What a way to start a dinner party! At his final dinner with his disciples, the first words of Jesus name the conflict that is the elephant in the room. Judas is going to betray Jesus. We see in John's Gospel the other way that Jesus names the conflict in which he found himself, the conflict written deep into the whole social fabric of his day. He moves from the head of the table to the foot of the table, takes the place of the least and washes the feet of all the disciples (John 13:3–17). In doing so, he names the structural and systemic problem of his society. He turns the society upside down.

There is nothing sentimental or individualistic or pietistic about this meal. The meal is not privatized or spiritualized. There is nothing here that is romantic or escapist. At this Table we experience the real world, with real and deep conflict. Jesus sits at his last supper, under the shadow of the cross with the man who would betray him and eleven others who will desert him. Does that experience sound conflicted to you? And Jesus named it. Justice requires the naming. Truth requires the naming. Transformation requires the naming. What Jesus does next is remarkable, radical, and transforming in the context of his day and ours. After naming the conflict, he turns and offers everyone—Judas, Peter, everyone—bread and wine. Think about this gesture. He reaches over to Judas and gives him a portion of a loaf he has blessed, not cursed, and says to Judas, "Take; this is my body." He also gives this bread to Peter and all the others who would deny him. Then he takes a cup, and after giving thanks, he gives it to them, and all of them drink from it—*all* means Judas as well as Peter. He says, "This is my blood of the covenant, which is poured out for many" (Mark 14:22–24). The bread is the symbol of God's sustenance of God's creation best symbolized by the manna in the wilderness. The wine is a sign of the heavenly banquet (see 1 Cor 11:23–26; Matt 26:26–29). It is a sign of the new covenant between God and God's people—a covenant of forgiveness and reconciliation. The one cup symbolizes the unity of the body in Christ gathered at the table. Jesus names the conflict, but not in order to give a stone or to set the stage for retribution and punishment. He names it and then gives bread and wine. Indeed, he gives his life. Here Jesus reframes our whole reality and the way we are to respond to conflict, differences, and harm. The frame within which Jesus calls us to live out our lives is not the frame of naming to punish, but the frame of naming to give bread. At this Table I began to find the fullest response to my search for a better way than the adversarial retributive model. Here we move from blaming to naming, from punishment to accountability, from retribution to forgiveness. The naming becomes a different reality in the context of the gift of bread and forgiveness. When the second step in the process after naming is giving bread, the tone of the naming is changed. It does not have the tone of blaming or humiliation. It does not have the "feel" of a statement to punish or wound or humiliate or dismiss. It creates a difference in the speaker and in the hearer. It opens up a different spirit in the speaker. It opens up in the hearer, in large part because of this different spirit, the possibility of openness to real accountability as opposed to a purely defensive response. There is a judgment here, but it is the judgment of love.

In those circumstances where we fail to reconcile after leaving our gifts at the altar (Matt 5:23–24), what if we brought the person we should seek out and be reconciled with to the Table, where we could, in the presence and with the assistance of others in the community, listen to each other's stories, experience each other's joys and sorrows and pursue the journey of reconciliation together in community?

I have a dream, a dream for your church. When people walk by your church, you will hear them say: "Inside this church is a healing, restoring table. At this Table, you truly hear and experience the good news of God's love and forgiveness. You find people living out the call to a ministry of reconciliation. At this Table, you can be authentic, including dealing with your hurt and your conflicts. Conflicts are named, not in the spirit of punishment but in the spirit of getting to a good place together. My friend came to a good place with his family at this Table. Another friend came to a good place with his neighbor with whom he had been feuding. Folks gather around this Table to discuss the major issues of the day and to discern what God's love is calling us to do. This Table has become the center every Sunday of weekly celebrations of restoration, healing, and reconciliation. Everything becomes new at this Table. I want to be a part of this place with this Table. At this Table we can be well together." In my dream, your church has created, around this Table, a culture of justpeace.

Bibliography

Boyes-Watson, Carolyn. "Healing the Wounds of Street Violence: Peacemaking Circles and Community Youth Development." *Community Youth Development Journal* 2.4 (2001) 16–21.

Fisher, Roger, and William Ury. *Getting to Yes: Negotiating Agreement Without Giving In*. Edited by Bruce Patton. 2nd ed. New York: Penguin, 1991.

Heschel, Abraham J. *The Prophets*. New York: Harper and Row, 1962.

Marshall, Christopher D. *Beyond Retribution: A New Testament Vision for Justice, Crime, and Punishment*. Grand Rapids: Eerdmans, 2001.

Porter, Thomas W., Jr. *Engaging Conflict Well: The Spirit and the Art of Conflict Transformation*. Nashville: Upper Room, 2010.

———, Jr. *The Spirit and Art of Conflict Transformation: Creating a Culture of JustPeace*. Nashville: Upper Room, 2010.

Pranis, Kay. *The Little Book of Circle Processes*. Intercourse, PA: Good Books, 2005.

Pranis, Kay, Barry Stuart, and Mark Wedge. *Peacemaking Circles: From Crime to Community*. St. Paul: Living Justice, 2003.

Part II: Just Peacemaking as the New Paradigm for the Ethics of Peace and War

Stassen, Glen H., editor. *Just Peacemaking: The New Paradigm for the Ethics of Peace and War.* Cleveland: Pilgrim, 2008.

Tutu, Desmond. *No Future Without Forgiveness.* New York: Doubleday, 1999.

Wheatley, Margaret J. *Turning to One Another: Simple Conversations to Restore Hope to the Future.* San Francisco: Berrett-Koehler, 2002.

Whitney, Diana, Claudia Liebler, and David Cooperrider. "Appreciative Inquiry in Organizations and International Development: An Invitation to Share and Learn across Fields." In *Positive Approaches to Peacebuiding: A Resource for Innovators,* edited by Cynthia Sampson, Mohammed Abu-Nimer, Claudia Liebler, and Diana Whitney, 25–54. Washington, DC: Pact, 2003.

10

The Road to Forming a Gendered Understanding of Just Peacemaking and Intersections with Digital Peacebuilding

NAJEEBA SYEED-MILLER

AT THE AGE OF fifteen I returned to Srinagar Kashmir, my birthplace. I had not been in the area since I had left at the age of three. I was overjoyed with the experience of returning to memories that existed mostly in the nether regions of my psyche, and the smells, sounds, and sights came alive after more than a decade of separation from my region of origin. One other aspect of my visit was the daily exposure to a military presence that spanned nearly every inch of my hometown. The visual assault of the presence of the army and police force was emblazoned on my mind.

From that point onwards, I took a vow to Allah (God) and to my community that I would support peacemaking practices in any way that I could and wherever I was. This formative experience reminds me that the work of just peacemaking, interfaith or otherwise, can be informed not just by a motivation for abstract achievement of peace. A commitment to God was the impetus for me to continue to do perform acts of peacemaking as an expression of devotion to my community and to the Divine. My horizontal relationship with people and the way I engage mercifully with human beings was directly proportionate to my vertical relationship with my Creator. If I refused to show mercy to others, I would indeed then displease my Creator.

Muslims are instructed by Prophet Muhammad, upon him be peace,

Jarir bin Abdullah رضي الله عنه reported: The Messenger of Allah صلى الله عليه وسلم said, "Allah will not be merciful to those who are not merciful to mankind." [Sahih Bukhari, Volume 9, Book 93, Number 473]

Sometimes the trigger of seeing the apex of what happens with a lack of mercy, when devolved into having to utilize armed intervention to resolve conflicts, can make a peacemaker of a person. Interestingly enough, it was my very faith as a Muslim that caused me to be formed as a peacemaker. It is *because* of my beliefs as a Muslim and relationship to Allah that I am a peacemaker, not despite my status as a believer in Islam that I am engaged in this work.

As we consider the role of one's religious commitment and how it plays out into the disposition and interest in peacemaking, so too must we give care to the consideration of gender. How can interfaith just peacemaking be contextualized into the spiritual and educational formation processes of Muslim women? Are there unique iterations of piety that can enrich and add variables perhaps heretofore not considered in the religious educational process of Muslim communities and particularly Muslim women?

I will first address whether or not to consider a specific set of approaches to just peacemaking formation with the Muslim women's context, and then provide frames of reference and exploration that have been gleaned by my practice as an educator in Muslim and interfaith communities in peacemaking. The central theme of this essay will explore the need to particularize just peacemaking as a pedagogical approach and object of teaching within the cultural and religious contexts that Muslim women operate in on a regular basis. The first frame will seek to define the relevance of gender to peacemaking; the second will consider stages of spiritual formation and engagement with modes of piety and performance and the final will explore the new horizons of peacemaking through cyber/internet-based activism.

Gender and Its Implications in Just Peacemaking

The unfortunate consequences that are gender specific in war-related scenarios include rape. In some scenarios, "sexual violence against women becomes almost like a universal culture of militarism."[1] Other cases abound, such as the Bosnia-Hercegovina and the disproportionate impact of practices of war that target women. Hence the need to read into the ten practices

---

1. Ling, "Violence, Poverty, Justice and Peacemaking," 54.

of just peacemaking and determine how and if there is a further nuancing with a gendered lens is a topic for current and future investigation.

While there is much literature regarding violence against women, there is also an equal scholarly discourse on the role of women as agents of peacemaking. The role of women as agents for peacemaking has been eloquently articulated and investigated by many authors, including Etin Anwar's essay that explores both the specific implications of violence on women and the capacity for gender as one organizing platform both within and across traditions. Anwar identifies one approach (out of three) to peacemaking as gender, the "biological thread" that connects women, and the further bonding that moved them beyond their roles as mothers, even as their starting point of motherhood informed and "became a common cause for making peace."[2]

It is also interesting that as just peacemaking moves into the interfaith forum, the role of gender as a potential unifying principle across faiths could catalyze the ten practices into even further nodes for both research and on-the-ground intervention as reference points. In specific cases such as Nigeria, indigenous scholars point to the capacity for women to approach conflict resolution in ways that are "transpolitical, transnational, and aimed at reaching women in the opposite camp."[3]

A specific interfaith example can be identified in the Nigerian context in Kaduna, where Christian and Muslim women have utilized common language and convened meetings to advance peacemaking with a faith-based approach. According to one report, there is an Interfaith Council for women. It "comprises leaders and members of women's faith groups in Kaduna consisting of both Muslims and Christians. The Council's activities include promoting peace and understanding through interreligious dialogue, and capacity building through workshops, exploring women's common concerns and working with the media to amplify peace messages."[4]

To the degree that just peacemaking practices can engage and include gender as a variable in the development of models of education and engagement, it may be possible not just to expand the ten practices' breadth of engagement within one faith tradition, but also to move into a space that is also interreligious in ways that will have major implications for the many interfaith conflicts around the globe. Just peacemaking becomes a

---

2. Anwar, "Gendered Space and Shared Security," 32.
3. Ogolame and Ukpere, "Role of Women," 12714.
4. Mni, "Kaduna: Women Investing in Peace."

paradigm that will recognize the specificity of gender while also providing tools to promote peaceful resolution of conflicts in cases where women may often be the most targeted or genuinely affected parties to a war.

Best Practices in Just Peacemaking in Muslim Women's Religious Contexts

Sensitizing the Instructor to Piety and Its Expression in Some Muslim Women's Contexts

This essay will undoubtedly be limited in its implications for all Muslim women's environments or communities. There is a wide variety of forms of Muslim practice throughout the globe and varying levels of religious expression. I will merely provide some baselines for potential investigation and assessment to be considered when developing programs for those who identify as Muslim and are seeking to align themselves within that identity framework. Perhaps the greatest lesson we can glean from any of this work is the importance of assessing the particular conflict and the just peacemaking practices and determining with those who are closest to the conflict the most appropriate way of creating models of engagement with them as partners. This is especially the case when one adds identity performance variables such as gender, culture, national origin, etc.

In my own work of training hundreds of Muslim women in different scenarios, I have found that cultural competency of the trainers is especially important in terms of understanding how piety might be demonstrated in the communal religious setting. Saba Mahmood has explored the notion of public and private piety extensively in her *Politics of Piety* and her ethnographic study of the Egyptian women's piety movement. In relation to just peacemaking there are two principles I wish to extrapolate from her extraordinary study:

Performance of Ritual and Relation to Piety

Mahmood astutely identifies an inherent relationship that is manifested in the outward and inward spaces of piety and its performance in some Muslim contexts:

> The pious subjects of this book posit a very different relation-
> ship between outward bodily acts (including rituals, liturgies

and worships) and inward belief (state of the soul). Not only are
the two inseparable in their conception but more importantly,
belief is a product of outward practices, rituals and acts of worship rather than simply an expression of them.[5]

When considering the formation of just peacemakers in relation to all
ten practices, the state of piety is not just a focus on the inward development of the subject. Inherent in Mahmood's assessment is the reality
that inhabits both an inward manifestation and the dialectic between
belief, performance of ritual and the communal body that shapes those
practices and beliefs.

To put it into concrete terms, in my work with some Muslim women's
context when I am training in conflict resolution, I utilize specific examples
of practice that Prophet Muhammad manifested in his life that exhibited
an internal orientation in peacemaking. In addition to providing a set of
activities that promoted peacemaking, we actually practiced these in their
community contexts. So for example if the practice revolved around curbing
gossip and backbiting and promoting confidentiality as a basis for peaceful
resolution of conflicts, I would guide my students to exhibit this aspect of
Prophetic behavior both in class and in the time periods between class.

The act of performing this peacebuilding practice was meaning making for many of the participants precisely because the piety of the act was
not predicated merely on the belief that it was right, but also in its performance and recognition that the repetition of the act reached ritual status
and was integrated into the daily life of the students. In other settings, just
engaging in class role plays would be sufficient. What many of my students asked me for was actual guidance in the way that the prophet both
believed in and exhibited the mode of nonbackbiting in his daily practice.

To further mine this sense of piety as rooted in daily, repetitive practice I have found that the way to provide the most fruitful instruction in
peacebuilding in this context was a sustained pedagogical model so that
students could develop a daily modality for exercising a particular ritual
over a period of time and to test with me, their peers, and their larger
community how to perfect their ritual and belief.

The Qur'an commands Muslims to perform good deeds with 'ihsan
(5:93). 'Ihsan is variously often translated as excellence. So for those seeking
to develop peacemaking as a skill it is incumbent on them to recognize first
the relation that a practice has to their Muslim obligations generally, and
then to practice good deeds with excellence. The formation of a Muslim just

5. Mahmood, *Politics of Piety*, xv.

peacemaker is not a shallow endeavor for either the student or the teacher. It is holistic in the pursuit of the mind, the body and daily practice.

Formation of Muslim peacemaker behooves us to develop a pedagogy of daily performance. Al-Ghazali, one the great theoreticians of formation in the Muslim context, emphasizes that knowledge must be put into practice, and true knowledge affects the behavior of the student.[6] If the goal is to tie piety and peacemaking, it is important not just to replicate larger-scale practices of the ten presented in Stassen's texts. These practices can serve as a foundation for what in the Muslim context might be seen as "micro-practices."

How might we break down individual larger practices into reflective, digestible, performable forms of engagement that emanate directly from the uswah (example), of Prophet Muhammad and the Holy Qur'an? For example, Norm 3, "Using Cooperative Conflict Resolution," might be envisioned in three levels, building on Mahmood's definition of piety: 1) Reflection on passages in the Qur'an and sayings in the Hadith that speak to the inner state of mind necessary when performing acts of cooperative conflict resolution and how the state of heart and mind reflect ihsan, or excellence as the intention. 2) Engagement with everyday aspects of life and family for performance and practice of cooperative conflict resolution based on examples that Prophet Muhammad manifested in his lifetime. 3) Aggregate larger social and cultural frameworks for cumulative performance of pious acts of conflict resolution.

> All of these instructional modules should include ways for the teacher to model the act and a time period for the student to reflect and integrate these practices into their own sense of both identity and communal piety. Mahmood terms this "pedagogy of ethical cultivation" as a "behavioural pedagogy."[7] This leads us to the other aspect of formation that is extremely important in the Muslim context: Contextual formation of the communal corpus of the Muslim community.

Individual Formation As Community Development

As is often the case in viewing Muslim women, the rubric of liberation that is applied can often reduce women who are the subjects of the research

---

6. Al Ghazali, *Ihya ulum al din*, 3:61–62.
7. Mahmood, *Politics of Piety*, xvi.

project to being judged as "passive, obsequious and uncritical."[8] The notion of Muslim women organizing in mosque-based movements pushes aside the divides that might govern the discourse regarding social movements that engage Muslim women. This very act of creating a movement in which faith becomes the galvanizing force "necessitates a whole series of affective and sensible reorientations, some of which are undertaken systematically and others of which are acquired through social and cultural exposure and imbibing."[9]

How might one theologize and theorize the spiritual formation of a whole Muslim community? Within the Islamic framework there is a very useful tool to utilize. It is the twenty-three-year journey of the Prophetic mission, and the Muslim community he led till his death. As Mohammad Hashim Kamali points out, the early revelation of the Qur'an in the period in which the Prophet lived in Makkah is devoted to "matters of belief and the Oneness of God." Later revelations that were primarily in Medina at the later stage of the Prophetic mission were much more focused on legal rules.[10]

The focus of this essay is not on the implications of the Qur'anic injunctions vis a vis the chronological order of revelation. Rather, the train of inquiry is on how to form a community in the tradition of peacemaking? In the Muslim context, the existing example of starting with larger themes of holistic spiritual development is helpful not just with the individual but also with the whole community. Prophet Muhammad's mission was to be ultimately a mercy to all of mankind (21:107). If his central mission is to be a source of mercy, then the process of operationalizing his mission is not just in his teachings but also in a manifestation of *how* he taught his community.

Some specific suggestions we might draw upon based on this Prophetic spiritual formation track is to reorder the ten just peacemaking practices from the larger, more inwardly focused development processes to the legalistic and structured ways of seeing the world. In my own work when teaching Muslim perspectives on peacemaking, I start with the "Acknowledging Responsibility for Conflict Resolution and Injustice and Seek Repentance and Forgiveness," Norm 4.

The reason for this is that introduction of a Muslim pedagogy is most useful if staged in the way that Muslims themselves learn their religion and understand their faith as a community. If one begins with largely

8. Ibid., xii.
9. Ibid., xiii.
10. Kamali, *Principles of Islamic Jurisprudence*, 17.

legal examples then the inner formation both of each individual and the collective do not utilize the religiously competent trajectory for community-based spiritual formation and an understanding of how a Muslim community explores and coheres into a new stage of religious practice and piety.

We will now explore the frontiers of religious and spiritual formation as evidenced in the activism of Muslim women in the online world.

Digital Peacebuilding: Intersections of Spiritual Formation and Activism

Gamal Abdu-Nasser, Anwar Sadat, and Hosni Mubarak all were at the gates of heaven. They were asked, how did you each die? Nasser said, "Poisoned." Sadat said, "Assassinated." Mubarak replied, "Facebooked" (Egyptian street joke, circulating in April 2011).

It is clear that the presence of social media has forever altered the landscape of communication and culture in the Muslim publics within the United States, Europe, and the Middle East. Fundamental to this movement has been the presence of Muslim women in cyberspace, both as producers of content and leaders of new modalities of thinking and action related to a wide range of topics. Muslim women are actors in this virtual reality, embodied in a world that is often dislocated from a physical locale or designation.

However, a social media presence cannot be conflated with full participation in the decision-making. Even the revolutions that may be spawned from the intricate web of relationships established by new media may not result in women playing a role in post-revolutionary government and social structures. I will explore the definitions of Muslim publics, crystallize the relevant battlegrounds of public participation by Muslim women, and share the narratives of individual case studies that exemplify the current and future struggles of Muslim women in contemporary media.

This section of the essay is most related to Norm 5, Advancing Democracy, Human Rights and Interdependence, and Norm 10, Encouraging Grassroots Peacemaking Groups and Voluntary Associations. We will explore how Muslim women utilize the online world to hold governments and structures accountable in nonviolent ways, and also to organize in many situations for human rights in ways that might not have been possible in previous times without the use of online tools.

Defining Muslim Publics

There has been much debate regarding which Muslim publics utilize the Internet and social media tools. My focus here is on the use of social media sites, Facebook and Twitter, in particular. Because the emergence of these two social media tools is very recent, much of the existing literature focuses on the use of Muslim-oriented websites, which differs greatly from social media sites that are essentially crowd-sourced tools that capture the etchings of imagination of many people simultaneously.

The first issue that is often debated is the importance of the Internet as whole for different Muslim publics. Is it more a part of the fabric of Muslim societies in the U.S., Europe, or the Middle East? Earlier researchers contended that "the Internet is changing the fabric of Muslim communication patterns, and at this stage, the Internet is likely to be of more benefit for Muslims living in Western countries than their counterparts in Muslim countries."[11]

Percentages of usage have clearly increased over the past few years in the Middle East and North Africa (MENA), with the most dramatic rise in Egypt. The percentages of Muslims who engage in online activities are still limited in MENA, with women making up less of the total usage compared to the United States or United Kingdom.[12] However the dominance of male usage and ascent of female users is not limited to the West. In 1997, 75 percent of Internet users were male in the U.S., but the number of female users climbed to 52 percent of Internet users.[13] My main focuses here are on the Muslim publics of the United States and the MENA.

Another development that often creates a challenge for scholarship is that academic research and texts fall far behind the creation of social media tools. While Twitter and Facebook were central to the discourse on and instrumental in the Arab Spring, most of the literature on Islam and technology focuses on the single mode of websites that provide information and may have comments sections, but are not forums of massive public exchange. The web of the 1990s has evolved into the Internet 2.0 model. The

---

11. Abdulla, *Internet in the Arab World*, 62.

12. There are now fifteen million Facebook users in the Middle East and North Africa (this figure excludes Iran, Israel, Pakistan, and Turkey). Only 37 percent of Facebook users in this region are female (compared with 56 percent in the USA and 52 percent in the UK). Only Bahrain and Lebanon Facebook communities approach gender equality, with female users accounting for about 44 percent of total users (Malin, *Middle East and North Africa*, 3).

13. Herbst, "Masters of the House," 138.

software platforms that exist now share these modalities: (1) user-defined linkages between users and content; (2) simple mechanisms to share multimedia content; (3) prominent personal profiling; and (4) intertechnology applications, enabling interfaces with services and features on other sites.[14]

These types of software platforms are the ultimate manifestation of open source knowledge creation and dissemination. The actual web-based participatory venues are creating elements of knowledge that were heretofore only disseminated. For the premier scholar in the area of Islam and technology, the "notion of Islamic knowledge development through history also had an open source element. The development of the scholarship of sayings and traditions associated with the Prophet Muhammed, known as Hadith, required scholars to network between centers of knowledge production in order to collect and transmit the Hadith that they acquired."[15] Bunt acknowledges that this form of open source knowledge production can be "disruptive, chaotic and at times dangerous."[16]

The horizontalizing of the field of production of Islamic knowledge is one that may afford opportunities to those who were excluded in the earlier iterations of cohorts whose contemporary sharing and participatory processes led to the canon of Islamic sciences.

Social Media Participation as Dawah within the Muslim Community

There are many varying opinions on Muslim women's participation in social media sites. It seems that the most commonly acceptable form of participation fulfills the role of a Muslim woman as a transmitter and educator of others, especially as a reminder to her own community. Early Muslim forays into cyberspace were devotional in nature, and came from the obligation to spread knowledge about the traditions as a form of witnessing of faith. Anderson explores the genealogy of an Islamic presence in cyberspace: "Among the first to bring Islam to the Internet were students who were sent abroad in the 1980s for study in technical fields. . . . As pious acts for witness for Islam, they scanned and posted translations of the Holy Qur'an and translations of the Hadith, that together are the

14. Cormode and Krishnamurthy, "Key Differences," 6.

15. Bunt, *iMuslims*, 66.

16. Ibid.

principal sources of sharia, the practical guides to protect beliefs and practices, and created a series of online discussion forums."[17]

The acts of seeking knowledge as the inquirer and the response are in fact forever inextricably linked because of the public space in which the material is presented. The very act of sharing knowledge becomes a form of expression of practice of a component of faith in a way that has not been seen before in the Muslim community. As Eikelman and Johnson identify, "New media share some of the properties of ritual in that they are perfomative. Media do not merely convey messages, they are a part of the message."[18]

Muslims' discourse on "the development of Islamic netiquette is part of an ongoing process that includes the application of principles drawn from primary texts and the interpretation to meet contemporary needs and contexts. . . . This approach suggests a form of ijtihad."[19]

I would argue further that the concept of netiquette as described by Bunt finds its parallel in Islamic jurisprudence in the concept of *adab*, which is translated in many ways including conduct. Scholars and popular Muslim authors will continue to use the baseline of *adab* that is outlined in the Qur'an as the backdrop for their application to the modern realm of the Internet. So for example, as we've seen, the interaction between men and women via the Internet continues to be juxtaposed against the Qur'anic injunctions such as "Say to the believing men that they cast down their looks and guard their private parts. Say to the believing women that they cast down their looks and guard their private parts" (Qur'an 24:31). The concept of netiquette finds its roots in the firmly established 1400-year-old system of adab that will inform how those within the Muslim community choose to embrace, refine or define their cyber-future.

Social Media Participation as Revolution in Nonviolent Form

As the Internet both in MENA and the United States feminizes, it will be utilized as a tool for potential liberation for women who are often not at the table. Here I will focus on two forms of liberation via cyberspace. One will outline the role that Muslim women have had in the MENA Spring, and the second will focus on how Muslim women are utilizing social media to push the boundaries of interpretation and practice within their cultural and religious contexts.

17. Anderson, "Internet Islam," 301.
18. Eikelman and Anderson, "Redefining Muslim Publics," 5.
19. Bunt, *iMuslims*, 417–24.

First, one must recognize that the Internet is still an environment that grows out of a male-dominated discourse and professional context. Dorer assists us in understanding the results of the germination process of women engaging both in the online world and the professional setting that creates this world. "Contrary to the assumption that female pioneers in the new technologies might break open men's domains, it seems that gender boundaries are redrawn in way of assigning gender domains and attendant value, such as high or low prestige."[20] Hierarchy continues to be a part of this new reality, and it is the backdrop against which social media tools are developed and built.

This intersection of masculinity, Islam, and technology for personal use can be found in the phenomenon of Islamogaming. Much of the early use of technology for personal use, in addition to the aforementioned religious education purposes, was for "first person shooter games, which focus on enacting violence on the enemy."[21] As Campbell points out, the reasons for this may be a "response to the objectification of Muslims as villains in other video games."[22]

In the area of social media, Muslim women have utilized this tool to formulate many alternative narratives, both for the general depiction of Muslim women and the elision of Islam and violence as embodied in forms of Islamogaming. Furthermore, Muslim women, especially those in the MENA, are now uniquely situated for the enterprise. Alshejni, writing before the advent of social media's dominance, says that the general Arab response to the Internet was one of cultural protectionism and that "the Internet could be a very positive space for Arab women obliged to silence in public debates. Internet could be a tool for women to break away from the protectionism that has dogged their movement since its inception."[23]

While the role of Muslim women in the uprising in Arab Spring has been attracting a great amount of media attention, there is a nascent movement of Saudi women who are challenging specific religious rulings that directly affect their everyday lives. The costs of doing this are very great. Fatima Sidiya, in an Arab News article, points out that the use of Facebook amongst those in Saudi Arabia has increased more than three times from 2008 to 2009. In the article, she interviews Eman Al-Nafian, who runs the Saudiwomans Weblog. Al-Nafian says that on Twitter and

20. Dorer, "Internet and the Construction of Gender," 78.

21. Campbell, "Islamogaming," 69.

22. Ibid.

23. Alshejni, "Unveiling the Arab Woman's Voice," 217.

Facebook women "encourage each other and make each other more bold." In Al-Nafian's estimation, Saudis who utilize social networking are most concerned about "corruption, political transparency, discrimination against women, women's treatment by government, the issue of women being allowed to drive and the need to ban child marriages."[24]

Those who call for these rights are criticized by three groups, according to Al-Nafian: "Men who look down on the call, women who feel such comments malign the country, and conservatives who feel that women should be subservient to men."[25] This dynamic is clear in the case of Manual Al-Sharif, a Saudi citizen who was arrested for driving a car and then posting the event on Facebook. Al-Sharif's arrest has aroused protest in Saudi Arabia, including a petition signed so far by 1000 Saudis stating:

> We also believe that the time has come to clearly resolve the issue of women driving cars. It is unjust to say it is a social issue and that our religion does not prevent ladies from driving, while simultaneously arresting a woman driving her car. We are in need of a clear system, either to prevent women from driving, or, in case female driving is allowed, a clear indication that ladies are permitted to drive cars in Saudi Arabia.[26]

Social media reflect the debate in the "street" of whatever culture it emanates from. However, the ability to amplify that debate and gain international attention and produce accountability in a participatory manner forever changes the way governments may do business. Gender is one factor in the discourse, so too is the nationalist consciousness expressed in the realm of social media both in this case and other women's cyberactivism. Margot Badran articulates one major thrust for women's activism in Muslim majority countries, "the conviction that building an educated citizenry, especially educated female citizens, was integral to achieving solid independence and preserving national identity."[27]

The Saudi women's driving campaign does not happen within a social vacuum. Many scholars have blogged about changes within the Arab world that create conditions for change. Gema Martin-Munoz, in her public scholarship and texts, has identified many factors that contribute to the potential equalization of women, including high percentages of women in higher education, distribution of wealth into the hands of

24. See Sidiya, "Saudis Use Facebook and Twitter."
25. Ibid.
26. Ibid.; Sidiya, "Manal Al-Sharif."
27. Badran, *Feminism in Islam*, 105.

women in Arab states, and a reduction in family size.[28] Here I mention again the form of public scholarship through the Internet because those who are the very subjects of this scholarship can in ways that were never possible before also be consumers of this information. Not only are the conditions for social change present, the recognition of these conditions via the Internet itself becomes a tool for those organizing for social justice.

Muslim women's cyberactivism has also created what I term "cultural translators" across national boundaries. The very popular altmuslimah.com is essentially an American portal for Muslim women. It has also become an aggregator for news affecting the Muslim world, and the packaging of this information for a Western audience creates expanded public discourse on topics such as the "Fatwas against Facebook" article. The website has specific articles on issues such as domestic violence both within the Muslim world and the West. Activists can find mutual support and indeed, even a religious justification for their struggles, because these websites provide an analysis both of the social as well as doctrinal issues that underpin many of the struggles of Muslim women today.

The same may be said of Facebook and Twitter. Many Muslim women in the United States affected the actual policies of American media and are now sought out as advisors for U.S. policy. Mona Eltahaway, via her Twitter account, received many bookings on media outlets in the United States, and is credited with having affected the CNN terminology for the Egyptian freedom movement from "chaos" to "uprising."[29] Muslim women with a hyphenate identity are able to play an ambassadorial role. They will have to play the dance of ethics of representation and ensure that they are able to amply reflect the concerns of those that they are reporting about in the capacity of native informants. Fatemah Kesharvaz discusses this dilemma of being an internal informant to a larger audience and the dance it takes to amply represent the voices and the risks one takes of reducing or conflating the representations of those who are in a conflict zone into essentialist, hegemonic narratives.[30]

28. Martin-Munoz, "Arab World's Silent Feminist Revolution."

29. See Mona Eltahawy, twitterfeed; for Yemen see Ahlam Said, twitterfeed; for Syria see www.twitter.com/ProfKahf. For an Eltahawy CNN appearance see the YouTube video "Mona Eltahawy to CNN."

30. Keshavarz, *Jasmine and Stars*, 53.

Conclusion

One of the sayings of Prophet Muhammad, as reported to Abu Said was, "The Most excellent jihad is the uttering of truth in the presence of an unjust ruler."[31] The stories of the women outlined in this paper may best exemplify a new form of nonviolent jihad that is emerging: cyberjihad that calls on the utterance against oppression in the direct, public and open way that can only happen via the Internet. Through the public participation that the Internet allows, solidarity between local and international players magnifies the urgency of the issues and holds those in power accountable to change. Just Peacemaking is amplified by women in these virtual and real spaces through bolstering the norms of just peacemaking focused on advancing human rights, democracy, interdependence, and grassroots efforts. Indeed, this frontier for just peacemaking will be deepened not just by increasing participation across genders, but also bringing wider breadth through information dissemination and activism through the internet. The more important factor in our analysis is that the wider web-based community provides the spiritual and emotional support for the formation that is necessary both individually and communally to continue to develop just peacemaking practices and engagement. A person who may be struggling to access the inner resources to perform acts of peacemaking is now no longer alone, barriers of gender or otherwise that might have made an enterprise of peacemaking solitary now are performative acts that are communal in nature, public in their scope and exponential in their participation with others who have similar concerns across the globe. We might say that just peacemaking is by nature a collective activity both in performance as well as in formation of the individual to prepare him/her for activities and in order to *sustain* any actions long term a community must be built for support and reflective practice.

There will be continued struggle for obtaining full participation in the real world. While in Tunisia, women may obtain a 50 percent quota in future parliamentary bodies it is unclear within all the parallel struggles in other countries whether women will achieve a place at the decision-making table.[32] Further questions for exploration might be: 1) Will the social media effect of creating horizontal relationships translate into increased engagement of Muslim women in the traditional settings of Islamic education? How will this affect traditional notions and

31. Ali, *Manual of Hadith*, 398.
32. Xan Rice et al., "Women Have Emerged."

processes of spiritual formation within specific communities? 2) Will women who have developed legitimacy via their social media presence be viewed as authoritative by mainstream Muslim societies? Will this allow for greater engagement in peacebuilding activities? 3) How will the ongoing hesitation of some Muslim individuals to engage in social media based on religious interpretations of modesty, etiquette and gender relations limit the participation of Muslim women specifically? 4) How has and will Islamic hermeneutic principles and fiqh be altered by the Internet and social media? Will the leveling of the playing field between scholar and student, mujtahid (scholar qualified to perform ijtihad) and muqallid (follower) create chaos, or a greater level of social coherence? How will just peacemaking be configured as an element in this scholarly and popular discourse as a legitimate, indigenous concept?

The challenge of scholarship in this field is that there will continue to be technological innovations that outstrip the ability of researchers to study them. We are always at least two steps behind. Within a few years, Facebook and Twitter may indeed themselves become obsolete and these studies might also be marginal in applicability. This is the central challenge with Islamic jurisprudence, the pace of change needs scholars who are willing to engage in new media to offer sound rulings. Finding scholars and jurists who have the experiential component is also a rare combination. In the twenty-first century, a publicly involved intellectual must also be one who is willing to understand and experience what is quickly becoming the reality of choice: cyberspace.

There will be continued ways for Muslim women to develop an agenda for peacemaking whether in community, individual or online formats. The challenge that remains for us to consider as scholars of peacemaking is how to contextualize our pedagogical styles to keep pace with the needs of Muslim women who themselves are agents of nonviolent modes of communication, and who potentially will expand just peacemaking into areas that will bring greater peace for generations to come.

Digitizing peacebuilding education and encounters is a key component to the future success of just peacemaking. For example in Nigeria a country with great need and potential for interreligious and gender based peacemaking as noted earlier, digital peacebuilding holds this type of promise: "Proper use of new digital media in peace education keeps people engaged and is proven to be a useful tool for academic activities in peace education. It also serves to increase positive social interactions. With the help of churches, mosques, and other religious institutions, schools may embark on public peace campaigns utilizing new digital media technologies in the country."[33] The institutions of worship and religious organizations can be at the forefront of forming new peacemakers, supporting existing efforts and forwarding the capacity for interfaith just peacemaking that is inclusive of gender based considerations and with an invigorated framework for sustainable, just peace.

Bibliography

Abdulla, Rasha. *The Internet in the Arab World: Egypt and Beyond.* New York: Lang, 2007.

Al Ghazali. *Ihya ulum al din.* http://www.ibe.unesco.org/fileadmin/user_upload/archive/publications/ThinkersPdf/ghazalie.pdf.

Ali, Muhammad. *Manual of Hadith.* Northampton, MA: Olive Branch, 1978

Alshejni, Lamis. "Unveiling the Arab Woman's Voice through the Net." In *Women@Internet: Creating New Cultures in Cyberspace*, edited by Wendy Harcourt, 214–18. London: Zed, 1999.

Anderson, Jon W. "Internet Islam: New Media of the Islamic Reformation." In *Everyday Life in the Muslim Middle East*, 2nd ed., edited by Donna Lee Bowen and Evelyn A. Early, 300–321. Bloomington, IN: Indiana University Press, 2002.

Anwar, Etin. "Gendered Space and Shared Security: Women's Activism in Peace and Conflict Resolution in Indonesia." In *Women in Islam*, edited by Zayn Kassam, 19–42. Santa Barbara, CA: ABC-CLIO, 2010.

Badran, Margot. *Feminism in Islam: Secular and Religious Convergence.* Oxford: One World, 2009.

Bunt, Gary R. *iMuslims: Rewiring the House of Islam; Islamic Civilization and Muslim Networks.* Chapel Hill, NC: University of North Carolina Press, 2009.

Campbell, Heidi. "Islamogaming: Digital Dignity via Alternative Storytellers." In *Halos and Avatars: Playing Video Games with God*, edited by Craig Detweiler, 63–74. Louisville: Westminster John Knox, 2010.

Cormode, Graham, and Balachander Krishnamurthy. "Key Differences between Web 1.0 and Web 2.0." *First Monday* 13.6 (2008) n.p. Online: http://firstmonday.org/article/view/2125/1972.

Dorer, Johanna. "Internet and the Construction of Gender: Female Professionals and the Process of Doing Gender." In *Women and Everyday Uses of the Internet: Agency and Identity*, edited by Mia Consalvo and Susanna Paasonen, 62–89. New York: Lang, 2002.

Eikelman, Dale, and Jon W. Anderson. "Redefining Muslim Publics." In *New Media in the Muslim World*, 2nd ed., edited by Dale Eikelman and Jon W. Anderson, 1–18. Bloomington: Indiana University Press, 2003.

Eltahawy, Mona. "Mona Eltahawy to CNN: Call Egypt an Uprising." Uploaded 29 January 2011. Accessed 12 February 2012. http://www.youtube.com/watch?v=d_BS9IniwoQ.

---

33. Okolie-Osemene, "Towards Utilizing New Digital Media Technologies." See under "institutional responsibilities regarding new media."

———. twitterfeed. www.twitter.com/Monaeltahawy.

Herbst, Claudia. "Masters of the House: Literacy and the Claiming of Space on the Internet." In *Webbing Cyberfeminist Practice: Communities, Pedagogies and Social Action*, edited by Kristine Blair, Radhika Gajjala, and Christine Tulley, 135–52. New York: Hampton, 2009.

Kamali, Mohammad Hashim. *Principles of Islamic Jurisprudence*. Cambridge: Islamic Texts Society, 1991.

Keshavarz, Fatemeh. *Jasmine and Stars: Reading More Than "Lolita" in Tehran*. Chapel Hill, NC: University of North Carolina Press, 2007.

Ling, Samuel Ngun. "Violence, Poverty, Justice and Peacemaking: A Burmese Christian Response." *Ministerial Formation* (World Council of Churches) 104 (2005) 45–54. Accessed 1 June 2012. http://www.oikoumene.org/fileadmin/files/wcc-main/documents/p5/Ministerial_formation/mf104.pdf#page=46.

Mahmood, Saba. *Politics of Piety: The Islamic Revival and the Feminine Subject*. Princeton: Princeton University Press, 2005.

Malin, Carrington. *Middle East and North Africa Facebook Demographics*. Satwa, Dubai: Spot on Public Relations, 2010. Accessed 2 February 2012. http://www.spotonpr.com/wp-content/uploads/2010/05/FacebookMENA_24May10.pdf.

Martin-Munoz, Gema. "The Arab World's Silent Feminist Revolution," *Project Syndicate: A World of Ideas*, 9 December 2010. http://www.project-syndicate.org/commentary/munoz1/English.

Mni, Hajiya Bilkusi. "Kaduna: Women Investing in Peace." Inter-Faith Action for Peace in Africa (IFAPA) website. Accessed 1 June 2012. http://ifapa-africa.org/index.php?option=com_content&view=article&id=139&lang=en .

Ogolama, Fineface, and Wilfred Ukpere. "The Role of Women in Peacemaking, Conflict and Rehabilitation Management in Elele, Ukwerre Local Government of Rivers State, Nigeria." *African Journal of Business Management* 5.33 (2011) 12711–14.

Okolie-Osemene, James. "Towards Utilizing New Digital Media Technologies for the Promotion of Peace Education in Nigeria." *African Journal of Teacher Education* 2.1 (2012). Accessed 15 June 2012. http://journal.lib.uoguelph.ca/index.php/ajote/article/viewArticle/1936/2476.

Rice, Xan, Katherine Marsh, Tom Finn, Harriet Sherwood, Angelique Chrisafis, and Robert Booth. "Women Have Emerged as Key Players in the Arab Spring." *Guardian*, 22 April 2011. Accessed February 12, 2012. http://www.guardian.co.uk/world/2011/apr/22/women-arab-spring.

Said, Ahlam. twitterfeed: www.twitter.com/Ahlams.

Sidiya, Fatima. "Manal Al-Sharif: Testing Time." *Arab News*, 24 May 2011. Accessed 22 February 2013. http://www.arabnews.com/node/378573.

———. "Saudis Use Facebook and Twitter to Air Their Views." Arab News, 24 February 2011. Accessed 1 January 2012. Online: http://www.arabnews.com/node/369292.

11

Making Peace in a World of Violence

Families and Congregations Participate in Healing Hurt Kids

T. Laine Scales, Hope Haslam Straughan,
and April T. Scales

Imagine a six-year-old little boy, crying out into the dark night: As he screams, shouts, cries, and whimpers, his legs flail, he tugs on his ears, and buries his head deeper in the covers. The third "night terror" of the evening finds Mom racing from her room to his side once again, quietly offering prayers and comfort for her seemingly inconsolable son who cannot tolerate being hugged or even touched. In two short hours, she'll wake him to get ready for Sunday School. Can she really do this? Was it really supposed to be this hard?

WHAT THIS CHILD IS experiencing is not that unusual for a hurt child who has been adopted into a family and has a history of trauma, abuse and neglect. Adoptive parents and children are on a journey towards individual and collective peace due to the effects of these early life events, and community found within a congregation can be a healing component of this transformation.

Who Are We and Why Are We Writing This Chapter?

In this chapter, we share glimpses of our daily lives as a way to introduce some of the needs and concerns of congregants parenting children hurt by violence. We hope our stories will help readers involved in congregations and other communities of support to empathize with and assist adoptive families. We could not have survived our experiences nearly so well without the love of our congregations for our children and for ourselves as parents.

April, our co-author, is Laine's eighteen-year-old daughter. She has contributed to this chapter by offering experiences of her life as a hurt child living with Post Traumatic Stress Disorder. Listening carefully to first-hand statements of hurt kids is an essential beginning point and we are grateful to April for sharing her point of view in order to help other kids and families seeking peace.

Hope and her husband Jay adopted Matt and Billy in 2002, at ages three and four. Laine and her husband Glenn, partially inspired by their visits with the Straughan family and Hope's guidance through the CPS negotiations, adopted April in 2005 at age eleven.

Making Peace with the Past

The American Psychiatric Association (APA) introduced Post Traumatic Stress Disorder (PTSD) as a possible diagnosis when their 1980 diagnostic manual (DSM) defined a traumatic event as "occurring outside the range of usual human experience." The proposed revisions to the DSM forthcoming in 2013 include additional criteria that refine the definition by addition of two additional criteria: 1) "The person experienced, witnessed, or was confronted with an event or events that involved actual or threatened death or serious injury, or a threat to the physical integrity of self or others, and 2) The person's response involved intense fear, helplessness, or horror."[1] The forthcoming 2013 DSM diagnosis may introduce a new diagnosis, "Developmental Trauma Disorder" which will be important for children and teens as it points out how trauma affects physical, cognitive, psychological, (and, we argue, spiritual) development.

Children living with past traumas experience every-day events in dramatically different ways from the rest of us. Hurt children are in a constant struggle to make peace with their past. Greenwald describes a "trauma wall" behind which a person surviving trauma holds all the fear,

---

1. American Psychiatric Association, *Diagnostic and Statistical Manual*, 467–68.

anxiety, anger, and helplessness, rather than being able to "digest" it or process it along with other memories. This is especially true for children and teens who were pre-verbal at the time of trauma. Greenwald relates an example of an everyday experience of a traumatized teen:

> Most of us, when accidentally bumped in the hallway, will be slightly irritated, perhaps make a comment, but forget about it five minutes later. Now think about the twelve-year-old boy who has been routinely physically abused at home. Behind the wall is piled-up fear of being attacked, a sense of helplessness, and rage. When he is bumped in the hallway, the "sore spot" reaction from the stuff piled up behind the wall is so strong that he believes he is being attacked. Naturally, being angry and not wanting to feel helpless anymore, he defends himself. When he is sent to the assistant principal's office for "punching a peer with no provocation," he insists that the other kid started it.[2]

The person experiencing trauma may not be aware of triggers as they are happening. For example, a child who does not immediately understand how to do her math homework may give up easily, when she may be able to do it with a little more effort. However, she is already overwhelmed by a constant sense of helplessness lurking in the "sore spot" behind the wall. Students, parents, and teachers may not recognize how the sore spot is affecting seemingly ordinary school tasks.[3]

Making Peace with Oneself

At the same time a child is making peace with the past, she must move toward accepting and making peace with herself. Children who have been told from an early stage that they are "bad," or have been forced by adults to engage in behavior that our society has rejected as bad behavior, must come to terms with what they have done.

One of the important distinctions our professional study has helped us to discern is the difference between shame and guilt. Shame involves emotions of disgrace, humiliation, and self-blame. In healthy families, parents and children re-establish connection after misbehavior; parents assure the child she is still safe and loveable. However, in families with depressed, angry, neglecting, or rejecting parents, the child's shame leads

---

2. Greenwald, *Child Trauma Handbook*, 13.
3. Ibid.

her to feel worthless, inferior, and unlovable.[4] These children carry their shame with them, even when they are behaving appropriately. In moments of misbehavior, their shame reactions become extreme, leading them to defend themselves in the face of obvious lying or other infractions. They may withdraw and hide out of fear, refuse to apologize, rage against the person calling attention to the infraction, blame others even when it is obvious the fault is theirs, or avoid the offended people. All of these shame reactions are focused on protecting themselves and surviving.

Helping children learn to move toward guilt, rather than shame, when they have engaged in wrong behavior, is an important task in their healing. Attachment issues come to the fore when describing a guilt reaction: the offending child or teen focuses on the behavior itself and recognizes it as a behavior, not a character flaw. She is anxious to repair the wrong and to restore harmony in relationship. Desire for reparation is increased if she is attached. Apologies flow from guilt and remorse and right relationship can be restored.[5]

Avoiding a shame response seems almost impossible at times. Guilt and remorse, when expressed and acted on by the person experiencing it, can often lead to a freedom from those feelings, reconnection with those who have been wronged or hurt by the choices, and an ability to move on with the day with a steady mood and countenance. However, when small and large mistakes or missteps evoke shame, a child is internalizing a dark, powerful emotion of blame, self-destructive and negative thoughts that make it increasingly difficult to apologize, much less reconnect with the person interacting with them around these choices and behaviors. It often becomes a cycle, which is unable to be slowed down, stopped, or reversed.

For about two years, the primary goal Hope and Jay were working on with Billy and his therapist, was that most of the time, he would become able to make this terribly difficult shift away from his shame, yelling, and accusations to others which ultimately led to destructive self-talk. Instead, he would become able to move toward a short apology and an ability to reconnect with the rest of the family and re-engage in the evening activities, a response to his guilt reaction, and not shame. This goal was set after years of his extremely difficult behavior on most evenings of the week, which led to exhaustion, separation, and destruction of much self-esteem, of material property, and of relationships between the family members. Billy would get sucked up in that dark cycle of shame and self-blame, and

4. Orlans and Levy, *Healing Parents*, 53.
5. Miculincer and Shaver, *Attachment in Adulthood*.

often would miss dinner after stomping off to his room, yelling all the way, and barricading himself in his room. He'd fall asleep in a disturbed, exhausted state, without the relief of reconnected relationship, forgiveness and deep acceptance. To further the cycle, this lack of resolution before sleep led to very challenging mornings, as he'd awaken fatigued, embarrassed, and with inexpressible raw emotions.

Norah, Billy's therapist, helped the parents introduce simple "interruptions" to that dark cycle of blame and shame, including offering Billy a small cup of warm milk, using a squishy ball to throw, or squish to focus aggression and frustration in that contained manner. It took over a year and a half for Billy's successes to reach the level of "most of the time he's able to separate himself if need be, but then apologize, reconnect with people, and re-engage in the evening activities." Interrupting that dark and powerful shame and blame cycle remains one of the most important goals as the parents assist Billy in making peace with himself, and coming to a place of acceptance for who he is.

As is common with kids in foster care and adoption, Matt and Billy have additional arenas to make peace with in terms of race and ethnicity. Their biological parents were a mixed race couple: one parent was White and one parent was Black. The Straughans are a transracial family now, as Hope and Jay are both White, and their two sons are both White and Black. Matt looks fully African-American with beautiful, rich dark brown skin, and hair that is currently growing out in twists-becoming-dreads. Billy is much lighter skinned, appearing almost Latino in tone, with hair that is almost exactly like Hope's—full of body, brown, with loose curls.

Children move toward making peace with themselves in a context with those they are closest to, the feedback they receive, and what they "see" when they look around them. In the Straughan family's earliest days, Matt was deeply distraught because his skin was so much darker than anyone else in his new "forever family." He cried over it, begged his new parents to somehow change his hair so it could be more like Jay's—blonde, straight—and very unlike his own! Sometime later, Hope was stunned by a story Matt's kindergarten teacher recounted, having overheard it one morning. Ms. Kremer heard E.J. say, "Hey, Matt, why isn't your mom black like you and me?" Matt stopped his Lego building project, looked up to see Hope walking out of the classroom door, and after a short pause, he said, "I don't know, but her favorite color's black!" It seemed that in a short time Matt had found some level of peace with his own racial identity which allowed him to be completely open to any connection he and his forever Mom might have about black-ness.

Making Peace in a New Family

The primary tasks of a new family are to build new attachments and establish roles within the family. Such tasks are surrounded by years of storming, confusion, and grief. As one of our children's therapists put it "the time you need most to get away from your child, perhaps when they are pushing away, will be the time they most need you to come near." How does one move toward a child who is so rejecting? This is one area in which congregations and communities of support can help families the most.

Much of the literature on foster care and adoption points to the very difficult process of attachment, which we will define here as "the deep and enduring biological, emotional, and social connection caregivers and children establish early in life."[6] Attachment is a more complex human need which takes years to develop within adoptive families. Orlans and Levy remind us that attachment security has been shown to be the most powerful predictor of life success because it directly affects learning, brain development, self-control, trust, and impacts relationships throughout life. Hurt children have disrupted and damaged attachments leading them to focus on self-preservation and survival rather than entering relationships in more positive ways.[7]

Studies on the developing brain demonstrate that an infant's interaction with caregivers actually shapes the formation and operation of the brain, including the Neocortex, Limbic system, and brain stem. The parts of the brain most affected by neglect and/or abuse are the areas that regulate self control, the release of stress hormones, and the way genetic material is expressed. Add to these negative effects the mental illness, alcoholism, drug use, and other factors common among parents giving birth to hurt children, and the obstacles to healthy living, beginning in infancy, seem insurmountable.[8]

Neglecting or abusive parents fail to respond, or respond violently to the normal biological and social needs of their children. Setting up a situation where trust is replaced by mistrust and fear may face the infant with a lifetime of disrupted attachments. Orlans and Levy instruct adoptive

6. Orlans and Levy, *Healing Parents*.
7. Ibid.
8. Ibid.

parents of hurt children to practice what they call "corrective attachment parenting" to build later in life the attachments that should have been in place between parents and their infants.[9]

When children have attachment disruptions early in life, an unfortunate outcome is that the lack of affective attunement with a caring adult causes the child to have a distorted understanding of self in relation to others.[10] Children often find it difficult to discern a level of intensity or intimacy in relationship with others, such as between a "best friend" and a child they've played with for ten minutes at the local park for instance. This often plays out in the home as well, but with far more challenging results. The child with reactive attachment disorder (a rare, but very serious diagnosis), often reacts strongly, intensely and negatively to the mother figure in the home. For example, a child may bolt when going from the car to the school, or from the church to the car. In extreme cases, a child may become violent by hitting, pinching and throwing things along with utilizing verbal assaults.

As professional social workers, we were both quite prepared cognitively for this rejection, though nothing could have prepared us emotionally. We have spent our careers studying about psychological processes and teaching human behavior and human development courses. However, even that strong knowledge base could not prepare us for the human experience of being rejected by the child you so hope will love you. It requires a mother to transcend her own needs and emotions and continue to accept the rejecting child. During this phase, adoptive children often are particularly loving and preferential to the father figure, perhaps as a way to stay close to one adult, perhaps as a way to attempt to separate the parenting team.

Storms Will Precede Peace

It is not uncommon for children who lacked stable and consistent parenting from a young age to be impulsive, quick to anger, and easy to reach a point of out-of-control frustration.[11] When in the midst of one of these intense and terrifying episodes a child can be so utterly overcome with fear of being intimately accepted, loved, and deeply loved, that they do all in their power to ensure they will be rejected, sent away, and proven right that they are indeed unlovable. Of course, hurt children are not able

9. Ibid.

10. Hughes, *Building the Bonds of Attachment.*

11. Jewett, *Adopting the Older Child.*

to articulate or even realize that this is in their thoughts. Instead, what they express is very direct, painful and blaming thoughts and sometimes threats toward the parent.

As Keck and Kupecky point out, "One of the hardest things for many hurt children to let go of is the dynamic of anger they often experienced and participated in while in their birth family. They have an amazing ability to recreate this dynamic with their new parents, who once considered themselves patient and loving."[12] This was certainly the case with us. Both of us have experienced intensely dark seasons of life with our children. In order to keep peace, we made compromises that did not fit our ideals for family life. Maybe we did not ask a child a second time to hang up a coat or backpack, for fear of an escalated response. While trying to be consistent, maybe we allowed a day of respite from chores in particularly stressful times.

As mothers, we would wake up each morning during these dark seasons and become immediately tense, desperate to avoid our children's wrath and outbursts, or their ignoring us as if we were invisible. What we understand now that we are through this darkness and on the other side of it, is that children who are fighting their hurt, experiencing flashbacks, desperately trying to trust, and generally still in survival mode, will battle for control using any means possible. These dark seasons are opportunities for congregations to come alongside parents and help them stay grounded in reality. A congregation that knows a child and family well can remind parents how far the child has come, and instill hope that growth can still occur.

Ironically, children behaving their worst are often starving and desperate for someone else who is sturdy, strong, and consistent, to take over.[13] They fight for control at the same time they desperately want to relinquish control. There is wide consensus in the literature on attachment that the adoptive mother bears the brunt of the child's anger, fear, and testing. In addition, children may perceive fathers as strong, because they often have height, physical strength, deep and strong voices, and all the stereotypical signs of strength for our culture. Families should not face this alone; they must turn to their congregational community for support.

In Laine's family, the phase of April testing the attachment coincided with adolescence. Having passed through to the other side, April has the wisdom and insight to reflect on what was happening. She writes:

> *Every adult had failed me from the day I was born. My birth mother gave me away to CPS [Child Protective Services] when I*

12. Keck and Kupecky, *Adopting the Hurt Child*, 124.

13. Trout and Thomas, *Jonathon Letters*.

was four, every foster family I lived with was easily able to remove me from their homes without a second thought, and my first adoptive family abused me for four years after having told me myriad times that they "loved" me. My confidence had been shattered and my view on the world was beyond pessimistic. All people did was hurt others. There was no such thing as being able to love or care about someone. I came to learn that I was the only person I could rely on and the only person I could trust. Through much pain, I became an independent individual.

When I was adopted into Laine and Glenn's family, I wanted to be able to hope that they would never harm or leave me. However, I could not recollect a time when an adult treated me properly and cared for my needs. I had lost the last of my hope years before. Laine and Glenn told me that I could trust them and they loved me, but I had heard that millions of times. They insisted that we would be a forever family, but was there such a thing as forever?

Being a part of this forever family, I could no longer do as I pleased. I now had two people that I had no trust in telling me what they thought was best for me. Laine and Glenn would tell me to go to bed at a certain time or to do chores. Now I can see that they meant to add stability in my life and keep me healthy, but at the time I perceived the requests as ways to control me and strip me from the only thing I had left; myself.

As I became a teenager, my urge to claim independence became overwhelming. At fifteen, I was begging, pleading, and screaming to stay out until one a.m., be driven from place to place, and to not have chores. I was blessed with many privileges and opportunities that most teenagers were not. But I never believed it was enough. I wanted my full individualism back. When it was not given to me, I began threatening to move out or run away. My mom and I would spend hours yelling at each other and arguing . . . sometimes over the silliest things. Despite all the threats and curses I screamed out and the long arguments, my parents remained strong, stable, and loving. This was exactly what I had needed my entire life. Because of this, I am now a strong, wise, and mature teenager.

Supportive congregations can help adoptive families by simply staying attuned to parents who need respite, acceptance, or extra encouragement. The hurt children and teens also need to be accepted and to have their behavior viewed as a process that must occur on their journey to making peace with their new families. A loving congregation can support the rejected parent(s) without being overly critical or punishing of this hurt child who must pass through this process of testing and temporarily rejecting the parents in order to make peace in the new family.

Being Present with a Child Making Peace

Daniel Hughes, a clinical psychologist who specializes in child neglect and abuse as well as foster care and adoption, has crafted a theoretical model to guide helping professionals, parents, and other caregivers in the healing work of helping troubled children find peace within themselves, and among those surrounding them. The model is based on the five principles of acceptance, curiosity, being empathic, loving and being playful. When a child is railing against himself and talking about how little and how bad he is, Hughes acknowledges that the natural response of most adults is to contradict the child, and show how many ways that child is brave, strong, important, and loved. However, this response, once again, proves to children that they are not listened to, that what they feel so deeply is dismissed entirely. Instead, Hughes says that we should be 100 percent accepting of these statements, and in an empathic, curious manner, reflect back to the child that it must be so hard to feel such despair and sadness.[14]

This connection with hurt children around their very raw and real emotions is a great gift, which can lead over time to a letting go of some of that darkness, as they no longer have to experience it alone. Through the spontaneous use of playful interactions, and consistently loving communication, even in very hard and disruptive situations, a child can begin to experience healthy relationships and a renewed belief in themselves, and peace between themselves and others. We need to be reminded that change takes place over time, and is sometimes barely visible. The disruptions, violence, and challenging behavior found in many foster and adoptive homes often drives extended family and friends away, and they are fearful and blaming at worst, or questioning of the extensive shifts and new ways of interacting and disciplining that are often necessary to help these children heal at best.

> Parents must pass the many tests their child may devise to see if he can truly trust this new family. The tests lessen over time but may emerge when another trauma, large or small, occurs for the child of family. Trauma leaves vulnerable spirits.[15]

---

14. Hughes, *Building the Bonds of Attachment*.
15. Schooler, Smalley, and Callahan, *Wounded Children, Healing Homes*, 8.

Orlans and Levy recognize that adoptive parents will have three primary challenges, the child will push away love and support, the child will need help coping with emotions and stress, and parents must find ways to manage their own emotional reactions to this challenging process. Congregations can play an essential role in supporting adoptive families and assisting with these three challenges.[16]

Making Peace with God

While spiritual development may proceed differently for each child, the faith of hurt children will be deeply affected by the multiple crises they have survived. While adult onlookers may expect that children surviving trauma might be thankful to God for saving or rescuing them into a new family, this may not be the stance of the hurt child. As social worker and family ministry author Diana Garland reminds us:

> Crisis almost always creates questions about the meaning and purpose of human life. Did we cause our own suffering? How can a loving God let children get cancer? How can I be depressed if I believe in a loving, graceful God? And on and on—for every crisis there is a question, a belief system that may be under siege.[17]

Unfortunately, the unpredictable behavior of wounded children that stems from their anger and hopelessness may be labeled by others (even church members) as immoral or sinful. They are often more confused than other children about images of God as a loving parent, the sinful nature of persons, forgiveness, grace, and other theological ideas. Families and others working with hurt children may have difficulty suspending judgment or frustration. However, as Wayne Muller, in his book, *Legacy of the Heart, The Spiritual Advantages of a Painful Childhood*, describes these wounds may ultimately lead to a closeness to God and "a profound inner wisdom" as the child becomes an adult.[18]

> Deep within them [hurt children]—just beneath the wound— lies a profound spiritual vitality, a quiet knowing, a way of perceiving what is beautiful, right, and true. Since their early experiences were so dark and painful, they have spent much of

16. Orlans and Levy, *Healing Parents.*
17. Garland, "Response to Chavez."
18. Muller, *Legacy of the Heart*, xiii.

their lives in search of the gentleness, love, and peace they have only imagined in the privacy of their own hearts.[19]

If hurt children and teens have this potential for the "profound spiritual vitality" that Muller describes, how can families and congregations create environments to nurture this kind of faith development?

Making Peace with the Church

Christian families parenting hurt children must be able to lean on their congregations for support, tangible help, and guidance in spiritual matters. We have learned about this experientially from receiving the good love of our own congregations. We did not know what we needed and could not ask for it. However, our churches were sensitive to our needs and responded.

When Laine and Glenn first met their daughter-to-be (April), she was eleven years old and attended church regularly with her foster family. One of the most special moments of the second visit with her was when she leaned her sweet blonde head against Laine's arm during the worship service. Her leaning was so tentative that she barely put her little ear against Laine's shoulder, seemingly afraid to rest her full head, lest she be rejected. Of course Laine responded by embracing her; their first mother-daughter touch. Laine recorded the memory in a few lines of a poem called "Love Decides."

> Little ear on my shoulder in church
> Arms open to surround you and
> Will never close
> Forever family is born.[20]

The journey of this new family included church services right away as a time to be close and to love. In fact, the church pew was always a special place where they sat together as a family of three: girl in the middle surrounded by a loving parent on either side. That December, as a way to celebrate this new family, the pastor invited them to light the advent candles, recalling Christ's coming. This newly formed family of three mirrored Mary and Joseph welcoming the new baby.

In addition, the new family created a religious ritual together to celebrate their beginnings. By writing a family covenant that became the center of an "entrustment ceremony" in which the foster family and others

19. Ibid., xiii.
20. Scales, "Love Decides," 25.

entrusted the care of April to her new parents. The covenant spelled out promises to April from her parents: they promised to stay with her, to help her remember her families of the past, to be present in her joys and sorrows, and that she will always have a place in their home and in their hearts, even after she is grown.

The parents drafted the ceremony and asked April to edit the manuscript. They invited the adoption caseworkers and therapists to attend the ceremony and affirm that they trusted this would be a good family. The current foster family articulated a "letting go," noting how much she had grown healthier and stronger during the year she spent with them. April's friend from her current church, Anna, came to the ceremony. The parents' church provided a candle arrangement and the family lit candles to represent April's past families, her siblings, and others she would continue to love and remember. The ritual closed with the foster parents and nine foster siblings reading a benediction to April; a prayer from the parents' wedding ceremony. Each year the family celebrates Entrustment Day with special treats and family togetherness.

The Straughan family ritualized their entrustment in a similar way and both families celebrate these anniversaries with special treats and family togetherness. By ritualizing and celebrating yearly our transitions with promises and prayers, blessings and benedictions, our families have created special memories (and DVD recordings) of our lifelong commitments that we can return to as we wish. While we did not hold these ceremonies in our church's buildings, our current and former congregations were present in the candles, the blessings, and the friendships represented in the ceremony.[21]

Reaching Out to Other Hurt Kids

From preschool through adolescence, April experienced numerous traumatic events within the church. As she continues to search for peace following these events, has sought positive experiences outside of a formal congregation. She wonders, as many wounded people do, why God was not there in her time of need: if God had been there, how could God allow her to be abused? It may take a lifetime and more for her to be able to find peace about that question, but as her narrative reveals, she is seeking:

21. Leiberman and Bufferd, *Creating Ceremonies*; Mason, *Designing Rituals of Adoption.*

The day I lost my faith in God is a day I will never forget. It was the day I finally realized that the B's, my first adoptive family who kept me for 3 years before tossing me back to CPS, did not love me or care about me. That was the day I finally realized that no one did or ever would care:

Tina slammed the pantry door closed. Darkness. Vomit mixed with Horseradish and bits of blood covered the tiny, tiled pantry. My adoptive mother was forcing me to sleep with my head in the vomit. I turned my head to face the ceiling. The smell was revolting. I had been taught by this supposedly "Christian" family to listen to Christian music. I began singing Call on Jesus.

"When I call on Jesus,
All things are possible . . .
. . . Cause he'll move heaven and earth
to come rescue me when I call
la la la . . ."

My voice faltered and tears welled in my eyes. My heart felt as if someone was squeezing it as hard as they could. Anguish. Who was I kidding? I had prayed for years and no one had ever listened. What kind of God would let me suffer so much? My body tensed as I tried to keep my cries inside. All I allowed out of my mouth was air that struggled to be released. I began hitting and clawing my body. Why couldn't I just die? No one loved me. No one would miss me or care. I was just a mistake. I cried until my body was worn, tired, and could no longer produce any more tears. I laid there feeling numb and cold. Finally, I closed my eyes and drifted into an uncomfortable sleep. I was all alone.

After I moved in with Laine and Glenn, we attended church every Sunday and some Wednesdays. During Sunday School, I was fine. We didn't talk much about God. Instead, we did art projects, sang, or prayed. But I dreaded going to the sermons. Not because the preacher wasn't good, but because I was horrified by the God-talk. The sermons were tragic reminders of what the B's did to me and why. During the service, I would lay on my mom and sleep or I'd read; anything to get my mind away from reality for that hour. I would constantly ask what time it was and when church ended. I'd count down how many items we had left on the bulletin.

As I got older, I asked my mom if I could attend Sunday School only. For a while, this worked. But once I became old enough to enter the youth group, almost all we did was talk of God. My mind would wander off and when the youth minister requested I read a passage, my body would tense and my mouth would become dry. I really felt like God was being shoved at me when what I needed was space and time to heal. I couldn't heal when I was constantly being flashed into the past and reliving all the memories I had gone through with this family that claimed to be Christians.

Eventually, I moved to a different youth group in a new church, hoping that they might be different. But, they weren't. It was the same every Sunday morning. So I stopped going Sundays and only attended the Wednesday youth activities. Slowly, I even removed myself from that and quit church all together.

For a couple years, I avoided anything related to God. I allowed myself the time and space I needed to heal. I was given the opportunity to work through all the horrors I had experienced.

Now, I am still in between the lines of Atheism and Christianity. However, a few weeks ago, I was able to give the most sincere and heartfelt prayer I had given in six years. I have had a renewed interest in God. A different God than the one the B's told me of. This God is a God that does not believe I am a mistake. . . . A God who forgives and loves all people. The steps I must take are tentative and shaky today, but with time, they will become strong and confident.

One of the opportunities for April to work toward some resolution to her questions is embodied in the ministry she and Laine started together through their church. Creating a satellite of the prayer shawl ministry, they gathered young people and taught them to knit and crochet, producing blankets for foster kids in transition to new homes. Noting that much charitable attention is given to adopted babies while older children often go unnoticed, their group focuses on children and teens age 10 or older. *Kidz Komfort* offers opportunities for April to pay it forward as she once received a homemade quilt from a group of church women in one of her new foster homes.

While meetings are held outside the church walls, this ministry offers a venue for April to share her story at whatever level she feels comfortable with and to do something tangible, comforting, and meaningful in the context of her own journey. She shared a few thoughts with her congregation one Sunday morning about the uses of a blanket:

At night, when they are in a strange place, kids can pull the blanket close to them and know "someone was thinking of me." It lights a spark of hope in the kid's heart. . . . God stitches our lives together, putting us together like a crocheted blanket. You still have mess ups, some holes are bigger than others. We are not perfect. But the blanket can still be useful and keep you warm. Also, some kids don't like to be hugged by people, but they enjoy being cuddled by a blanket. I felt that way sometimes; I didn't want to hug or be close to a person because I knew I'd just have to leave them in a few weeks or, at the most, a couple of months. But being hugged by a blanket is like being surrounded by God's love for you. You always have it.

Families and congregations can encourage and facilitate this type of ministry that blesses the giver as much as the recipient. And hurt kids need to give; to see themselves as worthy of being a giver and strong enough to share something of themselves without threatening their own survival. April had an opportunity to describe the ministry in the church newsletter and several church members donated yarn or joined the group.

Congregations Can Help

From our own experiences as adoptive families, we have compiled the following list of suggestions for how congregations can support adoptive families and our children have added to the list. We believe you will recognize how the suggestions relate to the stories we have shared in this chapter. The list is not exhaustive; your congregation will imagine additional ways to help hurt children and families on their journey together toward peace:

Supporting Individual Children and Teens

1. Understand delayed or unusual expressions of psychosocial development. An older child joining a new family will want to cuddle, lay in a parent's lap, and do other things similar to a toddler. Behavioral issues in the nursery or in Sunday School may mirror children younger in years.

2. As children and teens begin to consider church membership or confirmation, recognize ways in which prior spiritual traumas may affect their perspectives. They may be exceptionally reluctant to trust, or overly eager to join the church without full understanding of their long-term commitments.

3. Create art. Art is therapeutic for children experiencing trauma during a pre-verbal stage of life. Sunday School, Vacation Bible School, and other artistic opportunities for children and youth are essential. This focus should continue into the teenage years.

4. Create sound and movement. Children recovering from trauma must have opportunities to sing, play instruments, dance, and join in other creative activities. Watch for what is being expressed and be available for discussion as needed.

5. Create opportunities for dramatic expression. Plays, pageants, musicals, and other opportunities offered in churches provide excellent opportunities for hurt children to express themselves and try on new or different roles and identities.

Supporting Adoptive and Foster Families

1. Find ways to help families ritualize their life transitions while acknowledging God's blessings. Some examples include entrustment ceremonies, adoption-day celebrations, child dedications, and families leading worship in song or scripture readings.

2. Offer respite care to adoptive families of hurt children. Families in the congregation may take the children for a weekend or even a Saturday, offering parents needed rest.

3. Protect private stories. Children and youth may tell stories of their past in an effort to bond with their congregation or youth group. Members should be warned of the personal nature of these often dramatic stories of abuse or violence so they are not repeated. The child needs a safe space to tell his or her story without it being repeated.

Support from the Entire Congregation

1. Join faith communities from across the country in the Children's Defense Fund-sponsored Children's Sabbath, in celebration of children as sacred gifts of the Divine. This communal celebration provides the opportunity for houses of worship to renew and live out their moral responsibility to care, protect and advocate for all children. This celebration is part of a broader movement to improve the lives of children and families, while working for justice on their behalf.[22]

2. Encourage children and youth to minister to others. For example, April and Laine's *Kidz Komfort* became a featured ministry in the church newsletter and members supported the ministry by donating yarn.

22. Children's Defense Fund, "National Observance."

3. Work through local agencies to advocate for abused children. When the church reaches out to address child abuse, hurt children of the congregation learn productive ways to express their anger and frustration at a world where innocent ones can be violated. The church's advocacy combats the hopelessness that hurt children and youth may feel. In addition, hurt children, if they are comfortable, can be excellent sources of information for others in the congregation who do not understand trauma and abuse. Proceed with caution.

4. As ministers and lay workers work with children and teens, they must recognize and respect the various ways in which a child's trauma may affect spiritual development. Ministers, social workers, and others in the congregation can help identify readings and resources to enhance a layperson or minister's knowledge base regarding abuse.

5. Adopt children as a congregational effort. This requires a large and well considered, long-term commitment, and can range from supporting multiple families within the church who have adopted children, supporting families financially who seek to adopt.[23]

Conclusion: Making Peace for a Lifelong Journey toward Healing and Wholeness

Children and teenagers who have been hurt in violent homes may spend the rest of their lives trying to make peace: with themselves, their past, their new families, and with God. Peace is the theme of this chapter and this collection of readings, and we will repeat what has been stated by several authors throughout this volume: peace, as described in the New Testament, is not passive, it is active. Foster and adoptive families, along with their congregations, must assist hurt children to make peace.

In describing the psychological and spiritual lives of all children and teenagers, developmental psychologists such as Eric Erikson point to conflicting inner urges as well as external demands that are at work to form the personality. As a child pushes away the parts of her life that are "unacceptable" and "not me," those darker parts still remain to be integrated and dealt with in development. This integration may be called "peace" or harmony, and according to White, the achievement of peace "becomes a pressing issue for every child but is, perhaps, the least recognized need."[24]

23. "Church Adoption Funds"; World Orphans, *Our Church to Church Model.*
24. White, "Role of the Home," 235.

If inner turmoil and the pushing away of the darker "not me" is the developmental task of every child and teenager, imagine how insurmountable this task can be for a child who has been told she is the embodiment of the devil. How impossible might this task be for the boy who has been raped? He knows instinctively that the sexual act has to be "not me," and yet remembers being present during the rape. One of the common symptoms of Post-Traumatic Stress Disorder, a common diagnosis of abused and hurt children, is disassociation. This is an exaggerated "not me" reaction as a child tries to deal with horrendous and unspeakable acts. The disassociating child tries to escape being present, using the mind and spirit to remove her "self" until safety returns. How hard it must be to find peace in one's lifetime under these circumstances.

White describes the biblical peace as "one which finds its center within the person as that person relates to Christ."[25] However, peace does not stop there, because from that center the Christian develops peace in her relationships to others. For White, the home provides "the greatest power in the development of peace in any person's life."[26]

For hurt children, their earliest homes often held the chaos and battlegrounds that destroyed their families. In their new foster or adoptive families, a child may be able to move toward peace as she experiences the trust and commitment described above, along with discipline and limit-setting that is loving and consistent.[27] As we have tried to demonstrate by sharing our own stories of adopting hurt children, the spiritual development of the child as well as the support of the adopting family can be an essential part of the congregation's ministry to families. The church is called to lift up, support, develop, and instruct families as they seek to nurture peace within children whose prior homes have been destroyed by violence. The church is also called to advocate peace on earth and freedom from violence for every child.

What we have written grows out of our own experience, of course, and not out of deduction from just peacemaking theory. But it involved all four of the initiative practices (nonviolent action that began to create the peace and justice all children need, independent initiatives, conflict resolution, acknowledgment, forgiveness and repentance). It certainly involved fostering the justice and human rights that all children and all

25. Ibid.
26. Ibid.
27. White, "Role of the Home."

persons need. And it absolutely required patient and consistent efforts to create community with love, with important support from church groups.

Our prayer is that the peace that passes all understanding may come to the world's children, including our own hurt but healing kids.

Bibliography

American Psychiatric Association. *Diagnostic and Statistical Manual of Mental Disorders.* 4th ed. Washington, DC: American Psychiatric Association, 2000.

Children's Defense Fund. "National Observance of Children's Sabbaths Celebration." Washington, DC: Children's Defense Fund, 2010. Accessed 12 December 2010. http://www.childrensdefense.org/programs-campaigns/faith-based-action/childrens-sabbaths.

"Church Adoption Funds." *The ABBA Fund Blog.* 2011. Accessed 7 April 2011. http://abbafund.wordpress.com/church-adoption-funds/.

Garland, Diana R. "Response to Chavez." *Social Work and Christianity.* Forthcoming.

Greenwald, Ricky. *Child Trauma Handbook: A Guide for Helping Trauma-Exposed Children and Adolescents.* Binghamton, NY: Haworth Reference, 2005.

Hughes, Daniel A. *Building the Bonds of Attachment: Awakening Love in Deeply Troubled Children.* 2nd ed. Lanham, MD: Aronson, 2006.

Jewett, Claudia. *Adopting the Older Child.* Boston: Harvard Common, 1977.

Keck, Gregory C., and Regina M. Kupecky. *Adopting the Hurt Child: Hope for Families with Special-Needs Kids.* Colorado Springs: Pinon, 1995.

Leiberman, Cheryl A., and Rhea K. Bufferd. *Creating Ceremonies: Innovative Ways to Meet Adoption Challenges.* Phoenix: Zeig, Tucker & Co., 1998.

Mason, Mary Martin. *Designing Rituals of Adoption: For the Religious and Secular Community.* Minneapolis: Lutheran Social Services, 2002.

Miculincer, Mario, and Phillip R. Shaver. *Attachment in Adulthood.* New York: Guilford, 2007.

Muller, Wayne. *Legacy of the Heart: The Spiritual Advantages of a Painful Childhood.* New York: Simon & Schuster, 1992.

Orlans, Michael, and Terry Levy. *Healing Parents: Helping Wounded Children Learn to Trust and Love.* Washington, DC: CWLA, 2006.

Scales, T. Laine. "Love Decides." *Family and Community Ministries: Empowering through Faith* 22.2 (2008) 25.

Schooler, Jaune E., Betsy Keefer Smalley, and Timothy J. Callahan. *Wounded Children, Healing Homes: How Traumatized Children Impact Adoptive and Foster Families.* Colorado Springs: NavPress, 2009.

Trout, Michael, and Lori Thomas. *The Jonathon Letters: One Family's Use of Support as They Took In, and Fell in Love with, a Troubled Child.* Champaign, IL: Infant-Parent Institute, 2005.

White, Ernest. "The Role of the Home in the Religious Development of Children." *Review and Expositor* 80 (1983) 231–43.

World Orphans. *Our Church to Church Model.* Accessed 7 April 2011. http://www.worldorphans.org/church-to-church-model.php.

1 2

Religious Peacebuilding
and Economic Justice

Nimi Wariboko[1]

Introduction

THIS CHAPTER ADDRESSES THE concrete issues of peacebuilding and economic justice. As the eminent African-American ethicist Peter Paris admonishes: "We must remember always that social justice is not an abstract idea. Rather it is an empirical reality; it is specific, concrete, visible, and quantifiable."[2] Thus, I aim to approach my assignment not with the philosopher's interest in conceptual and analytical categories, but to fashion perspectives on justice and peacebuilding that can help us to comprehend their links and connections in empirical reality. In my discussion I will make peacebuilding the measure of communion and economic justice the plumb line. If peacebuilding is about eliminating (addressing) injuries based on injustice, acknowledging and correcting neglect to establish and sustain right relationships, and paying attention to dynamics of history, then economic justice is one veritable instrument to gauge its progress. Peace and economic justice are interactive. Each conditions and is conditioned by the other. Any approach to the study of peacebuilding that privileges peace at the expense of justice or vice versa is inadequate.

1. Lecture for course taught by Petersen, Helmick and Porter.
2. Paris, "Meditation on Love," 3.

My approach is not only to highlight the interplay between peace and justice, but also to argue that the network of expected, aleatory, interstitial "personal encounters" in all forms of human coexistence constitute their generative and unifying principle. Encounters within any given community are informed by the authority of virtue-guided, tradition-formed communities. There is no such thing as an "encounter as such," that is, an encounter prescinded from all historical and cultural context. In Paul Tillich's words,

> Man [sic] becomes man in personal encounters. Only by meeting a "thou" does man realize that he is an "ego." No natural object within the whole universe can do this for him. Man can transcend himself in all directions in knowledge and control. He can use everything for his purposes. . . . But there is a limit for man which is definite and which he always encounters, the other man. The other one, the "thou," is like a wall that cannot be removed or penetrated or used. He who tries to do so destroys himself. The "thou" demands by his very existence to be acknowledged as a "thou" for an "ego" and an "ego" for himself. This is the claim which is implied in his being.[3]

The network of personal encounters in any given society is the locus of the *real* for peace and justice. The freedom of personal encounters keeps every system and structure of peace and justice open, opened to complexities, and emergent. This network is a duplicitous intersection of autonomy, and *an-archy*.[4] The network of personal encounters is the *matrix* and *moloch* of justice and peace: possibilities and actualizations are born, emerge, evolve, and disappear, only to re-emerge in new forms in it. Every personal encounter—every network of actions and reactions—includes an excess that it can never incorporate nor comprehend. It is never complete and this incompleteness makes infinite creativity possible in all social relations.

My deployment of the notion of network of personal encounters as the generative and unifying principle of concrete peacebuilding and justice in this essay is informed by a teleological commitment: actualization of human potentials and communal flourishing. It fits the third set of just peacemaking practices—those that focus on community. I will say more about this in the following pages.

3. Tillich, *Love, Power, and Justice*, 78.

4. "In this context, the term *anarchy* does not mean the absence of form and thus disorder, confusion, or chaos. Rather, an-archy suggests the absence (*an*, "without") of any beginning (*arkhe*) and by extension the lack of an originary foundation. That which is anarchic is groundless" (Taylor, *After God*, 102).

I have based the following discourse on peacebuilding and economic justice on certain key theological presuppositions common to them. My thinking follows from these four theological-philosophical presuppositions:

a. Human dignity. Every human being has an inherent inviolable dignity as one created by God. Every person in any form of human sociality should interact with others without compromising human dignity (his/her own or that of the others). Persons are to be always treated as subjects, and never merely as objects; they are to be always treated with due respect for their worth.

b. Nature of the human person. A person is one in the process of becoming, actualizing his or her potentials through his or her own agency that is always grounded, mediated, and aided by community.

c. Social nature of human beings. Individuals need community to become persons. Community is essential for self-realization and human flourishing.

d. Participation and membership. Every person, by virtue of his or her membership in a community, has the right to active participation in the process of seeking and ordering the common good of the community.

These presuppositions allow us to address peace and justice in terms that go beyond proceduralism and are made concrete in the ten justpeace practices.

Nowadays every discussion of justice is directly or indirectly haunted by this question: Does justice require a substantive content or establishment of procedural requirements for fairness of actions or transactions? This vital question equally applies to peacebuilding. When we think of peacebuilding are we merely concerned with procedures for peace or do we have a substantive understanding of it?

In these remarks I offer a substantive account of peacebuilding and economic justice—a view of peacebuilding and its attendant notion of justice that are derived from a teleological commitment. The search for the basic meaning of peacebuilding and justice must be undertaken as part of the search for basic meaning of the actualization of human potentials and communal flourishing. Life, as Tillich taught us, is the process of actualization of potentials. The obligation or unconditional command that lies at the root of all forms of human coexistence is the moral imperative to allow persons to become whatever it is that they have the power to become in the context of harmonious communal relationships. Peacebuilding and justice are *ways of being* for life. For the religious person it is a way of being for life that is oriented toward the ultimate, toward the unconditional. Religious peacebuilding should not just be about retrieving moral and reconciliatory resources that promote and guide feuding parties to peace, but also about understanding the theonomous dimensions of all forms of human sociality and justice.[5]

First I will address the concept of peacebuilding. Next I will attempt to develop a notion of justice that can guide our discussion. Based on these sections, I will endeavor to explore the connection between peacebuilding and economic justice. Concluding remarks follow in the final section.

1. The Notion of Peacebuilding

Peace is a perfect obligation. By perfect obligation, I mean that if a community deserves or has a right to peace, the rest of us (persons, organizations, and nations) have the duty not to fracture its peace. Peace is a property that a community can claim as moral right from the rest of us, and every community fundamentally has this right. This claim demands efforts at peacebuilding from all of us; that is, at least an investment in the well-being of the members of the community.

Peacebuilding is a continuous process of individual self-actualization and movement toward increasing communion. It is also about the preservation or rebuilding of a community in ways that ensure that individuals and groups in a particular community, acting alone or in concert with other communities, can be all that they can be under the conditions of existence. Its practical implementation takes two basic forms. First, peacebuilding is about the continuous proper ordering and balancing of powers in community or communities to sustain harmonious relationships and acknowledgment of the worth of persons. Disproportion of power (especially economic and military) leads to injustice, as Reinhold Niebuhr has shown us.[6] Injustice is a threat to both peace and economic development. Peacebuilding creates possibilities for economic growth, whereas economic injustice denies possibilities of participation to a group or class and thus chafes against the very idea of peace. Second, there is the peacebuilding effort that is directed at rebuilding, restoring, or repairing a preexisting harmony that has been shattered.

5. I have based my thinking in this paragraph on Paul Tillich's approach to morality in *Love, Power, and Justice*. See especially 72–125.

6. Niebuhr, *Nature and Destiny of Man*, 1:223, 2:262; Tillich, *Love, Power, and Justice*, 36, 199, 173.

These two forms are informed by what I will call *primary peace* and *secondary peace*.[7] To declare that members of a community are at loggerheads, at disharmonious state of relationships, is to imply that there is a way of coexisting that is peaceful. This way of relating together, letting lives hang together, we will call *primary peace*. The peace that consists in restored or repaired fissures, cracks, and breakdowns in relationship is *secondary peace*. These two forms of peace or peacebuilding are premised on two forms of justice. Take the case of a victim and the accused (perpetrator of a crime) for an illustration. According to Nicholas Wolterstorff, there is a way in which the accused would have treated his or her victim that would not have been an infraction of justice; there was a way of relating that would have been just from the outset. This he calls *primary justice*. It is only when this did not happen that a judge is called to render just judgment as a way of dealing with charged or threatening breakdowns. "The justice that consists of rendering just judgment is *secondary justice*, in the sense that it deals with infractions of primary justice, accusations of infraction, or disputes over what would be an infraction."[8] So far it looks as if peace is primarily an outcome of justice. But it is germane to state that the relationship between them is interactive, mutually influencing one another. To seek peace is to find justice, to find justice is to seek peace.

Often in peacebuilding efforts issues about retributive justice need to be considered. How far do you go to account for past injustice? What compensations need to be paid for past offenses? It is important to point out that compensations cannot really take care of injustice because the initial violation and suffering cannot be undone. Let's say that a daughter is murdered and the murderer agrees to compensate the parents according to orders of a competent court. If the parents take the money, it only means that they are forgiving the offender for the un-payable. There is no amount of money that can bring their daughter back or undo the initial loss and trauma they suffered. Justice cannot strictly be an "eye-for-an-eye" exchange; there is always (and must be) a surplus in order for justice to work. It is in this realm of surplus that we have forgiveness, hope, and the space where social energies can restore harmony and unleash creative and transformative acts of change.[9] This is why the just peacemaking

---

7. Here I am alluding to Nicholas Wolterstorff's idea about primary and secondary justice. See his "Is There Justice in the Trinity?," 177–78.

8. Wolterstorff, "Is There Justice in the Trinity?," 179.

9. See Friesen, Langan, and Stassen, "Introduction," 1–28.

practice of acknowledging responsibility for conflict and injustice, and seeking repentance and forgiveness, is crucial for peacemaking.

In working to create the necessary space for peacebuilding, we must be sensitive to differences and otherness. Philosopher John Rawls argues that we must close our eyes as we go into justice and that differences between people or groups do not count in crafting a system of fairness. He suggests that we make moral decisions behind a "veil of ignorance." Theologian Miroslav Volf has argued that one does not need to cultivate systematic blindness to build a just consensus but needs to keep one's eyes wide open to note and respect small and big differences; one needs to move away from blind impartiality and toward sensibility for differences.[10] As he puts it: "If our identities are shaped in interaction with others, and if we are called ultimately to belong together, then we need to shift the concept of justice away from an exclusive stress on making detached judgments and toward sustaining relationships, away from blind impartiality and toward sensibility for differences."[11]

Instead of following the great Rawls, we need to create spaces where both victims and perpetrators are visible to one another to start the process of re-connection. One may venture to say that the whole point about peacebuilding is to make room for the other within either small or large places to coexist and flourish. It is about making spaces in people's opinions, identities, and lives for the other—mutually giving themselves to one another in love. Volf calls this kind of peace, *embrace*.[12] And I will add that if there happens to be no space for the other, we must create the space for movement and expansion. Cutting-edge peacebuilding efforts must create the space into which they expand, just like the universe. With what "forces" does an expanding galaxy of peacebuilding activities unfurl the subsequent space it will inhabit? "Double vision" or the "art of enlarged thinking" and economic justice are some of the factors that will do the magic. This is how Volf explains the "art of enlarged thinking":

> [W]e enlarge our thinking by letting the voices and perspectives of others . . . resonate within ourselves, by allowing them to help us see them, as well as ourselves from their perspective, and if needed readjust our perspectives as we take into account their perspectives. Nothing can guarantee in advance that perspectives will ultimately merge and agreement be reached. We

10. Volf, *Exclusion and Embrace*, 203.

11. Ibid., 225.

12. Volf, "Forgiveness, Reconciliation, and Justice," 27–49.

may find that we must reject the perspective of the other. Yet we should seek to see things from their perspective in the hope that competing justices may become converging justices and eventually issue in agreement.[13]

It is vitally important to mention that there will be times when "enlarged thinking" may not even be enough or when it will be seen as another version of "colonizing thinking." Such times may call us to construct multiple ways of thinking that will press us into multiple ways of seeing and coexisting.[14]

Economic justice expands the spaces for survival and flourishing of the other—the poor, the marginalized, the weak, the disinherited, and the victimized in our midst. This is about making room in the economic table (or constructing a whole new table of which the primary economic players today are not the chief architects and custodians[15]) for them to develop their capabilities so as to become the agents of their own development. Such spaces are purposely created to acknowledge their human dignity and right to life as well as to honor their community's commitment (obligation) to their well-being. When economic justice takes root in a given community, it reduces inequality, expands the overall well-being of the community, and promotes peace.

Economic injustice is the opposite of what peacebuilding stands for. It is a symbol of exclusion; contrary to embrace—and substantively so. While peacebuilding is about healing relationships and making them sturdier, economic injustice is about fracturing relationships and keeping them as open festering wounds and yawning gaps in the social fabric. Spiritual formation sensitizes us to these fissures. This is precisely what is addressed in the just peacemaking practices.

2. The Notion of Justice

We begin our investigation of the meaning of justice by making a distinction between the ultimate end and ultimate principle of justice. The ultimate end of justice is the preservation or rebuilding of a community, a social group.[16] But the ultimate principle of justice, according to Tillich, is the "acknowl-

13. Volf, *Exclusion and Embrace*, 213.

14. I am grateful to my colleague, Professor Sharon Thornton, for telling me that "enlarged thinking" is not always enough.

15. Once again, I thank Professor Thornton for this idea of constructing a new table.

16. Tillich, *Theology of Peace*, 160.

edgment of the dignity of everyone as a person, from which follow human rights and obligations in the encounters of one with other."[17]

Tillich, in his usual manner, has packed a lot of insights into this short sentence. Let us try to unpack them by exploring four key terms: *dignity*, *rights*, *obligations*, and *encounter*. I will address dignity briefly as most of us as Christian theologians or seminarians or just plain Christians understand it well. The theological idea is that persons enjoy inherent *dignity* because they are created in the image and likeness of God, endowed with reason and freedom, ransomed by Christ, and destined for communion with God as heirs to eternal glory.

From the writings of Immanuel Kant and John Stuart Mill to contemporary Catholic social teachings it is clear that *rights* refer to the minimum conditions necessary for safeguarding the dignity of every human being, so that each person will be treated as a subject and not as an object.[18] They are rights not just because we can merely refer to minimum conditions documented in one tome, but because individuals can legitimately claim these conditions from us, society, institutions, and organizations, and we are perfectly *obligated* to honor the claim. If I have a right to life I can make a claim on society for this right, and society and I have an obligation to honor it. What is my right to life, if my society will not take actions to protect me, or will allow me to be killed by anyone at will? Such a right has no real meaning. If a woman has the right not to be raped, not to be made an object of the orgiastic pleasure of a man, it means that we cannot leave it to her alone to protect herself from rapists. We must create the minimum conditions in society to prevent rape and when rape occurs we are obligated to prosecute and punish the rapist. We are saying to the woman, your right imposes an unavoidable claim on the part of others and society.

The *encounter* of one with others is the *classical site* of justice. Martin Buber in his 1958 book, *I-Thou*, argues that the human is not an individual, but a person, related, *ek-static* being, who has no ontological content apart from communion. The "I" can only be properly understood in the context of social relation, the "Thou." In the encounter of one with the other, the person is to be treated as a *Thou*, a subject, and not an *It*. The encounter (which is always located within particular tradition-formed communities) breeds, nurtures, limits, and transforms rights. For the sustenance of rights, especially the continuous duty of the state and communities to

---

17. Ibid., 174.
18. Allman, "Thick Theory of Global Justice," 109.

honor the obligations appertaining to them, always presupposes particular practices, social institutions, and virtues.

Tillich shares a similar view, arguing that we become persons in encounter with others in a community and that the content of the moral aim or imperative is to become a person within a community of persons. This moral imperative demands giving each person his or her due so as to become what he or she is essentially (to actualize his or her human potentialities), and also demands performing the creative and transformative acts of reuniting the separated.[19] Here, we see that the ultimate principle and ultimate goal are related; the person can only realize him or her self within a transformative and creative community.

Still pressing on the value of encounters within a community for understanding justice, let me present an African perspective on justice that will further clarify the connection between the ultimate goal and ultimate principle of justice. Here I will draw from my 2008 book, *The Depth and Destiny of Work*, where I examine the Kalabari (Niger Delta, Nigeria) indigenous notion of justice.[20] The cosmological thought of traditional Kalabari community gives central place to justice because it is not only a relational virtue, but it also relates to all other virtues. A person is considered just if the moral impact of his or her practical activities and his or her exercise of all other virtues contribute to the good of the community, that is, the preservation and promotion of community and communion.

The Kalabari view of justice as rooted in relationships places great emphasis on establishing and sustaining connections between people, connecting self to the other, and making room on the inside for the outsider. Justice is the quality and mode of connectedness in a given set of social relations. Justice is at the heart of all relationality because it asks for the recognition of the value of the other (the one excluded from the in-group, from power), it regards the intrinsic claim of the other as a person, and it adjusts the relationship toward reciprocity, equality, mutuality, and solidarity. Justice's purpose is to deepen relation, care, and nurture; to extend the network of relationships; and to embody community. Justice is nurturance. Doing justice is "righting wrong relationship,"[21] restoring fractured relationships, and expanding the space for participation in the network of social relations by the poor and marginalized. What is "participation space"? It can be defined as a room in socioeconomic relations

19. Tillich, *Morality and Beyond*, 19–25.
20. Wariboko, *Depth and Destiny of Work*, 133–34.
21. Harrison, *Making the Connections*, 19.

that allows the disadvantaged, poor, marginalized, and outsiders to gain resources for developing full human capability without jeopardizing the sustainability of the economy.

There are two crucial features of justice in the Kalabari social ethical system. Justice works to bring into deeper communion and fellowship many who are excluded or separated from an embracing community. There is the power of *eros*[22] within justice that drives the network of relations toward the ultimate goal for all engaged in it. The process of deepening and widening relationships also strives toward higher levels of flourishing, catholicity, and meaning. Second, justice works toward the fulfillment of all humans within the network of relationships.

Peacebuilders want personal encounters to be just, harmonious, and supportive of human flourishing. In bringing people together, to encounter one another in the spheres of life, peacebuilders explicitly or implicitly work from two philosophical orientations. These two approaches explain in very different ways the nature and epistemology of the *real* that is the network of personal encounters. The approaches are discernible from two basic answers provided to this one question: Unity or difference, which one is ontologically more real and more morally compelling in the encounter of persons to persons? Each answer ensues in different ways of *figuring* the real in the *material, formal, efficient,* and *final* dimensions of building peace in a given situation.

To help us think through the answers, I extend Tillich's essay on the traditional arguments for the existence of God and their two types of theology. In his essay entitled, "Two Types of Philosophy of Religion," he states that:

> One can distinguish two ways of approaching God: the way of overcoming estrangement and the way of meeting a stranger. In the first way man discovers *himself* when he discovers God; he discovers something from which he is estranged, but from which he never has been and never can be separated. In the second way, man meets a *stranger* when he meets God. The meeting is accidental. Essentially they do not belong to each other.[23]

In peacebuilding too, practitioners make basic assumptions about the relatedness of parties in conflict. Do they believe that they are reuniting

22. *Eros* is "the drive towards the other, towards an ultimate goal, striving of the person or subject for union with that which it is separated from though it belongs to it." *Eros* "strives for a union with that which is a bearer of values because of the value it embodies." See Tillich, *Love, Power, and Justice,* 25–30.

23. Tillich, "Two Types of Philosophy of Religion," 10.

people who are essentially united, but now estranged, or that they are join-ing people who essentially do not belong to each other? How we think about persons and their *a priori* relations to one another as important in the process of envisioning peace, justice, and community? From one per-spective, the unity peacebuilders seek is the conclusion of the reconcili-ation effort. In the other, it is the presupposition of peacebuilding. One presupposes cleavage, estrangement, and alienation as ontological to hu-man relationality. The other presupposes primal unity, which is believed to be always present in every form of separation. Here one is reminded of Saint Augustine's critique (in *The City of God*) of *Pax Romana*, which was founded on *a priori* violence; peace in Rome and in the empire emerged after the violent defeat of preceding disorder. Peace in the thinking of the people of the *earthly city* is something achieved after defeating someone else. But a Christian imagination of peace, according to Augustine and now John Milbank (in *Theology and Social Theory*), begins with ontologi-cal peace whose end is the realization of justice for all.

I believe that persons essentially belong to each other (they are all grounded in the groundless "power of being"). Thusly, justice or peace is the movement toward communion of the estranged, a movement from unity through opposition and division to reconciliation and reunion. Now identity becomes differential rather than oppositional; unity and identity are inclusive rather than exclusive. This reunion is a complex unity that does not dissolve differential identities. The engine of this movement from estrangement to complex unity is *participation*. The peacebuilder then is a man or woman who is helping to *figure* the conditions of possibilities for the "presencing" of the reunion (unity, *koinonia, shalom*) in and between groups (communities, socialities).

To say that human beings are grounded in primal unity is not to insist that differences are epiphenomenal or to exclude otherness. Unity is both the result and presupposition of personal encounters. To be is to be in com-munion, as the Greek Orthodox theologian John Zizioulas argues in his 1985 book, *Being as Communion*. Back home here, we recently heard the same message being heralded by Columbia University theologian Mark C. Taylor in his 2007 book, *After God*, where he argues that to be is to be con-nected. Indeed, persons are integrally rather than externally related. A true peaceful order is not wrought by the defeat of enemies or "complete strang-ers" but by identification with others through participation in practices that incorporate (estranged) individuals into social bodies.

3. Peacebuilding and Economic Justice

I have argued that justice is individual self-realization within the confines and responsibilities of the *embrace* (in unity with the whole in which he or she belongs). Justice, although it is the principle of peacebuilding, is at the same time the outcome of peacebuilding. Justice is the concrete principle of peacebuilding in conditions of existence characterized by wrongdoings and conflicts. It is an expression of the substance of peacebuilding, the actualization of the human potentialities in ways consistent with human dignity and with the unity of the community. As stated above, peacebuilding is a continuous process of individual self-realization and movement toward increasing, uniting communion. The separation that arises by each individual dynamic actuality of life is overcome or limited by its realization within the whole and mutual participation in one another's life.[24]

Justice is a principle of peacebuilding because it represents, shows, and points to a specific and concrete alternative way of human coexistence to be followed in order to establish and sustain harmony. The praxis of justice involves the *transforming initiatives*[25] that we take to practically participate in weaving or reweaving the threads of relationships that sustain our communities.

Peacebuilding—and not just interpersonal conflict resolution—is communal, involving structures beyond the personal and interpersonal. Peacebuilding is about making the legal, political, social, and economic structures of cooperation and brotherliness sturdier to sustain love, which as Tillich once put it, is the drive toward the unity of the separated. Justice is the structures of society that make love on a communal level possible; transforming love from sentimentality to forms and dynamics of interactions that uphold human dignity and foster participative and fair economic development. Justice is the public (communal) dimension of love that acknowledges the empirical realities of power and self-interest in any community and sets up institutions (of law, procedure, accountability, restraints, charity, rewards, punishment, and coercion) to reduce, minimize their destructive tendencies.

Economic injustice deprives an individual of the creative freedom to actualize oneself within the community in which one belongs. A just order enables an individual to actualize her potentials—to be what she essentially is, and its absence is tantamount to the denial of her human

---

24. Tillich, *Theology of Peace*, 94.
25. Friesen, Langan, and Stassen, "Introduction."

dignity and the destruction of her humanity. The fact that one person can deprive another person of the capabilities and conditions of possibility needed to actualize one's potentials is founded on power differentials. This is also true at the international or global level.

The encounter of persons is in a certain sense a vexing encounter of political, social, and economic powers. Reinhold Niebuhr tells us that if there is a huge imbalance of power there is bound to be injustice, and minorities and the weak cannot achieve the necessary freedom to fulfill their lives, to *act*, and participate fully in the community.[26] He argues for the reduction of the imbalances of power and the setting up of structures of justice to protect the powerless or the not-so-powerful in society.

One of the central problems of the international economic system, as I have shown in my 2008 book, *God and Money: A Theology of Money in a Globalizing World*, is the imbalance of power between a few powerful nations and the rest of the world, especially those in Africa, Latin America, and South Asia. So instead of enhancing relationality and flourishing life, the international economic system gives the poor nations an abjectly Hobbesian hand. The life of poor nations in the global economic system is solitary, poor, nasty, brutish, and short. This is, perhaps, even an understatement. Instead of dealing life to developing nations, the international economic system often deals death to them. The system is not organized for them to live, to *act*.[27] It needs to be reshaped toward a more democratic

26. Niebuhr, *Nature and Destiny of Man*; Niebuhr, *Love and Justice*.

27. Hannah Arendt identifies three activities of life: labor, work, and action. Labor as an activity is concerned with the mere reproduction, survival, and biological processes of life and is caught in the endless, repetitive cycles of nature.

> While nature manifests itself in human existence through the circular movement of our bodily functions, she makes her presence felt in the man-made world through the constant threat of overgrowing or decaying it. The common characteristic of both, the biological process in man and the process of growth and decay in the world, is that they are part of the cyclical movement of nature and therefore endlessly repetitive; all human activities which arise out of the necessity to cope with them are bound to the recurring cycles of nature and have in themselves no beginning and no end, properly speaking; unlike *working*, whose end has come when an object is finished, ready to be added to the common world of things, laboring always moves in the same circle, which is prescribed by the biological process of the living organism and the end of its "toil and trouble" comes only with the death of the organism. . . . Whatever labor produces is meant to be fed into the human life process almost immediately. (Arendt, *Human Condition*, 98–99; see also 118, 125).

Work as an activity transcends this level and tries to achieve some permanence in the perpetual flux of life through the making of things. Arendt states that humans are in a perpetual struggle to create products of work and not the products of labor. "The

structure, one that is more supportive of life. The global economic system should be used to create, enhance, and sustain relationships between persons and nations in the global community, rather than allowing it "to steal, and to kill, and to destroy." The book *God and Money*, in highlighting the importance of relationality and sociality in economic interactions, points to an alternative to the current predatory global economic system that would take participation and human sociality seriously. The re-imagined alternative (the "Earth-Dollar System") aims to enable individuals and nations to participate fully in the preservation and progress of life and for their local and global communities to operate through their own agencies and in cooperation with others.

I have shown that peacebuilding and economic justice are integral aspects of one and the same coin. Peacebuilding is the metal of the coin and justice is the form adequate for it. What lies beneath the coin is social relations, personal encounters. The generative energy that keeps the coin in circulation and in good use is the *eros* of participation. Participation is the gum that holds together the kind of relationships that we have said is necessary for peacebuilding, network of care, and justice. Participation is the antidote to alienation, disconnection, and apathy. In our efforts to promote peace in both thriving and beleaguered communities we should emphasize the idea of people acting together, having the right/duty to share in the common good, and being able to play active roles in the life of their communities. Such right also makes a claim on society and decision-makers to consult persons on policies, projects, and decisions that affect them and/or their communities. The source of this right for an individual to be an active agent of and the source of duty to be in solidarity with others in the process of seeking and ordering the common good is, simply, membership in the community.

---

products of work," she argues, "guarantee the permanence and durability without which a world would not be possible at all. It is within this world of durable things that we find the consumer goods through which life assures the means of its survival" (p. 94).

In life activity as an action, the individual leaves traces of his or her existence for future generations and has the potential to add something novel to the world. At this level of activity, life is about doing great acts that involve possibilities of transcendence and immortality. To Arendt, action is what truly distinguishes human beings from animals and nature. She is careful enough to note that the individual cannot engage in the pursuit of greatness if he or she has not secured the necessities of life. This acting takes place in the public realm, and it is boundless because of human interrelatedness.

The question for us is this: is the set of relations and relatedness in the international economic system organized in such a way that developing economies can act in the international public realm and join others in the common pursuit of greatness, or are they forever condemned to mere survival and necessities of biological life?

Here once again, I resort to Catholic social teachings as a veritable source of clarifying my understanding of the theology of participation.[28] Participation is an inviolable and inalienable right of every member of the community—meaning it cannot be taken or surrendered. It flows from the understanding that the human being is a *social being* and participation is essential for his or her self-realization and flourishing; a person self-realizes, self-actualizes through acting together with others. Participation enables the individual to participate in the life of God and in God's creative and sanctifying activity over the earth and its inhabitants, and in ordering the universe and the common good of society.

Insofar as human beings are essentially social in nature, beings-in-communion, human dignity and participation are best addressed in social relationships in community. Everyone is required to participate in the production of social goods, the creation of the common good. And society is to enable each and every person to acquire the capabilities that will allow him or her to so participate. This means that caring for the poor and victims in the peacebuilding process is not just about meeting their needs, but giving them enough power to meet their needs. In summary, at the societal level it involves two things: capabilities (which Reinhold Niebuhr did not particularly address, but Amartya Sen, the Nobel-prize winning economist, did) and power (that is ensuring a balance of power between classes which Niebuhr addressed, but Sen did not).

Participation in the economy of one's community or country is the principle means of participation in all modern societies. Participation in the economy (economic justice) is an excellent moral lens for examining and assessing peacebuilding and social justice. According to the United States Catholic bishops, "the ultimate injustice is for a person or group of persons to be treated or abandoned passively as if they were nonmembers of the human race. To treat people this way is effectively to say that they simply do not count as human beings."[29] The persons are both wronged and harmed by their exclusion from participation.

Participation and economic justice are not about equality of economic outcomes among all citizens. It is about arranging the basic structures of society to protect the poor, weak, and marginalized. It involves a combination of *perfect* and *imperfect obligations* which generates three principles or policy guidelines. First, to safeguard human dignity and provide for the necessary minimum levels of participation in the life of community

---

28. I am relying on Allman, "Thick Theory of Global Justice," 183–202.

29. National Council of Catholic Bishops, *Economic Justice for All*, para. 77.

we must establish a floor of human flourishing and regard it as an obligation society must honor. Primary justice requires it. Second, in order to encourage risk taking and entrepreneurship necessary for economic development we have to create incentives to spur on additional efforts and allow people to maximize their own outcomes. Finally, in maximizing one's outcome or income the conditions of others should not be worsened by one's actions. There is a prohibition against doing harm to others or their situations in the process of an individual acquiring his or her own possession. The second principle constitutes an imperfect obligation and the third is a perfect obligation.

4. Concluding Remarks

I have treated peacebuilding and economic justice in very similar terms. They are both rooted in personal encounters. I have also presented both of them as goods that members of society, a social whole, have a right to enjoy. The absence of peace and justice in any given community means that persons in it have their moral status and well-being altered or diminished. Peacebuilding is an excellent way of restoring and even improving their moral status and well-being. Just peacemaking practices offer a concrete way to actualize this. Peacebuilding constructs an environment for persons to be treated with respect and creates the conditions of possibilities for the actualization of human potentials. It is vitally important to add that the building of peace is not only about setting up structures and stabilizing situations that give life meaning and purpose and flourishment, but also about disrupting, dislocating, and disfiguring structures of society and forms of sociality that negate or thwart life. It is also about persons (including victims and perpetrators) "discerning the body" in which they are incorporated. "Discerning the body," as Saint Paul informs us, is about being sensitive to issues that cause alienation, divisions, fractures in social body, alert to the sufferings of its weak, marginalized, and disinherited members, and being compassionate enough to care for the harmony of the whole body under the impact of the *Spiritual Presence*.

Bibliography

Allman, Mark J. "A Thick Theory of Global Justice: Participation as a Constitutive Dimension of Global Justice." PhD diss., Loyola University of Chicago, August 2003.

Arendt, Hannah. *The Human Condition.* Chicago: University of Chicago Press, 1958.

Friesen, Duane K., John Langan, SJ, and Glen H. Stassen. "Introduction: Peacemaking as a New Ethic." In *Just Peacemaking: Ten Practices for Abolishing War*, edited by Glen H. Stassen, 1–28. Cleveland: Pilgrim, 1998.

Harrison, Beverly Wildung. *Making the Connections: Essays in Feminist Social Ethics.* Edited by Carol S. Robb. Boston: Beacon, 1985.

National Council of Catholic Bishops. *Economic Justice for All.* Washington, DC: US Catholic Conference, 1986.

Niebuhr, Reinhold. *Love and Justice: Selections from the Shorter Writings of Reinhold Niebuhr.* Edited by D. B. Robertson. Louisville: Westminster John Knox, 1957.

———. *The Nature and Destiny of Man: A Christian Interpretation.* 2 vols. New York: Scribner's Sons, 1964.

Paris, Peter J. "A Meditation on Love." *Princeton Seminary Bulletin* 26.1 (2006) 1–4.

Rodney Petersen, Raymond Helmick, and Tom Porter. Lecture delivered at the seminar course "International Conflict and Ministry of Reconciliation," Boston University, 30 March 2009.

Taylor, Mark C. *After God.* Chicago: University of Chicago Press, 2007.

Tillich, Paul. *Love, Power, and Justice: Ontological Analyses and Ethical Applications.* London: Oxford University Press, 1954.

———. *Morality and Beyond.* Louisville: Westminster John Knox, 1963.

———. *Theology of Peace.* Edited by Ronald Stone. Louisville: Westminster John Knox, 1990.

———. "The Two Types of Philosophy of Religion." In *Theology of Culture*, edited by Robert Kimball, 10–29. New York: Oxford University Press, 1964.

Volf, Miroslav. *Exclusion and Embrace: A Theological Exploration of Identity, Otherness, and Reconciliation.* Nashville: Abingdon, 1996.

———. "Forgiveness, Reconciliation, and Justice: A Christian Contribution to a More Peaceful Social Environment." In *Forgiveness and Reconciliation: Religion, Public Policy and Conflict Transformation*, edited by Raymond G. Helmick, SJ, and Rodney L. Petersen, 27–49. Philadelphia: Templeton Foundation, 2001.

Wariboko, Nimi. *The Depth and Destiny of Work: An African Theological Interpretation.* Trenton, NJ: Africa World, 2008.

Wolterstorff, Nicholas. "Is There Justice in the Trinity?" In *God's Life in Trinity*, edited by Miroslav Volf and Michael Welker, 177–90. Minneapolis: Fortress, 2006.

13

Just Peacemaking in
Light of Global Challenges

Involving Islam and Muslims

MARTIN ACCAD

IN EVERY ERA, EVENTS, realities, movements, and ideologies that turn out
to represent significant challenges to peacemaking in the world seem to
emerge. Fundamentally, however, biblical cosmology and anthropology
seem to indicate that the most entrenched challenge to peacemaking is
related to internal human factors rather than to external circumstances.
This recognition renders the challenge both more perplexing and at the
same time more hopeful. Perplexing because it is always easier to blame
problems on external factors: colonialism, economic injustice, manipulative foreign policies of hegemonic nations, communism, the establishment of the State of Israel, Islamic terrorism, arms proliferation, rogue
states . . . etc. More hopeful because the problem to which the Bible
points belongs to the realm of our own influence, namely our own sinful
nature and God's deliverance.

The present chapter proposes to consider this century's greatest challenges to peacemaking with reference to the Islamic religion. The danger
with such an approach, however, is that we may be setting out to find blame
in a particular source for all of the world's great challenges. It is therefore
fitting to frame this conversation within a reflection on discipleship. How

does a twenty-first-century disciple of Jesus need to be equipped in order to face this era's challenges, knowing that faithful and effective discipleship is first and foremost about the transformation of oneself before searching for the speck in our brother or sister's eye?

Islam entered twenty-first-century Western popular consciousness with a bang, and this as early as the first year of the century, 2001, on September 11. In this dramatic event that inaugurated our century, I see the manifestation of four great challenges that will be with us for at least a few decades to come. They are (1) the rise of radical Islamist ideology, (2) the polarization of the Israeli-Palestinian issue along religious lines, (3) the reductionist perception of Islam (including in our churches), and (4) the consolidation of what I call the "culture of resistance" bloc.

I also allege that what has now been firmly baptized with the label of "Arab Spring," but which we may want to consider calling more neutrally "Arab Uprisings," bring in an additional twist to the plot, which further both highlights and exacerbates the significance of these four challenges. Since the present analysis concerns discipleship, this chapter will not stop at diagnosis, but will move at each stage to a consideration of options toward resolution, based on an evaluation of the 10 practices for "Just Peacemaking." In conclusion, there will be a further assessment of the 10 practices and some closing practical guidelines that bring constructive transformative action down to the level of each one of us as individuals within our communities of faith.

The Rise of Radical Islamist Ideology

Radical Islamism must be viewed in the context of what has become known as late nineteenth-century post-colonial Islamic revivalism. The colonial era had led to a process of soul searching within the Muslim world, which was faced with its own failure to catch on with western technological progress during the Ottoman period. By the turn of the century, the writings of reformers such as Jamal al-Din al-Afghani (d. 1897), Muhammad Abduh (d. 1905) and Muhammad Rashid Rida (d. 1935), reveal that the colonial era had left the Muslim world with a deep sense of dissatisfaction with itself and the place that Islam had been given as an organizing principle in society.

This self-criticism was, however, accompanied at the same time with some very mixed feelings and often frustration toward the West and what it had brought to the Muslim world. For some, the benefits of western industrialism and scientific progress had exposed the failures of the Muslim world and even of Islam and triggered a desire to imitate the West and promote a more secularist approach to reality. Others saw the colonial era as characterized by abusive policies that allowed colonial nations to accumulate wealth at the expense of colonized nations and peoples. It is within this latter, more reactionary stream of post-colonial Islam, that radical Islamist ideology found its roots.

A key trigger that gave particular impetus to this movement was the collapse of the Ottoman Empire, and with it the abolition of the Islamic caliphate at the hand of Mustafa Kemal Ataturk in 1924. This single act, interpreted by the more religious as deeply humiliating and shameful, had a profound impact on the popular Muslim psyche. Islamic history until then, with its consistent line of successive empires and dynasties, had never witnessed a time without some form of centralized representative leadership (albeit never fully united beyond the beginnings of the second century of Islam). This deep sense of loss was fertile soil for the anti-Western, moralizing ideology of Hassan al-Banna (1906–49), founder of the Muslim Brotherhood in Egypt. It was Sayyid Qutb (1906–66), however, who became the Muslim Brotherhood's chief ideologue. An intellectual who was initially drawn to Western-style modernism and reform, Sayyid Qutb became a harsh critic of Western society and morals after a two-year visit to the United States in 1948.

Besides its post-colonial reactionary message, the ideology of the Brotherhood had also adopted the religious (hermeneutical) methodology of the earlier Muslim reformers, which was deeply subversive of the traditionist approach to the Islamic disciplines. The prospect of bypassing fourteen hundred years of monopoly by traditional scholars on the founding religious texts of Islam, with its promise of retrieving the model "authentic" community of primeval Islam, had a tremendous appeal for the masses in the Muslim world. Late nineteenth-century reformers had agreed that the traditional interpretation and application of Islam had failed. By the early decades of the twentieth century, some in the Muslim world sought to remedy that failure by experimenting with secularist ideologies, such as Ataturk's Turkish nationalism, and later Abd al-Nasser's Arab Nationalism in Egypt as well as Baathism, particularly in Syria and Iraq.

Nationalism and Islamism in a variety of manifestations were the two experimental ideological streams that competed, often violently, for the attention of the Muslim world during much of the twentieth century. It was in the prisons of Abd al-Nasser, often under cruel conditions, that the ideology of the Muslim Brotherhood developed. Islamist organizations remained largely underground for a good part of the twentieth century, until the Iranian revolution in 1979 set a precedent for successful Islamist political takeover and changed the fortunes of radical Islamist ideology for the rest of the century, at the expense of the nationalists.

Al-Qaida's ideology that emerged in the late 1980s is itself considered to be inspired by the Muslim Brotherhood. It certainly is driven by the common desire to restore Islam to its former glory by seeking greater political control, but this time on a global scale. In addition, it is fueled by a powerful pro-Palestinian and anti-Western discourse, and as such it is very much a fruit of the late twentieth century. The centrality of the Israeli-Palestinian conflict to the ideology of al-Qaida, and its connection with anti-American feelings, was pervasive in the public statements of Osama Bin Laden. In view of the impact that Bin Laden's statements have had on the psyche of Muslim populations at the grassroots, the implications of this ideology has to be considered very seriously.

After Iraq's invasion of Kuwait in 1990, King Fahd of Saudi Arabia required the *'Ulama* (official Muslim scholars) to endorse the arrival of American and other foreign troops on Saudi soil. In response, the Chief Mufti of Saudi Arabia, Bin Baz, issued two decrees: the first on August 14, 1990, authorizing U.S. deployment (Operation Desert Shield), and the second in January 1991, permitting Muslim troops to join in the attack on Iraq (Operation Desert Storm). Bin Baz's initiative led to a great gulf between the *Sahwa* (dissident theologians) and the official *'Ulama* of the Kingdom. The following statement of Osama Bin Laden was addressed as a letter to Bin Baz on Dec 29, 1994. It represented his first public pronouncement for a wider audience:[1]

> And it seemed as if you were not satisfied with abandoning Saudi Arabia, home of the two Holy Sanctuaries, to the Crusader-Jewish forces of occupation, until you had brought another disaster upon Jerusalem, the third of the Sanctuaries, by conferring legitimacy on the contracts of surrender to the Jews that were signed by the traitorous and cowardly Arab tyrants (ref. to the Oslo Accords, signed on Sept 13, 1993, between Israel and the PLO). These contracts constitute a serious and dangerous calamity containing deceit and deception from a number of different perspectives.
>
> The legal duty regarding Palestine and our brothers there— these poor men, women, and children who have nowhere to go—is to wage *jihad* for the sake of God, and to motivate our

---

1. Lawrence, *Messages to the World*, 9.

umma to *jihad* so that Palestine may be completely liberated and returned to Islamic sovereignty.

Steps toward a Solution

Addressing this first challenge today requires a great deal of humility. In line with the fourth practice of Just peacemaking, this begins with an acknowledgment of colonial and post-colonial responsibility in creating a situation of helplessness for Muslim countries, as well as in the creation of the Palestinian problem. Of course this needs to be followed up by practical steps, otherwise it will only exacerbate the problem. Obama's speech at the University of Cairo on June 4, 2009, is a case in point. The title itself, "A New Beginning," contained an implicit recognition that the old approach had been a failure. His humble, lucid and balanced treatment of seven critical issues was unprecedented. Among these featured (1) "violent extremism in all of its forms" and (2) "the situation between Israelis, Palestinians and the Arab world," in addition to (3) "nuclear weapons," (4) "democracy," (5) "religious freedom," (6) "women's rights," and (7) "economic development and opportunity."

I believe it would be fair to say that the speech was received with a significant level of enthusiasm in the Arab street. Following the event, I visited a few of my Muslim leader friends to get a sense of what they thought. Despite American-Arab relations being at one of their lowest point in our history, the main reaction I received I would describe as "cautious positivism." Their fear, however, was that there would be a huge gap between talk and action and, sadly, they were right. But what struck me most was how quickly the anti-Western, anti-American feelings in the Arab world could be healed given some serious follow-up in actions of a more humble approach to our world's most serious problems.

Other practical steps to peacemaking that present themselves to us may be: taking independent initiatives toward resolving the Israeli-Palestinian conflict (practice 2), since this is an issue that fuels the radical ideology; cooperating with moderate trends within Islam in order to find a solution to the radicalization problem by seeking to understand their motivation and concern (practice 3); supporting non-violent direct action (practice 1) by the moderate currents in Islam in order to counter the culture of violence; replacing the arrogant tradition of interventionism with just and sustainable economic development (practice 6) in countries where extremism is, or even risks being, on the rise; and finally, no longer arming paramilitary factions in the hope that they will serve our agenda against our enemies (practice 9), for history teaches us that these factions themselves are likely to become tomorrow's enemies.

The Polarization of the Israeli-Palestinian Issue Along Religious Lines

In one sense, the Israeli-Palestinian conflict has deep roots in history, deriving from centuries-long tensions between Muslims and Jews that find their roots in the Qur'an and the Islamic tradition. During the time when he resided in Mecca, Muhammad had adopted a rather conciliatory tone towards Christians and Jews:

> Surely those who believe,[2] and those who are Jews, and the Christians, and the Sabians, whoever believes in Allah and the Last day and does good, they shall have their reward from their Lord, and there is no fear for them, nor shall they grieve (Sûrat al-Baqara [2] 62).[3]

The Qur'anic evidence suggests that, during that early period, Muhammad had viewed his message as a natural extension of the Judeo-Christian message, and he seems to have expected that it would be received with open arms:

> And when they hear what has been revealed to the messenger you will see their eyes overflowing with tears on account of the truth that they recognize; they say: Our Lord! we believe, so write us down with the witnesses (of truth) (Sûrat al-Mâ'ida [5] 83).

Extensive interaction between Muhammad and the Jews, however, most likely only began after his migration (*hijra*) from Mecca to Medina in the year 622 AD. Upon arrival to Medina, Muhammad established a pact of brotherhood (*al-mu'âkhât*) between the *Muhâjirûn* (the Meccan "immigrants" who had accepted his message and migrated with him to Medina) and the *Ansâr* (the Medinan "supporters" who had accepted his message and joined his community), as well as with the Jews, who belonged to the ruling tribes of Medina. The Jews were to benefit from the same status,

2. This expression in the Qur'an is a reference to Muslims, in other words those who believe in God's message to Muhammad.

3. All Qur'anic citations are from Muhammad Habib Shakir's translation of the Qur'an (he uses less archaic English than most other translations); Tahrike Tarsile Qur'aan, Inc., P.O. Box 1115, Elmhurst, New York 11373.

support and protection that members of the new community offered each other. It is clear that initially, Muhammad had no intention of using violence against them. However, we read in Muhammad's biography (*as-Sîra an-Nabiwiyya*), which is the main source for our knowledge of his life and ministry, that enmity soon arose between Muhammad and his followers on one side and the Jews of Medina on the other:

> About this time the Jewish rabbis showed hostility to the apostle
> in envy, hatred, and malice, because God had chosen His apostle
> from the Arabs.[4]

Whatever trust we place in the historical accuracy of this account, one thing seems clear. Until then, the Jews had controlled religious, social, economic, and political life in Medina, and it is not surprising if they felt threatened by the rising star of Muhammad, who was now forming a cross-tribal alliance, setting accountability to the *umma* above any natural tribal kinship. These tensions, we are told, eventually led to all-out battle and finally to the extermination of some and the exile of others of the Jewish tribes of Medina. In practice, there is a striking liturgical shift that takes place in this early period in Medina that no doubt reflects this growing rift between Muhammad's community on one side and Jews and Christians on the other. Initially Muhammad and his followers had carried out their daily prayers by prostrating themselves in the direction (Arabic: *qibla*) of Jerusalem, following the custom of the Jews and Eastern Christians. Not too long after arriving in Medina, however, after both Jews and Christians had come to reject the authenticity of his message, the direction of prayer was itself changed:

> It is said that the Qibla was changed in Sha'bân at the beginning
> of the eighteenth month after the apostle's arrival in Media.[5]

This liturgical shift seems to reflect a change in Muhammad's self-perception, initially viewing his message as an extension of the Judeo-Christian tradition, but later affirming its independence and novelty. It did not take very long after the death of Muhammad in 632 AD until more serious and definite conflicts emerged between the new movement inaugurated by Muhammad and the Jews and Christians. But even before that, in the Qur'an itself, his statements about them became gradually more negative and aggressive. The following verses belong to the later period of Muhammad's life:

4. Ishâq, *Life of Muhammad*, 239.
5. Ibid., 289.

And the Jews will not be pleased with you, nor the Christians
until you follow their religion. Say: Surely Allah's guidance, that
is the (true) guidance. And if you follow their desires after the
knowledge that has come to you, you shall have no guardian
from Allah, nor any helper. (Sûrat al-Baqara [2] 120)

O you who believe! do not take the Jews and the Christians
for friends; they are friends of each other; and whoever amongst
you takes them for a friend, then surely he is one of them; surely
Allah does not guide the unjust people. (Sûrat al-Mâ'ida [5] 51)

Despite these rugged beginnings, however, in geographic Palestine,
Jewish, Christian, and Muslim populations had been able to maintain a
certain level of peaceful coexistence. Of course, one may point to some
periods of intense conflict, but these tend to be connected with specific
political events that inflamed relations, such as the early Islamic conquest
of Palestine (following the Battle of Yarmuk in 636 AD), the capture of the
region by the Crusaders in 1099, and the recapture by Saladin in 1187.
In the modern period, the tension was considerably exacerbated by historical developments that began in the late nineteenth century, namely the
gradual yet massive immigration of Jews to Palestine, fostered by Zionist
ideology, and justified with the spurious propaganda that Palestine was "a
land without people for a people without a land." The statement was in fact
a rash misrepresentation of the demographic realities. In fact, from 1851
to 1925, the Palestinian population had grown from 327,000 to 765,000.[6]
Meanwhile, the Jewish population in 1851 represented less than 5 percent
of the population, at about 13,000, spread over Jerusalem, Tiberias, Safed,
and Jaffa. But this would quickly change under the concerted efforts of
the Zionist movement, which would find a very favorable atmosphere to
accomplish its goals under the British Mandate, particularly following the
Balfour Declaration of 1917, which affirmed that the British government
now viewed "with favour the establishment in Palestine of a national home
for the Jewish people." Over the same period, the Jewish presence would
grow to over 100,000. Centuries-long anti-Semitism in Europe, culmi-
nating in Nazi exterminationism, convinced Jewish leaders of the need
for a Jewish homeland. By 1947, under the UN Partition Plan, Jews, who
represented 31 percent of the population owning 6 percent of the land,
were given 52 percent of the land. By contrast, the Palestinians, who represented 69 percent of the population, were given 48 percent of the land. In
1948, when the State of Israel was established, 700,000 Palestinians either

6. Refer to Cole, "The Map." See also McCarthy, *Population of Palestine*.

fled or were driven out of their homes, and Israel took over a further 25 percent of the land. In 1967, the Six-Day-War led to the annexation of East Jerusalem and the occupation of the West Bank, Sinai, and the Golan Heights. Although UN Resolution 242 that followed required "withdrawal of Israeli forces from territories of recent conflict" based on "the inadmissibility of the acquisition of territory by war," this requirement has yet to be implemented.[7]

While the Israeli-Palestinian conflict started largely as a political conflict, involving Arab support for the Palestinians against the establishment of the State of Israel, over the latter part of the twentieth century, there was a gradual shift from the notion of an "Arab-Israeli" conflict to an "Islamic resistance" to the Israeli occupation of Palestine. This is symbolically reflected in comparing the two Intifadas. During the First Intifada (1987–93), the means of Palestinian uprising were mainly peaceful protests and stone throwing. The leadership of that protest, even when involving religious members, used a largely secular rhetoric, and included Palestinian Christians, such as Hanan Ashrawi, as well as Muslims.

The Second Intifada was a different matter. To begin with, it took on the highly symbolic name of the "Al-Aqsa Intifada" (2000–2005), conveying the sense of being an Islamic cause, championed by Hamas, and centering on Islam's third most holy site in Jerusalem (al-Aqsa mosque). If the First Intifada was chiefly Palestinian and nationalist in nature, the very name of the Second Intifada was designed to have a powerful appeal on the Muslim masses of the entire Islamic world. *Intifadat al-Aqsa* was Islamic and regional in nature, calling for the endorsement of the entire Islamic *Umma*.

Steps toward a Solution: Suggested Peacemaking Practices

The most intricate conflict of modern times, and cause of so much global conflict, is not going to go away overnight. But here again, steps toward conflict resolution must be considered. Western countries can support nonviolent direct action (practice 1), such as the "Gaza Flotilla" of 2010 and 2011. Seeing to the success of such action may be the only way to defuse Hamas and Hezbollah rhetoric that the only language that Israel understands is the language of force, as well as to put an end to communal punishment of all Gaza inhabitants, which empowers Hamas.

7. For a comprehensive and balanced coverage of the conflict, see Chapman, *Whose Promised Land?*

Friends of Israel need to encourage it to take independent initiatives that will demonstrate seriousness about making peace (practice 2). The more powerful party in a conflict is in a better position to take effective independent initiatives. Of course the danger is that this would be perceived as weakness, but in light of the decades of conflict, surely this must be a risk worth taking. Solutions to the conflict need to be sought cooperatively (practice 3). The resumption of "direct negotiations," such as the ones attempted in September 2010 is key. But unfortunately the talks quickly stalled due to the resumption of settlement building. And finally, just and sustainable economic development needs to be fostered (practice 6), which will benefit the Palestinian population. This needs to be carried out through and in collaboration with non-government organizations, along with close anti-corruption monitoring and training in transparency and accountability.

Grass-root resistance movements like Hamas and Hezbollah thrive and grow in popularity through the establishment of social services, particularly education and healthcare. These are of great service to neglected communities, but unfortunately they are also used as a tool to keep entire populations captive to radical agendas. The international community had better invest much more in community development, particularly in education, and much less in armament. Unfortunately, this message does not seem to be getting through. The U.S. continues to deliver $1.3 billion annually to Egypt in weaponry, and about a fifth of that in economic development aid. Perhaps if we stopped calling armament "military *aid*," we would see more clearly into the absurdity of such policy. I do understand that arms trade is important for the U.S. economy, and that cancelling these deals would create a serious problem to any presidential hopeful, as pointed out by a recent New York Times article.[8] But that's just the problem with foreign policy that is driven by U.S. presidential campaigning interests.[9]

The Reductionist Perception of Islam (Including in Our Churches)

From the two great global political challenges of recent history identified above, let us now move to a more intellectual and "internal" challenge that has also affected our churches more directly. September 11, 2001 was a turning point for Islam's perception in the world. Immediately after the attacks on the Twin Towers and the Pentagon, Islam was identified as the

---

8. Myers, "Aid to Egypt Is Restored."
9. See the Op-Ed article of Thomas Friedman the following day: "Festival of Lies."

ideological system behind the terrorist act. The assumption was made that violent militant radicalism is the only authentic manifestation of Islam's defining texts. In an Op-Ed just preceding the tenth anniversary of September 11, 2001, Robert Fisk, Middle East correspondent for *The Independent* daily, pointed out how much had been written analyzing the attacks, while the motivations of the nineteen bombers was ignored.[10] Although it immediately became clear that "the 19 murderers of 9/11 claimed they were Muslims," and that "they came from a place called the Middle East," Fisk points out that we have simply avoided asking ourselves the obvious question: "Is there a problem out there?" Fisk does make note of a book that stands out for its unique treatment of the motivations; it highlights the fact that "All the evidence . . . indicates that Palestine was the factor that united the conspirators—at every level." Soon after the attack, it was discovered that one of the organizers expressed his belief that the attack on the Twin Towers would force Americans to pay attention to "the atrocities that America is committing by supporting Israel."

As indicated in the section on the "Rise of Islamism" above, the Palestinian problem and the unquestioning support of Israel in US foreign policy was a recurring theme in Osama bin Laden's speeches as well. How is it, then, that there has been so little reflection on these connections over the past ten years? This is perhaps not surprising. Faced with such a shocking event at home, it was much easier for the White House to identify Islam as the source of its tragedy, rather than putting into question decades of foreign policy unquestioningly supportive of Israel. Thus the tragic conditions of the Palestinians both inside historic Palestine and in refugee camps of neighboring countries could continue to be ignored.

The problem, of course, with this reductionist approach, is that it continues to strengthen the hand of violent extremists and to weaken the voice of the moderate majority of Muslims, thus exacerbating conflict. Indeed, a 2007 Gallup Poll that sought to survey the views of Muslims around the world about violence and terrorism discovered that only 7 percent of the respondents thought that the 9/11 attacks were "completely" justified. Though this number may sound high when one thinks that it reflects an endorsement of such a dramatic event as 9/11, we must remember, nevertheless, that it is not pointing to a group of Muslims that are committing acts of violence. What it points to is a group that is angry enough about the role of the U.S. to have feelings of revenge toward it. The group may also be where violent agents may be recruited. It is interesting,

10. Fisk, "For 10 Years."

however, also to note that the anger towards the U.S. is not limited to this group. Among the majority—those who thought that the attacks of 9/11 were not justified—as many as 60 percent said that they viewed the U.S. unfavorably. This nevertheless did not lead them to *endorse* the use of violence against it.[11]

In 2007, I carried out a simple experiment using the website Amazon.com. I ran a search for books with the word "Islam" in their title. I ran the search twice, once by limiting my search to all books published before September 2001, and the other by limiting my search to all those published after September 2001. The result was quite enlightening. While books published before 9/11 were for the most part of an academic, informative nature, those published since 9/11 were popular and polemical in their very titles: *Antichrist: Islam's Awaited Messiah* (Joel Richardson: 2006), *The Day of Islam: The Annihilation of America and the Western World* (Paul L. Williams: 2007), *Unveiling Islam: An Insider's Look at Muslim Life and Belief* (Ergun Mehmet Caner: 2002), *Answering Islam: The Crescent in Light of the Cross* (Norman L. Geisler and Abdul Saleeb: 2002), *Islam and Terrorism: What the Quran Really Teaches About Christianity, Violence and the Goals of the Islamic Jihad* (Mark A. Gabriel: 2002), *Religion of Peace?: Why Christianity Is and Islam Isn't* (Robert Spencer: 2007), *Islam Unveiled: Disturbing Questions about the World's Fastest-Growing Faith* (Robert Spencer: 2003), *Religion of Peace?: Islam's War Against the World* (Gregory M. Davis: 2006), *Understanding Islamic Terrorism: The Islamic Doctrine of War* (Patrick Sookhdeo: 2004). Is it any wonder that the Western world's understanding of Islam has grown towards more and more prejudice following 2001, if these are the books we're reading? I ran the search again in the course of writing the present paper and was pleasantly surprised that our readings on Islam seem to be returning to a more balanced, analytical and academic agenda, even though it will no doubt take time for perceptions to return to some balance.

To see how this intellectual reductionism actually affects practice, let us reflect briefly on the "Burn-a-Qur'an" saga that developed in the run-up to the 9th anniversary of 9/11 in 2010, which at the time also became related to the "Park 51" (or so-called Ground Zero Mosque) controversy. Granted that Terry Jones is not the representative of mainstream Christianity; nevertheless, despite the fact that many Evangelical leaders publicly condemned Jones' plan to burn Qur'ans on the anniversary of 9/11, I suspect that many did it primarily out of utilitarian motives rather than out

11. Esposito and Mogahed, "What Makes a Radical?"

of a conviction that the Qur'an does deserve our respect. Many arguments were leveled by way of expressing disapproval of Mr. Jones' intention. Some said it would put U.S. armed forces at risk in Iraq and Afghanistan. Others argued that it would become breeding grounds for the recruitment of violent Muslim extremists. It will place the lives of Americans at risk in the U.S. It will cost tens of thousands of dollars to ensure the safety of Mr. Jones and his little congregation in Florida. It will provoke the persecution of Christians in Muslim lands. The lives of Americans and other Westerners living in the Muslim world will be placed at risk.

Mercifully, it was also pointed out that burning the holy book of any religious group is not proper civil behavior, especially for someone claiming to be a Christian, let alone a Christian pastor. Some Christians condemning the impending act insisted that it was completely unaligned with Jesus' teaching on loving one's neighbor, or even one's "enemy." Many observed what a serious blow this act would deal to Christian-Muslim relations and peacemaking, and were already contemplating the disastrous consequences on humanity for decades to come.[12]

Clearly, then, the reaction to Jones' plan had been diverse. Although we shouldn't ignore the appropriate responses, we nevertheless need to recognize that there is also a strong element that condemned the action out of a purely pragmatic fear of consequences rather than out of principled objection. And the thinking behind this attitude, I would allege, is this reductionist view of Islam that does not believe that Islam is capable of anything other than violent action as well as reaction.

The Terry Jones saga became directly connected with the "Park 51" controversy, another issue that illustrated the dangers of stereotypical views of Islam. The issue of building the "Cordova House" project at Park 51 was made into a "controversy" apparently by conservative bloggers, such as Robert Spencer (jihadwatch.org) and Pamela Geller (Atlas Shrugs). The way that the issue was represented in the media (particularly the question of its proximity to Ground Zero) possibly began with Robert Spencer calling the "Cordova House" the "Ground Zero Mosque." The description would have had us imagine that the project was going to be built on the very site of the former Twin Towers when, as a matter of fact, Park 51 was going to be about 6 blocks away. In addition to being most likely intentionally misleading, the media also reminded us of some statements that Imam Faisal Abd al-Rauf (in charge of the project) had made in the past about the U.S., suggesting that it had caused more deaths

12. See Cave and Barnard, "Minister Wavers."

among Muslims than al-Qaida had caused among non-Muslims. One of the great reductionist comments that were made in this regard, as well as stereotypical assumptions with regard to Islam's responsibility for 9/11, was the statement made by Newt Gingrich: "Nazis don't have the right to put up a sign next to the Holocaust Museum in Washington. We would never accept the Japanese putting up a site next to Pearl Harbor. There's no reason for us to accept a mosque next to the World Trade Center."[13] Through a sweeping statement like this, Gingrich essentially cast the burden of responsibility for 9/11 on the entire Muslim community as well as on Islam as an entire ideology.

Sadly, this reductionist attitude and understanding of Islam has become deeply ingrained in the church, where in many quarters Islam has become vilified and demonized to an extreme. In many cases today, missionary individuals and organizations as well as other Christian bodies are being asked to take a clear stance towards issues like the so-called "insider movement" and "Christian-Muslim dialogue," and to make this clear in their policies. Too often this has taken the shape of a "witch hunt" rather than a prayerful intellectual pursuit informed by realities on the ground. I also believe that the debate on one side is driven primarily by hatred for Islam (although proponents usually claim they love Muslims), driven by the reductionist understanding of the religion as a monistic reality, similar to the phenomenon described above, rather than by a comprehensive and fair historical, theological and practical exploration. Many missionaries and organizations are actually losing their financial support because their views and approaches are perceived to be "too friendly" toward Islam.

Steps toward a Solution:
Suggested Peacemaking Practices

The best way to move beyond a reductionist approach and understanding of an ideological "other" is to move them out of our theoretical "lab" and approach them as persons and neighbors. The reductionist approach "objectifies" individuals and movements, whereas I believe that as Christians we are called to approach people subject-to-subject, and their ideas as dynamic realities, rather than as objects of exploration. In an effort to practice this approach, we are called to take independent initiatives that build permanent channels of communication with Muslim communities

13. "Fact Check: Islam Already Lives Near Ground Zero," http://www.huffington-post.com/2010/08/19/islam-already-party-of-gr_n_687639.html.

in our neighborhoods (practice 2). This will put a "human face" to Islam and reduce prejudice among Christians, and equally important, it will offer Muslims a positive experience of their Christian neighbors, which I think is an invaluable contribution that we can make to building peaceful societies for the future.

In parallel, we need to start establishing cooperative interfaith platforms to address issues of inter-communal conflict and abuse (practice 3). Too often, people of faith resolve their grievances by pointing the finger to the harm provoked by members of other faiths. We are primarily concerned about those in our own community whose rights are being abused. If our concern for human rights abuse were driven by a love of neighbor, then we would also be concerned by the abuse of the rights of members of other faiths. Interfaith platforms of advocacy would then form a front against all forms of abuse, based on fundamental principles of ethics, not on ethnocentric or religion-centric tribalism.

Thirdly, we can encourage grassroots (and church-based) peacemaking groups and voluntary associations (practice 10). Members would be educated about Islam in a fair and balanced manner. The motivation would not be fear, but the desire to understand Islam in all of its diversity and complexity.

Finally, we need to educate to purge our churches from a mentality that supports war (practice 9)—war as a solution to "terrorism," war as a solution to Israel's security. Instead, we need to develop a more sophisticated understanding of our current problems that is interested in examining and addressing root causes. We need to tell our governments to take *preventive* measures that address the root cause of conflict, rather than dealing *preemptive* strikes against countries that are already inflamed with anger due to past grievances.

The Consolidation of a "Culture of Resistance" Bloc

The Iranian revolution in the late seventies became the epitomic symbol of resistance to the West, and particularly to America, whose foreign policy in the Middle East region had come to be viewed as driven by a neo-colonialist agenda, oil-driven self-interest, and a duplicitous attitude toward the Israeli-Palestinian question. This fourth challenge brings us back full circle to the first challenge of the rise of Islamism. The success of the Islamic Revolution in Iran represented the first time that Islam was able to take back political power since the abolishing of the

Caliphate in the early 1920s. Symbolically, in the minds of many Muslims, this represented a huge comeback for Islam and a first step toward restoring Islam's "honor" and "sense of pride" in the world. These two words, *karâma* (honor) and *'izza* (pride), are two important catchwords that Hezbollah, in Lebanon, regularly uses in its appeal to the masses in the honor/shame societies of the Middle East. Their appeal becomes particularly significant when one understands first the deep sense of humiliation that the abolishing of the Caliphate had brought about in the Muslim world some fifty-five years before the Iranian Revolution.

Hezbollah emerged in the early eighties as a movement of resistance against the Israeli occupation of Lebanon. It quickly began to play a significant role in furthering this ideology of "resistance" inaugurated by Khomeini. Hassan Nasrallah, General Secretary of Hezbollah, often speaks of the need to transform Lebanon into a "society of resistance" with a "culture of resistance." As I write these paragraphs on May 11, 2012, Nasrallah has just made a televised appearance on the occasion of the completion of the "most beautiful promise" (*al-wa'd al-ajmal*) operation, the reconstruction of the Southern Suburbs of Beirut after its near-total destruction by Israel's bombings in summer 2006. No surprise in the fact that these large-screen appearances take place in the new and massive quadrangle that Hezbollah has named the "*Pride and Honor Quadrangle.*"[14]

In the late 1980s, this same ideology was taken up by Hamas in its own struggle against the Israeli occupation of the West Bank and Gaza. Though Hamas is a Sunni group, more closely affiliated in its political ideology to the Sunni Muslim Brotherhood of Egypt than to the Shiite ideology of Khomeini, it is the "resistance" dimension of this stream of Islam that joins two groups like Hamas and Hezbollah together ideologically, beyond the historic Sunni-Shiite enmity. The bloc is joined by Shiite movements in Iraq in the first decade of the twenty-first century. I am referring to this bloc as the "culture of resistance" bloc.

A description of the "culture of resistance" bloc would not be complete without a word on the Syrian regime. The support of resistance movements against Israel has been a major pillar of the Assad regime since the eighties. It is worth noting, however, that this united "resistance front" has begun to crumble over the Syrian manifestation of the "Arab Spring." Indeed, Hamas has found itself faced with a huge loyalty dilemma. The Assad regime's Damascus has been the only Arab capital willing to host

14. A report on Nasrallah's speech at the occasion can be found here (http://news. qawem.org/impnews/7144–41.html) on Hezbollah's website.

the Hamas political bureau and its chief, Khalid Mishaal, since 2001. Yet since the start of the demonstrations in Syria, Hamas has gradually shifted its primary allegiance back to the Syrian Sunni Muslim Brotherhood and supported its uprising against the Assad regime. Whatever the outcome of the Syrian "Arab Spring," it would seem that the "culture of resistance" bloc, which once consisted of Iran-Hezbollah-Syria-Hamas, will come out considerably weakened. It will lose either Syria and Hamas, if the Assad regime is overturned, or at least Hamas, if the regime manages to survive.

"Culture of Resistance" and "Culture of Affluence" on the Lebanese Scene

The "culture of resistance" in Lebanon had to reckon with the emergence of another powerful force in the 1990s: money and affluence. After the end of its Civil War (1975–91), from about 1992–2004, Lebanon was governed by powerful business-minded Prime Minister Rafic Hariri. The climate was one of post-war reconstruction and the culture that Hariri cultivated was a "culture of affluence," which lasted a little over a decade. For a while, in the mid-nineties, Beirut was attested as the world's largest building site! The massive financial investments that poured into Lebanon toward reconstruction kept Hezbollah in check for a time.

In February 2005, however, Hariri was assassinated and Hezbollah's ideology and worldview began to reemerge. For the past seven years, the country has been torn in half, unable to govern itself, because of successive governments that have been deeply divided along conflicting values: the "culture of affluence," represented by those who want to get on with life and grow economically in harmony with the international community, and the "culture of resistance," represented by those who accuse the international community of economic selfishness, hypocrisy toward the Palestinians, and double standards toward Israel. The Syrian "Arab Spring" has further deepened the divide, with the two Lebanese factions pitted against each other in their stance toward the Assad regime.

The "Culture of Resistance" on the Global Scene

The emerging geopolitical reality described above, manifested in the alliance between Lebanon's Hezbollah, Assad's Syria, Iran, Southern Iraq, and certain Shiite-majority Gulf countries, has given rise to what is increasingly seen as the geopolitical threat of the "Shiite Crescent." As I see it, however, the greater threat emerging globally is not so much Shiite ideology as it is this "resistance" ideology. Both the *Islamist* and the *resistance* ideologies are driven by many of the same motivations: a reaction to Western neo-colonial ambition, the Palestinian cause, anger against the U.S., etc. But whereas the "radical Islamist" ideology (first challenge) tends to manifest itself primarily through violent acts perpetrated by an extremist elite, the danger of the "culture of resistance" challenge is that it is gradually pitting two worlds against each other: West and East, Shiite and Sunni, Christian and Muslim, affluence and resistance. It does so through a resilient "boycott" of Western political, social and economic ideological influence and less through lethal action. But there are likely to be longer-term consequences, as the rift between these two ideological worlds goes much deeper.

The Principal Features of the "Culture of Resistance"

I would summarize the principal features of the "culture of resistance" that I've been seeking to trace above as follows:

1. A deeply-entrenched anti-Americanism (and to a large extent anti-Westernism)

2. Sharp criticism of American (and to a lesser extent other Western) political hegemony and the double standards toward Israel and the Arabs

3. A perception that the U.S. claims to democracy and freedom are nothing but thin air that dissipates to the benefit of selfish economic interests

4. A loss of trust in the international community and its representative bodies like the United Nations

5. Claims to stand for the cause of the weak and oppressed, in the face of neo-colonial Western powers

6. Militancy for the Palestinian cause

7. In the West, a growing resistance among immigrants to integrate culturally, sociologically and certainly religiously within their host communities

Steps toward a Solution: Suggested Peacemaking Practices

The "culture of resistance" has emerged out of a conviction that the "enemy" understands only the language of force. It has also emerged out of deep grievances against what is perceived as the West's double standards in judging the worth of human life in Israel/Palestine, Iraq, Afghanistan, and elsewhere. The only way perhaps to begin changing that conviction is to support nonviolent direct action (practice 1), which will hopefully set some precedents for a successful and just resolution of conflicts and unjust situations.

Independent initiatives (practice 2) may be taken in reducing whatever fuels this ideology of "resistance"—the Israeli-Palestinian conflict being the chief issue. Israel's restoration of occupied land to Syria and Lebanon would take away some of Hezbollah's justification for its own existence as a group that has emerged in resistance to occupation. The establishment of an independent Palestinian nation-state would go a long way toward removing some of the fodder that feeds the "culture of resistance." I am not suggesting that militant Islamist groups would suddenly disappear if such steps were taken. But it would place alternative cultures on higher moral ground than they currently are, and greatly increase their ability to grow in strength and numbers.

Leaders of the two opposite cultures—the "culture of resistance" and the "culture of affluence"—need to initiate cooperative efforts (practice 3) and seek a common agenda in key areas of disagreement, beyond simply finding temporary "common enemies." An attempt by each side to empathize with the grievances, concerns and interests of the other would go a long way toward relieving some of the tension and distrust. In the case of Lebanon, this approach, combined with an agreement to move towards some mutual concessions, might help in restoring the ability to govern the country and move out of the current status quo and deadlock.

Looking further at the situation in Lebanon, which we have identified as an important pole in this "war of cultures," if parties in Lebanon acknowledged their respective responsibility for wartime crimes (practice 4), particularly in connection with the Lebanese Civil War, this would potentially restore some trust between them and help them work toward common goals with mutual benefits.

Due to the pervasiveness of "cultural blindness," which we all suffer from, we need to encourage the emergence of peacemaking groups (practice 10) at the grassroots, whose chief agenda is to learn how to see each other's perspective. Seeing from the eyes of the "other," without necessarily endorsing their view, is a precious quality for the resolution of cross-cultural conflict. But it requires the highest level of self-awareness and capability for empathy, as is emphasized by the practice of cooperative conflict resolution. Most of us are too entrenched within our own cultural worldview even to admit to the existence of legitimate alternatives.

Problematic Aspects of Some of the Just Peacemaking Practices in the Context of Global Religious Challenges

In the present section, having examined the applicability of the ten just peacemaking practices on the three global challenges involving Islam and Muslims, I want to explore briefly the limitations of three of these practices in the particular context that we have been discussing.

Practice 4: Acknowledge Responsibility for Conflict and Injustice and Seek Repentance and Forgiveness

Although the principle of acknowledging responsibility is important, and that of seeking repentance and forgiveness is profoundly biblical, I would like to advance that the practice of communal repentance is very delicate in the context of honor and shame cultures. Beginning in 1996 and in the run up to the year 2000, a group of Christians from the West retraced the steps of the Crusaders from the heart of Europe, all the way to Jerusalem, asking forgiveness for the crimes committed a thousand years earlier.[15]

The concept as a whole was attractive and moving. Certainly many people were touched by the novelty of the initiative. As we read some of the accounts on the website indicated above, I am sure that those who were the direct object of the meetings were moved by the humility and kindness of the groups visiting them from the West. But I remember asking various people at the time what they thought of it. Reactions I got ranged from skepticism to puzzlement. In a culture of honor and shame, you might apologize for your own mistakes, but apologizing for your ancestry brings shame to your group. And generally speaking, people that belong to honor/shame cultures want to relate to people that they consider "honorable."

Furthermore, after such a dramatic act, if you are not able to maintain the repentant behavior, the consequences are even worse than before. Shortly after the reconciliation walks, following the attacks of September

15. Further details may be found in ReligiousTolerance.org, "Christian Apology."

11, 2001, the "Western world" went to war against the Muslim world again, as a sort of repeat to the Crusades. Or at least that is how the wars in Afghanistan and Iraq were widely viewed in the Muslim world. Further, such initiatives did nothing to address the Palestinian question, which is the main grievance of the Muslim world today.

Repentance and seeking forgiveness is a dangerous business. If it is not followed through with change of behavior, it leaves the wound even rawer and the relationship sore. Apologizing for the treatment of the Palestinians, and actually doing something about all the pro-Israel and pro-Zionist ideology of the Western church, which continues to be at the expense of the Palestinian people, would go much further in reconciling East and West. I am of course not advocating that feelings of enmity toward Israel should now be fostered in our churches. I believe, on the contrary, that the unquestioning support for political Israel, with no concern for the Palestinian people, is extremely harmful to Israel in the long run. Those who want to save Israel need to start addressing the Israeli-Palestinian question with much more fairness and balance. The continued abuse of Palestinian rights, both in Palestine and in the terrible conditions of decades-old refugee camps in neighboring countries has frightening consequences. These are sins that need to be acknowledged, followed by repentance and reparation. Short of this, global communal initiatives of repentance remain at best symbolic, and at worst hypocritical.

Practice 5: Advance Democracy, Human Rights and Religious Liberty

Powerful voices in the Muslim world today mock Western powers' use of these notions because of the perceived self-serving double standards. Again the question of Palestine here jumps to mind. Israel is described as a thriving democracy in the Middle East, yet Palestinians there have been living like second-class citizens or worse for decades, while the separation wall is fencing them in like sheep in an enclosure.

As for the Western claim in the first decade of our twenty-first century that the wars in Iraq and Afghanistan were going to usher in democracy and human rights and liberty, the logic was so ridiculous that I find no better description for it than the sign that a woman was holding during an anti-war demonstration (once a famous picture in the media) "bombing for democracy is like f***ing for virginity!" The thought that forcing democracy and liberty upon a people is an option reflects a deep lack of understanding of realities on the ground.

Democracy is a system that requires that a large proportion of a population would be educated and have experienced a certain amount of personal freedom, to the point where they have a desire to work toward the common good. When you've been deprived of your freedoms for decades by a dictatorial regime, have grown up in a tribal society where the interests of your clan or religious sect come before the interests of your national state, what will make you desire democracy is not more bombs, but more liberal education, more taste of personal freedom of choice, and a level of experience of the benefits that come from a society that works together for the common good.

Furthermore, certain aspects of democracy, human rights, and religious liberty are understood differently in the Muslim world. These differences need to be respected for what they are as a starting point, and inter-civilizational dialogue may then allow for differing notions to influence each other. If the development of these concepts is to occupy a global agenda, then we need to begin by exploring Muslim understandings in order to overcome and avoid patronizing attitudes.

Islam has deeply-rooted understandings of principles of consultation (*shûra*) and consensus (*ijmâ'*), and it places high value on the sanctity of life. But not having gone through the liberal secularization waves that much of the western world has gone through, what Muslims refer to as the "right of God" still stands in judgment of human rights and personal freedoms in Muslim societies. Simply manifested, it was more important to defend the "right of God" in the face of the slanderous Danish caricatures than it was to defend the individual right of the cartoonist to draw whatever he pleased. These value priorities are culturally driven and culturally relative. There is no point in trying to argue that one is better than the other. All we can do is dialogue about these priorities, try to understand the motivations behind them, and agree on certain boundaries that respect the values of the one without robbing the freedoms of the other.

Practice 8: Strengthen the United Nations and International Efforts for Cooperation and Human Rights

The United Nations is supposed to be a higher authority that holds various world powers accountable, and that guarantees that the interests of weaker entities are not abused. But many in the Muslim world today have lost faith in the UN because it has often failed to impose its will on superpowers. Its Security Council resolutions have too often been trodden upon by all sides, such as in the Palestinian-Israeli conflict. And more recently, in the case of the International Tribunal for the assassination of Lebanon's Rafic Hariri, its international legal system is being made into a mockery by voices emerging from the "culture of resistance."

Greater consistency in supporting the UN, and the endorsement and implementation of ALL its resolutions by leaders of the international community is called for. Perhaps this would go some way toward remedying the current negative attitude toward the UN that is prevalent in many circles, and toward restoring its position as a leading authority and arbiter globally.

Just Peacemaking and Twenty-First-Century Discipleship: Small Practical Steps

As noted in my introduction, discipleship involves not only diagnosis but needs to be followed by a suggestion of practical solutions. In each of the sections above, I have suggested how some of the ten Just Peacemaking practices are helpful in providing action steps toward a solution to the challenges identified. In this closing section, I want to suggest even more specific steps that may be used by each individual among us as we seek to be part of a solution to today's great challenges that face us as we seek to be peacemakers globally. The suggestions come from a quick survey among friends who are active in bettering relations between Christians and Muslims around the world.[16]

1. Endeavor to see all Muslims as people first, made in the image of God.

2. Assume the best of your Muslim friends and of Muslims in general, taking them at their word and taking their statements as genuine reflections of their beliefs, rather than assuming that they are being politically correct or hiding some sinister beliefs that some in your community tell you "they all" believe.

3. Consider yourself welcome at your local mosque during prayer times and other special Qur'anic study times. Make friends with the local sheikh or imam and hear for yourself what he is teaching your Muslim neighbors. Do this transparently and without pretense to be who you are not. Muslims are generally very welcoming of non-Muslims

16. Special thanks to Jared Holsing and Michael Ly for returning many of these suggestions that they practice in their own lives.

at the mosque, but most would be uncomfortable for you to engage in Muslim prayers publicly if you are not a professing Muslim.

4. Take pastors and other Christians with you to the mosque to meet Muslims and Muslim leaders. Take along your spouse and your children, so that they too can develop friendships with Muslims from their social groups.

5. Encourage Christian and Muslim community leaders to host interfaith dialogues at their church and mosque buildings. Help them pick topics where honest and respectful dialogue can happen, such as Jesus, love, peace, justice, human rights, etc.

6. Attend fund-raisers for mosques or Muslim organizations and show support for the Muslim community. If you live in a country where Christians are the majority, this is the time to be hospitable to Muslims. It is when you are in the majority that your outreach and hospitality efforts are most effective, when you don't actually "need" the other.

7. Besides reading your Bible, also read the Qur'an to understand personally and first-hand what it actually says. Then ask a Muslim friend or imam when you have a question.

8. Attend community gatherings and celebrations to make new friends in the Muslim community. Accept invitations to the mosque and Muslim homes and initiate invitations in return.

9. Invite leaders and members of the Muslim community to your home for friendly conversations and to share meals, as well as to your own community's celebrations. Invite some of your Christian friends and pastor to share those meals as well in order to foster friendships between the two communities.

10. Read widely from various sources and perspectives, attempting to see the world through the eyes of a Muslim.

11. Be a bridge between the Christian and Muslim communities in your neighborhood. Teach a balanced understanding of Islam in your church and in Christian organizations when asked. Take a Muslim friend or teacher along where possible.

12. Comment in your social networks (Facebook, twitter, blogs, etc.) and engage in sustained dialogue with your non-Muslim friends in order to be an alternative, positive and loving voice in their lives regarding Muslims.

13. Go out of your way to build friendships with Muslims in your neighborhood and at work.

14. Ask questions of your Muslim friends in order to understand better their daily life realities. Ask about holidays, beliefs, family, fasting, politics, poetry, culture, music, hopes, fears, etc.

15. Share the love, forgiveness and assurance of salvation you have found in Jesus Christ and enjoy an open dialogue about this with your Muslim friends. Strive to shape your life on the model of Jesus in values, thoughts, attitudes, and behavior.

16. When your Muslim friends suggest books, articles, videos that you ought to read or watch, follow through and learn as much as you can. Engage in an open and sustained dialogue with them. As you do this, assume that you both love God, that you both are grateful for the tradition in which you have been raised, that you both have questions, and that you both have found answers that you each find deeply compelling. Remember that these are conversations among friends.

17. Meet regularly with other followers of Jesus and pray specifically for Muslims in your neighborhood and in the world. Pray for justice and peace. Pray that people of faith everywhere would come to a greater and more intimate understanding of the way of Christ and of the implications of his teaching and life on their own reality.

Bibliography

Cave, Damien, and Anne Barnard. "Minister Wavers on Plans to Burn Koran." *New York Times*, 10 September 2010. http://www.nytimes.com/2010/09/10/us/10obama. html?pagewanted=all.

Chapman, Colin. *Whose Promised Land?* Grand Rapids: Baker, 2002.

Cole, Juan. "The Map: The Story of Palestinian Nationhood Thwarted after the League of Nations Recognized It." *Informed Comment* (blog), 6 March 2010. Accessed 9 May 2012. http://www.juancole.com/2010/03/map-story-of-palestinian-nationhood.html.

Esposito, John L., and Dalia Mogahed. "What Makes a Radical?" Excerpt from *Who Speaks for Islam? What a Billion Muslims Really Think*. New York: Gallup, 2007. Posted 13 March 2008. Accessed 12 May 2012. http://www.gallup.com/poll/104941/What-Makes-Radical.aspx.

Fisk, Robert. "For 10 Years, We've Lied to Ourselves to Avoid Asking the One Real Question." *The Independent*, 3 September 2001. Accessed 11 May 2012. http://www.independent.co.uk/opinion/commentators/fisk/robert-fisk-for-10-years-weve-lied-to-ourselves-to-avoid-asking-the-one-real-question-2348438.html.

Friedman, Thomas. "A Festival of Lies." *New York Times*, 24 March 2012. Accessed 10 May 2012. http://www.nytimes.com/2012/03/25/opinion/sunday/friedman-a-festival -of-lies.html?_r=1.

Ishâq, Ibn. *The Life of Muhammad*. Edited and translated by Alfred Guillaume. London: Oxford University Press, 1955.

Lawrence, Bruce, editor. *Messages to the World: The Statements of Osama Bin Laden*. New York: Verso: 2005.

McCarthy, Justin. *The Population of Palestine: Population History and Statistics of the Late Ottoman Period and the Mandate*. New York: Columbia University Press, 1990.

Myers, Steven Lee. "Once Imperiled, U.S. Aid to Egypt Is Restored." *New York Times*, 23 March 2012. Accessed 10 May 2012. http://www.nytimes.com/2012/03/24/world/ middleeast/once-imperiled-united-states-aid-to-egypt-is-restored.html?_r=1.

ReligiousTolerance.org. "Christian Apology for the Crusades: The Reconciliation Walk." Accessed 13 May 2012. http://www.religioustolerance.org/chr_cru1.htm.

14

Dealing with the "Disposable People" of the Globalized Economy

Just Peacemaking and Immigrants, Refugees, and Displaced Persons

Juan Francisco Martínez

Introduction

TODAY'S GLOBAL ECONOMY IS called an information economy. Much is made of the fact that information workers are at its cutting edge. But little is said of other segments of the workforce that maintain the global economy. This same economy that depends on information workers, also depends on the work of those on the bottom of the labor force, be they low wage factory workers, part of the service industry, agricultural workers or other similar employees.

Many of these low-wage tasks can be exported to poor countries that compete with each other to offer the lowest wages to multi-national corporations. But many jobs cannot be outsourced, and do not get paid at a living wage. In many countries, even people toward the bottom of the economic ladder do not want to do many of these jobs either because they are too labor intensive or because they are badly paid.

This is the space filled by migrant workers. In today´s economic and political situation many of these workers are either undocumented or marginally documented. They often have few or no legal rights and are at the mercy of their employers. Undocumented workers are clearly the "disposable labor force" of Marxist interpretation. They have rights only where they do not need them, and no rights where their labor is serving the host economy. The undocumented are politically powerless and voiceless; because they have no legal standing they are at the mercy of all of those around them.

Because of the complicated current economic situation, most political powers find it easier to use the undocumented as scapegoats than to address the economic systems that "require" their labor, but despise their presence. Even people who want to help them often treat them as objects of their goodwill, becoming their voices, instead of empowering them to speak for themselves.

Displaced peoples and refugees find themselves in a similar legal and political limbo. Any goodwill they receive usually depends on the political interests of those who have the means, and they are completely at the mercy of political decisions over which they have no control and in which they have no voice. If a specific displaced group cannot obtain an outside representative who will speak effectively on their behalf, their needs will simply be ignored. Some displaced peoples and situations seem "sexier" and more marketable than others. But all displaced peoples find themselves in a similar situation. Even those who are willing to help them often only see the displaced as objects of their efforts.

Here, in these unequal situations, is where Just Peacemaking can play a crucial role in creating change. Those who would use just peacemaking practices among "disposable peoples" need to remember that they will be most useful to people with few rights if they empower them to be the subjects of their own future. It is not enough to work on their behalf; just peacemaking must help the disposable find their own voices and be subjects of their own future.

Common Framings for Dealing with Immigrants, Refugees, and Displaced Persons

For those who do not live or work among these disposable people, the "normal" response to their situation is indifference. Most people in the middle and upper classes of the majority world can simply ignore the existence of these persons. The undocumented wish not to be noticed. The displaced and the refugees are often in places far from the centers of power or media attention.

When they manage to get some attention the responses usually go in one of two very opposite directions. On the one hand some people respond with compassion. The situation of these people creates an emotional response and a willingness to provide some type of limited action, such a donation to help people in a refugee camp in a distance country. But if the people are too close "for comfort," sometimes the attention creates the opposite response. For example, the undocumented are perceived as a threat and the displaced and refugees as a drain on resources, particularly if they are in the same country as those who have to respond to them. Any potential goodwill is quickly overtaken by frustration, anger and/or fear.

A small percentage of people respond to these situations with a desire for justice. They recognize that things are not right and that someone has to work to bring change. Their view may be merely from a legal perspective, but their desire is for justice on behalf of the disposable.

Some from this latter group of people are motivated by a preferential option for the disposable. Much like liberation theology they have opted for those in need. But often people like this find themselves in a situation similar to what happened to liberation theology in Latin America. Liberation theology opted for the poor, but the poor opted for Pentecostalism. They want to help those in need, but the disposable do not see them as a response to their situations. The disposable are objects of their concern and action, but are not empowered to become agents of their own future.

Going beyond Common Framings

People committed to Just Peacemaking might respond much the same way as many others have responded to the poor and the disposable. But it is not enough to want to use these practices to help the disposable. What is needed is a different perspective where a preferential option for the poor becomes a preferential option alongside the poor.

The disposable need people who will speak on their behalf. But most of all, they need the help of people who will recognize that migrants, refugees, and the displaced can become framers of their own history and future. They need to be empowered, not disempowered, once again, even by those who want to help them. As long as the displaced, the refugees and the migrants are seen only as victims, they will elicit responses of mercy from the well-intentioned. But only as they are empowered will they be able to break out of the "victim" status and take responsibility for themselves.

Of course those in power, and those in locations of power who often feel disempowered, will often feel particularly threatened by the powerless when they become subjects of their own reality. For example, in 2006 and 2007 immigrants in the United States took to the streets to claim their rights in the country that was benefiting from their labor. Yet a large percentage of people in the U.S. saw this as a threat. Even many of those in favor of immigration reform felt that it was best that the undocumented not march publicly. The disposable became subjects of their own reality and the larger population complained or became afraid.

CHIRLA, the Coalition for Humane Immigrant Rights of Los Angeles, works among the undocumented in southern California and beyond. One of their key actions is to educate the undocumented in the rights they do have. The undocumented are empowered because they become aware of what they can do to make their situation better and to take responsibility for themselves and their children. They model a style of working among the undocumented, instead of principally for them.

Just Peacemaking as Paradigm Shift in Thinking about Migrants, Refugees, and the Displaced

Several practices of just peacemaking can be particularly useful to the disposable if people willing to work alongside them, not for them, put them into practice. At least four just peacemaking practices would be particularly useful for migrants, refugees, and the displaced.

Cooperative Conflict Resolution

The practice of cooperative conflict resolution assumes that there are two sides that recognize and want to resolve a conflict, and that the different cultures of each can make contributions toward resolution, if respected as potential assets rather than as obstacles. Cooperate with Latino loyalties and cultural learnings, don't dismiss or bypass them. The problem with the disposable is that most people do not perceive them as having the right even to speak into their situations. They are either seen as a people at the mercy of others or as lawbreakers who can make no claims on their host country. Many migrants, refugees or displaced peoples also assume that they have no voice and therefore no place from which to seek to resolve the conflict.

People committed to using the practice of *cooperative* conflict resolution recognize that there are very important "pre-practices" that they must be involved in before there can be a cooperative conflict resolution process. The initial task is to bring non-participants, who do not see a "problem," to the table. To do this they must be both educators and advocates. On the one hand, they have to create the space among those in power. They must advocate for the disposable so that a resolution process can develop. This means confronting the systems of power and those who benefit from them. Until those who benefit from not changing the situation are willing to "come to the table," there can be no conflict resolution.

But they must also work with the disposable. Victimized peoples often lose sight of their role and power. Since they assume they have no voice, they allow others to speak for them and sometimes conclude that only outside forces can address their situation. Education includes informing them about their rights, but also teaching them how to find their own voices. For example, the majority culture could learn much from Latino loyalties to faith, family, and community that could bring helpful correction to the rampant Ayn-Rand-like individualism and privatism of many in the majority culture. And these community values could become an asset in seeking solutions. Policies that seek to banish one or even two parents while children remain in the United States without their parents are destructive to everyone, including the future of the United States. The destructiveness of such policies is clearly demonstrated by Kathleen Stassen Berger, the developmental psychologist who has written the widely used (including at Fuller Theological Seminary) textbook, *The Developing Person*. By contrast, a future United States with increasing influence of Latino and Asian-American voters and leaders may become a United States whose policies and culture are more family-friendly and more supportive of community loyalties and the common good.

Because of the significant power differential, those involved in this type of conflict resolution need to be active participants in the process. They constantly have to "right the balances" so that the voiceless are empowered. But this will always create some tension since those with rights and power can easily feel they are being disempowered if the powerless are given the right to be at the table.

The *Red de Pastores y Líderes del Sur de California* (LA RED) is actively involved in setting up the framework so that the undocumented can find a place at the table in the discussions about their future. This network of pastors and leaders in southern California includes many people who are undocumented. The first step in empowering them is to give them a voice in the process of working toward immigration reform. The undocumented are encouraged to tell their own stories, particularly to those with whom they would not normally interact, such as Christians from majority culture churches or African-American churches. By creating spaces of hospitality where these stories can be heard, but also places to hear the concerns and fears of others, the undocumented begin to become agents of their own future.

A second step is educating the undocumented so that they can know what rights they do have in relationship to the U.S. legal system. In the LA RED model not only do pastors and leaders learn about their rights, they also begin to share this information with their parishioners.

Thirdly, the immigrant and native-born Christians have begun working on projects together on behalf of the undocumented. By working together they have been able to build relationships, but also to value each other as persons of worth before God and in the task of working toward immigration justice.

All of these actions are "pre-practices," opportunities to lay the groundwork so that in the future there might be a space for actual conflict resolution. But without these pre-practices there will never be an opportunity for cooperative conflict resolution. It is precisely pre-practices of this sort that the authors of *Just Peacemaking* intend when they name the practice *cooperative* conflict resolution, not merely Enlighten-rationalism-style conflict resolution. (See *Just Peacemaking*, chapter 3.)

Advance Democracy, Human Rights, and Religious Liberty

The practice of advancing democracy, human rights, and religious liberty needs to have a specific focus when speaking of the disposable. These rights are usually protected and enforced by national governments. Transnational or global bodies only have as much power as are granted to them by national governments. This makes the task of advocating for the rights of migrants, refugees and the displaced particularly difficult. In some cases their home country is the principal cause of their problems. In others it is the host country that limits the rights of foreigners, particularly those without legal standing. Sometimes the worst abuses occur where national governments are little more than failed states.

Working on behalf of these rights for those who cannot appeal to a national state to protect and defend them means being willing to work in situations where the state, even a state that grants these rights to its citizens, is a key part of the problem. All states will assume that they have the responsibility to grant and protect these rights for their citizens, but that foreigners of any type have only the rights that the state feels like granting at any given time, based on internal political realities, and that those rights will always be less than the ones enjoyed by citizens.

Because in the current global situation the nation-state is the primary political structure, this creates a particular dilemma when wanting to employ this just peacemaking practice on behalf of the disposable. Working toward the rights of the disposable will imply speaking the truth to democracies, not only to states where these rights do not exist among its citizens. This means that the first commitment of those involved in using this just peacemaking practice will be the moral commitment to protect these rights for the disposable, even when it goes against the laws of national governments who protect those rights for their citizens.

In his widely respected major work, *Spheres of Justice*, Michael Walzer argues convincingly that a country like Germany that relies on "guest workers" from another to get the work done that benefits that country is obligated to provide a workable path to citizenship for those workers. This does not require automatic citizenship: requirements like learning the history and culture of the host country and having some length of residence are reasonable, on the basis of the fundamental right of community that belongs to all persons and nations. A nation has a right to ask potential citizens to be able to contribute to that nation's community culture and tradition. It also means a nation has a right to limit the number of immigrants who may enter. But the very same fundamental right to community requires that guest workers have a path to citizenship, a path to the right to vote, a path to having a voice in shaping the justice and culture of the nation that is benefiting from their labor. Presently, the path to citizenship in the United States is so clogged, so infinitely long, that it is not functioning in any realistic way for America's "guest workers." If we are to apply the practice of cooperative conflict resolution to the pressing question of immigration, and to the pressing question of justice and community both for immigrant workers and for U.S. community as a whole, then we absolutely need comprehensive immigration reform that respects liberty and justice for all. All are created in the image of God. All are loved by God, who gives all warm sunshine and life-giving rain. All are endowed by their Creator with the human rights of life, liberty, and the happiness of dignity in community. These are basic human needs, not to be denied.

Foster Just and Sustainable Economic Development

Clearly economic interests drive many of the decisions that create displaced peoples, refugees, and undocumented aliens. The globalized economy drives salaries in a downward spiral in poor countries as they compete to underbid each other for low wage jobs. Rich nations push for "open" markets, but then force small countries to purchase their subsidized products (such as U.S. corn) and destroy the local economies. Mineral-rich countries often find that the interests of the powerful displace people from areas with mineral wealth rather than developing that wealth on behalf of their citizens. The rich countries find it easy to blame unjust governments for these injustices, but refuse to recognize that their consumption of natural resources creates the environments that make people disposable.

If there were more balance in economic development, and more justice in the usage of natural resources, then there would be fewer disposable people. Fewer people would migrate out of need and fewer would be displaced for the economic benefit of the powerful. People would be able to support their families and dream about a better future while staying in their countries and regions of birth. If there were sustained and balanced economic development, people would have the freedom to move for new opportunities, but they would not have to migrate out of need. The currently disposable could become agents of their own future and the future of their children.

The principal challenge with enacting this just peacemaking practice, particularly as it relates to the disposable people of the world, is that it militates against the advantages created for the centers of economic power in today's globalized economy. Any changes in favor of the disposable will likely affect the profits of multinational corporations and raise the prices of some products people have gotten used to buying at a cheap price.

This situation illustrates the profound changes that need to happen in a globalized economy. The public "advantages" of this economic system make it difficult to think of true alternatives. Things like micro loans and "fair trade" products provide small opportunities to help those at the bottom. But the just peacemaking practice of just and sustainable development also means greater respect for local economies and a willingness to recognize that current economic systems create the concentration of wealth almost by their very existence.

Work with Emerging Cooperative Forces
in the International System

Currently the groups working with and for the disposable are either based in the United Nations or are non-governmental organizations with commitments to respond to specific types of needs or crisis. The UN agencies all have to deal with the fact that the member nations have national interests that usually conflict with the types of long-term solutions needed by the undocumented, the refugees or the displaced.

On the other hand, NGOs are usually most effective in responding to the immediate needs of refugees or the displaced. Many organizations are ready to enter the most complex and dangerous situations to help those in immediate need. Some are also involved in the next level of development as people attempt to rebuild their lives.

But the task of those who would work on this just peacemaking practice is to be willing to serve over the long term. Most proposed solutions respond to the immediate need, but those in charge then change directions when the next crisis hits. This might be sufficient for people who are able to return to their homelands and continue their lives. But for the undocumented or long-term refugees this practice will be effective to the extent that someone is ready to continue working with the various cooperative forces as they are pressed to respond to new needs or find themselves under pressure from national governments with changing political interests.

Palestinian refugees, the undocumented or marginally documented in countries around the world (though principally in the US and Europe), displaced religious minorities, citizens of failed states and others in similar situations, present problems that are not easily resolved by existing international entities. Each of these confronts conflicting interests that make it very difficult to find solutions people are willing to accept. Working with cooperative forces in the international system will mean a long-term commitment and a willingness to continue to look for new ways of giving status and rights to those who do not have them because of the ways our national systems work.

Conclusion

Just peacemaking provides the tools for responding to the injustices and structural violence suffered by migrants, refugees, and the displaced. Those who commit themselves to work among these groups of peoples will find that these practices can provide specific ways of addressing various aspects of the challenges faced by the disposable of our world today.

But just peacemaking tools will be most helpful if used to help these people become agents of their own future. If the disposable learn and use the tools of just peacemaking they will gain their own voice and work toward a better future for themselves.

As immigrants, refugees and the displaced who learn to be agents of their own future will need those committed to just peacemaking to walk alongside them. For these practices to be effective in extremely unequal power situations, we will be need people to create the spaces and extra support necessary to "level the playing field." As we walk alongside those who have been marginalized by political and economic systems, we can work together to create new realities that provide hope and a future for us all.

15

Just Peacemaking on the Korean Peninsula

Kim Dae-jung's Sunshine Policy

HAJUNG LEE

A NOBEL PEACE PRIZE laureate and former South Korean president, Kim Dae-jung struggled to overcome mistrust and hostility on the Korean peninsula and to bring about peace under the Sunshine Policy. The divided Korean peninsula technically remains at war, because a peace treaty has still not been signed. Under Kim Dae-jung's Sunshine Policy, the two Koreas opened up the road toward peace that had been blocked off since the division after World War II. The implementation of the Sunshine Policy built cooperative momentum towards reconciliation between the two Koreas after the South-North Summit in Pyongyang on June 13–15, 2000.[1] The two Koreas agreed to promote unification and move towards reconciliation and cooperation by adopting the June 15th South-North Joint Declaration. The summit talks eased five decades of tensions in Korea and opened a new era of warm reconciliation. After the summit, North Korea immediately ceased propaganda broadcasts

---

1. Kim Dae-jung and North Korean former chairman Kim Jong-il (of North Korea's National Defense Commission) met in Pyongyang from June 13 to June 15, 2000. The South and North recognized coexistence and agreed to promote unification through the joint efforts of the Koreans. They also agreed to lead exchange visits by separated families between the two Koreas. They promised to establish mutual trust through balanced economic development between the South and the North and to hold dialogues in order to implement the agreements.

against the South. In July 2000, the South-North ministerial talks were held, and in August 2000, separated family members were reunited for the first time after a half-century of division. At the opening ceremony of the Sydney Olympics in September 2000, athletes and officials from the two Koreas marched together holding a unification flag. The Gyeongui Line, the railroad that connected Seoul and Pyongyang before the division of Korea, was reconnected for the purpose of transporting South Korean workers and materials to the Kaesong Industrial Region, located about six miles north of the DMZ.[2] It was a historic reconciliation project, connecting roads and railroads across the DMZ. The inter-Korean summit meeting became a turning point for the two Koreas, and it was spurred by Kim Dae-jung's unprecedented initiative towards peacemaking on the Korean peninsula. Kim Dae-jung never gave up on the Sunshine Policy, even though he was relentlessly vilified by the Korean media over its implementation.

In this chapter, I will argue that Kim Dae-jung's Sunshine policy is not merely a theoretically idealistic policy, but an effective alternative model of Just Peacemaking practices in a Korean context. In analyzing this policy, I will primarily refer to Kim's unification doctrine, as stated in his book, *Kim Dae-jung's Three-Stage Approach to Korean Unification*, his Sunshine Policy, and some exemplary peacemaking activism in his life.

Kim Dae-Jung's Unification Doctrine and His Sunshine Policy

In 1995, Kim Dae-jung synthesized his unification doctrine in his book, *Kim Dae-jung's Three-Stage Approach to Korean Unification*. He proposed three stages of unification—confederation, federation, and complete unification, based on the principles of self-reliance, peace, and democracy.[3] Kim Dae-jung stressed gradual restoration and reconciliation during the first stage of confederation.[4] In this stage, Koreans would focus upon the gradual reduction of arms and the establishment of a cooperative economic structure, paving the way to co-prosperity as "one nation, two states, and two independent governments."[5] In the second stage of federation, a Unification Constitution would be enacted

2. Miles, "Command Supports Peace, Prosperity."
3. Kim Dae-jung, *Kim Dae-jung's "Three-Stage" Approach*, 15–17, 22–23, 25.
4. Ibid., 14, 43, 115.
5. Ibid.

through the democratic process, reflecting public opinion and setting up "one nation, one state, one system, and two autonomous regional governments."[6] In the third stage, the two Koreas would be completely unified. In developing his theory, Kim contrasted peacemaking ("positive pacifism") with peacekeeping ("passive pacifism") that merely opposed war, and he was a proponent of a "positive pacifism" that actively pursued the "creation of peace" through international cooperation.[7]

The term "Sunshine" originated in Aesop's fable on "wind and sunshine."[8] In this fable, a traveler drew his cloak closely about him in a strong wind, but he took it off in the warmth of the sun. Kim Dae-jung believed that gradually increasing interaction with North Koreans through "Sunshine" would be more effective than "the strong wind" of confrontation and isolation.[9] The Sunshine Policy was implemented from 1998 to 2007 during the presidencies of Kim Dae-jung and Roh Moo-hyun. During this period, South Korea undertook multiple humanitarian actions toward North Korea and encouraged the international community to embrace North Korea. Kim's peacemaking practices were based on the biblical values of love, justice, and peace.[10] During the Pyongyang summit, he emphasized the importance of South Koreans and North Koreans having a burning love for one another.[11] Kim Dae-jung, a devout Catholic Christian who believed peacemaking to be a God-given mission, based his practices of peacemaking on his commitment to biblical values, and his policies model Just Peacemaking in the Korean context.[12]

6. Ibid.

7. Ibid., 12. Kim used the expression "positive pacifism," which is equivalent to "peacemaking," and the expression "passive pacifism," which is equivalent to "peace-keeping." See also Lim, *Peacemaker*, 165–66. Lim Dong-won, a South Korean former Unification Minister and key architect of the Sunshine Policy along with Kim Dae-jung, used the expressions "peacebuilding" and "peacekeeping."

8. Chung-in, "Understanding the DJ Doctrine," 37.

9. Ibid.

10. Kim Dae-jung, "Challenge, Response and God."

11. Kim Dae-jung, "June 15 South-North Summit Speech."

12. Kim Dae-jung, "Challenge, Response and God."

Kim Dae-Jung's Sunshine Policy
As Just Peacemaking Practices

Kim Dae-jung's Sunshine Policy, his reunification doctrine, and his peace activism concur with Glen Stassen's Ten Practices of Just Peacemaking Theory.[13]

First, Kim's life *demonstrates strong support of nonviolent direct action.*[14] Kim Dae-jung was a champion of human rights and democracy with passion. Before his presidency, he was a nonviolent activist and protester against the military dictatorship in South Korea. He spent six years in prison and survived a death sentence and several suspected assassination attempts by the dictator in the 1970s and the 1980s. Kim believed that nonviolent direct action was a powerful means for social change and for supporting human rights in the face of violence and injustice. He respected the nonviolent activism of Martin Luther King Jr. and Mahatma Mohandas Gandhi.[15] During his presidency, Kim explicitly supported the non-violent direct actions of pro-democracy civilians in Burma and East Timor.[16]

Second, Kim *implemented independent initiatives* through the Sunshine Policy.[17] Through Kim's initiative, 20,000 families separated since the Korean War experienced temporary family reunions. Kim provided North Korea with over 500,000 tons of food and 300,000 tons of fertilizer to abate North Koreans' food shortage sufferings by December 2000.[18] Under the Sunshine Policy, many South Korean civilian organizations voluntarily provided humanitarian aid to North Korea. According to Kim, this began to transform North Korean hostility towards South Koreans into friendly feelings.[19] Even though North Korea did not proportionately reciprocate, Kim Dae-jung persistently implemented independent initiatives to reduce hostility.

Kim emphasized active partnership with North Korea as a means to decrease threat perception and distrust by acknowledging the co-existence of the two Koreas and listening to North Korea's stated needs. He asserted

13. Stassen, *Just Peacemaking: The New Paradigm*; Stassen and Gushee, *Kingdom Ethics*, 169–73; Stassen, homepage.

14. See chap. 1 in Stassen, *Just Peacemaking: The New Paradigm*.

15. Kim Sung-jae, "Kim Dae-jung's Life and Thoughts." http://www.kdjpeace.com/kdj_news_view.asp?idx=1600&gotopage=1&words=&sel=

16. Kim Dae-jung, "Night for Democracy in Burma."

17. See chap. 2 of Stassen, *Just Peacemaking: The New Paradigm*.

18. Kim Dae-jung, "Nobel Lecture."

19. Simion, "Sunshine Policy in the Life and Work," 3–7.

"peaceful co-existence and exchange" as early as the 1970s, when South Korea merely ignored the legitimate existence of North Korea. Because this assertion was too radical in the Cold War era, he has been stigmatized as a politician who appeased communists. Unlike his predecessors, who used confrontation and anti-communist propaganda, Kim Dae-jung asserted de facto unification, in which the two Koreas could peacefully co-exist in reconciliation and cooperation with the goal of ultimate unification. By rejecting unification by absorption and proposing a prolonged stage of peaceful coexistence, Kim Dae-jung led the agreement to jointly promote unification at the first summit. Kim treated North Korean leadership with respect as a co-existing partner in order to reduce threat and build peace.

Third, Kim Dae-jung made efforts to *use cooperative conflict resolution*.[20] Kim firmly believed that cultural and human exchanges between the two Koreas would allow them to experience each other's perspective and prevent future conflict, similar to the Helsinki Treaty, which successfully resulted in gradually demolishing stereotypical images of Western society in Eastern European communist nations through human exchanges.[21] For example, the Hyundai project and Mt. Kumkang project have resulted in cultural and human exchanges through cooperative economic opportunities. About 1.9 million South Koreans visited Mt. Kumkang for touring in North Korea. Kim encouraged economic exchanges at a civilian level rather than a governmental level, so as to maximize the opportunities for Koreans to be exposed to each other's stories and culture, a foundational step towards conflict resolution. The total amount of South Korean aid to the North dramatically increased at the civilian level once the policy of engagement was implemented. The total amount of civilian-level aid to the North in 1996 was 1.55 million dollars, mainly through the International Red Cross.[22] By 1998, the total amount of civilian aid was 20.85 million dollars.[23] In 1999, this civilian aid was offered through many diverse organizations, whereas it had been monopolized through the International Red Cross until 1998.[24] Kim Dae-jung expected both Koreas to gradually experience each other's perspectives through such human exchanges. This also reveals a significant paradigm shift from a government-centric

---

20. See chap. 3 of Stassen, *Just Peacemaking: The New Paradigm*.
21. Kim Dae-jung, "Sunshine Policy, the Road to Success."
22. Ki-Jung and Deok, "Beyond Mt. Kumkang," 130–31.
23. Ibid.
24. Ibid.

policy towards North Korea to a civil-centric policy.[25] Kim rejected any discrimination between the two Koreas, and recognized the significance of cooperative conflict resolution as part of the peacemaking process.

Fourth, Kim *acknowledged responsibility for conflict and injustice* towards North Koreans and *emphasized repentance and forgiveness.*[26] He sought repentance and forgiveness toward enemies as an extension of God's message.[27] According to Kim, every person should recognize himself or herself as a person who also needs to be forgiven before forgiving others.[28] He recognized repentance and forgiveness as imperatives, not merely charity or rights.[29] Facing a death sentence in 1980, he wrote to his second son to express his willingness to love and forgive the dictator who brutally persecuted him and sentenced him to death.[30] At his inauguration speech, Kim declared the cessation of the "politics of retaliation" and promised to pardon the former dictators who repressed the democratic movement and massacred civilians in Gwangju in 1980.[31] Kim refused revenge and transformed his human desire for retaliation into forgiveness by practicing politics of forgiveness.[32] He also made efforts to reconcile with Japan, which had oppressed Koreans during the colonial period.[33] Kim acknowledged forgiveness in order to transcend religious, ethnic, and racial conflicts and achieve global peace. Kim recognized the responsibility of the inter-Korean conflict for human suffering and injustice and raised awareness of the international responsibility to embrace North Korea. He urged the international community to support a policy of engagement and restore North Korea as a member of the international community. As mentioned above, Kim Dae-Jung expanded human exchanges between the North and the South, so that more South Koreans would become aware of North Koreans' destitution, empathize with them, and realize their responsibility to seek forgiveness and reconciliation. This was intended to lead to collective forgiveness between the two Koreas.

25. Ibid., 107.

26. See chap. 4 of *Just Peacemaking: The New Paradigm.*

27. Kim Dae-jung, "Challenge, Response and God"; Kim Sung-jae, "Kim Dae-jung's Life and Thoughts."

28. Kim Sung-jae, "Kim Dae-jung's Life and Thoughts."

29. Ibid.

30. Spanovich, "Way to World Peace"; See also Kim Dae-jung, *Prison Writings I,* 169–75.

31. Kristof, "New Kind of Leader."

32. Geyer and Shriver, "Acknowledge Responsibility," 98.

33. Kim Dae-jung, "Challenge, Response and God."

Fifth, Kim Dae-jung dreamt of a unified Korea that *advances democracy, human rights and interdependence.*[34] Democracy was one of Kim's three principles of unification.[35] He asserted that the entire process of unification should proceed under democratic procedures and democratic consensus.[36] He pictured the unified nation as a society that would honor and respect human dignity by accomplishing social justice and welfare.[37] Kim expressed his strong opposition to imperialism, which has a history of violating human rights,[38] Furthermore, Kim desired that the unified Korea would support "Global Democracy" wherein "all human beings live harmoniously with dignity," and specifically promoted democracy in third-world countries.[39] Kim also valued the human right to life and promoted the abolition of the death penalty, as he did not allow any executions during his presidency.[40] In addition, he sought economic interdependence between the two Koreas, promoting investment and trade, which both can contribute to decreasing the incidence of war.[41] Kim's government facilitated inter-Korean economic exchanges by expanding the list of approved items, avoiding double-taxation, and deregulating import permits to accelerate intra-Korean trade.[42] Kim also firmly believed that the growth of the middle class in the North Korean economy would contribute to democratization of North Korea in the future.[43]

Sixth, the Sunshine Policy *fostered just and sustainable economic development* through economic cooperation between the two Koreas.[44] Kim's unification strategy supports eco-justice and the protection of all living things.[45] In 2001, Kim Dae-jung agreed with former South African president Nelson Mandela's proposal to create a peace park in the Korean DMZ, which could become a symbol of peace as the last frontier of the

34. See chap. 5 of Stassen, *Just Peacemaking: The New Paradigm.*

35. Kim Dae-jung, *Kim Dae-jung's "Three-Stage" Approach,* 10. Three principles of reunification are self-reliance, peace, and democracy.

36. Ibid., 11.

37. Ibid., 27.

38. Ibid., 28.

39. Ibid., 12, 26–27.

40. Kim Dae-jung, "Challenge, Response and God."

41. Stassen, *Just Peacemaking: The New Paradigm,* 125–26.

42. Kim Dae-jung, "Nobel Lecture."

43. Simion, "Sunshine Policy in the Life and Work," 8.

44. See chap. 6 of Stassen, *Just Peacemaking: The New Paradigm.*

45 Kim Dae-jung, *Kim Dae-jung's "Three-Stage" Approach,* 12.

cold war, ecological sustainability, and biodiversity.[46] Kim transmitted this proposal to North Korean leadership.[47] Furthermore, Kim's economic policy was based on the principle of "growth and fair distribution of wealth" by creating equal opportunities and recognizing the need to protect the marginalized.[48] Under the Sunshine Policy, South Korea viewed its superior economic condition through the eyes of an elder brother, focusing upon North Korea's economic need.[49] As Kim Dae-jung mentioned in his speech, North Korea might be able to overcome devastating poverty by developing its rich underground resources (magnetite, tungsten, copper, and etc.), estimated to have an economic value of $2 trillion.[50] Kim made efforts to offer technology and capital and to create jobs in North Korea by considering their economic needs and attempting to reduce poverty. For instance, the Kaesong Industrial Project created about 43,000 factory jobs for North Koreans in 2010.[51] The Kaesong Industrial Region project also exemplifies the economic efficacy of such cooperative projects. Because North Korea has abundant natural resources and South Korea has technology and capital, both parties can benefit from cooperation with one another. Kim sought out economic exchanges and cooperative efforts with North Korea, motivated by the goal of benefiting both nations without absorbing the North Korean economy.[52]

Seventh, Kim Dae-jung acknowledged the significance of *internationally cooperative forces* in inter-Korean relations.[53] He stressed the importance of a multilateral and cooperative Northeast Asian security structure for affirming peace in Korea.[54] According to Kim, a unified Korea would understand its geopolitical position in Northeast Asia and attempt to secure regional stability as part of its national defense.[55] Kim also suggested

---

46. Mandela, "Message from Dr. Nelson Mandela."

47. Ke, "Preserving Korea's Demilitarized Corridor," 249.

48. Kim Dae-jung, *Kim Dae-jung's "Three-Stage" Approach*, 27.

49. The South Korean economy is the eleventh largest economy in the world, forty times as large as the North Korean economy.

50. Kim Dae-jung, "Six-Party Talks."

51. Miles, "Command Supports Peace, Prosperity."

52. Kim Dae-jung announced the Sunshine Policy at his inaugural speech on 25 February 1998. See Kim Dae-jung, "Sunshine Policy, the Road to Success."

53. See chap. 7 of Stassen, *Just Peacemaking: The New Paradigm for the Ethics of Peace and War*.

54. Kim Dae-jung, *Kim Dae-jung's "Three-Stage" Approach*, 66–67.

55. Ibid., 28.

that peace agreement talks should involve four or six parties.[56] Kim urged foreign nations to participate in the Arms Control process of inspection and verification.[57] He emphasized the importance of positive relations between the U.S. and North Korea, and he asked the U.S. to take humanitarian action toward North Korea through international NGOs.[58] He worked closely with U.S. President Clinton, who publicly supported the Sunshine Policy. The Clinton administration was inclined to normalize diplomatic relations with North Korea, which agreed to abandon nuclear weapon development.[59] However, in 2002, U.S. President Bush adopted a containment policy towards North Korea, which he described as part of an "axis of evil." The Bush administration initially rejected dialogue with North Korea. This policy did not improve access to North Korea, which became further isolated and repeatedly conducted nuclear testing. The Bush administration finally moved towards an engagement policy in 2007, because the policy of hard constraint had not made any improvement.[60] This change could be understood as a recognition that engagement through dialogue works better in reality than a policy of constraint and isolation.

Eighth, the Sunshine Policy led North Korea to begin *cooperating with the United Nations organizations.*[61] Because of the Sunshine Policy, North Korea became more willing to discuss its economy and humanitarian aid with the United Nations Development Program UNDP, UNICEF, and the World Food Program.[62] In 1998, North Korea amended its constitution to gradually introduce the free market economic system.[63] The North showed its willingness to learn how the free market economy works by sending scholars and economic bureaucrats to the outside world for capitalist market training.[64] The North Korean government requested training in the free market economy from IMF and World Bank, and the "Rajin Business Institute" was opened by the UNDP in 1998.[65] South Korea's Sunshine Policy built a

---

56. Ibid., 90.

57. Ibid., 100.

58. Spanovich, "Way to World Peace."

59. Ibid.

60. Cumings, "Back to the Future."

61. See chap. 8 of Stassen, *Just Peacemaking: The New Paradigm.*

62. Babson, "Economic Perspectives," 233–34.

63. Chung-in, "Understanding the DJ Doctrine," 51.

64. Ibid.

65. Chung-in, "Understanding the DJ Doctrine," 50; Babson, "Economic Perspectives," 234.

warm atmosphere for North Korea to be exposed to the free market econo-my through United Nations organizations. In addition, Kim revealed his de-sire to seek justice and human rights by proclaiming "Open Nationalism."[66] Unlike the "aggressive nationalism" driven by narrow national interests and supported by former presidents, "Open Nationalism" promotes peace and freedom for other nations, supporting collective international action to seek human rights.[67] In 2008, Kim Dae-jung participated in sending a message to UN Secretary General Ban Ki-moon, acknowledging an international responsibility to protect human rights and encouraging the UN to extend its support to Zimbabwe, Burma, and Sudan and uphold human dignity.[68]

Ninth, Kim Dae-Jung supported *reducing offensive weapons and weapons trade.*[69] The vicious cycle of violence has created a world in which the two Korean nations possess excessive military forces and arms. This has led to a tremendous waste of national resources on both sides. The North Korean people have experienced extreme economic deprivation, while their government has spent an enormous amount of money on its military. Kim Dae-Jung recognized this vicious cycle of arms buildup and proposed a concrete way to break this vicious cycle by an "Arms Con-trol" plan.[70] He argued that the capability for unexpected attack should be removed by eliminating offensive weapons. As part of his unification doctrine, Kim proposed gradually reducing military forces on the Korean Peninsula and creating a peace-oriented military balance that would serve as a defensive force structure.[71] He asserted that the Demilitarized Zone should be changed into a "Limited Deployment Zone (LDZ)" that would be an offense-free zone of peace.[72] Kim fully acknowledged the need for a concrete and specific plan to reduce military forces and build an order of peace in Korea. He also stressed the importance of inspection and verifica-tion, as well as strict reciprocity in the process of implementation.[73]

Tenth, Kim *encouraged grassroots peacemaking groups and voluntary associations.*[74] He emphasized the importance of the active participation of

66. Kim Dae-jung, *Kim Dae-jung's "Three-Stage" Approach*, 12.

67. Ibid., 12; Stassen, *Just Peacemaking: The New Paradigm*, 172–73.

68. Kim Dae-jung Peace Center, "Message to UN General Secretary Ban Ki-moon."

69. See chap. 9 of Stassen, *Just Peacemaking: The New Paradigm*.

70. Kim Dae-Jung, *Kim Dae-jung's "Three-Stage" Approach*, 78.

71. Ibid., 63–64.

72. Ibid.

73. Ibid., 65.

74. See chap. 10 of Stassen, *Just Peacemaking: The New Paradigm*.

all Koreans in the unification process through diverse civil peacemaking organizations. In order to absorb these diverse opinions into official statements, Kim urged minority groups, including women's grassroots peacemaking groups, to raise their voices and participate in civilian movements. Influenced by his encouragement, groups such as the "Women Making Peace (WMP)" group began vocalizing women's perspectives concerning unification during Kim Dae-jung's regime.[75] The Sunshine Policy recognized not only the importance of top-down policy but also the bottom-up approach of mobilizing citizen participation through grassroots peacemaking groups.[76]

In sum, Kim Dae-jung's approach to unification and the Sunshine Policy contributed to peacemaking on the Korean peninsula by creating momentum toward inter-Korean collaboration, forgiveness, and reconciliation. While the South Korean Unification Ministry officially declared the Sunshine Policy a failure in 2010, Kim's unification strategy and his Sunshine Policy paved the way for the application of Just Peacemaking Theory to future Korean conflicts. Kim's Sunshine Policy has been harshly denounced by his political opponents, even though it visibly increased inter-Korean exchanges and cooperation. Kim's initiation of a peaceful approach towards North Korea is a meaningful exemplar that peacemakers may emulate.

Future Direction of Just Peacemaking
in the Korean Context

Kim Dae-jung's Sunshine Policy has encountered strong domestic opposition, due to the lack of public consensus, vilification by the mainstream conservative press, and Kim's party's minority standing within the national assembly in South Korea. In order to overcome these difficulties and revive the Sunshine Policy, the following practices should be implemented. First, a future Sunshine Policy should be persistently implemented over a longer period of time to bring gradual reconciliation between the two Koreas. South Korean conservatives and progressives need to jointly create a bi-partisan long-term Sunshine Policy so that the government may sustain a prolonged engagement policy, regardless of which party holds political power. South Koreans should patiently and constantly offer humanitarian assistance to the north without expecting immediate and instantaneous reciprocity. Considering current North Korean destitution and the past severe mistrust and polarized conflicts during the Cold War,

75. Women Making Peace (WMP) website http://www.peacewomen.or.kr/.

76. Lim Dong-won, *Peacemaker*, 336.

South Koreans should understand that the time frame of North Korean reciprocity can be flexible, and that the process of resolving conflicts and restoring justice and peace inherently takes a long time, as Kim's three-stage unification strategy acknowledges. Future policies should allow for the alternative possibility of lag time for reciprocal returns from North Korea. The South Korean government should also have a concrete alternative strategy for unexpected hostile situations, while affirming security. It should flexibly and sensitively adjust the pace of the implementation of the policy. The two Koreas can patiently embark on this uncomfortable and long process, based on a firm belief in the efficacy of Just Peacemaking practices.

Second, in order to receive South Koreans' public support for Sunshine Policy, peacemakers should offer peace education regarding unification. Offering peace education to schools was a dream of Kim Dae-jung that was not successfully fulfilled during his lifetime. Peace education in public schools may stir up public interest in the issues of peace and unification. Grassroots peacemaking organizations can also actively facilitate peace education without being limited by the political creeds of different governments. Religious organizations, in particular, can effectively lead voluntary peacemaking movements. Peace education may increase the capacity of peacemaking, challenge a culture of violence and militarism, and create a culture of peace. Many people of the old generation, in particular, linger in a conservative anti-communism paradigm and strongly oppose the Sunshine Policy, largely because they lived through the extremely polarized Cold War period. Raising public awareness of the importance of peace and unification issues would help overcome the vilification of the Sunshine Policy by the conservative mainstream media. Without the support of the South Korean population, any future policy of engagement is likely to face the same obstacles as Kim Dae-jung's policy faced.

Third, future sunshine policy requires strong support from the international community. The South Korean government should actively encourage its allies to strengthen ties with North Korea. Opposition to the Sunshine Policy by the George W. Bush administration, accompanied by that administrations' decision to cut off oil shipments to North Korea to replace its shutting down of its nuclear reactor as promised by former president Jimmy Carter's peace agreement and carried out by North Korea, and also by the Bush administration's refusal of negotiations, helped undermine Kim's Sunshine Policy. It also led to North Korea's enrichment of sufficient uranium for approximately four nuclear bombs, and their testing a nuclear bomb and delivery missiles. These decisions have clearly brought bad out-comes for all sides. If a new Sunshine Policy is attempted by a future South Korean administration, it will need steady support by the U.S. government at that time.[77]

The six-party talks involving the U.S., Russia, China, and Japan, who have historically held enormous influence over the security of Korean pen-insula, are encouraged to resolve the North Korean nuclear issue.[78] These four power members should agree to guarantee the security of Korea in collaboration.[79] Kim Dae-jung proclaimed a goal of denuclearization of the Korean peninsula through peaceful dialogue with international community. He mentioned that North Korea has developed nuclear weapons, not for the purpose of possessing nuclear weapons but for the purpose of using them to secure an opportunity of dialogue with the U.S. and to enhance the ties with the U.S., so that the U.S. would remove economic sanctions.[80]

Conclusion

Although Kim's Sunshine Policy was not as highly effective as he had hoped during his short presidency, such a policy is the only way to build peace on the Korean peninsula. The Korean unification process should be based on a long-term Sunshine Policy, accompanied by the understanding of the necessity of peace among Koreans. Regardless of South Korea's economic fluctuation and domestic political climate, it is essential to remind South Koreans of the importance of human rights, justice and peace, and to en-courage them to engage in humanitarian action with North Koreans, who remain in a state of extreme economic deprivation. For Korean Christians, in particular, participating in just peacemaking offers an opportunity to follow Jesus Christ by forming a renewed peaceful life.

The current get-tough policy has increased intra-Korean hostil-ity through containment and isolation. Military confrontation with and isolation of North Korea may cause repeated vicious cycles of hostile interactions between the two Koreas. In order to bring about peace and

77. Yang Sung-chul, Korean Ambassador to the United States from 2000 to 2003, has stated, both in a public speech and in personal correspondence with Glen Stassen shortly thereafter, his expectation that a future South Korean administration is likely to return to efforts for peacemaking with North Korea (Yang, "Looking Backward to Go Forward").

78. Kim Dae-jung, "May 15 Democratic Uprising."

79. Ibid.

80. Kim Dae-jung, "Will the North Korean."

reconciliation on the Korean peninsula, a modified Sunshine Policy needs to be implemented. Koreans should envision a unified Korea that can play a significant role as a stabilizer for peace and justice in Northeast Asia. As Kim Dae-jung understood, bringing about peace on the Korean peninsula requires warm sunshine rather than cold wind.

Bibliography

Babson, Bradley O. "Economic Perspectives on the Sunshine Policy." In *Kim Dae-jung Government and Sunshine Policy: Promises and Challenges*, edited by Chung-in Moon and David I. Steinberg, 231–39. Seoul: Yonsei University Press, 1999.

Chung-in Moon. "Understanding the DJ Doctrine: The Sunshine Policy and the Korean Peninsula." In *Kim Dae-jung Government and Sunshine Policy: Promises and Challenges*, edited by Chung-in Moon and David I. Steinberg, 35–56. Seoul: Yonsei University Press, 1999.

Chung-in Moon and David I. Steinberg. *Kim Dae-jung Government and Sunshine Policy: Promises and Challenges*. Seoul: Yonsei University Press, 1999.

Cumings, Bruce. "Back to the Future: The Two North-South Summits in Historical Perspective." Lecture delivered at the event commemorating the eighth anniversary of the June 15 South-North Joint Declaration, Seoul, South Korea, 12 June 2008. http://www.kdjpeace.com/615_8th_2.asp.

Geyer, Alan, and Donald Shriver. "Acknowledge Responsibility for Conflict and Injustice and Seek Repentance and Forgiveness." In *Just Peacemaking: The New Paradigm for the Ethics of Peace and War*, 2nd ed., edited by G. Stassen, 98–115. Cleveland: Pilgrim, 2008.

Ke Chung Kim. "Preserving Korea's Demilitarized Corridor for Conservation: A Green Approach to Conflict Resolution." In *Peace Parks: Conservation and Conflict Resolution*, edited by Saleem H. Ali, 239–60. Cambridge: MIT, 2007.

Ki-Jung Kim and Deok Ryong Yoon. "Beyond Mt. Kumkang: Social and Economic Implications." In *Kim Dae-jung Government and Sunshine Policy: Promises and Challenges*, edited by Chung-in Moon and David I. Steinberg, 105–34. Seoul: Yonsei University Press, 1999.

Kim Dae-jung. "Challenge, Response and God." Nobel Peace Lecture, delivered at the University of Portland, Portland, OR, 17 April 2008. Accessed 17 April 2008. http://www.kdjlibrary.org/kdj/engweb/presidentkdj/newsView.jsp?pkid=47&currentPage=3&searchField=&searchValue.

———. "June 15 South-North Summit Speech at a Dinner Hosted by Chairman Kim Yong-nam of the Standing Committee of the Supreme People's Assembly." Speech, Pyongyang, North Korea, 15 June YEAR. Accessed 13 June 2000. http://www.kdjpeace.com/talk_first_speech_3.asp.

———. *Kim Dae-jung's "Three-Stage" Approach to Korean Reunification*. Los Angeles: Center for Multiethnic and Transnational Studies, University of Southern California, 1997.

———. "The May 15 Democratic Uprising and Peace on the Korean Peninsula." Keynote address at the opening ceremony of the 2006 Gwangju Summit of Nobel Peace Laureates, Gwangju, South Korea, 16 June 2006. http://www.kdjlibrary.org/

kdj/engweb/presidentkdj/newsView.jsp?pkid=21&currentPage=6&searchField=
&searchValue=.

———. "A Night for Democracy in Burma." Keynote address at commemoration of the
seventh anniversary of Kim's receiving the 2000 Nobel Peace Prize, Seoul, South
Korea, 4 December 2007. http://www.kdjpeace.com/nobel_7th_1.asp?p=4.

———. "Nobel Lecture." Lecture delivered at Nobel Peace Prize Award Ceremony,
Oslo, Norway, 10 December 2000. http://www.nobelprize.org/nobel_prizes/
peace/laureates/2000/dae-jung-lecture.html.

———. Prison Writings I. Seoul: Sidae, 2009.

———. "The Six-Party Talks and the North Korean Economy." Keynote address at the
World Peace Lunch, Hilton Portland, Portland, OR, 18 April 2008. http://www.
kdjpeace.com/kdj_news05_view.asp?idx=608&gotopage=11&words=&sel=.

———. "The Sunshine Policy, the Road to Success." Keynote address, Harvard Kennedy
School of Government, Cambridge, MA, 22 April 2008. http://www.kdjlibrary.
org/kdj/engweb/presidentkdj/newsView.jsp?pkid=50&currentPage=3&searchFie
ld=&searchValue=.

———. "Will the North Korean Nuclear Issue Be Resolved?" Keynote address, World
Affairs Council at Arlene Schnitzer Concert Hall, Portland, OR, 18 April 2008.
http://www.kdjlibrary.org/kdj/engweb/presidentkdj/newsView.jsp?pkid=49&curr
entPage=1&searchField=&searchValue=.

Kim Dae-jung Peace Center and Participants of the Event Commemorating the
Eighth Anniversary of the June 15 South-North Joint Declaration. "Message
to UN General Secretary Ban Ki-moon." 12 June 2008. http://www.kdjpeace.
com/615_8th_4.asp.

Kim Sung-jae. "Kim Dae-jung's Life and Thoughts: The Road to Peace." Lecture at Kim
Dae-jung's Legacy Conference, Seoul, South Korea, 12 August 2010.

Kristof, Nicholas D. "A New Kind of Leader for Korea, and Asia Too." New York Times,
23 February 1998. http://www.nytimes.com/1998/02/23/world/a-new-kind-of-
leader-for-korea-and-asia-too.html?pagewanted=all&src=pm.

Lim Dong-won. Peacemaker. Seoul: Joongang, 2008.

Mandela, Nelson. "Message from Dr. Nelson Mandela to the International Conference
on the Conservation of Korea's Demilitarized Zone". The DMZ Forum for Peace
and Nature Conservation website. http://www.dmzforum.org/aboutus/nelson_
mandela.php.

Miles, Donna. "Command Supports Peace, Prosperity along Korean DMZ." US
Department of Defense website, 22 March 2010. Accessed 22 March 2010. http://
www.defense.gov/news/newsarticle.aspx?id=58426.

Simion, Marian. "The Sunshine Policy in the Life and Work of President Kim Dae-jung:
A BTI Visit and Interview with Former President of the Republic of Korea, and
2000 Nobel Peace Laureate." Bulletin of the Boston Theological Institute 8.1 (2008)
3–7.

Spanovich, Gary A. "A Way to World Peace: The Sunshine Policy of President Kim
Dae-jung." Keynote speech at the First Kim Dae-jung International Peace
Conference, Kim Dae-jung Presidential Library & Museum, Yonsei University,
Seoul, South Korea, 8 December 2011. www.kdjlibrary.org/common/upload/
notice/20111208–11.pdf.

Stassen, Glen H. Homepage. http://www.fullerseminary.net/sot/faculty/stassen/cp_
content/homepage/homepage.htm.

————, editor. *Just Peacemaking: The New Paradigm for the Ethics of Peace and War.* 2nd ed. Cleveland: Pilgrim, 2008.

Stassen, Glen H., and David P. Gushee. *Kingdom Ethics: Following Jesus in Contemporary Context.* Downers Grove, IL: InterVarsity, 2003.

Women Making Peace (WMP) website. http://www.peacewomen.or.kr/.

Yang Sung-chul. "Looking Backward to Go Forward: On Future Korea-U.S. Relations." Lecture delivered at the University of Oregon, 14 May 2010.

16

Just Peacemaking and Overcoming Violence

Formation for Ministry

Rodney L. Petersen

Jesus and the Gospel writers, the Desert Fathers, the monastic and cathedral schools of medieval Europe, their temporal equivalences in the East along the "Silk Road"—and their contemporary manifestations—all of these have seen spiritual formation as a tension between being and becoming, an end in itself or as a means to an end. Such is also the case for contemporary sodalities of faith, whether Orthodox sketes, Catholic orders, or Protestant and Evangelical cell groups.

Pictured in Jesus' descent from the Mount of Transfiguration is an interest in tying together *being* and *becoming*, or spiritual formation for the work of ministry: *good news to the poor, freedom to prisoners, recovery of sight to the blind, and release to the oppressed* (Luke 4:18–19; cf. Isaiah 61:1). These are practices of just peacemaking. This work fosters a culture of life as much in the twenty-first century as earlier. The ten practices of just peacemaking draw together formation and ministry in ways acknowledged throughout this volume.[1] With such a conjunction in mind theologian David Tracy writes, "Of all the disciplines theology is the one where action and thought, academy and church, faith and reason, the

---

1. See Chapter One and elsewhere in this volume.

276

community of inquiry and the community of commitment and faith are most explicitly and systematically brought together."[2]

This search for coherence of word (*as formed in us*) and action (*as proceeding from that word*) might be found in the origins of moral theology that can be said to have been grounded in the Libyan Desert. It was there that St. Anthony (ca. 251–356) went to fight the demons—and it was there that he found them in himself. Commonly called the Father of Monasticism, Anthony dealt with the temptations of pride, envy, lust, greed, anger, gluttony, and sloth—oft-cited *Seven Deadly Sins*—in a way that has marked spiritual formation in overcoming violence from his day to our own.[3] Early monasticism was rigorous in its attempt to direct life entirely to God and to deal with the violence of life that would deter that effort. Overcoming violence through meditation or listening prayer became the first mark of spiritual formation in Christian tradition ever since—even in its self-conscious failure.[4]

Spiritual formation among Christians finds its first point of definition in the recognition of the resurrection of Jesus. Consciousness of this point of departure was so powerful that worship became organized around what was referred to as the Lord's Day or Sunday in recognition of the resurrection of Jesus. The early church gathered together not only for worship on this day but for the weekly collection for the poor (1 Cor 16:1–2), providing continuity with the emphasis on the deep inner connection between worship and ethics in Judaism (Isa 58:6–14; Mark 2:23–28). This Sabbath gathering with prayer and collection for the poor is the second mark of spiritual formation. It follows from the two tables of the law, love of God and love of neighbor (Matt 22:37–40). Whether as monastic communities or local assemblies of the faithful then or as communities of faith today, this Sabbath/Sunday gathering was a kind of summary of faith and "covenant renewal" within a defining narrative.[5] It forecast the life of prayer and

2. David Tracy, "On Theological Education: A Reflection." This lecture was given on the occasion of the 35th anniversary of the Boston Theological Institute.

3. Schimmel, *Seven Deadly Sins*.

4. Such spiritual exercises, *askesis*, as fasting, systematic and ceaseless prayer, study of Scriptures and the lives of the saints, charitable activities, all-night vigils, confession, and communion are recommended. See for contemporary reflection Markides, *Inner River*, 26. The question of the decline (Steven Pinker), prevalence (Robert Jay Lifton), or recurrence (Robert Muchembled) of violence in the twenty-first century is the topic of Green, Petersen, and Massaro, "Teaching Overcoming Violence."

5. The value of the Sabbath in the teachings of Jesus remains unbroken. An understanding of the Sabbath as a "covenant renewal" finds grounding in Jesus' teachings and Jewish practice. Karl Barth's argument adds theological rationale for this: that "the

work through the week, providing a rhythm for spiritual vision and character formation.[6] Sabbath/Sunday observance provided the community a place and a time to work out the inevitable conflicts of life. Finally, it gave scope to the recurring challenges of how to live in community, how to live with the earth, how to understand the meaning of economy, and how to engage others.

I. Character Formation

Whether as monastic communities then or as communities of faith today, this Sabbath/Sunday gathering gave structure to a life of prayer and manual work, not as an end in itself but as an aid to the moral journey. By giving attention to what would become the catalogue of virtues and vices, rhythm was found for the cultivation of character. Anthony's near contemporary, Palladius, a monk from Palestine, wrote a brief survey of monastic practices in his "Lausiac History." Here Palladius records that Abba Pachomius spent much time in striving with devils like a true athlete, after the manner of St. Anthony. Like Pachomius and others following him, Palladius would pray on the night of the Sabbath, as if to await the resurrection dawn on Sunday morning.[7] The monks and nuns, whether eremitic or coenobitic, would gather together for community renewal and Communion.[8] Sunday as the Lord's Day in the life of the Christian community gave structure through the weekly liturgy for the journey of the soul, tying it to a social context that avoided an abstract spiritualism.

Anthony's journey into the desert to fight the demons became paradigmatic for a life of faith in formation. It built upon the belief in the classical world that the nature of one's response to crisis gave evidence of the state of one's moral character. The strong person (*vir*) who struggled with vice (*vitium*, "failing or defect") was defined by a range of qualities such as prudence or wisdom, self-control, justice, and courage. These virtues defined character. They were the moral compass of the virtuous person, a theme made popular even today in the contemporary fantasy role-playing game, *Dungeons and Dragons*. In the context of Christendom and monastic culture, the classical virtues became widely referred to as the four

---

Sabbath commandment explains all the other commandments, or all the other forms of the one commandment. It is thus to be placed at the head" (*Church Dogmatics* 3:53).

6. Allen, "Lord's Day."

7. Waltke, Houston, and Moore, *Psalms as Christian Worship*, 185.

8. Dalgairns, *Holy Communion*, 155–56.

cardinal virtues joined by the three theological virtues, faith, hope and charity. Living by these as more fully elaborated in moral theology defined what it meant to live with a moral compass before God (*coram deo*).

The era of monasteries and monastic spirituality was further shaped by the evolution of moral theology (the *moral* or tropological reading of scripture), and through the development of spiritual direction, penitential practices, and the rise of the sacrament of confession. This spirituality was democratized in late medieval devotion and in the subsequent Protestant Reformation. With the emergence of theological academies and seminaries in the aftermath of the Protestant and Tridentine reforms, moral theology became caught up in religious polemics and became a subchapter in the Wars of Religion. For their part, varying Protestant traditions took their cue for the moral life from the sermons and examples of early Lutheran and Reformed leadership. Protestant moral life became shaped not only by the binary character of Ramist logic but, in the work of early Puritanism, by Calvinist and Arminian polemics. Caroline, Moravian, Pietist, and Wesleyan models of spirituality followed. The systematic presentation of moral theology in Catholic seminaries for the purpose of training priests for the sacrament of confession formed educational practices for religious leadership from the thirteenth century to the present shaped as well by new Orders and Oratories. In the twentieth century, Vatican II recognized the need to renew moral theology: "Special care should be given to the perfecting of moral theology. Its scientific presentation should draw more fully on the teaching of Holy Scripture and should throw light upon the exalted vocation of the faithful of Christ and their obligation to bring forth fruit in charity for the life of the world."[9] In contemporary church practice this has drawn the laity more fully in view.

Following the work of philosopher William James (1842–1910), general interest in the nature of the moral journey was increasingly shaped if not defined by the new discipline of psychology. After the ground-breaking work of psychoanalysts like Sigmund Freud (1856–1939) and psychiatrist and founder of analytical psychology Carl Jung (1875–1961), others working in the new field of psychology would follow: Lawrence Kohlberg's (1927–87) stages of moral development constituted an adaptation of the psychological theories on identity formation of Swiss psychoanalyst Jean Piaget (1896–1980). Carl Rogers (1902–87; person-centered psychotherapy) and Abraham Maslow (1908–70; hierarchy of needs) carried this

9. Norris, *Decree*, #16.

thinking into a more inclusive arena, as also theories of character developed by persons such as James Q. Wilson (1931–2012).

The book *Celebration of Discipline* (1978) by Quaker Richard Foster happily recovers older insights of moral theology—the inward disciplines of prayer, fasting, meditation, Bible study, along with such outward disciplines as simplicity, solitude, submission and service in the context of contemporary psychological sensitivities.[10] Grounding these practices in the weekly rhythm and "covenant renewal" of Sabbath/Sunday observance does much to shape character in the interests of a culture of life. Ritual, temporal rhythm and the encouragement of community can embolden what Eugene Peterson has called *"a long obedience in the same direction."*[11] The holistic, interactive, embodied character formation raised up in this volume is a further step in the work of formation for life. It raises up the importance of context (James Rast) and intentional community (Jonathan Haidt) for purposes of character formation.

II. Character Formation in Community

Gathering in community on the Sabbath/Sunday is exactly that—the gathered assembly. It provides the community a place and time to work out the inevitable conflicts of *life together.*[12] The liturgical rhythm of the week, anchored in the Lord's Day, provides a wealth of stories and models of faith through which a community might find insight to deal with conflict. The practices of just peace provide a way to mobilize the classical virtues around transforming communal initiatives, justice and love and community. They avoid idealistic and Platonic terms such as principles or ideals, and instead focus on practices, actions, and transforming initiatives.

Character formation through the lens of community life provides a different perspective on the individual's moral journey. As we turned to Anthony to begin our thinking on individual character formation, we might turn to another monastic for guidance on character formation in community—Dorotheos of Palestine (Gaza), a sixth-century monastic. Dorotheos frames and visualizes the theological foundation for community life, conflict transformation, and peacebuilding.[13]

10. Foster, *Celebration of Discipline.*

11. Peterson, *Long Obedience.*

12. Bonhoeffer, *Life Together.* The term is from this classic expression of personal prayer, worship in common, everyday work, and Christian service.

13. I am grateful to Thomas Porter for drawing my attention to Dorotheos of

The story is told that one day the monks of his monastery came to him complaining, "We have had it. We can't worship God in the company of our fellow monks." They argued that each other's "ordinary, irritating presence" got in the way of positive community life. As Roberta Bondi tells this story, Dorotheos responded by asking them to visualize the world as a great circle whose center is God, and upon whose circumference lie human lives. "Imagine now that there are straight lines connecting from the outside of the circle all human lives to God at the center. Can't you see that there is no way to move toward God without drawing closer to other people, and no way to approach other people without coming near to God?"[14]

In other words, in order to get close to God we need to get closer and closer to our fellow human beings and in order to get close to our fellow human beings we need to get closer to God. Roberta Bondi writes, "There is something implied in the very shape of his imagined chart, however, that Dorotheos did not draw to the attention of his listeners—that in the movement toward love, whether of God, or of another human being, there is an open space so close to the center of reality, that human and divine love becomes indistinguishable."[15] However, in the monastic tradition the "ordinary, irritating presence" of the other can often contribute to communal conflict and the growth of resentment. Resentment can lead to gossip or to ways that violate the dignity of the other. The author of the Letter to the Hebrews writes: "Make every effort to live in peace with everyone and to be holy; without holiness no one will see the Lord. See to it that no one falls short of the grace of God and that no bitter root grows up to cause trouble and defile many (Heb 12:14–15, NIV)."

How do we get closer to others in shaping community? It is abundantly easy for the "ordinary, irritating presence" of the other to become that root of bitterness cited by the author of Hebrews. Whether through slights or resentment, inadvertent wounding or outright hostility, one's dignity is easily challenged. Psychologist Donna Hicks delineates ten temptations that lead to the violation of the dignity of the other: taking the bait, saving face, shirking responsibility, seeking false dignity, seeking false security, avoiding conflict, being the victim, resisting feedback, blaming and shaming others to deflect your own guilt, and engaging in false intimacy and demeaning gossip.[16]

Palestine. See his book *Engaging Conflict Well*, chap. 2.

14. Bondi, *Memories of God*, 201.

15. Ibid.

16. Hicks, *Dignity*, 98–176.

Each of these violations can lead to a sense of disrespect, perhaps even shame, a frequent entree to communal violence. In reflecting on such subsequent social violence, psychiatrist James Gilligan writes that "All violence is an effort to do justice or to undo injustice."[17] The implication of Gilligan's insight into the basic yearning for justice is to deepen our understanding of the social psychological dynamics inherent in violence in civil society, particularly in cross-cultural relations. His observation opens up an important perspective on the nature of violence, its relation to justice, and the fundamental need for social justice, or just peace in society. Gilligan calls us to a view of justice as restorative justice, and toward the creation of societies characterized by "justpeace." Shaming and the absence of a perception of justice find their political counterpart in many conflicts in the world today.[18] As Evelin Lindner describes it, "As a weapon of war and a tactic of torture, the power of humiliation to destroy everyone and everything in its path makes it 'the nuclear bomb of the emotions.'" She goes on to write that Thomas Friedman, *New York Times* columnist, for example, in many of his texts, pinpoints "humiliation" and "dignity" as being *the* issue in the Middle East, and the driving force behind the "Lesser Jihad" of violence.

Yet, if humiliation is the driving force behind global jihad, how valuable it is to place conflict and the absence of just peace in the context of communal moral failure and, it might be added, in the absence of the "Greater Jihad" of cultivating moral virtue, as advocated by present-day Muslims and by St. Anthony. This journey of the "character in community" has led Desmond Tutu to argue that there is "no future without forgiveness."[19] Forgiveness can foster the onset of a spiritual journey through the gates of restorative justice and reconciliation to community. It is part of the fourth just peacemaking practice—acknowledge responsibility for conflict and injustice and seek repentance and forgiveness. What is pictured so well by Dorotheos in a monastic setting takes on meaningful political and prophetic character in our world today.[20]

This is seen in the value being put on public theology and shaping a politics of reconciliation in a number of our religious traditions. It takes shape around the formation of persons and societies intent upon forgiveness, restorative justice and reconciliation. The end of public theology is

17. Gilligan, *Violence*. Compare with Muchembled, op. cit., and male aggressiveness, codes of honor, and nature of violence among those in contexts of privilege in contrast with those living on the margins of privilege.

18. Lindner, *Making Enemies*.

19. Tutu, *No Future without Forgiveness*.

20. Narvaez, *Political Culture*. 15.

community or a healthy civil society—the "beloved community" envisioned by Martin Luther King, Jr.[21] Ministry, formed in the spirit of Anthony and Dorotheos, extends itself in the spiritual formation of persons toward community. It recognizes that the identity of each is shaped by the identity of the other. Effective ministry is concerned about the spiritual formation of persons and is characterized by a prophetic realism that will not flinch from the truth about ourselves and about ourselves as related to the other. The ten practices of just peacemaking are a way of conceptualizing good moral theology, *being* extended into *becoming* in the interest of personal and communal moral maturation. In good Augustinian fashion, the minister is an educator, and formation is one of the four "arts of ministry" along with theology, the interpretation of scripture, and history, each to be cultivated by those doing the work of ministry.[22] The Apostle Paul writes of equipping the saints "for the work of ministry, for the building up of the body of Christ," (Eph 4:11–15).[23] All of the minister's efforts are bent toward human maturation, the rhetorical resonance of the human with the divine.[24]

So what of the gates through which one might pass on the journey to community, even the "beloved community": forgiveness, restorative justice, and reconciliation?

Forgiveness

Different people have offered a variety of interpretations of the word "forgiveness," this first gate on the journey to community. No one has brought

21. The term "beloved community" comes from the philosophical idealism of Josiah Royce and was picked up first by the Fellowship of Reconciliation and then by Martin Luther King Jr., reflecting a community characterized by social justice as shaped by faith. See the argument of Marsh, *Beloved Community*.

22. Augustine, *On Christian Teaching*.

23. Paul's conception of Jesus as the Christ implies that union with Christ through faith imparts the divine nature upon the believer as a member of Christ's body and involves the believer abiding in Christ for growth in grace and service (cf. Col 1:15–29). Thomas F. O'Meara, OP, writes of ministry as "(1) doing something, (2) for the advent and presence of the kingdom, (3) in public, (4) on behalf of a Christian community, (5) as a gift received in faith, baptism and ordination, (6) and as an activity with its own limits and identity existing within a diversity of ministerial actions." While the cultural ramifications of ministry may be wider than O'Meara appears to allow, he makes room for a cooperative model of ministry through the enabling work of the Holy Spirit, in *Theology of Ministry*.

24. On different models of maturation, such as those of Fowler, Kegan, etc., see James E. Loder, who compassionately sets such thinkers as these in context with analysis from theologians like Barth and Pannenberg in *Logic of the Spirit*.

the term into public currency more than Anglican Archbishop Desmond Tutu from South Africa. As each person nuances the word differently, we see how various aspects of forgiveness shape our self-understanding, our relationships with others, and the nature of emerging patterns of community.

Forgiveness might be seen as a commitment to a way of life and practice (L. Gregory Jones). It might be defined as a commitment of the will (Marjorie Suchocki). It may also imply liberation from the past (Geiko Müller-Fahrenholz). Forgiveness might focus upon and be seen as applicable to the secular realm and public policy (Donald Shriver), or it might be seen as focused upon motivations that reduce interactions with one who has hurt us (Everett Worthington). One researcher, Joanna North, writes, "Forgiveness is a matter of a willed change of heart, the successful result of an active endeavor to replace bad thoughts with good, bitterness and anger with compassion and affection." Another (Michelle Nelson) writes of stages of forgiveness, detached, limited, and complete along a road toward healing.[25] Journalist and political philosopher Hannah Arendt writes of Jesus as the "discoverer" of forgiveness.[26]

Consider the following example: Geiko Müller-Fahrenholz writes:

> To understand what forgiveness does to our relationships we need to see the bondage that evil creates. In *Song of Solomon* the African-American novelist Toni Morrison writes, "If you take a life, you own it. You are responsible for it. You can't get rid of nobody by killing them. They are still there, and they are yours now." This is a forceful way of saying that every act of transgression constitutes a bondage that keeps the perpetrator and victim locked together. The more violent is the transgression, the deeper the bondage.

Müller-Fahrenholz writes that forgiveness generally refers to a specific act of pardoning. "Someone repents, someone forgives. 'Repentance' and 'forgiveness' are taken as the two sides of a process in which the perpetrator of an evil act confesses his or her remorse and the victim of that act grants pardon. Two elements explain why forgiveness has become so cheap a notion: its triteness and its inconsequentiality."[27]

Note how "forgiveness" defines the church: Forgiveness is essential to worship (Matt 5:23–24). Forgiveness defines the material identity of the church (John 20:21–23). Forgiveness, as it tends toward reconciliation,

---

25. Enright and North, *Exploring Forgiveness*, 63–74, 95–105.

26. Arendt, *Human Condition*, 239.

27. Müller-Fahrenholz, citing Toni Morrison in *Art of Forgiveness*, 3, 24.

defines vocation (2 Cor 5:19). Indeed, it might even be said that just as there are degrees to which we are willing to forgive so, too, there are degrees to which we might find community.

Restorative Justice

Forgiveness finds life in restorative justice, a second gate through which we pass on the journey to community. The term "restorative justice," originating in indigenous communities and among sociologists and legal scholars, implies that attention be given to the effects of judicial procedures upon victims, offenders, and the community; i.e., that victims' needs are met, that offenders learn responsibility, and that communities find safety through just relationships.[28] Restorative justice is the basis for the fifth and sixth practices of just peacemaking—human rights and sustainable economic development. Our moral vision shapes our practices of just peacemaking, how we deal with conflict toward the ends of improving civil society.[29]

Forgiveness moves toward reconciliation, and reconciliation moves toward patterns of life that are based in trust and are just and equitable. Just peacemaking moves us from "what we would *like to think*" to "what we *are actually doing*"; from "toward" an ideal state of "just peace" to participation in an actual process of peace*making*. This is Hebraic Jesus language, not Platonic idealistic language. This would appear to be the conclusion of Psalm 85:10—the meaningful meeting place of truth, mercy, justice, and peace (John Paul Lederach).[30] Such relationships might be called restorative, or we might use the term "restorative justice." To be reconciled to another, not merely to tolerate the other, means that change is required on the part of both parties as we seek the restoration of each other, something we or the other may or may not be prepared to do (Miroslav Volf).[31] Another way to refer to such new patterns of relationship is to use the term "reparative" justice or even "transformative" or "delivering" justice. This perspective about how we might live together draws upon the Hebrew Bible, on both Old and New Testament assumptions—and also upon the best wisdom traditions of indigenous peoples and other religions or faith traditions. It emphasizes the

28. Zehr, *Changing Lenses*, 181.

29. See Stassen, *Just Peacemaking: Transforming Initiatives*; Lederach, *Moral Imagination*; and Pranis, *Peacemaking Circles*.

30. Lederach, *Building Peace*, 30.

31. Volf, *Exclusion and Embrace*.

humanity of both victims and victimizers. It seeks to repair social connections, to foster peace rather than retribution against offenders.[32]

Most agree that restorative justice promotes healing, but the kind of healing depends upon the nature of the breach. One focus is to see crime as more than simply law-breaking, an offense against governmental laws and regulations. Instead, restorative justice advocates also see crime as causing multiple injuries to victims, the community and the offender.[33] Another lens is to view the criminal justice process as one that should help repair the injuries brought about by crime. Still others protest the government's monopoly over society's response to crime. Victims, offenders, and their communities must also be involved as early as possible and as much as possible.[34]

Consider the following example: Carolyn Boys-Watson, director of the Center for Restorative Justice, Suffolk University, defines our term in the following way: Restorative justice is a broad term which encompasses a growing social movement to institutionalize peaceful resolutions to criminal and human rights violations. These range from international peacemaking tribunals such as the Truth and Reconciliation Commission of South Africa to innovations within our courts, jails, and prisons, such as victim-offender dialogue, community justice committees, and victim impact panels. Rather than privileging the law and the state, restorative justice engages the victim, the offender, and the affected community in search of solutions that promote repair and reconciliation. Restorative justice seeks to build partnerships to re-establish mutual responsibility for constructive responses to crime and wrongdoing within our communities.[35]

Reconciliation

A third gate through which we pass on our journey toward community is reconciliation. Reconciliation is the resolution of violence. It begins to happen when we participate in positive relations with previous enemies.[36] This is the community theme of the last four practices of just peacemaking. The term "Reconciliation" (*katallagé*), as used by the Apostle Paul (2 Cor 5:16–21; Eph 2:11–22), was a word used for

---

32. Minow, *Between Vengeance and Forgiveness*, 92.

33. Zehr, *Changing Lenses*, 181–86.

34. Van Nes and Strong, *Restoring Justice*, 31.

35. Boyes-Watson, "Reflections."

36. De Gruchy, *Reconciliation*.

monetary exchange in the Hellenistic world. It meant "the making of what one has into something other" or, by extension, one becomes a new person by exchanging places with another. It is not without effort (Matt 5:38–41); it implies agreement after estrangement, with the apparent theological premise that sin has separated humanity from God but that God purposes to aid God's enemies. Such biblical paradigms of reconciliation imply great cost: that of Joseph and his brothers in Egypt (Gen 50:15–21), the embrace of Esau and Jacob (Gen 33:4) or, finally, Jesus' death on our behalf. Here, one becomes a new creation because a power from without enables one to be other than what one was before.[37]

The *Kairos* Document of South Africa talked of "cheap reconciliation," in analogy to Dietrich Bonhoeffer's "cheap grace," implying reconciliation without justice.[38] It raises the question of the temporal sequencing of justice and reconciliation and whether justice as perceived by all parties can ever be finally determined. We have a need for truth, as we are bound in patterns of victim and perpetrator. In this light, we might speak of "national reconciliation" and wonder about "collective healing" and the pursuit of "political unity," as Donald Shriver argues in *Just Peacemaking: The New Paradigm*. Or, in personal relations, we stumble on the term the "forgiveness bypass" (Judith Herman), a short-changing of justice in inter-personal relations on the way toward reconciliation. Everett Worthington writes that "Forgiveness happens inside an individual; reconciliation happens within a relationship."[39] Miroslav Volf, substituting the term "embrace" for "peace," claims four points about the relation between justice and embrace: 1) the primacy of the will to embrace, 2) attending to justice as a precondition of actual embrace, 3) the will to embrace as the framework of the search for justice, and 4) embrace as the horizon of the struggle for justice. These views, taken from the domain of national life and inter-personal relationships, remind us of the Latin root for reconciliation, *concilium*, or a deliberative process in which conflicting parties meet "in council."[40]

> Consider the following example: John Paul Lederach envisions reconciliation as a meeting place where Truth, Mercy, Justice and Peace come together (Psalm 85:10). He writes how in his work in Nicaragua, the locus for these terms as he used them

37. Schreiter, *Reconciliation*.
38. Volf, "Forgiveness, Reconciliation, and Justice," 35–36.
39. Worthington, *Dimensions of Forgiveness*, 129.
40. Müller-Fahrenholz, *Art of Forgiveness*, 3.

took on revelatory and reconciling potential. He adds, "Reconciliation can be thus understood as both a focus and a locus. As a perspective, it is built on and oriented toward the relational aspects of a conflict. As a social phenomenon, reconciliation represents a space, a place or location of encounter, where parties to a conflict meet."[41] John Dawson outlines numerous areas in need of reconciliation as he encourages us to think from the perspective of our given social location.[42]

III. Community Formation

For character formation in community, community—even the "beloved community"—is the end of the journey. We have seen from the start of this volume that the nature of our relationships shapes our identity. We have also seen that holistic, interactive character formation constitutes the quality of our just peacemaking, enabling community to happen. Good social science and good theology lead us to understand that we are designed to live in community, and for Christians this reflects the complex nature of divinity.[43] Further, the Sabbath/Sunday gathering, whether for monastic communities or communities of faith today, becomes a symbolic summary of faith and a time for "covenant renewal." It gives scope to the recurring challenges of four communal dimensions of life: how to live within community, how to live with the earth that sustains community, the meaning of economy within the community, and how to engage the communities of others.

By the end of Anthony's life two types of monasticism flourished in Egypt, villages or colonies of hermits (eremitical monasticism), and monasteries in which a community life was led (cenobitic monasticism)—later to give expression to much of European monasticism through the Rule of Benedict of Nursia (c.480—c.543). By engaging oneself in accordance with the established Sunday-rhythm of the week in prayer and manual labor, the Benedictine Rule proved to be a guide for how to live with these four challenges to community existence—life within community, with the earth, with an economy, and in relation to the communities of others.

41. Lederach, *Building Peace*, 30.

42. Dawson, "Hatred's End."

43. See Horvath, "Living into Biblical Community," esp. chap. 4 which lists reasons for participation in five different intentional communities in Greater Boston (USA).

Each of these challenges to community life forms a moral trajectory for just peacemaking practices in the twenty-first century. Laid out as they were by the International Ecumenical Peace Convocation of the World Council of Churches, these four areas continue to be alive for us today as we seek to be formed to become agents of just peacemaking.[44] They give scope to what are recurring areas of challenge in character and community formation, 1) how to live in community with others, 2) how to live in peace with the earth, 3) the meaning of economy, and 4) how to engage with the communities of others.

Peace in the Community

"Churches learn the complexities of Just Peace as we hear of the intersection of multiple injustices and oppressions that are simultaneously at work in the lives of many. Members of one family or community may be oppressed and also the oppressors of others. Churches must help in identifying the everyday choices that can end abuse and promote human rights, gender justice, climate justice, economic justice, unity and peace."

—*THE MESSAGE OF THE CONVOCATION* (MAY 2011)[45]

Civil society is one of the great achievements of the modern world. It is nurtured by healthy communities. However, these communities are subject to such divisions as gender, race and economy.[46] Nicholas Wolterstorff writes that when the Bible talks about justice and injustice it gives us a litany of victims, the wounded ones—the widows, the orphans and the aliens—not that of perpetrators.[47] The justice that God loves, writes Wolterstorff, consists in

---

44. The 2001–10 Decade to Overcome Violence (DOV) came to an end with an International Ecumenical Peace Convocation (IEPC) in Jamaica in 2011. It identified these four trajectories as subject to a just peace focus.

45. See the Raiser et al., *Just Peace Companion*, and World Council of Churches, *Message of the Convocation*, http://www.overcomingviolence.org/en/resources-dov/wcc-resources/documents/presentations-speeches-messages/iepc-message.htm (Retrieved March 2012).

46. Gunderson, *Deeply Woven Roots*, 64. Gunderson, formerly of the Carter Center, suggests mapping congregational connections in an effort to look for "patterns of need."

47. See Wolterstorff, "Contours of Justice."

the well-being of the weak, the vulnerable, and the lowly. Behind this justice are three elements: the fact that God loves all people, not just some; that God desires the shalom of all people; and God's justice seeks the shalom of all people because all have a right to the basic conditions that lead to peace. The unity of this message is found throughout the Jewish, Christian, and Islamic Scriptures and in other traditions.[48]

Many community tensions come together around issues of asylum, migration, and immigration. The twentieth century is noted for populations in movement: war, ethnic cleansing, economic and political unrest, and ecological disaster have combined to create an unparalleled human crisis of immigrants, refugees and asylum seekers that continues into the twenty-first century. Ruth Bersin, Director of the Refugee Immigration Ministry, describes this area of "border crossing" as she writes of the profound significance of spirituality and spiritual formation in the journey toward personal healing and social health.[49]

Peace with the Earth

"The environmental crisis is profoundly an ethical and spiritual crisis of humanity. Recognizing the damage human activity has done to the Earth, we reaffirm our commitment to the integrity of creation and the daily lifestyle it demands. Our concern for the Earth and our concern for humanity go hand in hand. Natural resources and common goods such as water must be shared in a just and sustainable manner. We join global civil society in urging governments to reconstruct radically all our economic activities towards the goal of an ecologically sustainable economy."

—*THE MESSAGE OF THE CONVOCATION* (MAY 2011).[50]

Monastic life, epitomized in the phrase "prayer and work" (*ora et labora*), laid a foundation for present concerns with "Peace with the Earth." Failure to foster earth care is as much a social disease as other areas of injustice.

48. Thistlethwaite, *Interfaith Just Peacemaking*. See prefaces representing the three faiths (ix–xvi).

49. Bersin, "Life beyond the Gates."

50. See Raiser et al., *Just Peace Companion*; World Council of Churches, *Message of the Convocation*.

As disciples discover the courage to be the body of Christ in the world, "stewards of the mysteries of God" (Col 1:9), they must also become as environmental researcher Calvin DeWitt challenges, "stewards of the earth" (Gen 2:15). Creation care is our oldest challenge. Creation, too, is recipient of God's mission as the whole *cosmos* looks for liberation to be what it was meant to be (Rom 8: 18–21). Personal and social salvations are aspects of a deeper ecological healing that is required of us and of our world. DeWitt draws attention to the interplay between the Biosphere and Missiology as he places importance upon putting our contemporary scientific understanding of the world into interactive relationship with missiology.[51] This is what the just peacemaking practice of *Just and Sustainable* economic development is pointing to for all creation.[52]

Peace in the Marketplace

"The global economy often provides many examples of structural violence that victimizes not through the direct use of weapons or physical force but by passive acceptance of widespread poverty, trade disparities and inequality among classes and nations. In contrast to unfettered economic growth as envisioned by the neoliberal system, the Bible signals a vision of life in abundance for all. The churches must learn to advocate more effectively for full implementation of economic, social and cultural rights as the foundation for 'economies of life.'"

—*THE MESSAGE OF THE CONVOCATION* (MAY 2011).[53]

The gospel adage, "Go, sell everything you have and give to the poor, and you will have treasure in heaven. Then come, follow me" (Mark 10:21) has impelled many disciples through history to live a life of poverty. One of the burdens of the twenty-first century is peacebuilding in relation to economic justice. As the eminent African-American ethicist Peter Paris

---

51. DeWitt, "Missiology and the Biosphere."

52. See the study of the World Council of Churches, "Justice, Peace and Integrity of Creation" (JPIC) and reflection on the term "creation" in Conroy and Petersen, *Earth at Risk.*

53. See Kaiser et al., *Just Peace Companion*; World Council of Churches, *Message of the Convocation.*

admonishes: "We must remember always that social justice is not an abstract idea. Rather it is an empirical reality; it is specific, concrete, visible, and quantifiable."[54] This is the sixth just peacemaking practice of just and sustainable economic development.

Peace and economic justice are interactive. Each conditions and is conditioned by the other. Social ethicist Nimi Wariboko argues in this volume that any approach to the study of peacebuilding that privileges peace at the expense of justice or vice versa is inadequate. In his chapter he lays out four theological principles: 1) Human Dignity: Every human being has an inherent inviolable dignity as one created by God. Persons are to be treated as subjects, and never merely as objects; they are to be treated with due respect for their worth. 2) Nature of the Human Person: A person is one in the process of becoming, actualizing his or her potential through his or her own agency that is always grounded, mediated, and aided by community. 3) Social Nature of Human Beings: Individuals need community to become persons. Community is essential for self-realization and human flourishing. 4) Participation and Membership: Every person, by virtue of his or her membership in a community, has the right to active participation in the process of seeking and ordering the common good of the community. "Discerning the body," as Saint Paul informs us, is about being sensitive to issues that cause alienation, divisions, fractures in the social body, alert to the sufferings of its weak, marginalized, and disinherited members, and being compassionate enough to care for the harmony of the whole body.[55]

Questions like, "*What do we mean when we say God?*" have a double edge in the context of economic deprivation. This question, raised by former priest and Haitian president Jean-Bertrand Aristide in his book, *Eyes of the Heart: Seeking a Path for the Poor in the Age of Globalization*, has a different resonance for one growing up in Cité Soleil, Port-au-Prince's largest slum, than for one living in Palm Beach, Florida, USA. But if "God" means "God," then the term has the same referent whether one is impoverished or wealthy. We can make no excuses for it, but the question of social privilege was and is one of the issues being played out in our world where many of the young are impoverished and without employment, or prospect of it. John H. Yoder observes that "The world of the twenty-first century will not be able to back away from having become one world."[56]

54. Paris, "Meditation on Love," 3.

55. Wariboko, *God and Money*. Wariboko explores the significance and ethical implications of money as a social relation in the light of the dynamic relations of the triune God.

56. *BTI Magazine*.10.2 (spring 2011) 2.

Peace among the Peoples

"History, especially in the witness of the historic peace churches, reminds us of the fact that violence is contrary to the will of God and can never resolve conflicts. It is for this reason that we are moving beyond the doctrine of just war towards a commitment to Just Peace. It requires moving from exclusive concepts of national security to safety for all. This includes a day-to-day responsibility to prevent, that is, to avoid violence at its root. Many practical aspects of the concept of Just Peace require discussion, discernment and elaboration. We continue to struggle with how innocent people can be protected from injustice, war and violence. In this light, we struggle with the concept of the 'responsibility to protect' and its possible misuse. We urgently request that the WCC and related bodies further clarify their positions regarding this policy."

— *THE MESSAGE OF THE CONVOCATION* (MAY 2011).[57]

The world has witnessed a new kind of tribalism since the latter decades of the twentieth century. That social healing can come, even in areas of racial and ethnic hatred, is our contention in this book. Group conflict, often engineered by cynical manipulative forces playing on group anxiety and historical grievance, make of religion a weapon for harm rather than healing.[58] The 10 practices of just peace offer a way to work at even the most intransigent of conflicts in seeking peace among peoples. Raymond Helmick's analysis of the dynamics within majority and minority groups, the direct nature of a conflict and the framework within which it occurs, can yield solutions in line with the learning of social psychology and principles of good ministry. Often *scapegoating* is fundamental to conflict in ways that mandate the need for understanding, and call for the potential of forgiveness in order to find reconciliation. The spirit of many of these conflicts seems to have become more cataclysmic following the 9/11 attack as the United States appeared to also be overcome by its own fear and rage.[59]

---

57. See Raiser et al., *Just Peace Companion*; World Council of Churches, *Message of the Convocation*.

58. Helmick, "Context of Group Identifications."

59. See the essays in Petersen and Simion, *Overcoming Violence*.

IV. A Postscript for Schools of Theology

Just Peacemaking and formation for overcoming violence is the work of all of God's people. Nevertheless, we might find in the modern seminary or school of theology a contemporary counterpart to early monastic education. A seminary education that places an emphasis upon formation for life, building a culture of peace rather than fostering a culture of death, is one that will grow and thrive. Such an approach will be enlivening of schools and supportive of an ecumenical vision.[60] Seminaries are literally "seed beds" for community life and a healthy civil society.

The ecumenical movement is about overcoming violence and building community. The shape of this work might look something like that outlined in the ten practices of just peacemaking,[61] but needs to accompany an equal emphasis upon the kind of covenant renewal in community as also outlined above. A unity of worship and the practice of social justice are grounded in Sabbath/Sunday practices (Isa 56 and 58, and Luke 6:1–10) and forecast the life of prayer and work through the week. This provides rhythm for spiritual vision and character formation. Sabbath/Sunday is a time of covenant renewal and enables character formation to take place in community. This rhythm provides the moral imagination for community formation in the context of the inevitable conflicts of life. Social ethics grounded in a worshipping community offers strength to deal with areas of social challenge: how to live in community with others, how to live in peace with the earth, the meaning of economy and material life, and how to engage with the communities of others. This is the stuff of *Life Together*, the book penned by Dietrich Bonhoeffer in 1939 as the world was about to become engulfed by hatred, suspicion and war.

> "Behold how good and how pleasant it is for brethren
> to dwell together in unity." (Ps 133:1)[62]

Bibliography

Allen, Horace T., Jr. "The Lord's Day as Anticipation and Promise in Liturgy and Word." In *Sunday, Sabbath, and the Weekend: Managing Time in a Global Culture*, edited

---

60. Enns, *Ökumene und Frieden*.

61. Stassen, *Just Peacemaking: Ten Practices*; and see Stassen, *Just Peacemaking: The New Paradigm*.

62. Bonhoeffer, *Life Together*, 23.

by Edward O'Flaherty, SJ, and Rodney L. Petersen with Timothy Norton, 93–104. Grand Rapids: Eerdmans, 2010.

Arendt, Hannah. *The Human Condition*. Chicago: University of Chicago Press, 1959.

Augustine. *On Christian Teaching (De doctrina Christiana)*. Translated by R. P. H. Green. New York: Oxford University Press, 2008.

Barth, Karl. *Church Dogmatics*, volume III, Part4: *The Doctrine of Creation*. Edited by G. W. Bromiley and T. F. Torrance; translated by A. T. McKay et al. Edinburgh: T. & T. Clark, 1961.

Bersin, Ruth. "Life beyond the Gates: Seeing Ourselves in the Other." In *Antioch Agenda: Essays on the Restorative Church in Honor of Orlando E. Costas*, edited by Daniel Jeyaraj, Robert W. Pazmiño, and Rodney L. Petersen, 223–37. New Delhi: ISPCK, 2007.

Bondi, Roberta. *Memories of God: Theological Reflections on a Life*. Nashville: Abingdon, 1995.

Bonhoeffer, Dietrich. *Life Together: The Classic Exploration of Faith in Community*. New York: HarperOne, 1978.

Boyes-Watson, Carolyn. "Reflections on the Purist and Maximalist Models of Restorative Justice." *Contemporary Justice Review* 3.4 (2000) 441–50.

Dalgairns, John Dobree. *The Holy Communion: Its Philosophy, Theology and Practice*. Toronto: University of Toronto, 2011.

Dawson, John. "Hatred's End: A Christian Proposal to Peacemaking in a New Century." In *Forgiveness and Reconciliation: Religion, Public Policy and Conflict Transformation*, edited by Raymond G. Helmick, SJ, and Rodney L. Petersen, 229–56. Philadelphia: Templeton Foundation Press, 2001.

de Gruchy, John W. *Reconciliation: Restoring Justice*. Minneapolis: Augsburg Fortress, 2002.

DeWitt, Calvin. "Contemporary Missiology and the Biosphere." In *Antioch Agenda: Essays on the Restorative Church in Honor of Orlando E. Costas*, edited by Daniel Jeyaraj, Robert W. Pazmiño, and Rodney L. Petersen, 305–28. New Delhi: ISPCK, 2007.

Enns, Fernando. *Ökumene und Frieden: Bewährungsfelder ökumenisher Theologie*. Neukirchen-Vluyn: Neukirchener Theologie, 2012.

Enright, Robert D., and Joanna North, editors. *Exploring Forgiveness*. Madison, WI: University of Wisconsin Press, 1998.

Foster, Richard. *Celebration of Discipline: The Path to Spiritual Growth*. 3rd ed. San Francisco: HarperSanFrancisco, 1988.

Gilligan, James. *Violence: Reflections on a National Epidemic*. New York: Vintage, 1996.

Green, M. Christian, Rodney Petersen, and Thomas Massaro. "Teaching Overcoming Violence." *Practical Matters Journal* 5 (Spring 2012). http://practicalmattersjournal.org/issue/5/teaching-matters/teaching-overcoming-violence.

Gunderson, Gary. *Deeply Woven Roots*. Augsburg Fortress, 1997.

Helmick, Raymond G., SJ. "The Context of Group Identifications and Their Conflicts: A Four-Factor Theory of the Dynamic of Conflict." In *Antioch Agenda: Essays on the Restorative Church in Honor of Orlando E. Costas*, edited by Daniel Jeyaraj, Robert W. Pazmiño, and Rodney L. Petersen, 287–304. New Delhi: ISPCK, 2007.

Helmick, Raymond G., SJ, and Rodney L. Petersen, editors. *Forgiveness and Reconciliation: Religion, Public Policy and Conflict Transformation*. Philadelphia: Templeton Foundation, 2001.

Hicks, Donna. *Dignity: The Essential Role It Plays in Resolving Conflict.* New Haven: Yale University Press, 2011.

Horvath, Katherine Kyte. "Living into Biblical Community through Healthy Conflict Resolution." DMin thesis, Gordon-Conwell Theological Seminary, 2012.

Jeyaraj, Daniel, Robert W. Pazmiño, and Rodney L. Petersen, editors. *Antioch Agenda: Essays on the Restorative Church in Honor of Orlando E. Costas.* New Delhi: ISPCK, 2007.

Lederach, John Paul. *Building Peace: Sustainable Reconciliation in Divided Societies.* Washington, DC: US Institute of Peace, 1997.

———. *The Moral Imagination: The Art and Soul of Building Peace.* New York: Oxford University Press, 2005.

Lindner, Evelin. *Making Enemies: Humiliation and International Conflict.* Westport, CT: Praeger Security International, 2006.

Loder, James E. *The Logic of the Spirit: Human Development in Theological Perspective.* San Francisco: Jossey-Bass, 1998.

Markides, Kyriacos C. *Inner River: A Pilgrimage to the Heart of Christian Spirituality.* New York: Image, 2012.

Marsh, Charles. *The Beloved Community: How Faith Shapes Social Justice, from the Civil Rights Movement to Today.* New York: Basic, 2005.

Minow, Martha. *Between Vengeance and Forgiveness: Facing History after Genocide and Mass Violence.* Boston: Beacon, 1998.

Müller-Fahrenholz, Geiko. *The Art of Forgiveness: Theological Reflections on Healing and Reconciliation.* Geneva: World Council of Churches, 1997.

Narvaez, Leonel, editor. *Political Culture of Forgiveness and Reconciliation.* Translated by James Arthur Lupton and Renato Rozende. Bogotá, Colombia: Fundación para la Reconciliación, 2010.

Norris, Frank B. *Decree on Priestly Training and Decree on the Ministry and Life of Priests of Vatican Council II.* Glen Rock, NJ: Paulist, 1966.

O'Meara, Thomas F., OP. *Theology of Ministry.* Mahwah, NJ: Paulist, 1999.

Paris, Peter J. "A Meditation on Love." *Princeton Seminary Bulletin* 26.1 (2006) 1–4.

Petersen, Rodney L., and Marian Gh. Simion. *Overcoming Violence: Religion, Conflict and Peacebuilding.* Newton, MA: BTI, 2010.

Peterson, Eugene H. *A Long Obedience in the Same Direction: Discipleship in an Instant Society.* Twentieth-anniversary ed. Downers Grove, IL: InterVarsity, 2000.

Porter, Thomas W., Jr. *Engaging Conflict Well: The Spirit and the Art of Conflict Transformation.* Nashville: Upper Room, 2010.

Pranis, Kay, Barry Stuart, and Mark Wedge. *Peacemaking Circles: From Crime to Community.* St. Paul, Minnesota: Living Justice, 2003.

Raiser, Konrad, et al. *Just Peace Companion.* Geneva: World Council of Churches, 2011.

Schimmel, Solomon. *The Seven Deadly Sins: Jewish, Christian, and Classical Reflections on Human Psychology.* New York: Oxford University Press, 1997.

Schreiter, Robert J. *Reconciliation: Mission and Ministry in a Changing Social Order.* Boston: Boston Theological Institute / Maryknoll, NY: Orbis, 1992.

Stassen, Glen H., editor. *Just Peacemaking: Ten Practices for Abolishing War.* Cleveland: Pilgrim, 1998.

———, editor. *Just Peacemaking: The New Paradigm for the Ethics of Peace and War.* 2nd ed. Cleveland: Pilgrim, 2008.

————. *Just Peacemaking: Transforming Initiatives for Justice and Peace.* Louisville: Westminster John Knox, 1992.

Thistlethwaite, Susan Brooks, editor. *Interfaith Just Peacemaking: Jewish, Christian, and Muslim Perspectives on the New Paradigm of Peace and War.* New York: Palgrave Macmillan, 2012.

Tracy, David. "On Theological Education: A Reflection." In *Theological Literacy for the Twenty-First Century,* edited by Rodney L. Petersen with Nancy Rourke, 13–22. Grand Rapids: Eerdmans, 2002.

Tutu, Desmond. *No Future without Forgiveness.* New York: Seabury, 2000.

Van Nes, Daniel W., and Karen Heetdirks Strong. *Restoring Justice: An Introduction to Restorative Justice.* 4th ed. Atlanta: Anderson, 2010.

Volf, Miroslav. *Exclusion and Embrace: A Theological Exploration of Identity, Otherness, and Reconciliation.* Nashville: Abingdon, 1996.

————. "Forgiveness, Reconciliation, and Justice: A Christian Contribution to a More Peaceful Social Environment." In *Forgiveness and Reconciliation: Religion, Public Policy and Conflict Transformation,* edited by Raymond G. Helmick, SJ, and Rodney L. Petersen, 27–49. Philadelphia: Templeton Foundation Press, 2001.

Waltke, Bruce K., James M. Houston, and Erika Moore. *The Psalms as Christian Worship: A Historical Commentary.* Grand Rapids: Eerdmans, 2010.

Wariboko, Nimi. *God and Money: A Theology of Money in a Globalizing World.* Plymouth, UK: Lexington, 2010.

Wolterstorff, Nicholas. "The Contours of Justice: An Ancient Call for Shalom." In *God and the Victim: Theological Reflections on Evil, Victimization, Justice, and Forgiveness,* edited by Lisa Barnes Lampman and Michelle D. Shattuck, 107–30. Grand Rapids: Eerdmans, 1999.

World Council of Churches. "Justice, Peace and Integrity of Creation." In *Earth at Risk: Advancing the Environmental Dialogue between Religion and Science,* edited by Donald B. Conroy and Rodney L. Petersen, 1–20. Amherst, NY: Humanity, 2000.

World Council of Churches. *The Message of the Convocation.* Geneva: World Council of Churches, 2011.

Worthington, Everett L., Jr., editor. *Dimensions of Forgiveness: Psychological Research and Theological Perspectives.* Philadelphia: Templeton Foundation, 1998.

Zehr, Howard. *Changing Lenses.* Scottdale, PA: Herald, 1990.

Subject Index